DEFYING
NAPOLEON

DEFYING NAPOLEON

HOW BRITAIN BOMBARDED COPENHAGEN
AND SEIZED THE DANISH FLEET IN 1807

THOMAS MUNCH-PETERSEN

SUTTON PUBLISHING

First published in the United Kingdom in 2007 by
Sutton Publishing Limited · Phoenix Mill
Thrupp · Stroud · Gloucestershire · GL5 2BU

British Library Cataloguing in Publication Data
A catalogue record for this book is available from the British Library.

Hardback ISBN 978-0-7509-4279-9
Paperback ISBN 978-0-7509-4280-5

Typeset in Photina.
Typesetting and origination by
Sutton Publishing Limited.
Printed and bound in England.

CONTENTS

LIST OF ILLUSTRATIONS

(between pages 138 and 139)

LIST OF MAPS

PREFACE

A good story needs no excuse, and the events surrounding the British bombardment of Copenhagen in 1807 make for an engrossing story. They are full of drama, incident and tragedy and involve some remarkable personalities – some famous, others obscure. The British expedition to Zealand to gain possession of the Danish fleet must rank as one of the most successful combined military operations in history – swift, ruthless and effective. And it is the first occasion in modern history when the gruesome expedient of terror bombardment was deployed against a major European city.

Some of the intelligence underpinning the British decision to strike against Denmark was inaccurate, and the operation is also a prime example of the principle of pre-emptive war in action. For a reader in the first decade of the twenty-first century, these two elements of the picture inevitably create some uncanny parallels with the invasion of Iraq in 2003. I suspect that readers will interpret the evidence about 1807 in their own ways and reach their own conclusions about the rightness of the British decision to attack Denmark – just as they have done over the invasion of Iraq.

The story is its own reward, but this book also throws light into a dark corner of the history of the Napoleonic period. Except in Denmark, the bombardment of Copenhagen in 1807 has largely been forgotten. Although there have been articles and chapters in larger studies dealing with aspects of the bombardment, this is the first book devoted to the subject. With the notable exceptions of John Holland Rose and Anthony Ryan, British historians have shied away from it. The victory was strategically brilliant but perhaps too easily won. And there is no getting away from the fact that the operation, whether justified or not, involved unprovoked aggression against a neutral state and the terror bombardment of a civilian population.

The choice of subject matter does not mean that this is a debunking book. The story is told essentially from the British point of view, and I have aimed to write with empathy for the fearful dilemmas faced by the British government in the summer of 1807. But outcomes were determined by the interaction between the decisions taken by all the major players in the drama. It is important to extend understanding to the other side of the hill and to see the governments of Denmark, France and Russia not just as threats to Britain but also as independent agents with their own fears and objectives.

The book is based on extensive original research in British and foreign archives and offers new evidence and new interpretations on many aspects of the story. But I have made space for anecdote and personality as well as the harsh march of events, and I have tried to present the story in a way that can appeal equally to the professional historian specialising in the Napoleonic period and to the general reader with an interest in the past. I take to heart George Trevelyan's remarks in the preface to the first volume of his *England under Queen Anne*, published in 1930:

> For my part, I cannot abandon the older ideal of History that was once popular in England, that the same book should make its appeal both to the general reader and to the historical student. In these latter days there tends to be division. It is right there should be division in some cases, but it is right in other cases that the older unity should be attempted.

That is an ideal to which I subscribe. The reader will decide whether I have lived up to it.

There are many historical narratives that can be constructed around the effects of underlying economic, social and cultural forces. The bombardment of Copenhagen in 1807 is not one of them. In this case, the role of chance and the individual are central. The ferocious will of Napoleon Bonaparte, the devious and nebulous ambitions of Alexander I of Russia and George Canning's determination to prove a worthy heir to William Pitt made a difference in 1807. They were all, of course, influenced by the political culture of international relations at the time, but other men would have reacted differently to the opportunities and dangers that confronted them in the summer of 1807.

The bombardment of Copenhagen is not a purely Anglo-Danish affair. It took place within the much broader context of a Europe at war from the Baltic to the Mediterranean. There had been a deterioration in relations between Britain and Denmark in the nine months before the British assault on Copenhagen, but this was not the fundamental cause of that assault. The real catalyst for the British attack on Denmark was the new alliance forged between Alexander I and Napoleon at Tilsit. That is why this book begins not in London or Copenhagen, but on the battlegrounds of eastern Prussia where French and Russian armies were locked in a desperate contest in the early summer of 1807.

ACKNOWLEDGEMENTS

I have accumulated many debts of gratitude while working on this book. I am most grateful to the Carlsberg Foundation in Copenhagen, the Dean's Travel Fund and the Faculty Research Fund of the Faculty of Arts and Humanities at University College London and the Scouloudi Foundation at the Institute of Historical Research, London, for generous financial support of the research involved in writing this book. In particular, I am indebted to my then head of department, Tom Lundskær-Nielsen, for significant monetary assistance from departmental funds to cover both research expenses and sabbatical leave to complete the book.

I have benefited enormously from contact with numerous scholars. Their help has ranged from tracking down obscure information and making photocopies of material in archives I could not visit in person, through practical advice to email correspondence and stimulating conversation. I list them in alphabetical order with my heartfelt thanks: David Aldridge, Hans Bagger, Michael Barnes, Simon Burrows, Carsten Due-Nielsen, Mike Durey, Charles Esdaile, Ole Feldbæk, Peter Foote, Robert Frost, Jan Glete, Janet Hartley, Andrew Lambert, Krzysztof Link-Lenczowski, Munro Price, Jean Rankine, Martin Robson, Jakob Seerup, Elizabeth Sparrow, John Townsend, Tim Voelcker, Harry Watson, Hubert Zawadzki. The French specialists who have helped me with the mysteries of d'Antraigues's handwriting – William Barber, Colin Duckworth, Philip Mansel, Wendy Mercer and Michael Worton – should be mentioned as a special category. I am grateful to my publishers, Sutton Publishing – in particular to Jonathan Falconer, Julia Fenn and Hilary Walford – for assistance and support over a wide front.

I must also thank the two research assistants who valiantly transcribed and copied research material on my behalf: Jenny Skipp in Leeds and Thomas Olesen in Copenhagen. In particular, I am grateful to Ole Feldbæk, who read the whole manuscript, and to Mary Hilson and Munro

Price, who read parts of it, for taking the time to proofread and comment on my work. It goes without saying that the usual caveat applies – I alone am responsible for this book and for any errors it may contain.

I am also indebted to several members of my family. My son David and my father-in-law, Viggo Roed, transcribed archival material on my behalf, and my wife, Jannie Roed, has been a pillar of strength – patient, supportive and understanding of the foibles of those engrossed in writing and research.

I am grateful to the owners and custodians of the following manuscript collections for permission to consult and quote from them: Her Majesty the Queen for material in the Public Record Office of the National Archive of the United Kingdom; the Earl of Harewood for the George Canning papers in Leeds District Archive; the British Library for the Grenville papers; Durham University Library for the papers of the Second Earl Grey; the National Maritime Museum at Greenwich for the Duckworth papers; the National Library of Scotland for the Murray papers; the Huntington Library at San Marino, California for the Thomas Grenville papers; the Danish National Archives in Copenhagen; the French foreign ministry for the Fonds Bourbons; the Czartoryski Library, Cracow; the Swedish National Archives; and the Finnish National Archives. I owe special thanks to the Royal Danish Naval Museum in Copenhagen for helping me to find relevant illustrations for this book and for permission to publish them.

NOTE ON SPELLING AND PLACE NAMES

I have modernised the spelling and punctuation of quotations from printed and manuscript sources, but the wording has never been altered.

I have used the modern spelling of place names (preferring the English version where there is one). There are a few exceptions, and I list the most significant place names in this category below.

1807	Present day
Cattaro	Kotor
Eylau	Bagrationovsk
Friedland	Pravdinsk
Königsberg	Kaliningrad
Memel	Klaipeda
Mitau	Jelgava
Reval	Tallinn
Tilsit	Sovetsk
Tonningen	Tönning

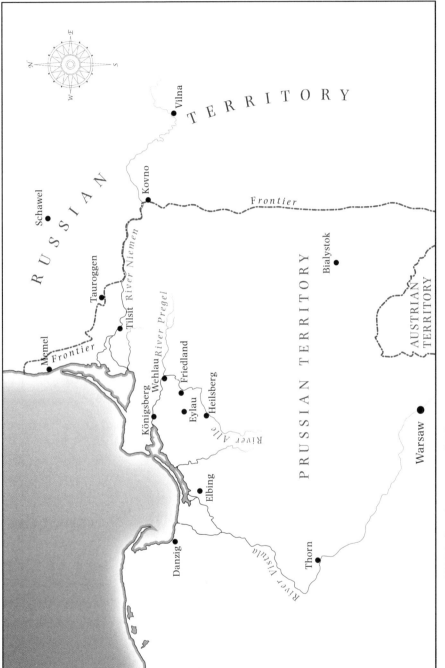

1. East Prussia in 1807 before the treaties of Tilsit

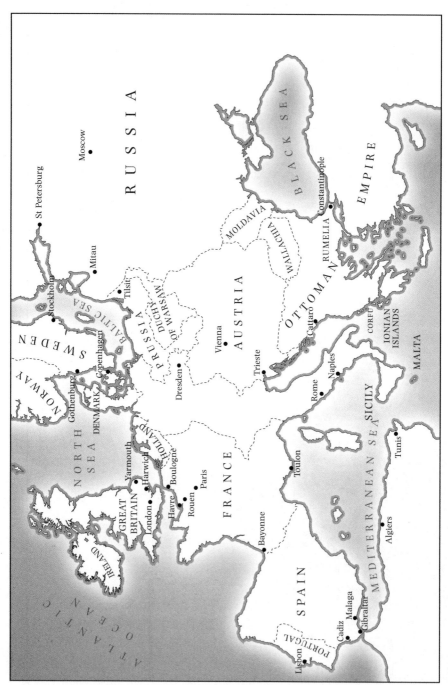

2. Europe after Tilsit

3. The Baltic and Scandinavia

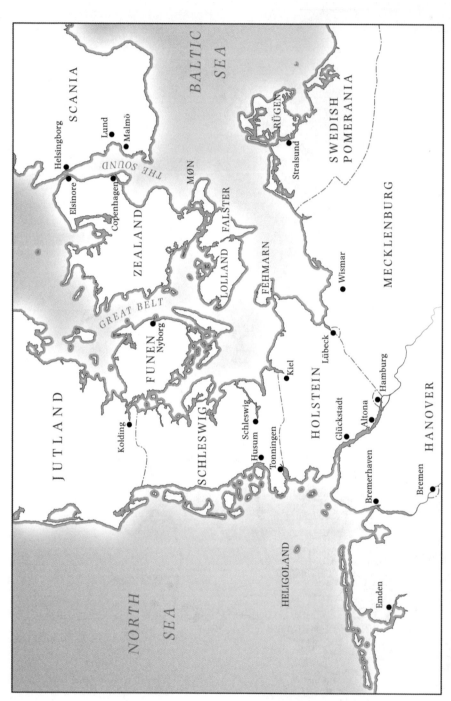

4. Southern Jutland and the Danish islands in 1807

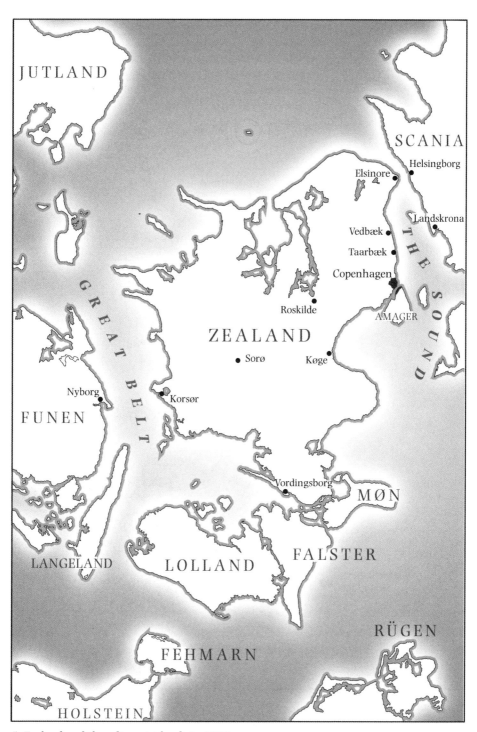

JUTLAND

SCANIA

Helsingborg

Elsinore

Landskrona

Vedbæk

THE SOUND

Taarbæk

Copenhagen

Roskilde

AMAGER

ZEALAND

GREAT BELT

Sorø

Køge

Nyborg

Korsør

FUNEN

Vordingsborg

MØN

LANGELAND

LOLLAND

FALSTER

RÜGEN

FEHMARN

HOLSTEIN

5. Zealand and the adjacent islands in 1807

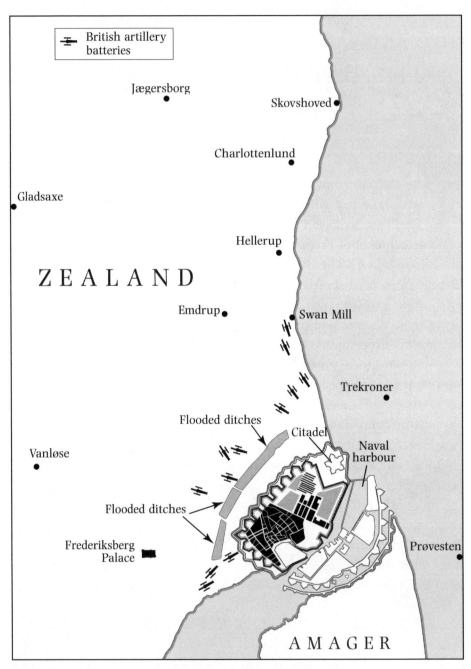

Jægersborg

Skovshoved

Charlottenlund

Gladsaxe

Hellerup

ZEALAND

Emdrup

Swan Mill

Trekroner

Flooded ditches

Citadel

Naval harbour

Vanløse

Flooded ditches

Frederiksberg Palace

Prøvesten

AMAGER

6. Copenhagen in 1807

THE BATTLE OF FRIEDLAND, 14 JUNE 1807

The Russian army had been marching for almost thirty-six hours with little rest when its advance guard reached the small town of Friedland in East Prussia on the afternoon of 13 June 1807. A small detachment of French cavalry in the town was driven off, and some prisoners taken. The Russian commander, General Levin August Bennigsen, arrived shortly afterwards. He was an experienced soldier, but in the course of the next few hours he made a decision that would lead his army to disaster and unleash a series of events that turned the power balance in Europe upside down.[1]

Bennigsen cut a sinister figure: 'a pale, withered personage of high stature and cold appearance, with a scar across his face'.[2] He was in his early sixties, a Hanoverian by birth, an example of those foreign soldiers of fortune who had taken service in the Russian army during the eighteenth century. He ultimately retired to his ancestral estates in Hanover and never learnt Russian properly, claiming with admirable complacency that his oath of allegiance had not required it of him.[3]

That oath had not prevented Bennigsen from being one of the ringleaders of the plot to murder Emperor Paul I in 1801. Few of the conspirators prospered in the new reign. Paul's son, Alexander I, had been privy to the plot, but affected or preferred to believe that its object had been to depose his father rather than kill him, and most of the assassins were eased out of positions of real power once Alexander had established himself firmly on the throne. But Bennigsen was an exception, and in January 1807 his career reached its peak when he was appointed commander of the Russian forces facing the French in East Prussia. This was no easy posting as his opponent was none other than Napoleon Bonaparte, Emperor of the French, at the height of his powers.

Since the resumption of large-scale warfare on the European continent in September 1805, Napoleon had defeated the two German great powers in turn with astonishing completeness and rapidity. Austria had been knocked out of the conflict in just over four months in late 1805. The following year, Prussia lasted little more than a month, her army crushed at the twin battles of Jena and Auerstädt on 14 October 1806. The Prussian king and the broken remnants of his army fled to the farthest corners of his kingdom to join up with the Russian forces lumbering painfully to their assistance. The Russian progress was too slow to prevent Napoleon's troops from advancing from the Oder to the line of the Vistula in November 1806.

The French took Warsaw on 28 November, but after that their progress slowed. Winter conditions, particularly the mud after sudden thaws, made movement difficult, the French supply lines had virtually collapsed and Bennigsen ceded little ground during the operations east of the Vistula between December 1806 and February 1807. Indeed, at the bloody battle of Eylau on 8 February 1807, he inflicted heavy losses on the French and fought Napoleon to a draw – the first real setback the French emperor had experienced in a great battle. After that, both armies retreated to their winter quarters and both commanders issued vainglorious proclamations professing victory.[4]

Bennigsen had many critics on his own side,[5] but he had not done badly against the most renowned general of his day and against the most fearsome military machine in Europe, Napoleon's *Grande Armée*. But appearances were deceptive. During the three-month lull that followed, Napoleon was reorganising his lines of communication and bringing up reinforcements. By the time that active operations resumed in the main theatre of war in early June 1807, Napoleon had 100,000 men guarding his rear and controlling Germany and another 220,000 to put into the field against Bennigsen's 120,000.[6]

Bennigsen made the first move with a tentative advance, but quickly fell back as Napoleon started to mount an enveloping movement. On 10 June Bennigsen inflicted another setback on Napoleon when he repulsed an attack on his entrenched army at Heilsberg on the west bank of the Alle. Napoleon had failed because he had attacked piecemeal with too few troops and without waiting for the rest of his army to come up. Despite this success, Bennigsen still faced the risk of envelopment by superior forces and, on the night of 11–12 June, he slipped away from Heilsberg, crossed the river and marched north along the east bank of the Alle. He hardly stopped before his advance guard of cavalry reconnoitred Friedland on the afternoon of 13 June. As he had done several times before over the preceding seven months, Bennigsen had given the French a bloody nose and then eluded them.

So far, so good, but it was now that Bennigsen made his disastrous misjudgement. Napoleon had established his headquarters at Eylau, only 20 kilometres from Friedland, on the previous day. Friedland lay on the west bank of the Alle and there was no natural obstacle between it and Eylau. The Russian army, however, was approaching on the east bank, shielded from the French by the river, and it was only the advance guard that had crossed the single bridge at Friedland and occupied the town. When some French prisoners were brought before Bennigsen and interrogated, they told him – quite truthfully – that there were only weak French forces in the immediate vicinity of Friedland. Additional prisoners taken in the early hours of 14 June confirmed this and added that Napoleon was marching in the opposite direction towards one of the last great Prussian centres not yet in his possession, the old trading town of Königsberg.[7] This last piece of information was untrue. Napoleon had detached a strong force of 60,000 men towards Königsberg, but the greater part of his army was headed for Friedland. In ignorance of this vital fact, Bennigsen took the fateful decision to send the bulk of his army as it arrived to the west bank of the Alle and to draw it up in the cornfields just outside Friedland.

It was a decision that proved devastating to Bennigsen's reputation as a military commander and he later tried to explain it away in the slippery, vague and mendacious account of the battle that features in his memoirs. He claimed that he sent his army across the river because he wanted to rest his exhausted troops for 24 hours and believed that no significant French forces could reach him within that time.[8] This explanation is self-evidently preposterous – 'one does not rest an army by marching it toward the enemy'.[9] If that had been Bennigsen's true purpose, he would have merely secured Friedland and its bridge and left most of his troops on the east bank of the Alle. Instead, he marched 46,000 men across the river. His real motive must therefore have been different. Perhaps he hoped to inflict another Heilsberg on Napoleon by crushing the small French force outside Friedland before slipping away and continuing his retreat. Perhaps his ambitions soared higher than that. On the morning of

13 June he had written to Emperor Alexander that he intended, once he had 'definite news' that Napoleon was moving against Königsberg, to recross the Alle and attack the enemy in the flank or from the rear.[10] Either way, he was marching his army into a trap of his own making.

For a start, the terrain was not favourable to the Russians. At this point, the Alle snaked lazily through broad flatlands between banks that were high and steep. The land to the west of Friedland where Bennigsen drew up his army was part of a small cultivated plain, which sloped gently uphill to a ring of forests. The rye and the wheat were tall at that season, and the day was oppressively hot. The French therefore had the advantage of being shielded by the woods and placed on slightly higher ground than their opponents. Marshal Lannes, who commanded the French forces outside Friedland on the morning of 14 June, certainly had far fewer men than Bennigsen – probably no more than 10,000 at the outset – but he was able to contain the Russians on the plain, while he sent desperate appeals to Napoleon urging him to hurry forward additional troops.

His first messenger, a Captain Marbot, found the emperor, already mounted and leaving Eylau. After he heard Marbot's report, Napoleon set out with him at a gallop towards Friedland. As he rode, he was cheered by the marching soldiers he passed, frequently calling back that 'Today is a lucky day, the anniversary of Marengo', when he had defeated the Austrians in northern Italy on 14 June 1800.[11]

Napoleon reached the village of Posthenen, which lay 3 kilometres before Friedland, on the fringe of the forest, around the middle of the day. He immediately ascended a hillock behind the village to survey the scene. He found it difficult to believe the evidence of his eyes. The main Russian field army, which had proved so elusive to his grasp, appeared to be drawn up on the plain outside Friedland. It seemed incredible that Bennigsen intended to fight a great battle with the river at his back. Napoleon sent General Savary, his aide de camp, to reconnoitre whether this was truly the case. Savary's report was unambiguous: Russian troops were still crossing the Alle at Friedland, where they had built three floating pontoons to supplement the single permanent bridge in the town.

It seemed as if the Russian army was at his mercy. Had he been a more religious man, the emperor might have thanked divine intervention for delivering the enemy into his hands. But Napoleon believed in his luck, his destiny, his star, more than any Christian deity. He rapidly drew up a plan of attack. If he could seize or destroy the river crossings at Friedland, cutting off the Russian retreat, a crushing victory was in prospect. The plain in front of him was bisected by a small stream flowing through Posthenen down to Friedland, separating the Russian left wing from the centre and right. The stream was not wide, but it was an obstacle to the free movement of troops, horses and guns. This natural feature of the landscape facilitated Napoleon's plan, which was simplicity itself. Once sufficient reinforcements had arrived, the Russian left would be overwhelmed and Friedland and its bridges captured. Only then would the rest of the French army move against the Russian centre and right, which would be driven back against the Alle with no means of escape.

But in the fog of war nothing is certain, and as he waited for more troops to come up from Eylau, the emperor was still not sure how he would proceed. Perhaps the enemy were present in greater numbers than seemed to be the case? At 3 p.m. he sent orders to recall most of the force that had marched against Königsberg, writing that if he 'were led to suppose that the enemy is in very great force, it is possible that he may rest satisfied to-day with bombarding him' and defer the main battle until the following day.[12] In the event, that did not prove necessary. By 5 p.m., sufficient reinforcements had arrived from Eylau for the emperor to signal that the attack should commence. Although Napoleon could not have known it for sure at the time, he now possessed not only the advantages of the terrain but also an overwhelming numerical superiority – 80,000 men to Bennigsen's 46,000.

By that time, the two armies had been facing each other across the plain at Friedland for about five hours without significant fighting beyond a desultory exchange of artillery fire. It is not clear when the penny dropped for Bennigsen, but it does not make much difference. Retreat would have been extremely hazardous: it had taken five hours for his army to cross the Alle, and if he tried to pull back in daylight, the French would fall on his retreating columns.[13] His best chance was to wait for nightfall in the hope that Napoleon would not attack him before then. Even so, he claims in his memoirs that when some of his officers ascended the church tower in Friedland and saw in the distance a great cloud of dust rising along the roads from Eylau, indicating the arrival of yet more French reinforcements, he did give orders for a retreat back across the Alle.[14] If so, it was too late – the French attack had already begun.

The Russian troops fought with their usual bravery and endurance, but there could hardly be any doubt as to the outcome of the fierce battle that began as the French right wing advanced down from the woods. The fighting was vicious: at one point thirty-eight pieces of French artillery were firing grapeshot into the massed ranks of the Russian infantry at sixty paces, mowing them down as with a scythe. Eventually, after a stubborn struggle, the Russian left was driven back into the town of Friedland. The bridges back across the Alle were afire. Accounts differ as to the cause: maybe they were set alight by French artillery, maybe by the Russians themselves either accidentally or to prevent pursuit by the French. Most of the Russian soldiers who tried to escape by swimming drowned in the river, dragged down by their heavy equipment. Only now, with the escape route through Friedland destroyed, did the French centre and left advance. The ruin of the Russians would have been total had they not discovered a previously unknown ford, deep and difficult but just usable, a little downstream from Friedland. Even so, of the 46,000 men who had crossed to the west bank of the Alle in the previous 24 hours, 18,000 were left dead or wounded on the battlefield. French losses were much lighter – 7,000 or 8,000 men. That night the French Imperial guard, surrounding the emperor, slept on the battlefield where the Russian centre had stood. Four days later, in the seventy-ninth bulletin of the *Grande Armée*, Napoleon declared with more than customary effrontery: 'Thus has Providence punished those, who instead of negotiating with good faith to bring about a salutary peace, treated that object with derision, and regarded the repose taken by the conquerors as a proof of timidity and weakness'.[15]

There was no close pursuit of the Russians. This helped Bennigsen to reassemble his broken forces on the east bank of the Alle and to march on 15 June to Wehlau, where he crossed the Pregel, putting another river between himself and the French. But he did not stop there. He destroyed the bridge at Wehlau and headed for the river Niemen, which his army crossed on 18 June at Tilsit over boat bridges, which were once again burnt behind them. Only now, almost on the borders of the Russian empire itself, did he stop. The French had entered Königsberg on 16 June. Apart from the city of Memel, virtually all Prussian territory was now in enemy hands, and only Bennigsen's beaten army stood between Russia and French invasion.

Chapter 1

LORD GRANVILLE LEVESON GOWER IN EAST PRUSSIA, JUNE 1807

ARRIVAL

On 9 June, five days before the battle of Friedland was fought, a British frigate, the *Solebay*, anchored in the roads of the Prussian port of Memel. It carried the newly appointed British ambassador to Russia, Lord Granville Leveson Gower. It had been a tiresome passage of nineteen days from Yarmouth against contrary winds, but Gower had almost reached his destination. Since early May, the Russian emperor and his closest entourage, including his foreign minister, General Andrei Budberg, had been based at the small Prussian town of Tilsit, just under 100 kilometres away.

Gower was thirty-three, the son of a marquis but hard up, a situation not improved by his taste for gambling.[1] As his later daughter-in-law put it, 'though reputed the best whist-player of the day, he was never a fortunate one'[2] and is said to have once lost £23,000 at a single sitting.[3] He was the long-standing lover of Henrietta, Lady Bessborough, twelve years his senior, mother of four by her husband and of another two off the record by Gower. As a younger son, Gower needed to make a good marriage, but had so far failed to land a suitable bride, even though he was regarded as among the handsomest men of British high society. His looks appear to have made little impression on the celebrated courtesan Harriette Wilson, who did not think he came up to scratch when she was looking for a new protector. According to her notoriously unreliable memoirs, she marched Gower up Primrose Hill on a sweltering London day and then down again, before dismissing him as unsuitable.[4]

Gower was also ambitious and here his family connections helped. His father, the marquis of Stafford, had been useful to William Pitt during the early days of his premiership in the 1780s, and Pitt took the young Gower under his wing, conferring on him a number of junior appointments in government service, usually of a diplomatic nature. Gower had also been a member of the House of Commons since 1795. His big break came in 1804, when he was appointed ambassador to Russia. He only served for little over a year, but he was a successful envoy and played a significant role in negotiating the alliance between Britain and Russia that was concluded in 1805.

Gower had another connection in political life that proved more important to him in the longer term than the patronage of Pitt, who died in February 1806. At Oxford, Gower had formed a close friendship with George Canning, another protégé of Pitt's. In March 1807, the government of Lord Grenville, the so-called Ministry of All the Talents, had fallen as the result of a dispute with the king over a question of domestic politics and had been replaced by an administration largely composed of the former followers of Pitt under the nominal leadership of the decrepit duke of Portland. The new foreign secretary, and a driving force in the new government, was Canning, who immediately urged Gower to accept reappointment as ambassador to Russia.

Gower had personal reasons for taking the post. On his former tour of duty, he had formed some kind of amorous attachment to a Princess Galitzin – referred to as 'the little Barbarian' or 'la Blonde' in his correspondence with Lady Bessborough – and a return to Russia might open up the prospect of marriage if she could divest herself of an inconvenient husband. Canning's exhortations were seconded by Lord Harrowby, Gower's brother-in-law, who supplemented the arguments of public duty with a glancing reference to Gower's marital interests by pointing out that the mission would give Gower 'the opportunity of settling the affairs of Europe as well as your own'. This second consideration weighed heavily with Gower. He told Lady Bessborough that he intended his mission to be brief and that his 'real motive' in accepting it was 'the persuasion that if I omit this opportunity of renewing my intimate and confidential intercourse [with Princess Galitzin] we shall be separated completely'. He added – perhaps to remind his mistress that she was his accomplice in this venture – that if he failed to go, there would be 'very little chance of the renewal of that friendship on which you have always agreed with me in setting so high a value'.[5]

Gower's 'real motive' for going to Russia may have been personal, but it was not, of course, the reason why Canning sent him. The foreign secretary had also entrusted his friend with a vital mission – to restore and solidify the alliance with Russia that he had helped to negotiate two years earlier. That alliance was now in jeopardy, though it is doubtful if either Canning or Gower yet appreciated how fragile it had become. The reasons why the Anglo-Russian alliance was at crisis-point by the early summer of 1807 lie in the march of events in a Europe that had experienced more than a decade of upheaval and war since 1792.

A EUROPE AT WAR

In the eighteenth century international relations had come to be dominated by five great powers.[6] Some, like Austria and France, were long-established as leading states, while others – Britain, Prussia and Russia – had emerged more recently as players of the first rank. The political culture of international relations was permeated by a set of attitudes and assumptions that favoured the great powers while turning middling and lesser states into their potential victims. The maintenance of a 'balance of power' – a state system where each great power was restrained and prevented from becoming dominant by the strength of the others – was treated as the overriding goal of international relations. This in its turn produced the principle of 'compensation' – that any increase in the strength of one great power had to be matched by an equivalent increase among other great powers that might feel threatened as a result. The ultimate expression of such a mindset was the three partitions of Poland of 1774, 1793 and 1795, which had incrementally wiped one of the largest states in Europe off the map and divided its territories between Austria, Prussia and Russia.

The fate of Poland involved a territorial revolution in eastern Europe, but far more wide-ranging changes were unleashed by the series of interlocking wars that started in 1792 in the wake of the French Revolution three years earlier. The revolution prompted an explosion of national energy within France that was ultimately channelled into military expansion. The revolutionaries proclaimed many new doctrines, among them that France was entitled to her 'natural frontiers' – the Pyrenees, the Rhine and the Alps. Achieving that goal intensified the more predatory practices of the old regime, and within a decade the former state system in western Europe had been overturned. Many old principalities had been eradicated. In Italy, the venerable republic of Venice had ceased to exist, partitioned by Napoleon to give Austria compensation for territorial losses elsewhere. And in Germany, the number of political units within the equally venerable Holy Roman Empire, itself abolished in 1806, had been reduced from several hundred in 1789 to about forty in 1803.[7]

France had been brought to a position of dominance in western Europe such as she had never enjoyed before. French expansion had not proceeded unchallenged, but opposition had been fragmented. The other great powers were divided by mutual tensions and rivalries, and it was not always self-evident to them that their interests would be best served by resistance to French expansion. Prussia, for example, pursued a policy of neutrality from 1795 to 1806, often hoping to achieve concrete benefits for herself through cooperation with France. Paul I only took Russia to war with revolutionary France in 1798 and soon pulled her out again. The sporadic involvement of Prussia and Russia underlines that these wars were not primarily ideological conflicts – though it occasionally suited the participants to present them as such. There was, of course, a tension between the values of old-regime Europe and the ideas of modernity represented, however imperfectly and at times savagely, by the French Revolution, but it was usually an undercurrent rather than a persistent cause of warfare. This was especially true after Napoleon Bonaparte seized power in France in 1799, initially as First Consul of the Republic and then, in 1804, as Emperor of the French. He never ceased to be a parvenu to the leaders of the traditional dynastic states, but he was also regarded as a statesman who had brought order and stability to France after the turmoil of revolution.

In the early years of his rule, it looked as if Napoleon had not only restored orderly government in France but also laid the foundations for peace with her neighbours. The most consistent opponents of French expansion among the great powers had been Austria and Britain through the 1790s. Austria had in effect borne the brunt of the war on the European continent after 1792. The price had been ultimate defeat and in 1801 Austria had made peace with France. Britain followed suit and concluded the peace of Amiens with France in 1802. Both states explicitly recognised France's natural frontiers and tacitly accepted French hegemony in southern Germany and northern Italy. In the case of Britain, any hopes of a durable peace were soon disappointed and war was renewed between Britain and France in March 1803, setting in train a new cycle of conflict that would continue until 1815.

For the first two-and-a-half years, Britain had faced France alone without a major ally, but she was reasonably well placed to cope with this position.[8] She held no territory on the European mainland, if we disregard the electorate of Hanover, George III's ancestral lands in Germany, which were indeed occupied by the French within months after the outbreak of war. Britain was unique among the great powers in that her strength resided in her navy and her financial resources as the greatest commercial, manufacturing and maritime nation in the world. So long as Britain retained naval supremacy, she was shielded from the ferocious might of the French army. Since 1792, the Royal Navy had repeatedly defeated the fleets of France and her allies, and British naval pre-eminence was decisively confirmed in October 1805 by Nelson's great victory over the French and the Spaniards at Trafalgar.

Matters did not look so clear-cut at the time. During the first thirty-two months of the war, the British public and the British political elite lived in fear of French invasion as Napoleon assembled a great army and built transports for his troops at Boulogne. And then there was Ireland. In 1798, the United Irishmen had risen in rebellion against British rule, and a French squadron had eluded the Royal Navy to land an invasion force in Ireland. Both the uprising and the invasion had been easily crushed, but British statesmen could never forget Ireland, the perpetual source of a nagging ache of anxiety. Even after Trafalgar, the fear of invasion lingered on: Napoleon certainly had not given up. He pushed on with a naval-building programme right up until 1813.[9]

Naval supremacy might prevent invasion, but it would never alone defeat France. The British army was small, by far the smallest among the great powers. During the wars of the 1790s, the major British contribution to the struggle on land had taken the form of money, subsidies or loans to her allies to ease the financial burden of war and to keep troops in the field. There was a school of thought within Britain that favoured a go-it-alone, 'blue-water' strategy of overseas colonial conquest and letting the continent go hang. This strategy had the advantage of

depending on British resources alone, and within the first few years after
the resumption of war in March 1803 the British had indeed seized many
of the colonies of France and her allies. But most of the British political
elite were not content with a policy of isolationist colonialism except as a
short-term expedient and looked to allies among the continental great
powers so that war could be renewed on the European mainland.

British attention focused on Russia in this respect, and the British
courted her assiduously in 1803 and 1804. At first, Alexander had been
unresponsive, more concerned with internal reform than foreign policy,
but he was gradually drawn towards renewed Russian involvement in the
affairs of western Europe by ceaseless French encroachments in Germany
and Italy and the French threat to Russian influence in the Balkans and
the eastern Mediterranean. The fears aroused by Napoleon's hegemonic
ambitions pushed Alexander towards Britain, the only state at war with
France. In late 1804 and early 1805 Britain and Russia negotiated a
treaty of alliance against France and the terms for an overall European
settlement. It was an ambitious programme, designed to confine France
west of the Rhine and to create restraining centres of power in Germany
and Italy under Russian protection to contain the French in the future.
Like Britain, Russia was unable to strike directly at Napoleon for
geographical reasons, so the alliance depended on bringing in other states,
in particular at least one of the two German great powers, Austria and
Prussia. In the course of 1805, this goal seemed close to achievement.
Sweden and Naples were coaxed into the coalition and so too – kicking
and shouting – was Austria, who would have to do the bulk of the hard
fighting. More remarkably, even Prussia edged towards joining the war
against France.

It was a great edifice of dreams built on sand. As soon as he got wind of
what was afoot, Napoleon broke up his camp at Boulogne and marched
the *Grande Armée* straight for the Austrian heartlands. Within months
Vienna had been occupied and the Austrians, along with the Russian
army sent to help them, had been crushed at Austerlitz on 2 December
1806. The small British and Swedish forces that had been landed to
operate in northern Germany were withdrawn and Prussia learnt of the
defeat in time to pull back. Alexander, who had been with his army at
Austerlitz, hurried back to St Petersburg and the Russian army was
withdrawn inside Russia's frontiers. As for Austria, she had little option

but to make peace at the price of serious, though not crippling, territorial losses in late December 1805.

Britain and Russia, along with their smaller partners, remained at war with France, but the elimination of Austria brought a temporary end to major operations on the European continent as both engaged in ultimately fruitless peace negotiations with France for the next eight or nine months. It was the outbreak of war between France and Prussia in October 1806 that reactivated hostilities in central Europe. The peace talks with France had just broken down, and the Russians sought to resume the struggle alongside Prussia. In the event, the rapid collapse of Prussia – even more rapid and complete than that of Austria the previous year – meant that the fighting took place on the borders of Russia.

The Russians held their own in East Prussia from December 1806 onwards, but their position was critical during that bleak winter and the spring of 1807 as supply and financial problems were added to the purely military pressure on the Russian army.[10] Nothing could have been more helpful to the Russian cause than Austrian intervention. Now that Napoleon was operating in East Prussia with lines of communication stretching back through Germany, Austrian re-entry into the war would place him at serious risk. But Austria held back, despite all the exhortations that Britain and Russia could bring to bear, and contented herself with repeated offers of mediation between the belligerents.[11] Alexander did not get much joy from Britain either. His request for a massive loan of £5,000,000 sterling in November 1806 was declined and the only monetary help he received was the remainder of the subsidy (£500,000) pledged in 1805, though some money was also made available to the Prussians.[12] Above all, the Grenville government in Britain was evasive and unhelpful in response to his pleas for a diversion – a British landing on the coast of western Europe – to relieve the pressure on the Russians in the east.[13]

Instead, Napoleon proved more successful at creating a diversion than his enemies did. In the last months of 1806 French influence at Constantinople led to a crisis in relations between Russia and the Ottoman Empire, which eventually prompted a Russian occupation of the two Danubian Principalities of Moldavia and Wallachia, followed by a Turkish declaration of war. The Turks were unable to dislodge the Russians from the principalities, but the war in the Balkans tied down substantial

Russian forces that were badly needed in eastern Prussia. As well as opening up a second front in the Balkans, Napoleon also took some steps to recruit the Poles to his side. He set up a provisional Polish government in Warsaw and encouraged the Poles to see him as a liberator. For the moment, he proceeded cautiously and restricted his activities to the Prussian-ruled provinces of former Poland that he had conquered. He did not want to provoke Austria or to rule out the chance of a compromise peace with Russia, but the spectre of a French-inspired revolt in Russia's Polish provinces was something that Alexander and his advisers could not forget.

It is likely that Alexander pinned excessive hopes on the benefits he would have derived from a British diversion. Napoleon anticipated and prepared for a British descent by sea on his flank. He calculated, correctly enough, that a British expeditionary force would not exceed 25,000 and he issued a stream of precautionary instructions for dealing with a British diversion from his headquarters in Poland.[14] Napoleon was certainly vulnerable to Austrian intervention, but much less so to a British landing on the coasts of France, Holland or Germany. But that did not prevent such a diversion from becoming an obsession with Alexander, a touchstone of British loyalty, by the spring of 1807.

Such disappointments and lesser sources of friction corroded Alexander's faith in Britain, but a recent scholar is doubtless correct when he observes that the Anglo-Russian alliance was being undermined by more than the ungenerous approach of Lord Grenville and his colleagues. Inter-state relations are not generally a sentimental business, and the reserved attitude of Britain reflected a change in the distribution of power between the two states. They had gone to war in 1805 on the basis that Austria and, if possible, Prussia would bear the brunt of the fighting, and this assumption no longer applied. Trafalgar had reinforced Britain's invulnerability, but Austerlitz and Jena had swept away Russia's.[15]

LORD GOWER AT TILSIT

Canning attached much importance to creating a spirit of greater harmony between Britain and Russia, and the appointment of Gower was one of his earliest actions after taking over as foreign secretary on 25 March 1807. But nothing could disrupt the primacy of domestic politics. Soon after Grenville had fallen, parliament was dissolved so that the new ministry could strengthen its position in the commons, and Gower needed to stay in England to get himself re-elected before he set off for Russia. As a result, he did not leave London until 19 May. Canning had written to Gower that his mission was one 'upon . . . which the fate of Europe in a great measure depends'.[16] But not only did Gower proceed to Russia at a leisurely pace. Canning also failed to provide him with very much that would satisfy the Russians.

Canning wrote a veritable booklet of instructions and letters for Gower between 16 and 18 May, running to over one hundred folio pages, on the eve of his departure. They covered many subjects, large and small, but their core concerned the maintenance of the alliance and what Britain could do by way of financial assistance and a military diversion to help her allies. Canning dealt with the perception that Britain had been selfish and aloof towards her allies over the previous six months by adopting a typical politician's approach – while ostensibly denying the truth of the perception, he implied that it was the fault of the previous government. Gower was to do all he could 'to destroy any impression, which may unaccountably have prevailed' in Russia, that Britain wished to withdraw from involvement with the continent and to treat her own interests as 'separate' from those of her allies. 'From whatever source this misrepresentation may have flowed', Gower was to do all he could to demonstrate that Britain regarded the independence of the continental powers as essential to her own 'welfare and security'. To this end, Gower was instructed to propose a treaty for the joint prosecution of the war until the conclusion of a general peace, involving all the powers at war with France.[17]

Fine words, but they did not amount to more than a reaffirmation of the marriage vows sworn in 1805. What about the nitty-gritty? On the matter of money, Canning was less forthcoming. His instructions are convoluted, but the bottom line was not particularly helpful towards Russia. A twenty-year loan of £5,000,000 guaranteed by the British government was still out of the question. The maximum available for other forms of financial assistance to continental powers for the remainder of 1807 was just under three million pounds. If subsidies to other allies like Prussia and Sweden were deducted, that would leave at most £2,600,000, but Prussia might need more, and above all the possibility that Austria might be 'induced or compelled' to join the war needed to be constantly borne in mind. Gower should therefore try and persuade the Russians to postpone consideration of their own needs until the possibilities of bringing in Austria had been fully explored and, if necessary, to go short themselves in order to secure Austrian involvement in the war.[18]

Nor was Canning able to adopt a particularly helpful tone over the central question of a British diversion. So much so that he felt obliged to write that it was 'painful to me' to be unable to give 'more distinct and positive assurances both as to the time and the amount of such a detachment'. Once again, it was handy – and justified – to be able to blame the Talents: the Grenville government had allowed the amount of tonnage available to transport troops to decline and it would take some time to reassemble the necessary shipping.[19] Things were different now that Canning and his friends were in charge. No exertion would be spared to collect the requisite amount of tonnage. Even so, no precise time was given as to when the British expedition might sail, and all Canning would say about its likely strength was that it would, he hoped, amount to not less than 16,000 men. There was no absolute guarantee that the expedition would sail at all. The British did not have a large enough force to justify a separate operation of their own in the north of Germany and therefore had to think in terms of cooperating with Sweden. The Swedes still held out in their province of Swedish Pomerania on the north flank of Napoleon's line of communications. Once a report had been received on the possibility of a joint operation with the Swedes, the British government would consider it with a view to action, but only in so far as that seemed 'consistent with the principles of military prudence'.[20]

It was not much with which to mollify a hard-pressed and aggrieved ally. Canning was sending Gower if not exactly naked, then scantily clad into the conference chamber. At sea, Gower kept busy by writing an abstract of Canning's despatches in French, and found 'upon this close examination of them that there are many points upon which I have not received sufficiently precise instructions, and upon which I am left to guess at the meaning and intentions of my employers'. He was confident that he was equal to the situation,[21] but he received a rude awakening when he reached Tilsit on 11 June, just three days before the fateful battle of Friedland.

Gower was shocked by his first – and, as it would transpire, his last – formal audience with Alexander. He found the emperor's 'language and tone . . . perfectly unexpected'. Gower had hardly presented his credentials and uttered a few customary banalities before Alexander raised his first and most pressing complaint: that the whole burden of the war had fallen on his armies. He had repeatedly urged 'the absolute necessity' of a continental diversion by Britain, and 'hopes had been held out' that a British force would be sent to northern Germany, but nothing had happened. After some talk as to how best the British expedition might be employed, Alexander abruptly ended the discussion of this subject 'by saying, act where you please, provided you act at all'.

It was, of course, beneath the dignity of a monarch to discuss financial details in person, but Alexander also took the opportunity to point out how much he resented as a slur on his honour the refusal of the British government to facilitate his loan of £5,000,000 in London. Gower did not find the audience a happy experience: 'I cannot say that the emperor appeared perfectly satisfied with the answers made by me, to the various complaints urged by him.' But Alexander, like Canning, was free with rhetorical assurances. Despite his grievances against Britain, he was determined not to change 'his present system of politics' and declared that 'No misfortunes . . . should make him stoop to Bonaparte, he would sooner retire to Casan or even Tobolsk'.[22] Rash and, as it proved, untruthful words.

THE ARMISTICE

On 14 June Alexander set off to review troops who were on their way to reinforce Bennigsen's army as they crossed the Russian border onto Prussian territory. He left Budberg and most of the imperial entourage at Tilsit. The next morning, alarming reports reached the town. There was no news yet of the disaster at Friedland, but it seemed that some sort of detached French force had got itself behind Bennigsen's army and might be within striking distance of Tilsit. Budberg therefore decided to withdraw to the safer vicinity of Tauroggen, just inside the Russian frontier. He clearly sensed that the position was critical and wrote to Alexander suggesting a meeting between him and the king of Prussia, along with their first ministers, to consider the situation.[23] Significantly, he did not propose inviting Gower to the meeting, and when Gower expressed a desire to accompany him to Tauroggen, Budberg discouraged the idea by saying that 'in all probability no lodging of any sort' could be found for him there. Gower evidently did not regard roughing it as a proper part of the diplomatic life and returned to Memel.[24] It would be a long time before he met a member of the Russian leadership again.

Alexander was at the little village of Olitcha on the Russian border on 16 June when he received a report on Friedland, written the previous day, from the Russian commander. Bennigsen played down the extent of his defeat shamelessly, but still described the opening of peace negotiations with the French as 'indispensable', if only to gain time. Alexander was not deceived. At the same time he saw a letter from the foreign ministry's representative attached to the army, which made it clear that the Russian losses had been 'immense' and that Bennigsen had sent him an extremely sanitised version of events. But the conclusion was the same: there was no choice but to propose an armistice as quickly as possible or to enter into peace negotiations, while the army and the reinforcements that were on their way still enabled Russia to obtain honourable terms.[25]

Alexander's reply to Bennigsen betrayed his sense of bitterness and humiliation – and his self-absorption. The letter was largely concerned with his own feelings. 'I was far from expecting, *mon général*, after entrusting you with such a fine army . . . the news which I have just received from you.' Having got in his rebuke, Alexander authorised Bennigsen to negotiate for an armistice, if he had no other way of escaping the awkward position in which he found himself, provided that he did so in his own name alone. Alexander ended with another reproach: 'You will understand how much it costs me to follow this road'.[26]

Alexander had lost confidence in Bennigsen and was not prepared to leave the arrangement of an armistice to him. Instead, he sent Prince Dmitri Lobanov-Rostovsky to the front to carry out this task. In his instructions to Lobanov, Alexander told him that he was not to take the initiative in proposing peace negotiations in addition to an armistice, but that if the French expressed a desire to put an end to the war, Lobanov might reply that this was also Alexander's wish.[27] The Russians made contact with the French on 19 June once they had completed their withdrawal over the Niemen. When Lobanov saw Napoleon's chief of staff, Marshal Berthier, that day at Tilsit, which was now in French hands, he received an affable, not to say greasy welcome. Berthier referred warmly to the prospect of peace and waxed lyrical when Lobanov said that Alexander would never consent to humiliating terms and in particular to any loss of Russian territory – it was, Berthier declared, to do Napoleon an injustice to suppose he had anything like that in mind. That evening, another senior French officer, General Duroc, crossed the river to Russian headquarters and spoke with Bennigsen, who saw him alone, leaving Lobanov waiting in vain for an invitation to join them. Duroc repeated that Napoleon wanted more than a mere armistice and that he wished to negotiate a definitive peace. Duroc also dropped remarks that could be interpreted as suggesting a personal meeting between Napoleon and Alexander.

The two sides were circling each other like wary wrestlers, but there was no disguising that the rituals of courtship were afoot. Alexander received reports on these discussions the next day at the little village of Schawel. His response was effusive. Lobanov was to tell Berthier that Alexander shared the desire for an end to the bloodshed and had authorised Lobanov to enter into discussions about peace as soon as an armistice of one month's duration had been concluded. Alexander had come a long way from his cautious and reluctant acquiescence in a mere armistice signed in Bennigsen's name alone four days earlier.

The king of Prussia, Frederick William III, and a couple of his leading advisers reached Schawel later on 20 June. Budberg had initially withdrawn to Tauroggen when Tilsit was abandoned, but Schawel was deeper inside Russia and therefore more secure. The Prussians agreed that peace with France was the only way, and believed that Alexander would allow them to take the lead in the negotiations on behalf of both themselves and Russia. Alexander appears to have paid lip service to this notion, but the discussions between the French and the Russians had already acquired a momentum that relegated Prussia to the sidelines.[28]

Lobanov was back at Tilsit to see Berthier on 21 June. The wording of the armistice was rapidly agreed. It was valid for one month, with both armies holding their existing positions, and stipulated that Alexander and Napoleon would nominate negotiators to conclude a definitive peace with the least possible delay. As soon as the armistice was signed, Lobanov was admitted into the presence of Napoleon, who greeted him warmly and invited him to stay for dinner. Champagne was opened, toasts drunk. They remained together for two hours. Napoleon was expansive, holding forth about his high regard for Alexander and how the mutual interests of France and Russia required an alliance between the two states. The *pièce de resistance* came when Napoleon led Lobanov to a table on which a map of Europe had been spread out. He traced the line of the Vistula with his finger and declared that it was the natural line of delimitation between the two empires. 'Your master must dominate on one side, and I on the other'.[29]

Now that the discussions with the French were under way, Alexander had felt safe enough to move south to Tauroggen, only 30 kilometres from Tilsit, by the time Lobanov returned with the armistice. He countersigned it and sent Lobanov straight back to Tilsit with the ratified document. Alexander, who tended to see everything through the prism of his own self-regard, was enthralled by Napoleon's remarks. Lobanov was to express to Napoleon how gratified Alexander was by all that the French emperor had said. The remainder of Alexander's instructions, hastily written in pencil, give us a glimpse into his excited state of mind. Lobanov was also to say

how much I desire that a close union between our two nations should repair all the injuries of the past. You will say to him that this union between France and Russia has constantly been the object of my desires and that I am convinced that it alone can assure the happiness and tranquillity of the world. An entirely new system must replace the one which has existed until now, and I flatter myself that we shall reach agreement easily with the Emperor Napoleon, provided that we negotiate without intermediaries. A durable peace can be concluded between us within a few days.[30]

When it came to laying it on with a trowel, Napoleon had met his equal.

On the evening of 23 June, once Lobanov had departed, Alexander left Tauroggen for the headquarters of Bennigsen's army on the north bank of the Niemen, almost facing Tilsit. It was as if 'an irresistible force were drawing him closer to the place where Napoleon was to be found'.[31]

The ratified armistices were exchanged that same night at Tilsit, but Lobanov was not granted a new audience with the French emperor. Instead, Duroc asked him whether he had been instructed to make any overtures regarding peace negotiations. Lobanov replied that a direct interview between the two sovereigns would doubtless help to bring the negotiations to a speedy conclusion. On 24 June Duroc appeared at Russian headquarters to convey Napoleon's salutations to Alexander and to propose a meeting between them the following day on neutral ground, namely a raft in the middle of the river Niemen. Alexander accepted the invitation at once.

Napoleon wrote the same day that the initiative for an interview came from Alexander and that personally he was fairly indifferent to the prospect, but would not refuse to meet him.[32] The first part of this statement was technically correct, but misleading. The initial oblique overtures had come from the French side – though the courtship rapidly became mutual. Once he had baited the hook at the audience he granted Lobanov, Napoleon had been able to let Alexander make the running. Either way, the stage was set for one of the most abiding images of the era, the famous meeting of the two emperors in mid-river. Today we would call it a summit conference. It was a meeting that had potentially sweeping consequences for the whole of Europe, and not least for Russia's most important ally, Britain.

Britain's man on the spot had been unable to play any part in the discussions leading to the meeting of the two emperors. When Gower left Tilsit on 15 June for Memel, Budberg promised to keep him informed, but he failed to do so. However, on 19 June, Gower learnt at Memel that the Prussian king, Frederick William III, and his foreign minister had been invited to meet Alexander at Schawel and were setting off the next morning. Though he had received no invitation, Gower decided to go to Schawel too.[33] His attempts to gate-crash the conference were unavailing. He had not even got half way when he learnt that the two sovereigns were leaving Schawel for Tauroggen. He was advised 'on account of the total want of horses upon that road' to return to Memel. The two sovereigns did not, in fact, leave Schawel for Tauroggen until two days later, and it is reasonable to assume that Gower was deliberately misled in order to prevent him from turning up on Alexander's doorstep.

Back at Memel, Gower heard 'strong reports' that an armistice had been concluded with the French and that peace negotiations were about to begin. He immediately sent a messenger to Budberg on 23 June with a letter requesting an interview and some definite information on the subject of the negotiations with the French. Budberg's reply confirmed that a one-month armistice had been signed, but he made no mention of peace negotiations or the impending meeting between the two emperors. As for Gower's request for an interview, it would give Budberg 'great pleasure' to comply with his wishes if only he could foresee where Alexander would stay even for a few days. As soon as they were more settled in one place, he would be in touch. Gower correctly surmised from all this that 'under the present circumstances' the Russians regarded the presence of the British ambassador as 'inconvenient'. A separate peace was clearly on the cards.[34] For Gower, the big freeze was on.

Chapter 2

TWO EMPERORS AT TILSIT, JUNE–JULY 1807

'THE FINE WORDS OF TILSIT'

Late in the morning on 25 June, Alexander arrived in a carriage on the banks of the Niemen opposite Tilsit accompanied by a numerous entourage.[1] Thirty minutes later, Napoleon reached the other bank, galloping between a double line of soldiers from his guard. At almost the same moment, Alexander and Napoleon set off in open boats for a raft in mid-river, each accompanied by five companions. The raft was large and had space for two wooden pavilions. The larger one was 'very nicely furnished', according to Budberg, who was there.[2] French engineers had toiled through the night to prepare the raft for its august occupants.[3] There is some uncertainty as to how they greeted each other. One source refers to a handshake, but Bennigsen and Napoleon in the 85th bulletin of the *Grande Armée* speak of a cordial embrace. The two emperors spoke alone for over an hour in one of the pavilions on the raft. They emerged, arm in arm and smiling. They parted with a handshake, having agreed to meet again on the raft the following day.

What passed between them is unknown, except that Alexander pleaded that his Prussian ally should be included in the negotiations. Throughout the interview, Frederick William sat on his horse on the river bank, watching the raft without uttering a word. At one point, driven by some inner compulsion, he spurred his horse chest-high into the water before returning to the bank.[4] Napoleon had refused to admit him to the first meeting, but he gave way to Alexander's pleas to the extent of agreeing that the king of Prussia might be present the next day, and when he returned to Tilsit he authorised Berthier to sign an armistice with Prussia. When the two emperors met on the raft for a second time on 26 June, Frederick William was there, but got a brusque reception from Napoleon, who excluded him from the invitation to dine in Tilsit that evening which he extended to Alexander. The two emperors also agreed that Alexander (but not the king of Prussia) would stay in the town of Tilsit for the duration of the peace talks, so when Alexander crossed the river on the evening of 26 June it was not just to dine with Napoleon but also to take up residence in the town. Tilsit itself was neutralised and each emperor was allowed to keep a small force there for his personal protection. Frederick William was eventually able to establish himself at a windmill in Tilsit with a small escort of troops on 28 June, and he joined Alexander at Napoleon's table for dinner each evening, but he returned to sleep the night at Bennigsen's headquarters on the north bank of the Niemen. Poor Frederick William. He was very much the fifth wheel on the cart.

The negotiations at Tilsit lasted about a fortnight and a peace treaty between France and Russia was signed on 7 July, but we do not have much by way of documentary evidence about their precise course. Alexander and Napoleon spent most of their time together. They went riding, reviewed troops and watched manoeuvres. They put in quality time poring over the maps that Napoleon loved so much. In the evenings, they dined with the king of Prussia, and then met again alone in Alexander's lodgings, having got rid of Frederick William on the pretext of retiring for the night – like two schoolboy friends who had shaken off a tiresome third party. The only task of the French and Russian negotiators charged with concluding a peace treaty was to record in writing the decisions reached by the two emperors face-to-face. It was only in the last stage of the negotiations, on 3 July, that some remaining points at issue led to the exchange of a few letters between them. These letters and the actual treaties themselves are almost the only hard information that remain about the negotiations, and it is scarcely surprising that many uncertainties surround what may in addition to the text of the treaties have been understood or half-understood between the two emperors. Much therefore depends on how we read the personalities and policy aims of the two men.

They made an odd couple. Napoleon was the classic outsider, the offspring of Corsican gentry who had been given his opportunity by the upheavals of the French Revolution to rise to supreme political power in France and to conquer most of western Europe. Few dispute that he possessed demonic energy and military, political and administrative skills that amounted to genius. But what were they for? What guiding purpose lay behind this extraordinary career? Opinions vary.[5] Some claim that he wanted to bring stability and peace and that he only fought to secure recognition of France within her 'natural frontiers' and French preponderance in western Europe. Others argue that, intoxicated with antiquity, he was driven by an imperial dream and sought to 'be the Emperor, not simply an emperor'.[6] Others again regard his restless search for power and glory as devoid of any real purpose or believe that the mentality of a mere *capo di mafia* lurked within his brilliant mind and that his foreign policy was no more than 'a criminal enterprise'.[7]

The debate about Napoleon's protean and promethean personality is ultimately irresolvable, because his words and actions can be used to support virtually all possible interpretations of his character and goals. But at Tilsit, it is not difficult to fathom his immediate and most obvious – if not his long-term – objectives. They grew out of the position in which he was placed and the opportunities laid out before him. Napoleon went into the negotiations without a written shopping list of what he intended to achieve, but it is clear that he had three pre-eminent goals. The first was to reap the fruits of the great victories he had won at Jena and Friedland over the previous nine months by consolidating his hold on northern Germany and Poland. His rough and contemptuous treatment of Frederick William was merely an affectation that served to signal his intentions in this respect. The tortuous course followed by Prussian policy in the twelve months before Jena had perhaps been impressively duplicitous, even by the standards of diplomacy in this era, but Napoleon – that past master of double dealing and bad faith – was hardly the man to complain. He had no real reason to feel more aggrieved towards Prussia than Russia,[8] but it suited his purpose to pretend to be so.

Another area of major concern to Napoleon was to remove the Russians from the eastern Mediterranean. He had been building up his position in this region for some years. The whole of mainland Italy was already under his control and he had also taken Istria and Dalmatia from Austria after Austerlitz. Ever since the great wars that Catherine the Great had waged against the Ottoman Empire between 1768 and 1792, Russia had been expanding southwards around the Black Sea and the vision of reconquering Constantinople for the Orthodox faith, the so-called Greek Project,[9] had played a vague but recurrent role in Russian foreign policy. Catherine had even christened Alexander's younger brother, the oafish

Constantine, as a genuflection to this vision. In the previous ten years, Russia had also established a foothold in the eastern Mediterranean. Russian troops occupied Corfu in the Ionian Islands and the town of Cattaro on the Balkan mainland, while a Russian fleet operated in the surrounding seas. Napoleon was prepared to humour Russian aspirations in the eastern Balkans to a certain degree, but he wanted them out of his way in the Mediterranean.

Finally, Napoleon sought Russian cooperation in his war with the British. His most potent weapon against Britain was the 'continental system', inaugurated through the Berlin Decree, which he had issued on 21 November 1806. The Berlin Decree declared the British Isles to be under blockade and prohibited all commerce with them. It aimed to bring Britain to her knees through economic strangulation – an appropriate weapon to employ on what Napoleon famously described as 'a nation of shopkeepers'. Alexander could help him to make the continental system more effective in the Baltic region, and that was why Napoleon could not be content with peace alone (as in case of Austria after Austerlitz). Peace suited him, to be sure. He had been away from Paris for ten months, and there was still a danger of Austrian intervention if he pressed on into Russian territory. But peace had to walk hand in hand with an alliance, and Alexander's response to the unsubtle blandishments that Napoleon had showered on him during the armistice negotiations suggested that an alliance was within reach.

Alexander felt the need for peace more keenly than Napoleon. There were few voices urging a continuation of the war. Budberg favoured fighting on, at least in the first few days after Friedland. And Bennigsen soon recovered his nerve and began to emit martial rumblings. On 21 June he wrote to Alexander, again minimising the extent of his defeat at Friedland and claiming that with the reinforcements which were arriving he would be in a position to resume hostilities if the peace negotiations failed.[10] At army headquarters, Bennigsen declared the following day that 'he would undertake to beat the enemy again and again with 60,000 men, but no one replied'.[11] His credibility was done. The *Grande Armée* was now on the borders of Russia herself. If the peace talks broke down, the French were within striking distance of Vilna, the third largest city of the Russian empire. There was a strong party, headed by Alexander's brother the Grand Duke Constantine and heavily represented within the officer corps, which called for peace. Constantine even urged Alexander to remember their father's fate if he persisted in the war against France.[12]

Alexander faced his gravest crisis since ascending the throne six years earlier. His character and previous record give us few clues as to how he would react. His personality is as elusive to us as it was to contemporaries, and it is difficult to dissent from the verdict of Russia's national poet Pushkin, who called Alexander 'a sphinx who carried his riddle with him to the tomb'. In June 1807 Alexander was still a young man, a few months short of his thirtieth birthday. He was tall and handsome, but moved awkwardly as the result of a childhood fall from a horse (an occupational hazard for royalty). Alexander's behaviour and attitudes always seem contradictory. He looked like an emperor, and attached great value to his dignity and honour, but he could be hesitant, secretive and devious. He professed half-digested enlightened ideas, but jealously guarded his autocratic prerogatives. He preached peace and harmony in Europe, but often treated them as dependent on a growth in Russian power and prestige. He was self-righteous, and had a predilection for grand but nebulous ideas in contrast to what one biographer describes as his disinclination towards 'logical analysis'. The same biographer argues that Alexander picked up the habit of dissimulation as a child when he had to adapt to the conflicting demands of two strong personalities who detested each other – his grandmother, Catherine the Great, and his father, Paul I.[13] Perhaps so – though psychological speculations in the absence of a live patient are notoriously precarious.

Whatever his shortcomings, Alexander rose to the occasion after Friedland. He did what was necessary and he did it with enthusiasm – either real or feigned. The pressures in favour of peace were overpowering, and they became doubly attractive when Napoleon signalled during the armistice negotiations that no surrender of Russian territory would be demanded and that a division of Europe into eastern and western spheres of influence might be on the agenda. Alexander acted decisively to end a war that had brought Russia no benefits and to explore what opportunities for expansion at the expense of the Ottoman Empire might be on offer.

In contrast to Napoleon, we do have some written evidence for Alexander's initial negotiating position, two memoranda drawn up in the days just before the first meeting on the raft at Tilsit.[14] They reveal that his imagination had indeed been fired by the prospect of pursuing Catherine's Greek Project. Napoleon should be made to explain his ideas about the Ottoman Empire and its eventual partition, and this would naturally lead the conversation onto the question of re-establishing the western and eastern empires and the limits between them.

But such broad vistas were accompanied by far more defensive considerations, and the two memoranda show that the restoration of Prussia, even if she suffered heavy territorial losses, was Alexander's overriding goal. Since coming to the throne he had established a close personal relationship with the Prussian royal couple – a relationship that attained a grotesque manifestation in November 1805 when he and Frederick William descended into the crypt at Potsdam, accompanied by the latter's wife, Queen Louise, in order to swear an oath of friendship over the coffin of Frederick the Great.[15] Alexander's stance over Prussia at Tilsit reflected this friendship and his sense of loyalty towards an unfortunate and humiliated ally. But it also reflected hard cold calculation. Prussia served as a defensive *glacis*, protecting Russia along her southern Baltic border. This point is underlined by the statement in one of the memoranda that Prussia should not merely be 'nominally' re-established. It was also essential that she should not become a vassal of Napoleon, which he could use as an instrument against Russia.

In return, Alexander was prepared to make sweeping concessions. He was willing – whatever long-term plans might be laid for the partition of the Ottoman Empire – to evacuate the Danubian Principalities and to accept French mediation in making peace with the Turks. He was also prepared to pull Russian forces out of Cattaro and the Ionian Islands, to sever Russia's alliance with Britain and proceed cautiously towards excluding the British from the Baltic.

What we can surmise about Napoleon and Alexander's aims when they met on 25 June suggests that an understanding was attainable, and one was in fact reached rather quickly. On every point where there was a divergence between what we may presume were French and Russian wishes, it was Alexander who gave ground and Napoleon who got his way. This is hardly surprising. It reflected the outcome of the war and the balance of strength between them.

The French and Russian plenipotentiaries signed three treaties at Tilsit on 7 July 1807 – a public treaty of 'peace and friendship', an accompanying set of seven secret articles and, finally, an 'offensive and defensive alliance'. The first was a public document, while the second two were to remain secret, but the three documents naturally need to be considered in conjunction if they are to be properly understood.[16]

The kingdom of Prussia was re-established by the treaties under Frederick William and the Hohenzollern dynasty. Napoleon chose to treat this as a generous concession on his part to the Russian emperor and was not too much of a gentleman to let the world know that this was the case. The public treaty stated that in this respect Napoleon was acting out of regard for Alexander and as a proof of his sincere desire to unite France and Russia by ties of confidence and amity. The territorial price of restoration was savage. Prussia lost almost half of her population and one-third of the territory she had held before the war with France in 1806 – including all her lands west of the Elbe river and most of her share from the three partitions of Poland. Two new states were carved out of the lands that were not restored to Prussia. One, the duchy of Warsaw, was created out of Prussia's lost Polish provinces and was to be ruled by Napoleon's obedient creature, the king of Saxony. The other was the kingdom of Westphalia, which was entrusted to Napoleon's younger brother Jerome Bonaparte and consisted of Prussia's former lands west of the Elbe.

The letters Napoleon and Alexander exchanged between 4 and 7 July mainly concern Prussia and show that her fate was the subject of hard bargaining. In one of them, Napoleon claimed on 4 July that he wanted his own immediate influence to stop at the Elbe so that the lands between that river and the Niemen could serve as a buffer zone separating the two empires and preventing petty conflicts between them.[17] But his subsequent actions showed that he intended to keep the restored Prussia and the duchy of Warsaw under his control no less than the new kingdom of Westphalia. A French force of 30,000 men was stationed in the duchy of Warsaw, while most of the restored Prussia remained under the occupation of 100,000 French troops for years to come. Evacuation was promised but made dependent on the payment of a huge indemnity, which the Prussian government was unable to raise.[18]

These later developments made the re-establishment of Prussia a hollow victory for Alexander – the kingdom was restored, but without the real (as opposed to nominal) independence that Alexander had sought. In contrast, Alexander's concessions in the eastern Mediterranean, which featured in the secret articles, were highly tangible. Russia promised to hand over Cattaro to the French and that the Ionian Islands would be possessed in complete sovereignty by the kingdom of Naples, yet another of Napoleon's satellite states. Alexander also undertook to withdraw his naval squadron from the Mediterranean. In his final letter to Napoleon on 7 July, the same day as the treaties were signed, Alexander assured him that couriers were ready to be sent concerning the Russian squadron in the Adriatic as soon as the 'documents' were signed.[19]

On the question of the Near East and the Mediterranean, the public treaty merely said that Russia would evacuate the Danubian Principalities, but that Turkish troops could not occupy these provinces until a definitive peace had been concluded between Russia and the Ottoman Empire. It was also stated that Alexander would accept Napoleon's mediation for the conclusion of such a peace. It was by no means certain that the Turks would prove amenable – a recent revolution at Constantinople had overthrown Sultan Selim III, and no one could be sure what policy the Turks would now follow. The secret alliance treaty stipulated that if the Turks rejected French mediation or if the negotiations did not lead to a satisfactory result within three months, France would make common cause with Russia against the Turks. In this event, they would come to terms in order to deprive the Ottoman Empire of all its provinces in Europe except the city of Constantinople and the province of Rumelia, a vaguely delineated region roughly equating to much of Macedonia and Thrace.

The mountain had given birth to a molehill. If we go by the letter of the treaties, Napoleon's great ideas about the future of the Ottoman Empire did not amount to much. Even under the most ambitious scenario, the Turks would still retain Constantinople and a substantial hinterland on the European continent. But Alexander would later claim that much grander vistas had been surveyed (perhaps while looking at one of Napoleon's beloved maps?) during the interminable conversations at Tilsit. This is very possible, but all his later actions show that Napoleon was not even half-serious when he spoke of a more complete and far-reaching partition of the Ottoman Empire. Above all, he was not prepared to contemplate Constantinople in Russian hands. Alexander clearly aired this possibility at one of their many meetings, and when he returned from it,

Napoleon exclaimed in front of his secretary: 'Constantinople! Constantinople! Never! That is the empire of the world!'[20]

The final major point covered by the Tilsit treaties was what to do about Britain. The public treaty merely stipulated that Alexander would offer his mediation for the conclusion of peace between Britain and France and that Napoleon would accept it provided that Britain did too within one month. But the secret alliance contained far less benign provisions. It envisaged that the peace between Britain and France would rest on two bases. The first was that Britain should recognise the principle that 'the flags of all the powers must enjoy an equal and complete independence at sea', and the second that Britain should restore all the French, Spanish and Dutch colonies she had conquered and that Hanover would be handed back to George III in return. If Britain refused to make peace on these terms by 1 November, Russia would present Britain with an ultimatum stating that if she did not accept them by 1 December, Alexander would make common cause with France.

In this event, France and Russia would act in concert to demand that Denmark, Portugal and Sweden should close their ports to British shipping and declare war on Britain. If one or more of these three powers refused, they would be treated as enemies by France and Russia. Denmark and Portugal were neutral states, but Sweden was at war with France and allied to Britain and still also, technically at least, to Russia. If Sweden refused, Denmark too would be forced to declare war on her. Napoleon's relentless obsession with the closure of continental ports to the British flag did not stop there. The secret alliance treaty also stipulated that France and Russia would 'insist' that Austria, another neutral state, should close her ports to British shipping and declare war on Britain. The peace treaty between France and Prussia imposed similar obligations on Frederick William and his government. Once the measures agreed at Tilsit had been fully implemented, Napoleon would have achieved his goal of closing the whole European mainland to British commerce.

Russia did not explicitly undertake to close her ports and declare war on Britain, but the promise to 'make common cause' with France if the British failed to fall into line by 1 December amounted to much the same thing. This was a huge concession from Alexander – stopping trade with Britain would be damaging to the Russian economy and unpopular at home. And that was not the end of it. The British might retaliate by sending a squadron to the Baltic to attack the Russian Baltic fleet and its great naval base at Cronstadt outside St Petersburg, and the Russians were aware that they were ill-prepared to defend themselves.[21] On this point, Napoleon allowed them a respite. The timescale envisaged in the secret alliance treaty gave them until 1 December before they had to face war with Britain, and by then the winter ice would protect them from a British attack in the Baltic until the following spring.

The timing of a future war between Britain and Russia was important because there was little prospect that the British would accept the peace terms Alexander and Napoleon had in mind. Exchanging Hanover for conquered colonies was a fairly obvious suggestion, but the demand that the flags of all countries should enjoy equal and complete independence at sea would be quite unacceptable to Britain. Beneath the fine and seemingly innocuous words lay a subtext that challenged the foundations of British power. The British had long exploited their naval supremacy to disrupt neutral seaborne trade with their enemies in times of war. This caused great resentment – not to mention financial loss – among states whose trade suffered as a result. There was no universally accepted corpus of international law covering such matters, and the legalities were subject to differing interpretations. Two questions stood out as matters of dispute – what constituted contraband of war, that is goods liable to seizure because neutrals were forbidden to carry them to the enemy, and the right of British warships and privateers to search neutral merchantmen on the high seas. The British insisted on a restrictive definition of contraband and an absolute right of search, whereas the opposite applied for the champions of neutral rights. The attack on neutral trade was not only an instrument of economic warfare against the enemy. It was also highly profitable to the men of the Royal Navy, who were able to combine patriotic fervour with pecuniary gain. Merchant vessels and contraband condemned by the Admiralty's prize court generated 'prize money' for the crews of the warships that had seized them. The lion's share went to the officers, but even an ordinary seaman could sometimes double his annual wages through prize money.[22]

The 'extravagant system of maritime oppression' Britain applied against the commerce of other nations provoked widespread hostility in Europe.[23] Russia had twice put herself at the head of a so-called league of armed neutrality, in 1780 and again in 1800, to uphold neutral maritime rights against British pretensions. On both occasions, there had been a political dimension to the Russian stand, a desire to increase Russian prestige and power through leadership of a grouping of states, but the Russians – like most continental Europeans – were also genuinely offended by British behaviour.[24] After the assassination of Paul I, Russia had been obliged largely to accept the British definition of neutral maritime rights in the Anglo-Russian convention of 17 June 1801,[25] but their submission was reluctant and the Russian government hoped to reopen the question in more favourable circumstances.[26]

Such circumstances seemed to have arrived at Tilsit, and the two Russian memoranda drawn up in anticipation of Alexander's meeting with Napoleon referred to the possibility that Russia might form, in conjunction with Denmark and Sweden, a maritime force 'capable not only of defending the Baltic but even of forcing England to adopt more liberal principles with regard to navigation and the freedom of the seas'.[27] The suggestion was in part a sop to Napoleon, a means of extenuating Russia's reluctance to face an immediate naval war with Britain, but it also drew on a long tradition of Russian resistance to Britain's maritime pretensions. And the formation of such a grouping under his leadership would confer prestige on Alexander, just as the armed neutralities had done for his grandmother and father. It would therefore be misleading to see the peace terms that were to be imposed on Britain as a concession by Alexander to Napoleon. In this respect at least, Alexander was a willing accomplice in Napoleon's plans against Britain.

And so the deal was done. But before the emperors could depart, the peace treaty between France and Prussia also needed to be signed. The Prussians had been rigidly excluded from the negotiations. Frederick William remained solid hardwood when he met Napoleon socially, and in desperation, Queen Louise of Prussia, a celebrated beauty, was summoned from Memel to deploy her 'admirable affability' on the conqueror. Then as now, it was a customary courtesy to exaggerate the physical charms of female royalty, but the unanimity of opinion from her contemporaries suggests that Louise's portraits do not mislead. Much to her distaste and discomfort, Louise was brought to soothe the ogre's wrath. One of the two Prussian negotiators at Tilsit cheered himself with the thought that, even if Napoleon was 'not accustomed to frequent the society of ladies of high education', he would doubtless be able to behave like 'a polite and well brought-up man'.[28] Louise dined with Napoleon at Tilsit on 6 July, but he was not impressed. He wrote to the Empress Josephine that the Prussian queen had wanted to squeeze concessions out of him. She was 'truly charming', but he added: 'Do not be jealous . . . it would cost me too dear to play the gallant.'[29] The next day, after the treaties between France and Russia had been signed, the Prussian negotiators were informed that there would be no negotiations with them – they simply had to accept the text of the peace treaty that they were given. They signed forty-eight hours later, on 9 July.[30] As Gower observed, Louise 'had gained nothing from her personal humiliation [other] than a few insipid compliments upon her beauty and dress'.[31]

The same day, the ratified treaties between France and Russia were exchanged, and the two emperors took their leave of each other amid elaborate ceremony. There were parades, orders were conferred and finally Napoleon escorted Alexander to the boat that would take him back to the other side of the Niemen. They embraced warmly, and Napoleon stood by the river, 'making gestures of farewell', until Alexander had reached the north bank. For his part, Napoleon set off for Königsberg at ten o'clock that evening.[32]

Historians have expended much energy on discussing who was fooling whom at Tilsit. The suggestion that Alexander bamboozled Napoleon by playing the simpering young acolyte is not very convincing. The contrary claim that Alexander, 'so often unsure of himself', surrendered to 'the magnetism of Napoleon's decisiveness'[33] is more plausible, but the letters the two men exchanged in the last phase of the negotiations give the impression of some fairly hard-nosed bargaining. In the last resort, we do not need to speculate about whether Alexander was genuinely dazzled by association with the towering figure of his age, since the agreements reached at Tilsit can be explained in terms of simple power politics. The *Grande Armée* stood victorious on the frontiers of Alexander's dominions. It was natural that the peace terms would reflect the wishes of the victor rather than the vanquished.

There was not much in the Tilsit settlement that was to Alexander's advantage, and all he got in return was some vague (and, as it proved, insincere) speculations on the future of the Ottoman empire. He fought hard to save something for Frederick William and Prussia, but he seems to have been happy to abandon Britain without compunction even before he met Napoleon. This attitude reflected both his bitterness at the lukewarm support he had received from Britain over the previous nine months and the long-standing Russian opposition to British policy over maritime neutral rights. Bennigsen is reported to have observed portentously from the vantage point of army headquarters: 'the two emperors have shaken hands; Europe has cause to tremble.'[34] No state had more reason to feel threatened than Britain.

LORD GOWER AT MEMEL

While the two emperors conferred, Gower kicked his heels at Memel, hungry for any news that percolated down to the coast from Tilsit. Away from the scene of the action, Gower spent much of his time at the Prussian court with Queen Louise until she was summoned to Tilsit in a futile bid to soften the conqueror's heart. It was a regime of walks, boat trips, games and dinners, but Gower professed to see underneath Louise's 'mask of affected gaiety great depression of spirits'. Lady Bessborough enjoined him: 'Do not in your anxiety to console a beautiful Queen fall in love with her.' By 7 July, even Gower's equable nature was rattled and he wrote to Lady Bessborough: 'Nothing can exceed the dullness of this place, and I feel it the more on account of the unpleasantness of my political situation here.' Nor did his marital affairs prosper. He had finally written to Princess Galitzin, but had received no reply: he was beginning to fear – as well he might – that 'she was affronted by that letter I wrote to her about divorced women not being received in England'.[35]

Gower made one last bid to regain access to Alexander. He learnt of the first meeting on the raft later the very day it occurred, and considered writing to Budberg to request an explanation of what was afoot, but decided against on the grounds that it might only create ill feeling.[36] Finally, Gower could no longer contain himself and wrote to Budberg on 28 June. The instructions with which Gower had been equipped before his departure from London had not rejected all thought of peace negotiations. Indeed, Canning had been prepared to defer on this question to Alexander, 'in proportion as he bears the brunt of the continental war', as the person 'best qualified, and best entitled to judge' whether such negotiations were appropriate or necessary. And Gower was authorised to say that Britain was prepared to make sacrifices for peace – a statement that we may take to be code for restoring at least some conquered colonies to France and her allies.[37]

But a peace settlement from which Britain was excluded was an entirely different matter, and this was the point that Gower pursued in his letter to Budberg. He pretended to disbelieve the 'rumours' of negotiations for a separate peace between Russia and France and expressed his confidence that the aim of the discussions was a 'general pacification' involving all the powers currently at war. He therefore reiterated his 'impatience' to receive an invitation to rejoin Emperor Alexander.[38]

Budberg's reply to Gower on 30 June dropped the diplomatic niceties. It rehearsed all Alexander's grievances against Britain – the long-promised diversion, the refusal of a loan and so on – and claimed that he would never have thought of changing his policies if he had received real support from other powers equally interested in resisting France. But they had instead 'exhibited tardiness and irresolution', and since he had been let down so badly by his allies – and by Austria too, for that matter – Alexander now felt entitled to look only to 'the glory and to the security of his empire'. Budberg concluded – and he made it sound like a magnanimous gesture – by offering Alexander's mediation for the negotiation of a peace settlement between Britain and France. He added that Alexander was certain that the offer would be accepted by France.[39]

'The tone and temper' of Budberg's letter with its 'acrimonious abuse' of the British government put an end to Gower's attempts to rejoin Alexander, even if he was impressed by 'the frankness, not to say effrontery' with which the Russians admitted 'the entire change of their political system'. It seemed as if 'Bonaparte has obtained complete possession of the mind of the Emperor Alexander', who had 'become the dupe of [his] insidious flattery'. Gower accepted that Russia was incapable of continuing the war and did not blame Alexander for making peace, but lamented his 'total forgetfulness of what was due to his own dignity' and his 'want of candour and frankness towards us, such as augurs ill for the renewal of the ties by which England and Russia were till this time connected'.

The only ray of hope which Gower could find was that when Alexander 'recovers a little from the intoxication produced by his familiar intercourse with Bonaparte', wiser counsels would prevail and recall him 'to a more just sense of the real interests of his country'.[40] Even so, he felt sure that if Britain remained at war with France, Russia would be 'drawn into measures if not of hostility at least of armed neutrality against us'.[41]

Gower hung on at Memel until 15 July. He heard nothing further from Budberg, but the little he learnt from Prussian sources gave no grounds for optimism. By 12 July he was convinced that Alexander had consented to the closure of Russian and Prussian ports to British shipping and that Denmark would be forced to follow suit. Personally, he favoured acceptance of the Russian offer of mediation to avoid 'the probability of a coalition of the whole continent against us'. He did not counsel yielding to 'dishonourable terms of peace', but he warned Canning that 'you must not conceal from yourself the difficulties that will follow the refusal to treat'.[42] He was more openly despondent with Lady Bessborough: 'I am in lower spirits that I can describe; every thing, both public and private is as disagreeable as possible. Not a line from the Barbarian.'[43]

He was much offended by Budberg's failure to inform him that a peace treaty with France had been signed and that Alexander had departed for St Petersburg. This 'personal incivility' towards him would make his position in the Russian capital 'extremely embarrassing'. He could not resist expressing his frustration by a swipe at Budberg, whom he had found 'proud and passionate with foreigners, and mean and cringing with the Emperor'.[44] On 15 July, as the horses were being attached to his carriage for the long journey to St Petersburg, he wrote two final letters from Memel, one to the foreign secretary and the other to his mistress. Once again, he warned Canning that 'unless you make peace England will be engaged in war with the whole of Europe'.[45] Once again, his language to Lady Bessborough was more dramatic: 'the most deadly blows are aiming at the very existence of the country; for be assured that the dangers which threaten England at this moment infinitely exceed what we ever before apprehended.'[46]

Chapter 3

A PRINCE OF DENMARK AT KIEL: DANISH NEUTRALITY, 1806–1807

'THE LONG TEMPORISING SYSTEM OF AN INFERIOR STATE'[1]

Prussia was the first victim of Tilsit and, as Gower correctly surmised, Britain was intended to be the second. The secret alliance of Tilsit also pronounced the doom of Danish neutrality: along with Portugal and Sweden, Denmark was to be forced to close her ports to the British flag and to declare war on Britain. In mid-July 1807, Denmark – oblivious to her fate – remained an oasis of neutrality in the Baltic region, but it was a neutrality that was living on borrowed time.

The regime that sought to uphold Danish neutrality was an absolute monarchy in which the king exercised virtually untrammelled authority. Real power, however, lay in the hands not of Christian VII, who was incapacitated from governing by mental illness, but of his son, Crown Prince Fredrick, the future Fredrick VI.[2] The legal framework of Danish absolutism did not permit the admission that the king was unable to rule, and the Danish archives are awash with royal decrees and decisions that bear the endorsement 'Approbated, Christian R', but Crown Prince Fredrick was regent in fact, if not in name.

In Denmark, power equated to mastery of the king's signature. Christian VII's madness had given rise to one of the great scandals of eighteenth-century Europe when control over the government passed in 1770 to the king's physician, Johann Friedrich Struensee, who was also the lover of the queen, Caroline Matilda. Struensee's dictatorship was short-lived and his downfall in 1772 took the queen with him. Struensee suffered a grisly public execution, and Caroline Matilda was divorced. She would have been placed under a sort of dignified house arrest in Jutland if it had not been for the strenuous and menacing intervention of her brother, George III of Britain. As a result, she was able to live out the few years left to her in Hanover. The four-year-old crown prince never saw his mother again.[3] Unlike his younger sister, Fredrick was not Struensee's child – he was conceived and born before the enterprising physician became acquainted with the royal couple.

By 1807 Fredrick was in his late thirties and the effective ruler of his country. He was something of a dull dog, physically unprepossessing and without any flicker of charisma, but he possessed a strong will to power and a strong sense of duty. That – combined with a capacity for hard work – placed the reins of government in his hands. He had a great love for all things military and the army was his abiding passion, but his supremacy extended to all areas of policy. It had not always been so. When he first assumed a leading position as a teenager in 1784, Fredrick had worked in harness with, and under the guidance of, a reform-minded aristocratic faction that controlled the council of state. This had paved the way for a period of government in the spirit of 'enlightened absolutism' and improvements in the conditions of the peasantry, but by the early years of the nineteenth century those days were over. The council rarely met, a tight censorship was maintained and Fredrick ruled alone in an increasingly conservative vein.

The Danish monarchy that Fredrick governed was not then the homogeneous nation-state of today, but a traditional multi-ethnic dynastic state of the *ancien régime*, which included not only the kingdom of Denmark proper but also Norway to the north and the duchies of Schleswig and Holstein in the south. Outside mainland Europe, Iceland, the Faroe Islands and parts of Greenland were under Danish rule, and the Danish state also held some islands in the West Indies and colonial outposts in Africa and India. Despite the geographical extent of the lands subject to the king of Denmark, the Danish monarchy counted as a power of the second rank in European affairs. Its major claim to consideration was the Danish navy, which consisted in 1807 of about twenty ships of the line, the heavy battleships that were the monarchs of the ocean, along with numerous smaller vessels – not much in comparison with the great fleets at Britain's command, but quite a significant force in Baltic affairs.

The days had long passed when Denmark aspired to a predominant position in the Baltic, and since 1720 she had largely succeeded in maintaining a position of neutrality in the frequent wars of the eighteenth century. But if Denmark had no real territorial ambitions, that did not protect her from territorial fears, and they were inspired by the second Scandinavian kingdom. The fundamental long-term problem of Danish security policy was the Swedish threat to Norway. One of the primary recurring goals of Swedish foreign policy since the early 1770s had been to break the centuries-old union between Denmark and Norway and to bring Norway under Swedish rule. For a hundred years, Sweden had been in retreat before the inexorable growth of Russian power and her frontier in Finland, which had been an integral part of the Swedish kingdom since the middle ages, had been successively pushed further westwards. If the human and material resources of Norway could be acquired, so the reasoning went, Sweden would be better able to resist Russia and to play a more assertive role in northern affairs.[4]

The Danish response to this threat had taken two forms. The first was to maintain a fleet that possessed an adequate measure of naval superiority over Sweden. This was essential, partly because Denmark had to be able to keep open her communications with Norway and partly because, in view of the difficulties of the Norwegian terrain, a Swedish attack over the sea against the heart of the Danish state, Copenhagen on the island of Zealand, was as much to be feared as a direct assault on Norway.[5] This was one of the reasons why the Danes boxed above their weight by sustaining a navy larger than might have been expected given Denmark's place in the European pecking order.

The second Danish response was to maintain a link to the great power that also had reason to regard Sweden as a potential enemy, Russia. The link was embodied in the treaty of alliance between Denmark and Russia of 1773, which committed both to assist the other if attacked. Denmark's association with Russia was the ultimate guarantee of her continued hold on Norway, and this dependence to a great extent had made Denmark a client of Russia. The central importance of the Russian alignment had compelled Denmark to join the two Armed Neutralities of 1780 and 1800, both created by Russia as an instrument to promote her own position in European politics.

On the second occasion, Denmark was not an entirely innocent camp-follower. Neutrality was not only prudent but profitable. The Danish monarchy possessed a merchant marine to match her navy and was well placed to benefit from neutrality in the frequent maritime wars between Britain and France. The pattern was always the same: as Britain asserted her naval supremacy, the seaborne trade of France and her allies passed into the hands of the neutrals. In the later eighteenth century, war was good news for those who could remain neutral and who possessed the shipping to fill the gap on seas swept clean of enemy vessels by the Royal Navy. These were palmy days for the great merchant houses of Copenhagen and for foreign ship-owners who could obtain – for a consideration, of course – false papers that enabled their vessels to sail under the Danish flag with cargoes certified as Danish-owned property.

This inevitably led to trouble with Britain over neutral maritime rights. As with other neutrals, the main bones of contention centred on the definition of contraband and the right of the British warships to search neutral vessels and to enforce a blockade of enemy ports. Naturally enough, the way the rules were applied tended to reflect the current balance of strength between the belligerent and the neutral at any particular moment. The growing conflict between Denmark and Britain over questions of this kind in the late 1790s led the Danish government to seek Russian support in August 1800. The Danes had little right to whinge when Paul I of Russia exploited their overture to fashion a confederacy, ostensibly dedicated to upholding neutral rights, but in reality a Russian-led power bloc directed against Britain.

The results were catastrophic for Denmark. The British sent a fleet to the Baltic, and it was Denmark, not Russia, that was first in the firing line. On 2 April 1801 the Danish defensive line drawn up in the roads of Copenhagen was defeated by a British fleet under Horatio Nelson at the battle of Copenhagen. To add further to Danish woes, the battle was fought to demonstrate Danish loyalty to a man who was already dead – though the Danes did not know that yet, of course. Paul I was murdered on the night of 23–24 March, and the new Russian government had no desire for war with Britain. Russia rapidly yielded to the British interpretation of neutral maritime rights on all the crucial points in the Anglo-Russian Convention of 17 June 1801. This was clearly a sell-out and the Danes duly cried betrayal, but it did them no good: in practice Denmark had no choice but to accede to the convention in October 1801.[6]

The events of 1801 were a bitter lesson to Denmark. After the outbreak of war between Britain and France in 1803, Denmark was more cautious in her dealings with Britain about seaborne trade and less inclined to follow Russia down hazardous paths. Strict neutrality was the order of the day: Prince Fredrick had high notions of national honour and dignity, and this had contributed to the clash with Britain in 1801, but he proceeded now with extreme caution. The renewal of hostilities created a new and immediate security problem for Denmark, because it was followed in June 1803 by a French occupation of George III's ancestral electorate of Hanover, which brought French troops perilously close to the borders of Holstein. Given the weakness of Denmark's land forces, it was inconceivable that the Danes could hold Holstein, Schleswig and the rest of the Jutlandic peninsula against a sustained French attack. The tenuous nature of the Danish hold on the Jutlandic peninsula was a fundamental factor in Danish foreign policy after June 1803. This latent French threat was a constant source of anxiety for the Danish government, but France's official policy towards Denmark was generally restrained between June 1803 and the last months of 1806, and serious diplomatic contact between the two countries was slight.[7]

Denmark's most frequent exchanges during these years were with the two great powers of the Baltic region, Russia and Prussia. Russia made several attempts to secure Danish cooperation in opposing French expansion, and Berlin was often interested in involving Denmark in a Prussian-led grouping of north German states, but neither applied strong pressure, and Denmark was able to evade all their attempts between 1803 and 1806 to enter into arrangements that would, in one way or another, have compromised her isolated neutrality.[8]

The only concrete result of these tortuous discussions was the Danish decision in September 1805, taken both as a measure of precaution and to please Russia and Prussia, to assemble a force of about 20,000 regular troops in Holstein to protect the neutrality of that province.[9] The crown prince – with his military enthusiasms – chose to command the force in Holstein in person from headquarters at Kiel, and that town became the centre of government for the next two years. This had a significant impact on the nuts and bolts of Denmark's relations with other powers. The foreign minister, Count Christian Bernstorff, accompanied Fredrick to Kiel and set up shop there, but foreign envoys were obliged to stay in Copenhagen and transact official business with his deputy and younger brother, Count Joachim Bernstorff, the 'director' of the foreign ministry.[10]

The Bernstorff brothers belonged to a family which originated in Mecklenburg and which still held estates there, but which had made its name in the service of the Danish crown. Christian and Joachim were the third generation to go down this road: their great-uncle and father had both in turn directed Danish foreign policy for many decades in the eighteenth century. The brothers were well acclimatised: they had grown up in Copenhagen and were bilingual in Danish and German. They were also young men with young wives, subject to the usual hazards of early nineteenth-century matrimony. Childbirth killed Joachim's wife early in 1807 and almost killed Christian's shortly afterwards.[11] Anxiety over Elise Bernstorff's illness may be the reason why Christian, who generally wrote to his ministers abroad twice a month, did not address a single despatch to the Danish envoys in London, Paris and St Petersburg between 21 April and 12 June 1807. Since his father's death in 1797, Christian Bernstorff had been in practice, if not at first in name, foreign minister, and he had shown resilience and courage during the desperate negotiations with Nelson after the battle of Copenhagen in 1801. He was an intelligent and skilful diplomat, but the last word over foreign policy – as on everything else – belonged to Prince Fredrick.

The separation of Christian at Kiel from the diplomatic corps at Copenhagen was an awkward arrangement, involving significant delay as Joachim referred matters to his brother, but it was by no means unusual – foreign diplomats had to remain at Paris while Napoleon and his *Grande Armée* charged across Europe, to take the most striking example. The arrangement probably also gave Joachim more influence than he ought to have possessed. His brother had already delegated to him day-to-day responsibility for questions of neutral trade, and he now became the main mouthpiece of the Danish government in its dealings with foreign envoys. He operated on the basis of instructions from Kiel, but enjoyed a fair amount of leeway – sometimes with unfortunate results as the younger brother seems often to have been in a testy mood when he spoke to foreign envoys.

Joachim's sparring partner on the British side was Benjamin Garlike, who was appointed to head the British mission at Copenhagen in April 1805. Garlike belonged to a less glamorous section of the British foreign service than Granville Leveson Gower. Not for him a plum posting like the embassy at St Petersburg in the first flush of youth. Garlike did not belong to a great noble family, but he had acquired some friends in high places. He owed his first break to the patronage of Lord Auckland, a prominent

British diplomat before the Revolutionary Wars with France, whom he served as an unpaid secretary on two foreign missions in the late 1780s. He also developed a connection with Thomas Grenville, the younger brother of Lord Grenville, probably while they both served at Berlin in 1799.

Since the 1790s Garlike had made a career as a professional diplomat, serving as deputy to the principal British envoy at most of the major capitals of the Baltic region – Stockholm, Berlin and St Petersburg. In all three places, he had acted as *chargé d'affaires* for a time, most notably for two years at Berlin.[12] His appointment as the fully accredited British minister to the Danish court as he approached his fortieth birthday represented a significant step forward in his modest but dogged career – especially at a time when the inexorable expansion of French power was closing down British missions abroad at a rapid pace and rendering many run-of-the-mill diplomats like Garlike unemployed. Garlike had his faults: he could be fussy and pedantic and he was the master of a prose style that was often confusing and soporific. But it is difficult to find much fault with the content of his reports to London, which generally presented a balanced and realistic picture of Danish policy.

The first eighteen months or so of Garlike's mission at Copenhagen were relatively untroubled as there were few causes of friction in Britain's relations with Denmark during the early phase of the Napoleonic Wars. There was no repetition of the disputes over neutral trade between Britain and Denmark that had characterised the previous Anglo-French war, and Denmark abided by the limitations placed on neutral maritime rights by the Anglo-Russian Convention of 17 June 1801.[13] Even with these restrictions, Danish trade, as Christian Bernstorff conceded early in December 1805, was 'more prosperous than ever'.[14] This was a cardinal point. Just as a French occupation of the Jutlandic peninsula would be a catastrophe for Denmark, so too would war with Britain. Her overseas colonies would be lost, her flourishing trade would be destroyed, and her communications with Norway would be placed in jeopardy. Only the successful maintenance of neutrality could shield Denmark from all dangers.

Denmark and Britain were also bound together by certain overlapping interests. The British had responded to the French occupation of Hanover by blockading the Elbe, and the Danish government protested formally both at the principle behind the blockade and at the effects on the two Danish ports located on the Elbe, Altona and Glückstadt.[15] In practice, however, the French occupation of Hanover and the British blockade of the Elbe rapidly created a mutually advantageous relationship between Britain and Denmark, as British goods that would previously have been shipped directly to Hamburg were diverted to the tiny Danish port of Tonningen on the Ejder river before they were transported in a semi-clandestine fashion to Hamburg and on into the heart of Germany.[16] The inhabitants of Schleswig and Holstein benefited from this trade, and so too did the finances of the Danish state, which received a significant revenue from tolls levied at Tonningen.[17]

Despite the armed clash between Britain and Denmark in 1801, Britain's diplomatic representatives in Copenhagen regarded Denmark after May 1803 as a friendly power, whose leading statesmen were genuinely well disposed towards Britain and would welcome a curtailment of French expansion in Europe.[18] Right from the start the British expected nothing from Denmark beyond 'a strict neutrality'. Even if 'a general confederation of the powers of the continent' could be forged, 'it would not be prudent that the King of Denmark should become a party to it until he could do so without danger to his own dominions'.[19] This was hardly a call to arms and represented a highly satisfactory attitude from a Danish perspective, but it is not a surprising one since continuing Danish neutrality served British interests well. It kept open the trade route through Tonningen and above all it ensured that British shipping could continue to pass unhindered through the Sound.

The Baltic was an essential source for Britain of certain vital imports – above all naval stores and grain – and in 1805 almost 6,000 merchant vessels passed the Sound on their way to or from British ports.[20] The Danish government had no interest in closing the Sound to the British flag – since the middle ages, the Danes had levied a toll on ships passing Elsinore, and the so-called 'Sound Dues' still accounted for about 15 per cent of the revenues of the Danish state.[21] But the French, of course, viewed matters differently, and rumours that they might demand the closure of Danish ports and the Sound to British shipping or even occupy Holstein regularly went the rounds after 1803.

These were the two flashpoints of British interest in Denmark – the ports of Holstein (Tonningen is just inside Schleswig, but British usage of the word 'Holstein' was somewhat elastic) and the free passage of the Sound. It is entirely symptomatic of Britain's outlook that the first significant flurry of anxiety in London over Denmark was occasioned by a perceived threat in these two areas. Garlike reported on 18 March 1806 that the Danish government feared 'the request of France to shut the ports of Denmark, and if possible the Sound itself against English and Russian ships' and expressed his own apprehension that Holstein might be occupied.[22] The British government reacted instantly. Charles James Fox, the foreign secretary, instructed Garlike to warn the Danes – naturally with all suitable expressions of British friendship and goodwill – that if Denmark closed her ports to the British flag, Britain would be obliged to regard this step as 'an unequivocal measure of hostility' and would retaliate. If, on the other hand, Denmark was attacked because she stood up to French demands, Britain would provide 'every support within [her] power'.

By the time he received these instructions, Garlike had already obtained assurances from Joachim Bernstorff that no demands had been presented to Denmark and that, if they were, Denmark would defend her neutrality and independence. This mini-crisis in Anglo-Danish relations rapidly blew over. By 6 May Fox was expressing 'the highest satisfaction' with Garlike's description 'of the excellent dispositions of the Danish government'.[23] Even so, British anxieties in April 1806 underline the fragility of the friendly relationship between Denmark and Britain and were a harbinger of worse to follow.

THE DANISH WITHDRAWAL FROM HOLSTEIN

The entry of Prussia into the war against France in October 1806 and her crushing defeat the same month placed Denmark in a far more exposed position than before. The Prussian collapse was followed by the French occupation of previously neutral areas of northern Germany like Mecklenburg and the three Hanseatic cities of Lübeck, Hamburg and Bremen. On 6 November, the same day as they took Lübeck, French troops in pursuit of a retreating Prussian force crossed the border onto Danish territory and clashed with the Danish advanced guard. Blood was spilled on both sides, and when he tried to negotiate, the local Danish commander received rough treatment from the French, who sent him and his adjutants back minus their horses.[24]

The incident was smoothed over, but at his headquarters at Kiel Prince Fredrick took it as an injunction to caution. Now that French troops were in secure possession of the whole area south of the Holstein border, the continued presence of a substantial Danish force in Holstein would imply a distrust of France that Napoleon might well find provocative, particularly since it would present some potential threat to his extended lines of communication into Poland. There was also the point that with French troops in Hamburg and Lübeck, the southern border of Holstein was not really defensible. Fredrick solved the problem through his decision on 19 November to withdraw the bulk of his troops in Holstein from that duchy, leaving only a light cordon of troops to police the frontier. The remainder of his forces took up a position behind the Ejder, the river separating Holstein from Schleswig, but in the course of December a few of these troops were pulled back to the island of Funen and more to the northern part of the Jutlandic peninsula beyond the duchy of Schleswig.[25]

The new positions occupied by the Danish field army were not merely less provocative to Napoleon. They would also make it easier to run for it and withdraw to the Danish islands in the event of a full-scale French invasion. Garlike reported that 'several leading persons' had mentioned the possibility of abandoning the whole of the Jutlandic peninsula and probably also the island of Funen in the event of a French attack in order to concentrate on the defence of Zealand and the other islands to the east of the Great Belt (Møn, Falster and Lolland).[26] There is no corroborating evidence from Danish sources for the existence of contingency plans of this kind beyond a sycophantic letter to Prince Fredrick in late November 1806 from Ernst von Walterstorff, the commander of the North Zealand militia. Walterstorff expressed pleasure at seeing the army drawn closer to the Danish islands and confidence that Zealand at least would always be defensible. Zealand, he declared, was 'the heart of Denmark, just as Your Royal Highness is its soul'.[27] This is not much to go on, but a withdrawal to the islands was plain common sense and Fredrick was often wary of committing sensitive matters to paper.[28]

Fredrick's decision to evacuate Holstein was hardly heroic, but it was well-timed. Two days after he made it, on 21 November, Napoleon instructed his foreign minister to urge the Danish government to pull back the Holstein corps from the frontier, but Fredrick's pre-emptive ingratiation had rendered the French approach superfluous by the time it was made.[29] Napoleon also signalled his displeasure at the border incident when he remarked – in passing, but in public – that this 'little prince should be careful'.[30] The remark was offensive, but for the moment it was mere swagger. For Napoleon, the decisive battlegrounds were now in eastern Prussia, and he had no desire to add to his enemies, even if they were puny ones. For the same reason, the renewal of alarming rumours in the second half of November that Napoleon would occupy Holstein or demand the closure of Danish ports and the Sound to British navigation lacked all foundation, and they gradually abated as the focus of the war shifted eastwards towards Poland. For Denmark, the danger of complications with France had receded, at least for the time being.

For their part, the British were not greatly concerned by the Danish withdrawal to the Ejder. In Copenhagen, Garlike could see nothing disturbing about it. The duchy was clearly indefensible against the French, and he regarded the idea of concentrating on the defence of Zealand and its adjacent island with evident approval.[31] And he had no difficulty in accepting Joachim Bernstorff's assurances that Denmark would resist if attacked by the French.[32] The British government took somewhat longer to adjust to the evacuation of Holstein. The executor of the Grenville administration's policy towards Denmark during the four remaining months of its short life was the foreign secretary, Charles Grey, Lord Howick.[33]

In the evening of his political career, Howick would go on to make a distinguished prime minister, but in the winter of 1806–7 he failed to shine at the foreign office. Fox had died in September 1806 and Howick had succeeded him both as foreign secretary and as leader of the Foxite Whigs. He still had youthful frolics on the fringes of radical politics and an adulterous affair with Lady Bessborough's elder sister (London political society was a small world) to live down. More to the point, Howick was inexperienced, testy and volatile. In mid-December 1806, he subjected Johan Rist, the newly appointed Danish *chargé d'affaires* in London, to an intemperate outburst about the Danish withdrawal from Holstein.[34] Rist was struck by how easily and passionately Howick surrendered in quick succession to opposing impressions, but believed that behind the hot-headed exterior lay an essentially benevolent attitude towards Denmark, which Howick had inherited from his friend and predecessor, Fox.[35]

This was an accurate assessment. Ministers were anxious about Denmark's possible 'future conduct', and on 9 December they alerted

George III that it might 'eventually' be necessary to seize the Danish
island of Heligoland in the North Sea as an alternative base to Tonningen
for smuggling British goods into Germany.[36] But the operative word was
'eventually', and when Howick instructed Garlike to obtain a full
explanation from the Danish government of what had happened and its
future intentions, he expressed an expectation that the Danish answer
'will be such as the friendship which has so long subsisted between the
two governments requires'.[37] By Christmas 1806 Howick's anxieties about
the nature of Danish policy had been largely assuaged. He had received
Garlike's reports on his conversations with Joachim Bernstorff and now
felt that 'the assurances hitherto given by [Fredrick] are of the most
satisfactory nature'.[38] Howick was also happy to endorse the idea that the
whole Jutlandic peninsula should be abandoned in the event of a French
attack on Denmark, and that for the moment she should pursue 'a
prudent system of neutrality'.[39]

LORD HOWICK AND THE DANISH NAVY

The Danish withdrawal to the Ejder did not, in short, lead to any real
problems in relations with Britain. But all was not sweetness and light.
The evacuation of Holstein coincided with a sudden expression of concern
in London about the future of the Danish navy. For Denmark, it was an
ominous and ultimately fateful development. The sea-going, operational
Danish fleet had not suffered significant damage at the battle of
Copenhagen in 1801. Instead, it had been jealously protected within the
harbour and the defence of the Copenhagen roads had been entrusted to
a motley collection of floating batteries, blockships and superannuated
battleships destined for the breaker's yard. Not one of the fleet's
serviceable ships of the line had been lost.[40] The Danish navy remained a
force to be reckoned with, and as such could not fail to attract the interest
of a state as dependent on its maritime supremacy and its access to the
Baltic as Britain.

Since the battle, the Danish government had been considering future
naval construction plans. The Danish admiralty was jealous of its sea-
going fleet and wanted to keep the emphasis on ships of the line, but the
army favoured a shift towards oar-powered gunboats that could lend
support to operations on land. Fredrick, with his great fondness for the

army, came down on its side in September 1806 and a new naval plan was adopted that called for the building of over 300 gunboats and a gradual reduction in the number of ships of the line to twelve by 1814.[41] Garlike got hold of what was afoot from a Danish source, albeit in a garbled form. He believed that if the plan went ahead, France would try to buy the surplus vessels, but that Denmark would prefer to sell to Russia.[42]

This was a distorted version of the new naval plan, which said nothing about selling warships to a foreign power, but it was the only one that Howick received and it alarmed him when taken in conjunction with the rumours of an imminent French occupation of Holstein. Howick jumped to the conclusion that the Danes might try to buy off Napoleon with some of their warships. On 3 December 1806, he wrote to Garlike that it would be impossible for Britain 'to acquiesce in any arrangement whereby the whole or any part of the Danish navy might be placed at the disposal of France . . . in order to secure the German dominions [i.e. Holstein] of the Crown of Denmark'. Howick expressed his confidence that Denmark was unlikely to submit to 'so humiliating a condition'[43] and for the moment nothing further was said, but for Denmark it was an ominous development. This was the first time since the resumption of war in 1803 that a British minister had referred to a risk that France might gain possession of all or part of the Danish navy. It would not be the last.

Just as the British government was adjusting to the Danish evacuation of Holstein, a new source of friction came to the fore – Danish military preparations in the Sound. They were prompted by the mutual antagonisms that divided the two Scandinavian kingdoms. As Garlike observed, the Danish and Swedish governments had 'prejudices on all that can occur'.[44] Sweden was a member of the coalition against France. Even after the French had overrun the rest of northern Germany, the Swedes still held out in the province of Swedish Pomerania, where the fortress of Stralsund was a valuable bridgehead for the anti-French alliance. Gustavus IV, the king of Sweden, professed to see the Danish retreat to the Ejder as a potential threat to southern Sweden regardless of whether the Danes were in secret league with the French or merely unwilling to stand up to them.

His fears may well have been genuine, but they also reflected his designs on Norway. Gustavus was a dull-witted player of the geopolitical game who ultimately proved to be a victim rather than a predator.[45] For the moment, he was keen to drip poison into the ears of the British government on the subject of Denmark. At all events, some of the Swedish troops on their way to Pomerania to fight the French were retained in Scania because of Gustavus IV's suspicions about Danish intentions after the evacuation of Holstein. Eventually, once Gustavus had cooled down, these troops were also shipped to Pomerania in early March 1807,[46] but at the time they caused a minor stir within the Danish government.

When the Swedish troop movements were noted by the Danish authorities, Prince Fredrick ordered that the defences of the sea batteries protecting Copenhagen and Elsinore should be placed on a higher level of preparedness. A week later, on 12 December, he added that the garrisons of some of the batteries should be augmented. As a result, there was a certain amount of visible activity as cannon were mounted, additional gunpowder was supplied and the number of guards on patrol increased.[47] These enhanced measures of precaution were fairly modest, but they did not pass unnoticed.

Howick suspected that the Danish preparations at Copenhagen and particularly at Elsinore were only ostensibly directed at Sweden and that their real target was Britain. He feared that their true object was 'to resist the power of England rather than that of France' and urged 'the most vigilant attention' on Garlike.[48] The reference to Elsinore, which lay at the narrowest point on the Sound, highlights the nature of Howick's anxieties. The strengthening of Denmark's coastal defences clearly suggested to him that the Danish government was anticipating a situation in which it might choose or be compelled to yield to French demands for the closure of the Sound to Britain's vital Baltic trade. Matters got worse when he received in early January 1807 a report on the current state of the Danish navy.

In December 1806 the British frigate *Astrea* suffered such severe damage when it went aground on Anholt Reef in the Kattegat that it had to be repaired at Copenhagen.[49] Garlike asked Captain James Dunbar, the master of the *Astrea*, to report on the condition of the Danish navy while his ship was in the dockyard, and on 20 December Garlike transmitted Dunbar's observations on the subject to Howick. Dunbar found that all the warships, large and small, were in excellent condition ('fine men of war') and that all the articles they needed to make ready for sea like rigging, sails and ropes were stored in the dockyard. It was his opinion that 'in one month in the proper season the whole fleet could be in the roads', though 'men no doubt for a time would be wanting', and that the Danes seemed particularly vigilant against the risk of attack from the sea.[50]

Dunbar had not actually said that there was anything new or unusual about the state of the Danish navy in December 1806, but that is how Howick interpreted his observations. The reality was that the Danish navy was kept in good repair and the naval arsenal well-stocked, but that the fleet had lain unrigged in Copenhagen harbour since the renewal of war between Britain and France in 1803. This served as an earnest of Denmark's pacific and neutral intentions, but also reflected the high cost of fitting out the whole fleet and the absence of a maritime threat to Denmark in these years. The foreign secretary, however, got his hand firmly around the wrong end of the stick, and proclaimed that Dunbar's report gave additional weight to the anxieties created by the measures taken to reinforce Danish coastal defences in the Sound. Howick saw these measures and 'above all the extraordinary state of preparation' of the Danish navy as a potential threat to Britain's Baltic trade through the Sound.[51]

Dunbar's report finally prompted the British government to take precautionary counter-measures. On 10 January 1807, the admiralty instructed one of the subordinate officers in the Mediterranean, Vice-Admiral Sir John Duckworth, to return to Britain 'without a moment's loss of time', since the admiralty intended that he should command a squadron that would be sent to the Baltic.[52] The first lord of the admiralty was Thomas Grenville, Garlike's friend and the prime minister's younger brother, and he had quite a formidable force in mind: 'ten or twelve sail of the line to be ready for the Baltic by the end of February or the beginning of March'.[53]

For the time being, of course, nothing more had been done than to summon home a naval commander for a squadron, not yet assembled, that would sail for the Baltic in the spring. With his mercurial temperament, Howick soon came round to a more relaxed view of Danish intentions. He did not dispute Garlike's emphatic assertion that no unusual naval preparations were afoot at Copenhagen,[54] and he found it difficult to believe that Denmark could be so blind to her own commercial interests as not to see that a rupture with Britain 'would destroy' the advantages that she derived from her neutrality.[55] And by late January he had accepted that the limited improvements in Danish coastal defences in the Sound were directed at Sweden rather than Britain.[56] For the time being, the immediate crisis had passed.

The consistent interest the British government had displayed in Denmark during December 1806 and January 1807 was followed by a lull in February and early March. No new reports of disturbing developments involving Denmark were received during this period, though it was widely believed in both London and Denmark that a British squadron would be sent to the Baltic in the spring.[57] That was still probably the intention, but hardly in any pressing way. On 23 February, Thomas Grenville wrote to his eldest brother, the marquis of Buckingham (who was not a member of the government), that 'Denmark is still amicable in language and my colleagues are not anxious yet for the Baltic squadron'.[58] After the alarms of December and January, Anglo-Danish relations moved for the time being into calmer waters. Even so, all the issues that would prove so destructive to harmony between the two countries in July 1807 had performed a dress rehearsal in those bleak winter months – the French threat to Holstein, the danger that Denmark was preparing for war with Britain, the risk that her fleet would fall into French hands.

THE BRITISH ORDERS IN COUNCIL

What reactivated British interest in Denmark was the thorny old question of neutral maritime rights. It had been quiescent since 1801 but the Danish reaction to the British Orders in Council of 7 January 1807 pushed them back onto the agenda. They presented the recently appointed Danish envoy in London, Johan Rist, with his second major challenge. He had done well in soothing Howick over the evacuation of Holstein and the coastal-defence preparations on the Sound, but the Danish protest at the Orders in Council proved too hard a nut for him to crack.

Rist was thirty-one when he took charge of the Danish legation in London in the autumn of 1806. As a Holsteiner, born just north of Hamburg, his education was entirely German, but he was a subject of the Danish king and he had come to Copenhagen in his early twenties to make his way in the world. While private secretary to the finance minister, he attracted the attention of Christian Bernstorff, who took Rist under his wing and gave him his first diplomatic postings as secretary of legation first in St Petersburg and then in Madrid. The move from Madrid to head the legation in London was a great step forward for a young man of limited diplomatic experience. It says much about Bernstorff's confidence in him – and also about Bernstorff's powers of patronage, even if he found it advisable to appoint his protégé as *chargé d'affaires* rather than as a full minister.[59]

The Orders in Council were the British response to Napoleon's Berlin Decree of 21 November 1806, which had declared the British Isles to be under blockade and prohibited all commerce with them. The Berlin Decree obviously applied to France and to the territories under French control, and its tenth article stated that it would be communicated to France's allies. However, the wording of the decree could be interpreted as meaning that it covered every nation of the world. There was, in fact, no attempt at this stage to impose the decree on neutral powers, but its contents were communicated to the Danish government accompanied by a suggestion that Denmark ought to support this attempt to curb the overbearing maritime power of Britain. In practice, so long as France did not demand Danish adherence to the Berlin Decree, the effect on Danish trade was slight. The Danish government did not make a formal protest, but the French *chargé d'affaires* in Denmark was told orally that Denmark had always disputed the British interpretation of the law of blockade and could not therefore officially recognise the validity of the Berlin Decree.[60] Joachim Bernstorff gave Garlike to understand that the French had been told that Denmark 'deprecated' the Berlin Decree.[61]

The British counter-measures declared all ships trading between any two ports from which the British flag was excluded as liable to seizure as lawful prize. The Orders in Council did not, however, forbid direct trade on neutral vessels between ports under French control and neutral states (which in effect meant Denmark and the United States of America). Rist was not therefore inclined to take the British measures too tragically and accepted that they had been provoked by the Berlin Decree.[62] On 4 February the Orders in Council were debated in the commons and they were strongly attacked by the Pittite opposition for their leniency, and defended with equal vigour by Howick and other members of the government.[63] Rist was pleased by what he regarded as the moderate and fair-minded attitude of ministers during the debate, and more or less said so to Howick in the course of an informal conversation on 7 February. In his despatch to Christian Bernstorff, Rist observed that Denmark had reason to be grateful to the opposition, since it had, 'by preaching too loudly the principles of maritime despotism and oppression', obliged the government to espouse the cause of moderation.[64]

Matters were seen rather differently at home, where the Danish government was keen to object in principle to the violation of neutral trading rights involved. When Garlike reported on 30 January about his first meeting with Joachim Bernstorff concerning the Orders in Council, he found that Joachim's 'anger so exceeded, that it almost deprived him of utterance'.[65] Even the more phlegmatic Christian Bernstorff gently reproached Rist and urged his protégé to protest at this violation of Danish neutral rights with more 'warmth and firmness'.[66] Garlike warned Howick that Rist would be instructed to deliver a sharply worded response to the notification of the Orders in Council.[67]

Garlike was quite justified in fearing that Rist would be instructed to protest in the strongest terms.[68] The lengthy note, dated 9 March, that Rist addressed to Howick argued that Denmark would suffer grave commercial consequences from the Orders in Council. As for the question of principle, the Danish government could never acquiesce in the Orders in Council and consequently hoped that they would be rescinded. It had 'protested solemnly' against Napoleon's Berlin Decree, 'whose example Great Britain seems but too ready to follow', and could not accept that Britain's right of retaliation entitled the British to interfere with Denmark's 'liberty of commerce'.

The claim that Denmark had protested strongly and formally at the Berlin Decree was intended as an olive branch (even though it was rather less than the unalloyed truth). So too were Rist's concluding remarks that his hopes of a favourable response were enhanced by 'a knowledge of the liberal way of thinking and acting of the enlightened minister' to whom the note was addressed and who had already been the 'advocate' of neutral rights.[69] All this cut no ice with Howick. He suspected (correctly) that Denmark had made no serious protest against the Berlin Decree, and the note was very different in tone from the attitude Rist had displayed over the previous two months. The parallels drawn between British and French conduct were offensive and, worst of all perhaps, the Danish note was a poor return for the public defence of a moderate line towards neutral trade that he had mounted in the commons on 4 February, despite the pat on the head with which Rist rounded off his communication.

Howick's reply to Rist emphatically rejected any notion that the Orders in Council should be withdrawn before the Berlin Decree had been 'publicly and formally repealed'. He was sceptical about Rist's claim that Denmark had protested against it and said so explicitly. In addition, his note contained several passing remarks which implied that the Danish government was not as impartial as it ought to be – he observed, for example, that a Danish corps had been maintained in Holstein while the forces of France's enemies were close to the frontier, but was 'immediately withdrawn on the approach of the French army'. Britain would have been perfectly entitled to retaliate against the Berlin Decree by declaring all the ports from which the British flag was excluded to be in a state of blockade, but she had instead restricted herself to very limited counter-measures. In short, Britain's 'forbearance and magnanimity' had been 'eminently conspicuous'.[70]

Rist was taken aback by what he called 'the harsh or rather bitter tone' of Howick's note.[71] Some weeks later, Rist told Christian Bernstorff that in the course of March Howick had 'developed a marked irritation towards us' and had spoken 'bitterly' to several foreign envoys in London about the Danish protest against the Orders in Council.[72] Howick certainly complained about it to the Swedish minister in London, Baron von Rehausen, who gleefully reported to Gustavus IV that 'in general the system of moderation hitherto pursued by the British government towards the Danish court seems to be at an end'. He added that a considerable squadron was being armed 'to oppose the intentions of the Danish court if they should prove to be in conflict with the interests of the allies'.[73] All this was doubtless music to the ears of Gustavus IV, but was it true?

It was certainly the case that in the aftermath of the exchange of notes between Rist and Howick concrete steps were finally taken to collect a British naval force for the Baltic. The Grenville administration fell in late March, and most ministers were replaced on 25 and 26 March, but the new first lord of the admiralty, Lord Mulgrave, did not take office until 4 April. Thomas Grenville was still therefore in office on 1 April when the Admiralty ordered Commodore Keats to proceed to Yarmouth to take command of a squadron of sixteen warships that was assembling in that anchorage and 'to hold yourself, and the said ships, in constant readiness to put to sea at a moment's notice' until he was joined by Duckworth, who would command the squadron in the Baltic.[74]

Howick was clearly angered and embittered by Rist's note of 9 March 1807, and the outgoing prime minister, Lord Grenville, later remarked that 'we had abundant proof before we quitted office' that 'the general dispositions of Denmark were hostile to us'.[75] The Danish protest against the Orders in Council proved the straw that broke the camel's back. Howick and his colleagues had absorbed all the seemingly alarming circumstances of December 1806 and January 1807 without altering their view that Denmark was fundamentally friendly. Now the dam broke and the repressed suspicions flowed out. But a policy of moderation had not been entirely abandoned, and Howick's last weeks in office were marked by a conciliatory approach over the application of the Elbe blockade.

Britain had blockaded the Elbe from 1803 to 1805 and again from April to September 1806. On both occasions, the Danes were able to obtain a series of relaxations in the application of the blockade for ships from the two Danish ports on the Elbe, Altona and Glückstadt. When Britain once again declared the Elbe to be under blockade on 11 March 1807, Rist protested formally at the question of principle, but concentrated on obtaining a renewal of the relaxations granted by the British during the two previous blockades. His representations were successful. On 21 March, Howick sent Rist a note agreeing to a number of concessions in the enforcement of the Elbe blockade for vessels from Altona and Glückstadt.

One of these concessions, namely the permission given to small boats to sail close inshore down the west coast of Holstein from Tonningen to the Danish ports on the Elbe, was equally beneficial to Britain in that it facilitated Britain's clandestine exports through Tonningen to Hamburg. The Berlin Decree and the French occupation of Hamburg in November ought, in principle, to have put an end to British trade with north-western Germany, but it soon became apparent that the French authorities in Hamburg could be bribed to turn a blind eye, and British exports via Tonningen between March and July 1807 were higher than ever before.[76]

This demonstrates that from a British perspective Danish neutrality remained a mutually beneficial arrangement. Indeed, after the row over the British Orders in Council, contacts between the two countries quietened down once again. Just as there had been a lull in Anglo-Danish relations between late January and early March 1807, so there was now another between late March and late May. When they were reignited, responsibility in London no longer rested with Howick but with a new foreign secretary – George Canning, a man equally irascible but possessed of far greater resources of guile and duplicity. It is time for us to become reacquainted with the leading man of our story – the hero or villain of the piece, as you will.

Chapter 4

GEORGE CANNING AND THE DANES, MARCH–JUNE 1807

THE RIST AFFAIR

Rist was glad to see the back of Lord Howick, and when he met his successor, George Canning, for the first time on 28 March 1807, he thought that Canning's 'experience, enlightened spirit and obliging manners' boded well for the future.[1] It is unlikely that many members of the British political class would have put it quite that way. The new foreign secretary attracted divergent reactions – admired for his brilliance and his oratorical skills, but disliked for his sharp tongue and his inability to separate the personal from the political. And he was not very effective at concealing an all-consuming ambition underneath its usual cloak of discreet denial.

Compared with many prominent politicians of the day, his origins were modest, and Canning was acutely embarrassed by his mother's career on the stage after his father's premature death. But his family background was 'respectable' on both sides, and thanks to a supportive paternal uncle he had attended Eton and Oxford, where he had formed many of the friendships and connections that sustained him through his political life. He was a loyal if bossy friend himself and attracted devoted friends in return (Gower is a case in point). Canning's inclinations sometimes coincided happily with his self-interest. His family connections were Foxite, but after Oxford he developed an enthusiasm for Pitt. He was also fortunate that he fell in love with an heiress and that she eventually reciprocated his feelings. Their marriage relieved him of his immediate financial anxieties and appears to have been a happy one, made closer perhaps by shared anxiety for a sickly child. At any rate, his name was never linked to another woman, though he may before his marriage have engaged in some sort of dalliance with the Princess of Wales, Caroline of Brunswick.[2]

The formation of a new government from among the former followers of Pitt in late March 1807 enabled Canning to advance to the centre of the national stage. The political atmosphere was exceptionally bitter after the fall of the Grenville ministry and Canning's taste for rhetorical invective matched the hour. The duke of Portland was too burdened by ill health to exercise effective authority as prime minister, and Canning at the age of thirty-seven was one of the driving forces in the new administration. In the longer term, the jealousies and rivalries dividing him and the other members of the younger Pittite generation – Lord Castlereagh, the war secretary, Spencer Perceval, the chancellor of the exchequer, and Lord Hawkesbury, the home secretary – would prove fateful to the government. But for the moment, they stood united behind the Pittite legacy.

That legacy was not without ambivalence – Pitt had not always advocated unrelenting resistance to French expansion – but in the spring of 1807 it meant a more effective prosecution of the war against Napoleon than the Grenville administration had achieved and a continuing commitment to the alliance with Russia that Pitt had forged two years earlier. Canning seems to have been regarded as particularly hawkish in his attitude to the war. Samuel Whitbread, a prominent member of the opposition, lamented his appointment to the foreign office on the grounds that 'his temper, his feelings, and the whole course of his political life' would discourage the renewal of peace negotiations with France.[3] It was certainly the case that Canning had absented himself from the commons rather than vote for the peace of Amiens with France in 1802, despite Pitt's support for the treaty, and several of Canning's followers actually voted against it.[4]

During his first two months in office, Canning seemed to justify Rist's high hopes by pursuing a conciliatory line towards Denmark. He continued Howick's policy over the Elbe blockade by granting further concessions to Danish navigation on the Elbe in the course of April and May.[5] Another possible source of friction was eliminated when the new ministers shelved Thomas Grenville's pet project for the immediate despatch of a squadron to the Baltic, though the warships that had assembled already were not dispersed.

The reasons are obscure, but, in the absence of evidence to the contrary, it seems probable that ministers simply concluded that a strong

naval presence in the Baltic was not a priority at that time. By 22 April
Castlereagh was speaking of no more than a token force of frigates and
light vessels to lend some practical assistance to Britain's allies in the
Baltic.[6] And in mid-May Canning went no further than saying that the
presence of a British squadron in the Baltic might *possibly* be required
later in the year. None of this meant, however, that Canning placed any
great trust in the Danes. Like Howick before him, Canning suspected that
Rist's note of 9 March about the British Orders in Council revealed the
true 'leaning and sentiments' of the Danish government and that 'the
strongest prejudices against the cause of the allies' lurked behind 'the
mask of a specious neutrality'.[7]

Rist seems to have been quite oblivious of these suspicions and
remained delighted with the change of ministry. In one report, he could
not resist a side-swipe at Howick, and appears to have developed an
excessive enthusiasm for his successor. After his first formal meeting with
Canning, he extolled his 'liberal way of thinking' and his 'moderation
[and] conciliatory manner', which had confirmed his previous view that
Denmark had only gained from his appointment to the foreign office. Rist
even defended Canning against accusations that his command of French,
the lingua franca of diplomacy, was insufficient for a foreign secretary.
Some of the newspapers had amused their readers with speculations
about how Canning managed to communicate with foreign envoys who
had no English, but Rist informed Christian Bernstorff that Canning spoke
French 'very well' but with 'difficulty or rather timidity' – a somewhat
backhanded testimonial.[8]

Rist had clearly misjudged his man, but there was more to it than that:
Canning had good motives for making himself agreeable. Even though he
was deeply wary of the Danes, Britain had no need for a gratuitous
quarrel with Denmark while the outcome of the great struggle in eastern
Prussia was undecided. The foreign secretary had every reason to be
genuinely conciliatory over relaxations of the Elbe blockade in Denmark's
favour – and he was, provided the principle of Britain's right to impose it
were not undermined. It was precisely the question of principle that
brought the first hint of trouble to the amicable relationship between Rist
and the new foreign secretary.

For Joachim Bernstorff, who dealt with questions of maritime trade at
the Danish foreign ministry, the good old principles of the Armed

Neutralities of 1780 and 1800 were hibernating rather than abandoned. He did not entirely approve of Rist's approach of pursuing piecemeal concessions from the British over the Elbe blockade, and instructed him – apparently without first consulting his brother and Prince Fredrick in Kiel – to protest formally against it.[9] As a result, Rist was obliged to write to Canning on 18 May in terms that could hardly fail to strike an ungracious note. He acknowledged the exemptions to Danish navigation that Britain had granted as a token of her friendly intentions, but described them as insufficient and registered his government's rejection of the blockade as incompatible with Danish sovereign rights. Having got in the protest, he softened the blow by indicating that Denmark could, however, just about live with the blockade if further concessions were granted to Danish navigation on the Elbe.[10]

Rist had a long meeting with Canning on 21 May to discuss his note, and each set out in some detail his government's position on the questions of principle raised by the Elbe blockade. Their accounts of the conversation are essentially the same, but each came away from it with a different impression. The way Rist told it, Canning had been charm personified, and they parted on the basis that Denmark could no more renounce her stand over neutral rights than Britain could abandon her rights as a belligerent, but that within this framework the British government was fully inclined to grant as much relief as possible to Danish navigation.[11]

That point was underlined the following day by a note from Canning agreeing to one of the further concessions for Danish shipping on the Elbe that Rist had demanded. Canning expressed the hope that Rist would appreciate this token of Britain's desire 'to encourage . . . a spirit of mutual accommodation and good will'.[12] Canning's account of the interview does not contradict Rist's, but nonetheless painted a less harmonious picture. He claimed he had mainly agreed to the meeting so as to dispel any notion that the concessions already granted over the Elbe blockade signalled any weakening of Britain's determination to enforce her belligerent rights, a point 'upon which His Majesty would never yield'.[13]

This was no more than the distant rumble of an approaching storm. What destroyed the personal relationship between Canning and Rist was a quite different question: the detention of Danish merchant vessels by

British warships. In 1805 only thirty-five Danish vessels had been detained and of these, only three had been condemned as lawful prize by the High Court of Admiralty. The number of detentions shot up to at least 154 in 1806 and remained at a high level when the sailing season resumed in 1807. The Danish consul in London grumbled that it seemed 'as if a net has been cast across the English Channel to catch all neutral ships which are conducting a lawful and peaceful commerce'.[14]

This state of affairs reflected both Britain's maritime supremacy and the great profits that the personnel of the Royal Navy could derive from the prize system. If the High Court of Admiralty found that a detained vessel had been carrying enemy property or contraband or attempting to enter a port Britain had declared under blockade, the cargo and, in serious cases, the ship itself were condemned as 'lawful prize' and the full value was divided between the crew of the warship that had brought it into port. The lion's share went to the officers, especially the master of the ship, but even the meanest rating got his modest cut. Even if the court eventually released the neutral ship, the captor received compensation for his trouble and effort if there were any formal error in the ship's papers (a nice little earner known as 'captor's expenses'). It was a sweet arrangement for the Royal Navy, and many British officers grew rich on prize money.[15]

It was all very well for the Danish consul to complain that it was 'lawful' for Danish merchantmen to sail to a port under French control provided that they did not carry enemy property or contraband, but we should be wary of seeing this simply as a case of the Danish David against the mighty British Goliath. The Danes had a very poor record from the eighteenth century of selling false ship's papers and carrying enemy property under a veneer of Danish ownership. Since the resumption of war in 1803, the Danish government had made a real effort to suppress rather than connive in abuses of this kind, but it could never be possible to prevent all Danish trade that contravened British prize law. Nonetheless, the assumption that all abuses had been eradicated was the basis on which the Danish legation in London had proceeded since 1803. It was standing policy to protest at all detentions without any attempt at discrimination between individual cases.[16]

Rist was merely following this well-trodden path when he wrote to Canning on 8 May to request the immediate restoration to their owners of fifteen Danish merchant ships detained in the English Channel since the middle of April. He wrote again on 26 May concerning the detention of a further thirteen ships in May and for a third time on 5 June with more general reflections on the workings of the British prize system. On each occasion, his tone became more offensive. The central thrust of his complaints was 'the frequency and frivolity' of these detentions. He claimed that the High Court of Admiralty awarded captor's expenses too easily and that as a result the detention of Danish vessels had become a 'lucrative occupation' for British warships. Unless this changed, the Royal Navy would continue to have an incentive to detain 'an infinity of vessels', which had no chance of being condemned as lawful prize, simply in order to be reimbursed for their supposed efforts and expenses, which in reality consisted of no more than bringing the ship into port before setting sail again in search of fresh prey.

Rist in effect accused the Royal Navy of operating a racket, with the connivance of the High Court of Admiralty, and rounded that off by describing this court as a 'semi-political' institution that often proceeded on 'instructions' from the British government. He was particularly exercised by the detention of two ships chartered by the Danish government to deliver the annual 'present' (it might also be described as protection money) Denmark paid to the rulers of Tunis and Algiers so that Danish commerce in the Mediterranean would be unmolested by the corsairs who operated from the so-called Barbary Coast of North Africa. It was true that the vessel bound for Tunis carried munitions, but Rist claimed that the ship's papers of both vessels were a sufficient proof of their destination. This was an incautious assertion, even if Rist probably only used it because the two ships were chartered by the Danish government rather than by private interests. Even so, it seemed to question the foundation of the British system of maritime warfare, which rested on the assumption that ships' papers were not to be implicitly believed and that Britain had a right to investigate when there were grounds for suspicion.[17]

Rist's three notes were extraordinarily clumsy, and it is difficult to fathom why he thought it advisable to write in such terms. He was doubtless genuinely incensed at the treatment Danish merchantmen were receiving at the hands of the Royal Navy. Perhaps Canning's previous friendliness made him incautious and led him to overestimate how far he could go. Perhaps he was seeking to ingratiate himself with his superiors, the Bernstorff brothers, who had both accused him of treading too softly over neutral trade in the past, by a demonstration of his zeal. Stir in the naivety and inexperience of a young man holding down his first big job, and we may have the explanation for his behaviour. Whatever the reasons, his remarks about the rapacious practices of the Royal Navy and the partiality of the British courts were offensive and provocative, and they prompted a savage reaction from Canning.

He was conciliatory over the detained vessels themselves, most of which had already been released or probably soon would be. But one had been taken attempting to enter Dieppe in breach of the British blockade, while the vessel bearing the annual Danish present to Algiers was carrying munitions and had an enemy port (Malaga) as its first destination. Canning urged Rist 'to discriminate with a little more precision than he appears to have exercised in these instances between the cases which he may think it his duty to make the subjects of complaint'. Indeed, 'the habit of complaining on all occasions with the same warmth, necessarily induces the risk of complaining often without just cause, and would therefore transfer the charge of "frequency and frivolity" from the captures of the British navy . . . to the complaints of the Danish mission'. As for the principle that a ship's papers were sufficient proof of its destination, which Rist had applied in the case of the ships bound for Tunis and Algiers, Britain would never accept it in any case where 'the apparent tenor of the papers is contradicted by any circumstances of suspicion', and Rist had acted 'unadvisedly' in citing it.[18]

Canning did not stop with rapping Rist over the knuckles. He also wrote to Garlike with copies of the notes exchanged between Rist and himself. He claimed that the 'tone and language' adopted by Rist were objectionable, particularly in 'a correspondence which has for the most part consisted in a succession of claims on the one side and concessions on the other'. He wanted Garlike to raise the matter with Joachim Bernstorff in the hope – it would seem – that Bernstorff would confirm what Canning at least pretended to believe, namely that the language adopted by Rist had not been 'dictated or authorised' by instructions from the Danish government.[19] Rist's removal from his post in London would be 'the best and surest manifestation that can be given of the good disposition of the Danish government'. Garlike was not to demand Rist's recall, but he was to insist that Rist should at the very least receive 'such an admonition . . . speedily and unequivocally as shall ensure a mode of executing his instructions less offensive than that which he has thought proper to adopt'. If instead Rist's conduct were approved by his government, then the only conclusion which could be drawn would be that 'Denmark is seeking a ground of quarrel with this country'.[20]

Canning had chosen to take the Rist affair very seriously. Why had he done so? No doubt he was genuinely aggrieved by Rist's notes, and his career shows both that he could be impulsive and aggressive, and that he always possessed a savage tongue and pen when it suited him. Some allowance should probably be made for all these characteristics. But there was sober calculation too. Canning was a politician to the core and on the level of domestic politics he could not allow himself to appear a softer touch in his dealings with the neutrals than Howick, who had boasted in the recent election campaign of the tough note he had sent to Rist in March.[21]

In diplomatic terms, Canning's overriding goal was to flush the Danes out, to force them to show their true colours. He regarded Rist's recall, or at the very least a stiff reprimand from his government, as a touchstone of Danish goodwill, a pointer to the underlying attitude of the Danish government towards Britain. Canning was 'almost afraid' that Rist's offensive behaviour was the result of instructions from his government, but it was better to treat it as the indiscretion of an individual rather than the 'ill-disposition' of the Danish government. He suspected that its reaction would be determined by the course of the war. If the Russians had gained a victory by the time copies of the correspondence reached Copenhagen, Rist would be 'disavowed and recalled'. In the contrary case, 'I suppose he will be supported – and I must look forward for a tedious controversy here to be terminated by nothing but a peace (which God forbid) or a fleet in the Baltic'.[22]

Canning had put the ball in the Danish court. In his eyes, it was now up to the Danes to react in a manner that demonstrated the absence of an 'ill-disposition' on their part towards Britain. Oddly enough, the individual who proved most inclined to do this was Rist himself, who belatedly realised that he had been boxing above his weight. That did not prevent him from being deeply hurt and outraged by Canning's remarks. He replied to Canning with pompous dignity that, as the foreign secretary had insulted him personally, he would hasten to transmit Canning's note to his government, 'the sole authority' entitled to administer reproaches to him.[23] That was the end of their correspondence over maritime law, and they did not have another formal meeting until September. It was also the end of Rist's crush on Canning – naturally enough after a note he described as 'so unconciliatory, couched in a language so uncommon in the transaction of business and also so calculated to wound my feelings as an individual'.[24]

But Rist was not blind to the seriousness of the situation. Normally, he reported on maritime questions to Joachim Bernstorff in Copenhagen, and reserved his despatches on political matters for Christian Bernstorff in Kiel, but on this occasion he wrote to both. He attributed 'the almost indecent language' Canning had adopted as an indication that the British government wished to silence all voices that had the temerity to draw attention to the abuses perpetrated by the Royal Navy and the British prize courts. Even so, he conceded Canning's point that the policy of protesting at *all* detentions and *en bloc* inevitably led to cases where the Danish complaint was unjustified, and claimed to have long felt that it was embittering relations with 'a friendly power'. He therefore requested new and precise instructions as to how he should proceed in the future. He also suggested that it might be advisable to appoint another Danish diplomat to fill his own post, someone – as he put it with a touch of self-pity – 'endowed with a character which will give the British a little more pause before they administer a reprimand in the extraordinary manner adopted by M. Canning'. He left it to Christian Bernstorff to judge if he, Rist, could be of any further use to Denmark in his present position after what had passed between him and Canning.[25]

The Bernstorff brothers found no merit in Canning's complaints and stood by their man in London. In a series of lengthy letters between Copenhagen and Kiel, they both took the line that Rist's complaints had been justified in all respects and Canning's response gratuitously offensive, though they conceded that Rist's choice of words might have been a little imprudent in places. It was in this unconciliatory spirit that Joachim discussed the matter on 27 June with Garlike, who came away fearing that the final response from Kiel would be coloured by 'the peevishness with which the Danish ministers are now deliberating'.[26]

It was more than a month after Joachim's meeting with Garlike before Christian Bernstorff conveyed his final decision. He excused the delay by referring to the weighty distractions that had prevented him from writing on matters of business in recent times – a reference presumably to his wife's illness. Christian left it to Joachim to reply to Rist as he thought fit, but made it clear that the reply should be supportive. However, behind the bluster, Christian did make an important concession to Canning. He suggested that Joachim should make it clear to Garlike on some suitable occasion that if what had transpired between Canning and Rist caused a tension in the future between the two that was detrimental to the transaction of business, then the Danish government would have to consider shifting Rist to another post.[27] This was not the disavowal and recall of Rist that Canning wanted, but it was something. This hint was never conveyed to Garlike, just as Joachim never sent Rist a reply to his request for fresh instructions, since great events soon overtook the rumblings of the Rist affair.

Christian Bernstorff's letter to his brother on 28 July would presumably have led over the following weeks to new instructions for Rist to tread more softly and an oral assurance to Garlike that Rist would be removed if he caused offence again in the future. This would more or less have given Canning the token of Danish goodwill that he had sought. But it never happened, because of the month-long silence of Christian Bernstorff. Canning had harboured strong suspicions about Danish attitudes and intentions from his earliest days as foreign secretary; they had been heightened by the Rist affair and nothing had been done to mitigate them. Like everyone else, politicians are subject to the power of immediate and sometimes trivial impressions. This is why the Rist affair is more than just a tiresome spat within the tiny world of diplomatic exchanges. As the great crisis provoked by Tilsit broke over the heads of the British government in early July 1807, the impression produced by Rist's notes was still alive in Canning's mind along with all the suspicions of Danish attitudes that it had reinforced.

BENJAMIN GARLIKE AND THE DANES

These suspicions were not effectively modified by the reports of our man in Copenhagen. The quiet life that Garlike had enjoyed at Copenhagen had come to an end with the Danish evacuation of Holstein, and throughout the first half of 1807 he was engaged in interminable wrangles with

Joachim Bernstorff. Joachim always found the British Orders in Council good for a grumble, and their relations were also bedevilled by frequent confrontations over the use of the port of Husum in Schleswig as a conduit for British correspondence with the continent. The post carried by the so-called packet boats that plied between Harwich and Husum were an important link in Britain's illicit trade with Germany and in her correspondence with British envoys abroad, and the Danes found themselves caught between the devil and the deep blue sea because of insistent French exhortations that access to Husum should be denied to British packet boats.

The Danes regarded a unilateral step of this kind as incompatible with their neutrality, particularly as it would represent a partial closure of a Danish port to the British flag, but they were too frightened of the French to reply with an emphatic 'no'. This left Joachim with the ticklish task of urging the British to discontinue the Husum correspondence voluntarily, while denying – with limited plausibility – that he was acting in response to a French pressure. Neither the Grenville nor the Portland government showed the slightest willingness to accede to the Danish request, and this set the scene for numerous heated discussions between Joachim and Garlike. Christian Bernstorff's ingenious and sneaky suggestion that the packet boats should unload their mail on the Danish island of Heligoland and that it should then be brought to mainland Denmark in Danish vessels foundered on his brother's insistence that such an arrangement would not satisfy France.[28]

The atmosphere between Joachim and Garlike was not improved by the former's intemperate nature and sharp tongue. Garlike often found him 'peevish and ungracious' and prone to 'ill-humour' and 'hasty expressions'.[29] He accepted that 'Count J. Bernstorff is not ill disposed towards England; and the violence of his manner is accompanied with proofs that he is not'.[30] Even so, the frequent unpleasantness of their exchanges potentially had unfortunate consequences, in Garlike's view, as Joachim's 'almost habitual . . . captiousness' and 'sore recollections of former quarrels' undermined the chances of 'for calm discussion in serious and critical moments'.[31]

What really mattered from a British point of view were the underlying intentions of the Danish government on the great issues of war and peace, and on this score Garlike presented a mixed picture. Far more important than the Husum question was British trade through Tonningen and other Holstein ports, and on this point Danish assurances were perfectly satisfactory. Joachim Bernstorff went so far as to declare on 29 May that Britain had no reason to fear the closure of these ports as the Danes would rather perish than consent to such a measure.[32] Joachim's rhetorical flourish was perhaps a little excessive, but it did echo the views of his brother at Kiel, who had written to him that 'so long as we are masters in our own land, our ports must remain open to the English'.[33] As Howick had done, Garlike also drew comfort from his awareness that for Denmark to allow herself to be drawn into open hostilities with Britain would 'expose her entire commerce, the guide and check of all her resolutions, to unavoidable ruin'.[34]

But all was not rosy: 'I have never looked without anxiety to the ultimate resolutions of this country as a minor state borne upon by the arts and ferocity of France.' Garlike had no doubt that the Danish government was sympathetic to the cause of the anti-French coalition and wished to see 'the independence of the continent' restored, but whether Denmark would manifest that disposition in concrete terms would depend on the means France possessed of exerting pressure on her.[35]

Garlike drew all the threads of his previous reports together in a despatch on 27 June, the same day as he discussed the Rist affair with Joachim, setting out his views on 'the real disposition of the [Danish] government'. The Danes genuinely wanted to cling to their neutrality and 'do imagine that they are steering a middle course' by their constant complaints about perceived offences against it. But it did not always look like that. In the nature of things, 'the vast increase in Danish commerce' was of necessity thwarted more by Britain than by France, so those complaints were directed far more against Britain than against France. Besides, 'the constant fear of sudden violence from France on the side of Holstein lowers the tone of their representations against the conduct of that power'. Despite such appearances, Garlike had 'little hesitation in saying that the disposition of the Danish government is friendly to Great Britain and to her cause'. And it was a question of self-interest as well as sympathy. The Danes were 'aware of the ruin that must follow a rupture with Great Britain from which it is more than probable that the islands of Denmark, with her continental provinces, Norway, and the foreign possessions could never rise again in their present united and flourishing state.'

These considerations should be 'expected to prevail at the proper moment in favour of Great Britain, the only power which could assist the government in preserving the sinews and resources of the country'. But – and here was the rub – Garlike had never thought that the pro-British sentiments of the government were to be relied upon 'under the pressure of sudden danger. I think it probable that much ill-judged resentment and pride would then take the lead of their interest and that Great Britain can rely only on the vigour and promptitude of those measures which may then be thought advisable.'[36]

Garlike never received any reply from Canning to his ruminations about the current and future conduct of the Danish government. Rist believed that Garlike was genuinely well-inclined towards Denmark, but that his views carried little weight in London.[37] Canning certainly had no great opinion of Garlike, but in fact Garlike's opinions were not so very different from Canning's, though they were a good deal more balanced and considered. They were both apprehensive of the line that Denmark would ultimately take. The main difference is that Canning supposed the Danes to be surreptitiously hostile to Britain, while Garlike took the opposite view but feared that they might in some circumstances be unable to resist French pressure. There was enough common ground for Canning to find in Garlike's reports the confirmation of his own suspicions that he was looking for. Canning claimed that Garlike's account of the 'disposition' of the Danish government was 'as unfavourable as possible', and that 'the whole tenor of Mr Garlike's despatches shows the Danish government to be in a state of ill humour and irritation against this country, which renders but too probable their compliance with any demand that France may make upon them'.[38] This was a selective, exaggerated and partial reading, but not a grossly distorted one.

Was Canning right? Were the Danes covertly hostile to Britain and her cause? The evidence of the Danish sources suggests that Garlike had read the Danes more accurately than the foreign secretary. Prince Fredrick, Christian Bernstorff and Danish envoys abroad rarely gave the ruler of France his imperial title in their correspondence. They occasionally call him 'Napoleon' or even 'the Emperor Napoleon', but most of the time they refer, in the same way as the British, simply to 'Bonaparte'. A trivial point perhaps, but more significantly the instructions that Christian Bernstorff sent to his envoys abroad are full of observations about the war and they contain no hint of Francophile sympathies. On the contrary, 'the preponderant and tyrannical power' of France had for far too long held the greater part of Europe in a 'state of ignominy and enslavement'. The outcome of the war against Napoleon would 'determine the destinies of Europe for centuries to come'. (Christian was not a man to eschew hyperbole.) Consequently, he experienced feelings of 'inexpressible satisfaction' at the setback Napoleon suffered at Eylau[39] and castigated Austria for clinging to her neutrality and her failure to intervene for 'the security and general good of Europe'.[40]

The same obligation did not, however, rest on Denmark. She could only lend the most insignificant support to the anti-French coalition and would place her very existence at risk by entering the conflict. Present circumstances imposed on her 'more imperiously than ever' that system of neutrality which had served her so well over the previous fifteen years of warfare.[41] And the survival of neutrality demanded an extremely cautious, not to say ingratiating, approach to 'the most absolute and powerful government which France has ever seen'.[42]

It was a caution born of fear, not any sense of affinity, and it in no way undermined Christian's overriding sympathy for Napoleon's enemies. But the focus of that sympathy was Russia far more than Britain. It was Emperor Alexander who would become not only 'the best of sovereigns' but also 'the avenger of mankind' if he triumphed over Napoleon.[43] (Christian had been at the hyperbole bottle again.) His attitude to Britain was more ambivalent. Not only was the British government 'haughty', 'easily offended' and prone to unwarranted prejudices against foreign powers. It was also absorbed by British internal affairs and often badly served by its representatives abroad. Above all, Christian disliked the arbitrary power that Britain exercised with such impunity at sea. And he was not at all happy at the prospect of a British squadron in the Baltic, though he recognised that Denmark could do nothing to prevent it.[44] The British should instead concentrate on mounting the much-delayed continental diversion that would relieve the pressure on the Russians in the east.[45]

The immense naval power that Britain deployed to enforce her own interpretation of neutral maritime rights damaged Danish interests, and this was the primary source of any distaste he felt for Britain. But his observations probably also bear testimony to a cultural divide between the two countries. He found it much easier to understand and relate to the traditional absolutist monarchies of the continent – Austria, Prussia and Russia. Britain, in contrast, was not only characterised by insularity in his eyes, but was also a parliamentary state. Christian deplored the instability occasioned by frequent ministerial changes, and he was no doubt equally disapproving when he read Rist's reports on the popular support attracted by the radical member of parliament Sir Francis Burdett from the electors of Westminster.[46]

Christian's feelings were hardly pro-British, but it was difficult to sympathise with the continental coalition against Napoleon without also extending some of that sympathy to Britain. More to the point, on the level of hard-headed self-interest Christian's analysis of Denmark's position coincided with Garlike's. Denmark would be 'ruined' the moment she came into conflict with Britain. He recognised that Danish neutrality was precarious, and accepted that Britain would become Denmark's natural ally if France attacked her or tried to impose demands that were incompatible with her independence.[47]

The evidence about Prince Fredrick's views is more fragmentary, but the letters he exchanged with his brother-in law, Duke Fredrick Christian of Augustenburg, in the first half of 1807 show that they entertained the same hopes and fears and sympathies as Christian Bernstorff.[48] In this respect, as in most others, the foreign minister was indeed his master's voice. Similar attitudes also appear at a more junior level. When Rist heard the first reports of Friedland, even while still smarting from the verbal thrashing he had received from Canning, his immediate reaction was that the consequences would be 'so baneful that one hardly dares yet to admit them to oneself, because the future offers no remedy'.[49]

None of this is compelling proof, of course, that Denmark would have chosen to side with Britain under what Garlike called 'the pressure of sudden danger'. A French ultimatum accompanied by a massed army on the frontier of Holstein would have presented the Danish government with terrible alternatives – the occupation by France of Jutland and the islands west of the Great Belt as against the destructive consequences of war with Britain. The alternatives were so terrible that Danish leaders seem not to have discussed them – at any rate, they have left no written record of having done so. Prince Fredrick's ideas of honour and national independence would probably have led him to resist France in these circumstances, but we cannot achieve absolute certainty two hundred years later any more than Garlike could at the time, since the question was never put to the test. Instead, when 'the pressure of sudden danger' was felt, it came from Britain, not France, and in a manner grossly offensive to all Fredrick's notions of honour. That would happen when the Danish navy, which had briefly attracted Howick's attention in the depths of the previous winter, became the focus of George Canning's interest. The first step in this process was the arrival of a piece of erroneous intelligence from Copenhagen.

LORD PEMBROKE AT COPENHAGEN

On 8 June, at the same time as he was writing to Garlike about Rist's objectionable conduct, Canning received a letter from Lord Pembroke, the newly appointed British ambassador to Austria. The mainland of western Europe was closed to British diplomats by French control of the continent, and Pembroke was obliged to follow a circuitous route to take up his new post – by sea from Yarmouth to Memel and then overland across Russia to Vienna. He reached Copenhagen on the morning of 28 May, and wrote to Canning the same evening. Those were gentler, less security-conscious days and he was allowed to walk through the dockyard in Copenhagen after his arrival. Pembroke thought that what he had seen was worth reporting to the foreign secretary.

Pembroke claimed that 'it was impossible not to perceive that every exertion was making to prepare against any possible attack' on Copenhagen from the sea. The main sea fort guarding the entrance to Copenhagen harbour from the north, Trekroner, was 'furnished with guns of the heaviest metal, so as to be absolutely crowded with them'. The same applied to the five large floating batteries within the inner harbour. There were also eight new gunboats 'on the stocks' in addition to those that had already been launched. Pembroke regarded the preparations as the result of the British attack on Copenhagen in 1801, which had produced among the Danes he encountered 'a dislike to and a jealousy of the English which is but too visible even to a resident of a few hours'. He also mentioned, almost in passing, that at least twenty Danish ships of the line (which meant in effect the entire fleet) were 'fit to go to sea with all their stores etc. named and numbered'.

Pembroke ended with the observation: 'I have nothing more to say and I am sure I may have already said more than I need have said'.[50] He had indeed said too much, because he was completely mistaken about the level of naval preparedness at Copenhagen. His claims are contradicted both by the Danish naval records and by the reports of several other British observers. Nor are they backed up by Lord Gower, who was also detained at Copenhagen by contrary winds on his way to Memel aboard another British warship at the same time as Pembroke, and who made no reference at all to the alleged Danish preparations in the letter he wrote to Canning from Copenhagen.[51]

The tables kept by the Danish naval authorities show that in the seven months between January and July 1807 inclusive, only two ships of the line, two frigates and three brigs were fitted out for service at sea. This was entirely in line with normal practice since the naval battle in the roads of Copenhagen in 1801. Each year, one ship of the line accompanied by one brig, which both sailed on 23 April in 1807, were used to exercise Denmark's naval cadets at sea, while one frigate was stationed in the Sound as a guard ship. Another ship of the line and one frigate were generally kept at Christiansand on the south coast of Norway, while one frigate was sent to show the flag in the Danish islands in the West Indies.[52]

The only unusual feature in 1807 was that a second ship of the line (the *Waldemar*) was equipped for a special service, namely to convey the Grand Duchess Maria Pavlovna, the sister of Alexander I and wife of the crown prince of Saxe-Weimar, from Copenhagen to St Petersburg. She had taken refuge on Danish territory, at Schleswig, when northern Germany was overrun by the French in late 1806 and wished to withdraw further from the vicinity of the war zone. The Danish government went to great pains to convey the grand duchess to Russia in some style, and Fredrick appointed one of his pet naval officers, Admiral Lindholm, to command the ship. Christian Bernstorff assured his minister at St Petersburg that 'all imaginable facilities' would be laid on.[53] But in the end she never went, because Tilsit made it possible for her to return to Weimar, and the *Waldemar* and its accompanying brig were decommissioned again.

The only fully equipped ship of the line Pembroke could have seen at Copenhagen on 28 May 1807 was the *Waldemar*. He also failed to take account of the question of manning. The two ships of the line actually at sea in 1807 – the *Princesse Louisa Augusta* (64 guns), which spent the year in Norway, and the *Prinds Christian Fredrick* (70 guns), which took the naval cadets to sea – both carried a crew of just over 500 men. If she had sailed, the *Waldemar* (80 guns) was due to carry 701 men.[54] The permanent establishment of the Danish navy consisted in this period of 6,000 to 8,000 men. Just over half were sailors or gunners. The remainder were employed for building, repairing and fitting out warships in the Copenhagen dockyard.[55] The Danish navy depended on a system of reservists, men with a greater or lesser knowledge of the sea, who could be called up in times of crisis or war. Two-thirds of them were enrolled on the reserve lists in Norway, and the most experienced among them were employed in the merchant marine. Somewhere between 11,000 and 15,000 of them would be needed, in addition to the navy's permanent sailors and gunners, to put the whole fleet to sea, and it was doubtful if such numbers could be found in practice, as opposed to theory.[56]

In November 1800, the Danish admiralty estimated that to provide crews for 10 ships of the line and 5 frigates, it needed to find 4,733 seamen. And in early 1801, when the Danish government expected a British attack in the spring, it had taken a desperate effort over three months to lay hands on the 5,000 or so men needed to man the floating defence line in the roads of Copenhagen – and this was at a time when the merchant marine was at home for the winter. About 1,500 Norwegian sailors marched overland through Sweden to reach Copenhagen just in time for the battle against Nelson. Even the corps of professional naval officers was too small to man the entire fleet for war – they were merely a nucleus of regulars who would be supplemented by experienced mates from the merchant marine drafted into the navy to serve on monthly contracts in times of tension or war.[57] Finding the crews was the Achilles heel of the Danish navy, and that – together no doubt with the cost – is why it was over forty years in 1807 since more than half of the fleet had been fitted out for sea at the same time. In the first seven months of 1807, there is no evidence at all that the Danish admiralty was calling up additional men for service in the navy.

Pembroke was equally wrong about the floating batteries. He claimed there were five in the harbour, when in fact there was only one. This was the accurately but unimaginatively named 'Floating Battery no. 1', which had fought the British in the roads of Copenhagen in 1801 and survived.

There is, however, a question of terminology here, and Pembroke may not be quite as mistaken as he sounds. Other British reports from the same period also speak of three or four floating batteries located in the inner harbour, so it is likely that the term is being used to cover the four armed barges (*stykpramme* in Danish), whose presence is recorded in the Danish sources.

As for the sea forts defending Copenhagen, the number of cannon remained fairly constant through to the summer of 1807, after the modest strengthening of their garrisons ordered by Prince Fredrick in December 1806. The only point where Pembroke was right was about the gunboats. The new naval plan adopted in November 1806 called for the construction of many small, shallow-draught gunboats, and a start had been made on building them by May 1807.

Pembroke's assertions were contradicted, and the evidence of the Danish sources confirmed, by the statements of two British naval officers. Lieutenant Hanchett, the commander of the *British Fair*, reported to Garlike on 2 May (about four weeks before Pembroke's tour of the dockyard) that there were 17 ships of the line, 11 frigates, 3 floating batteries and about 25 smaller vessels. 'The generality of the ships appear to be in good repair . . . All the vessels have their ballast in, and spars of every description on each side of the lower deck, no other stores of any kind are on board any of them.' The rigging, sails, guns and so on were 'all complete, but in store houses in the dock yard'. Hanchett concluded that 'you may place confidence in this report, as I have not only been in the holds of some of them, but have seen their stores of every description in their respective places in the dockyard'.[58]

The second British officer was Captain Francis Beauman of the *Procris*, and his report is dated 25 July off Elsinore. It stated that he had that day inspected the dockyard and ships at Copenhagen. He had found 18 ships of the line lying there, all 'in a state of ordinary . . . with their lower masts and part of their ballast in', except for one that was 'rigged' (the *Waldemar*). There were also 11 frigates, 4 floating batteries and numerous smaller ships. 'I went on board the greater part of the line of battle ships, and found them in the most perfect state of repair . . . and I am of opinion the whole of the Danish fleet might with the greatest ease *provided they had seamen* be at sea in six weeks from the commencement of their equipment.' Beauman concluded:

I beg you will not conclude from this statement that I mean to insinuate that a fleet is fitting out at Copenhagen. To the best of my knowledge and belief there is not the least sign of any unusual or active preparation. From what I could learn it has been the usual state of the Fleet ever since Lord Nelson's battle of the 2nd of April [1801], and I may venture to assert there is not at present the shadow of appearance for the equipment of a fleet, as it is impossible it could be hid from the eye of any naval officer.[59]

When he sent Hanchett and Beauman's reports to Canning, Garlike explained Beauman's point about seamen. Beauman had indeed confirmed orally that the entire Danish fleet might be got ready in six weeks if the Danish government had sailors available.[60] Captain Dunbar had in December 1806 put the time limit somewhat lower – he had believed the fleet could be in the roads in a month 'if able sailors were on the spot to begin the work'. But there was the rub – there were only about 800 sailors at Copenhagen, 'besides the dockyard men', and great numbers of Norwegian seamen were abroad serving in the Danish and British merchant marines.[61]

How did Pembroke get it so wrong? His claims bear a certain similarity to those made by Captain James Dunbar in December 1806 – no great surprise perhaps as the ship on which Pembroke was travelling to Memel was the *Astrea* and its commander was still none other than Dunbar. George Augustus Herbert, the eleventh earl of Pembroke, was an army man in his late forties, who had risen to the rank of lieutenant-general by 1807, on his first diplomatic assignment. He naturally had general military knowledge, but it is reasonable to assume that he was strongly influenced by Dunbar in his assessment of what he saw in the Copenhagen dockyard. At all events, Dunbar gave an equally alarming picture of the state of Danish naval preparations in a note he wrote some time afterwards about his second visit to Copenhagen.[62] The only semi-rational explanation that comes to mind is that Pembroke and Dunbar were deluded by their own suspicion of the Danes and saw in the dockyard what they expected to be there.

The obvious inference to be drawn from Pembroke's letter of 28 May was that the Danish government anticipated Denmark might soon be at war with Britain and was making active preparations to meet that eventuality. The Danes certainly did not need to strengthen Copenhagen's defences against attack from the sea on such a scale or to fit out twenty ships of the line because of anything the French might do. That was the conclusion which Canning ultimately drew from Pembroke's statements and it influenced his thinking heavily in the longer term. But at the time he received it, on 8 June, he paid very little attention to Pembroke's remarks about the Danish fleet. He did not even refer to them in his reply, which was entirely devoted to Pembroke's mission to Austria (Pembroke was after all on his way to Vienna).[63] When he wrote to Gower the following day, Canning mainly grumbled about Rist's offensive behaviour, which led him to fear that 'the disposition at Copenhagen is so unfriendly as to want nothing but the appearance of being able to insult us with impunity, to break out into open defiance'. He then added, almost in passing and without a word about the Danish fleet, 'such too seems to be Lord Pembroke's impression in a few lines which I had from him yesterday, written after he had been almost four and twenty hours at Copenhagen'.

The key to this almost studied indifference to Pembroke's observations about the Danish navy probably lies in Canning's belief that the ultimate attitude of Denmark would be determined by the outcome of the war in eastern Prussia.[64] In other words, Canning did nothing about Pembroke's letter for the same reason that he was willing to wait and see how the Danish government would react over the Rist affair. If Bennigsen gained the victory over Bonaparte, the Danes would not be a problem. Such judicious forbearance ceased to be an option when the news of Friedland reached London and its implications began to sink in.

Chapter 5

THE SECRET INTELLIGENCE FROM ALTONA AND NORMANDY, JUNE–JULY 1807

EDWARD THORNTON AT ALTONA

News travelled slowly in the early nineteenth century. Gower's reports from Memel took about three weeks to get to Canning in London, while Garlike's despatches from Copenhagen arrived after ten or eleven days. Much depended on the favour of the wind, and the time could be longer or shorter accordingly. Information in the public domain came a little quicker across the mainland of Europe through the medium of newspapers under French control. The battle of Friedland was fought on 14 June, but Canning spent the second half of June in happy ignorance of the fateful events that were unfolding in eastern Prussia. On 29 June rumours of a great battle that had gone badly for the Russians were circulating in London,[1] and by the next day Canning was in little doubt that this was so. He wrote to Gower that 'the afflicting intelligence of the disastrous result of the battle of the 14th' had reached London from The Hague and Calais.[2]

Canning's primary concern was that Britain should remain in step with Russia, and if that meant peace negotiations with France, so be it. The main thrust of the instructions with which he had furnished Gower back in May before his departure for Memel was focused on the prosecution of the war, but they also anticipated the eventuality of peace talks.[3] This was still Canning's line when he learnt of Friedland. The 'God forbid!' that he had attached to the prospect of peace a few weeks before was not quite to be taken literally.[4] He was confident that Gower would have anticipated the instructions he now sent (and he was correct in this assumption). They were straightforward: Britain would give Russia all possible support if she continued the war, as Canning hoped she would do, but was also prepared to join the Russians in negotiations for a general peace if that had now become 'inevitable' from Alexander's point of view.[5]

Canning's overriding priority was to maintain Britain's close connection with Russia whether in war or peace. So long as that connection remained in existence, it would prevent total French domination of the European continent and contain the seed of an alternative hegemonic alliance of Britain and Russia. The last thing he wanted was a separate peace between France and Russia from which Britain was excluded, and that, of course, was precisely what he got. And it was worse than that – not only a separate peace, but also a new, potentially hegemonic alliance at Tilsit between France and Russia, largely directed against Britain. The reality of what was happening in eastern Prussia remained confused for another week as some reports suggested that Friedland had merely been 'most bloody and indecisive',[6] but on 7 July the scale of Bennigsen's defeat was confirmed and the news that France and Russia had concluded an armistice hit London. The first strong evidence suggesting that not just a truce but a separate peace between France and Russia was in the making came not from any of Britain's diplomatic representatives in the Baltic but from our man in Altona, Edward Thornton.

Thornton belonged to a rare breed in the early nineteenth century: a self-made man in the diplomatic service. The orphaned son of an innkeeper, his gifts had won him a scholarship at Cambridge, where he had distinguished himself. This had led on to appointment as secretary to the British minister in Washington in 1793 and ultimately to a position of his own in the diplomatic service.[7] By the summer of 1807, Thornton was forty and had for two years been the British minister to the 'Hanse Towns and the Lower Saxon Circle'. He was an able and energetic man, an avid collector of intelligence with informants at different times in Berlin, Vienna, Munich and The Hague. His reports are overflowing with news of French troop movements and rumours circulating in northern Germany. He was also more inclined to offer advice to his political masters than the average envoy, and throughout the winter of 1806–7 he had repeatedly – and vainly – urged the advantages of a British landing on the continent and of fomenting rebellion in Germany.[8] This was a man after Canning's heart, and within a month of becoming foreign secretary, he had conveyed to Thornton 'His Majesty's approbation of your active and zealous exertions'.[9] No such encomium for poor Garlike.

Thornton's initial place of residence had been Hamburg, the commercial and news hub of the region, but he had fled the city when it was occupied by the French in November 1806 and taken refuge in Holstein, where his presence was 'tolerated' rather than recognised by the Danish government.[10] He moved around at first, but soon made Altona his permanent base. His displacement to Holstein did not greatly cramp his style, and his reports remained as informative as ever. He kept in touch with his friend, the Danish consul in Hamburg, and had a source inside the office of Louis Bourrienne, the highly venal French envoy in Hamburg.[11] At Altona, Thornton became acquainted with the duke of Mecklenburg-Schwerin, who had taken refuge in that town with his family after the occupation of his duchy by the French in late 1806. The duke had close ties with the Russian imperial house – indeed his son, the hereditary prince, had been married to one of Alexander's sisters, who had died in 1803.

Thornton's cultivation of the duke and his family paid off in the early days of July. After his first two meetings with Alexander at Tilsit on 25 and 26 June 1807, Napoleon made a conciliatory gesture by ordering that the duke of Mecklenburg-Schwerin should be restored to his domains.[12] Alexander wrote to his brother-in-law, the duke's son, on 29 June from Tilsit, communicating the happy news. Alexander's letter was carried by a Russian courier, who rode across northern Germany and reached Altona at noon on 5 July. The courier also brought a letter from Napoleon's headquarters at Tilsit to the French commander in Mecklenburg, informing him that the duke was to be immediately restored to his duchy. The hereditary prince allowed Thornton not only to read but also to transcribe the letter. Thornton hurried to send a copy to Canning in the belief that it could only portend an imminent settlement between the continental powers, 'because it seems to me that neither Bonaparte would have consented to the restoration of the duchy nor [Alexander] himself to have condescended to receive this concession at his hands, unless there had been a well grounded expectation that it would be followed by a peace'.[13] Thornton's point was well made, even if he could not yet bring himself to believe that 'at the first instant Russia will abandon her allies'.[14] This was an illusion he soon abandoned, and by 11 July he was speaking of 'the degrading indecency' with which Alexander had rushed into the arms of his 'late enemy'.[15]

The news of Friedland also prompted an entirely predictable renewal of the rumours, dormant since December 1806, that France was about to occupy all or parts of the duchies of Holstein and Schleswig and that their ports would be closed to British shipping.[16] The rumours were given a particularly extravagant form by the British consul at Tonningen, Alexander Cockburn. His letter has been lost, but Cockburn's claim appears to have been that France had already obtained permission from the Danish government to take possession of Holstein and that a French occupation of that province was imminent.[17] Cockburn was so alarmed that he ordered all the British vessels in Tonningen to leave the port and anchor at a point further down the river Ejder, where they could easily and rapidly reach the open sea if French troops suddenly arrived on the scene. As a result of Cockburn's panic, about forty British merchantmen immediately set sail for Britain either half-loaded or in ballast.[18] Further ingredients were added to the alarming brew of rumours from Holstein reaching London around 10 July by Britain's second agent at Altona, Sir Charles Gordon.

Although Gordon and Thornton were essentially involved in the same kind of intelligence-gathering activities, Gordon had no diplomatic camouflage and was altogether a more louche figure. He sent his reports to London by Thornton's messengers, but Thornton never acknowledged his existence in his own despatches. Gordon was the third son of a Scottish laird who had made a military career and who had acquired a good knowledge of Germany and the Low Countries in his youth. He came a cropper during a British expedition to capture the French islands in the West Indies in 1794. He was appointed governor of St Lucia, a conquered French colony, but was court-martialled for extortion and accepting bribes – he appears to have netted a cool £25,000, which he had to refund.[19] After that the best he could get was employment by the British government as an agent on 'the frontiers of Holland', though his place of residence shifted ever further away from The Netherlands with the spread of French power. In October 1806 he withdrew from Westphalia to Altona[20] and that is where he was on 1 July 1807, when he reported to Canning a statement by a French official that an army of 50,000 men was to be assembled on the Elbe, probably in order to 'overawe' Denmark and enforce Danish compliance with unspecified French demands.[21]

All these rumours were inherently improbable because it was not to be expected that Napoleon would turn his attention to Denmark until a peace settlement with Russia was well and truly in the bag. Nor were there any great numbers of enemy troops in the vicinity of Hamburg. The official French newspaper *Le Moniteur* had written on 30 April of 50,000 French and Spanish troops destined for the banks of the Elbe,[22] and Thornton reported frequently on the approach of Spanish troops summoned from Tuscany, but his despatches in June 1807 show that few had actually reached the Hamburg area. Instead, they refer to troops being withdrawn and the failure of the expected replacements to arrive. His informants also suggested that the Spaniards were not happy warriors in their new environment – 'persons who saw their march through Franconia' said 'they are very discontented with the mode of living and the climate of the country . . . and that is easy to be imagined'.[23]

Within a few days, Cockburn's order had been rescinded and normal British trade through Tonningen had resumed, while Cockburn himself eventually received a reprimand from Canning.[24] Thornton had become much more cautious about immediate French action against Denmark. The rumours, he said, appeared to have little foundation, and were being encouraged by French agents at Hamburg, who profited from the anxiety of merchants eager to get their goods out of Holstein and onto French-held territory as rapidly as possible by selling them French certificates of origin.[25]

In short, the rumours demonstrate the truth of the adage that where there is a tip, there is a tap. But even if the rumours were unfounded, it was natural to fear for the future, and Thornton regarded it as inevitable that a separate peace between France and Russia would be followed by the immediate French occupation of Holstein and the whole Jutlandic peninsula and the closure of their ports to the British flag. Indeed, if Britain allowed enough time to pass without counter-measures 'and if the timidity of the Danish government shall be worked upon', Thornton did not rule out the occupation of the Danish islands as well – 'and we shall then be really and literally excluded from the continent'. In view of this threat, Thornton felt constrained to offer advice, as he done on earlier occasions, excusing his presumption with the observation: 'We have had a long and unhappy experience that no foresight extends far enough to go beyond the projects of the enemy and to anticipate the rapidity of his movements.'

He suggested that Britain should hold sufficient land and sea forces in readiness to seize Copenhagen and the island of Zealand either with or without the consent of the Danish government as soon as she received news of a continental peace or at the very latest on the first appearance of a French force in Holstein. It would be imperative in that event that British warships were stationed in the Great Belt to prevent the passage of hostile troops to Zealand. The great virtue of his suggestion, he wrote, was that its execution was entirely within the power of Britain alone in view of her naval supremacy and did not therefore depend on the consent or cooperation of any other state. With Zealand in her hands, Britain would then command the Danish straits and control the Baltic along with the naval stores that were exported from its ports.[26]

The flurry of reports about an impending French move against Holstein in the first week of July 1807 from Cockburn, Gordon and Thornton were premature, as Thornton at least quickly recognised. But they exercised a powerful effect on Canning. In the first instance, they reminded him of the long-standing but slumbering French threat against Denmark and linked that threat to the growing probability of a separate peace between France and Russia. And, as Thornton pointed out, it was not merely Britain's clandestine trade with Germany through Tonningen that was endangered but potentially also her vital access to the Baltic through the Danish straits. Secondly, Thornton's letter of 1 July pointed to a means of solving the problem that Britain would soon face – a pre-emptive occupation of Copenhagen and Zealand. All these considerations had an important influence on Canning's thinking. Altona and Tonningen were not, however, the only sources of alarming news in these days. Equally if not more important were the reports received from Normandy.

GENERAL DANICAN IN NORMANDY

On the afternoon of 4 April 1807 a storm of sleet and snow passed over Paris, and it was bitterly cold when Charles Vitel faced the firing squad at the Barrière de Grenelle. The business was quickly transacted: an officer read out the military tribunal's sentence, the firing squad took aim and fired, and the body was immediately removed to the Vaugirard cemetery. Vitel was only twenty-seven, tall and good-looking, and the women of Saint-Germain market had felt a ripple of pity when they crowded round to watch him being taken from the Abbaye prison to his death.[27] That pity was well deserved and not only because of his youth and appearance – for if ever a pawn was sacrificed in a larger game, it was Charles Vitel.

The underground war between Britain and France aimed both at acquiring 'secret intelligence' and at fomenting domestic unrest, what we would call 'subversion', but the lines were blurred and the agents employed were often meant to perform both tasks. On both sides, the enemy within was a source of danger. In French eyes, Irish discontent with British rule always seemed to offer promising opportunities, while for the British, royalist sentiment in France was seen as the most fertile source of resistance to republican or Napoleonic rule. Napoleon may have restored order to France, but to the British government, he was still an usurper whose regime would always be inherently unstable. British ministers were easily attracted by signs of discontent and conspiracy, particularly of a royalist nature. Needless to say, the heavy reliance in Paris and London on enemy nationals, disaffected Irishmen and Frenchmen respectively, left the field open for a wide array of conmen, charlatans and double agents. It was into this murky world of intrigue, lies and half-truths that Charles Vitel had wandered.

He was the nephew of Louis Fauche-Borel, originally a printer and publisher from Neuchâtel who had become deeply involved in the French royalist cause.[28] As a result, Fauche-Borel spent over two years in prison in France and had fetched up – like so many of his kind – in London in the first days of January 1806. Within a few months he had become entangled in a protracted correspondence with an old chum, Charles Perlet, another Alpine royalist (Perlet hailed from Geneva) who had suffered transportation during the late 1790s but who had been allowed to return to Paris after Napoleon's seizure of power. Perlet claimed to represent a secret royalist committee dedicated to the overthrow of Napoleon. He could not, of course, divulge any names in writing, but its ranks included marshals of the empire, government ministers and senior members of the French police. The committee would act when the time was ripe, but in the meantime Perlet needed information on royalist and British plans for subversion inside France and a substantial sum of money from the British government to buy the complicity of less committed officials within the French administration.

It all sounds too good to be true – and, sure enough, it was. On his return to Paris after his release from transportation, Perlet had been pushed for money and found work with the Paris police. His letters to Fauche-Borel were dictated by his employers. It was a murky business, and it may be that initially at least Perlet tried to keep open the option of playing the triple agent and eventually coming down on the royalist side.[29] The scam seems so obvious that it is difficult to credit that anyone was duped, but in fact Perlet was taken seriously not only by Fauche-Borel himself but also by the British government and the advisers to the pretender to the French throne, the future Louis XVIII, who maintained a threadbare court in exile at Mitau in Courland.

When Perlet suggested that an agent be sent to Paris to meet the committee and assess the situation, Fauche-Borel wanted to travel to Paris himself, but he was eventually persuaded to let Vitel go in his place. At least that way he kept control of the correspondence in the family – and control as well of the flow of British money that would subsidise the preparations of Perlet's alleged secret committee. Vitel was also an acceptable choice to the British government since he had served in the British army for some years, most recently in India under Arthur Wellesley. When Vitel set off from London on 6 January 1807 to travel to Paris via Altona, he left with a promise from the foreign secretary, Lord Howick, of a lieutenant's commission in the British army on his return.

His uncle was devastated by his fate. Even Howick was shaken. Howick despised his successor, George Canning, and it perhaps says something about his distress that the only surviving draft letter to Canning in Howick's private papers was written on 1 April 1807 just after he had learnt of Vitel's arrest from Fauche-Borel. It asked Canning to do all he could to help Fauche-Borel secure his nephew's release. Howick then added 'It is of the utmost importance that whatever can be done to save this young man should be done without delay', but found this too effusive for a letter to his hated rival, scored it out and substituted the more terse sentence: 'It is necessary that no time should be lost'.[30] It was, of course, too late, far too late. From his headquarters in eastern Prussia, Napoleon had already pronounced Vitel's doom: 'this wretched agent' of Fauche-Borel was to be sent before a court-martial and shot.[31]

Perlet's principals probably assumed that the game was over with Vitel's execution and that Perlet's correspondents would break off contact with him. Not a bit of it! Fauche-Borel accepted Perlet's explanation that Vitel had been arrested *before* he got to Paris (an outright lie) and before he could come under the protection of the secret committee, and Portland's new government agreed that a second, more experienced agent would be sent to meet Perlet in Paris. The man selected for this task was General Louis-Michel-Auguste Danican,[32] a friend of Fauche-Borel. Danican has had a bad press as a vain and garrulous braggart, but he does not appear to have been significantly less effective or more shady than most of the French émigrés in British service. He was a man of relatively modest birth, a professional soldier in the French army before 1789, who had advanced to the rank of brigadier-general after the revolution. He claimed always to have been a royalist at heart and he surfaced prominently as such when he was appointed military commander of the unsuccessful royalist coup of *Vendémiaire* in October 1795. This brought him into direct confrontation with the young Napoleon Bonaparte. There are no prizes for guessing who won. The royalist forces, more of a mob than a military unit, were dispersed by 'a whiff of grapeshot' discharged along the narrow Parisian streets from the cannon of the opposing republican commander, General Bonaparte.

Danican escaped, but was condemned to death *in absentia* and spent many years knocking around the continent involved in various anti-republican schemes. In 1803 he arrived in London and was granted a British pension of £400 a year. A few months later, he set off on a secret mission to Paris, but his ship never reached France and ran aground in Norway after twenty storm-tossed days at sea. His paymasters were not impressed, and reduced his pension by three-quarters. This left him fairly hard up and keen for renewed employment. In October 1806 he had written to the British foreign office pleading for the restoration of his pension to its original amount – his creditors were pursuing him, he said, 'with an unparalleled rigour'. In return, he offered to go anywhere on a new mission abroad and recommended himself as 'a man able to divine the truth, to see clearly and to give a clear account in his reports'.[33] His plea does not appear to have produced immediate pecuniary results, but after making an offer such as this he would have found it difficult to refuse the mission of following in the footsteps of the unfortunate Vitel, despite its dangers for a man with an open death warrant against him.

The surviving evidence on the secret intelligence war between Britain and France is often fragmentary and elusive, but in the case of Danican's mission to the continent in 1807, we are reasonably well placed. Seven of the letters that he wrote while abroad have survived, either in full or in extract, in Canning's private papers, filed alongside other documents concerned with 'secret intelligence' relating to Denmark in 1807.[34] Only one of the seven is explicitly said to be from Danican, but cross references and other internal evidence show that all seven were written by the same person. We do not always know the identity of the recipient. It is clear from the content that three and possibly four were addressed to Fauche-Borel, but Danican also mentioned that he was writing to Charles Flint of the Irish Office, who had long played a central role in 'secret service correspondence',[35] and to George Hammond, one of Canning's two under-secretaries of state at the foreign office.

The way Fauche-Borel tells it in his memoirs, Danican's mission had the dual objective of obtaining information from Perlet on the current resources and needs of the secret committee and of discovering how and by whom Vitel had been arrested and why he had been shot.[36] Danican's letters show that he had a much wider remit from the British government than Perlet and his affairs. He was also to investigate the activities of Irish exiles in France, to gauge the state of French opinion and the opportunities for fomenting unrest and to activate a network of new or dormant agents.

Danican reached Le Havre by sea on 6 June from Altona, where he had taken ship on a Danish merchantman called *Die Christine* under the guise of being a German seaman. When he learnt of Danican's visit to France from Perlet, Joseph Fouché, the French minister of police, later denied in one of his daily reports to Napoleon that it had ever happened. No Danish vessel, he claimed, had called at Le Havre or any other port in the department of Seine-Inférieure in May or June, and in any case if Danican had tried to land, he would have been arrested before his feet touched terra firma.[37] Fouché was covering his back: Danican's arrival at Le Havre on 6 June is confirmed by an undated and unsigned letter from another British agent in France.[38] The real reason for Fouché's reticence was probably that he preferred not to explain to the emperor that the long-term interests of the Perlet scam required allowing the man of *Vendémiaire* to leave France alive. Shooting Vitel was one thing, but giving the same treatment to the second British agent to come knocking at Perlet's door as well would have overstretched the credulity of the British government.

Danican's stay in France was short. He was jumpy from the start. In his first letters from Normandy on 7 June he claimed that great efforts had been made to capture him at Altona and he was clearly apprehensive about going to Paris. Instead he set off for Rouen, travelling up the Seine by boat because he feared that he would be constantly stopped by gendarmes if he went by land. On 17 and 19 June he wrote to Fauche-Borel from 'Dondeville near Rouen', where he expected Perlet to arrive at any time. Danican evidently thought that he had persuaded Perlet to come from Paris to meet him in Normandy, but regarded a personal meeting anywhere as extremely dangerous. Perlet, however, seemed to lack any sense of risk (as well he might), in contrast to 'the fear' manifested by all the other royalists Danican had encountered. These were Danican's last letters from Normandy. He suddenly decided to run for it, and six days later he was in Brussels. By mid-July he was in the region south of Bremen and on 25 July, he was back in Altona, safe and sound again.

Danican later wrote to Perlet that he had decamped because his real identity was recognised at Rouen,[39] and this sounds perfectly plausible. As an attempt to make contact with Perlet, the trip had been a complete wash-out, and Fauche-Borel was duly miffed. It can be deduced from the sour observations in Fauche-Borel's memoirs that Danican now finally got his pension restored to £400 a year 'because he appeared to have exposed himself to danger', but Fauche-Borel regarded his mission as devoid of achievement.[40] That assessment arose out of Fauche-Borel's obsession with Perlet and his ignorance of the letters that Danican sent to Flint and Hammond.

If Danican is to be believed, he recruited or renewed contact with four agents who would send regular reports to England in the future – one at Le Havre, one at Rouen and two in Paris. As for public opinion, he was convinced both from his own direct observations and by his correspondents that there was no basis for fomenting unrest in France at the present time. The public mood was 'detestable' and Bonaparte was 'all powerful'. There were no royalist parties left in France – they only existed in the minds of intriguers and certain policemen in Paris 'who would like to see the English compromised once again'. Danican also passed on what he learnt from his contacts of wide-ranging French designs in the Balkans, Egypt and Persia, and against the British position in India (or 'Hindustan', as he called it).

These reports reveal an excitable, grasshopper mind, leaping promiscuously from one topic to another and back again, and they probably had little value as raw intelligence and proved of little long-term significance. But the first two letters Danican sent to London after his arrival at Le Havre had a powerful impact and immediate consequences. They are both dated 7 June and neither was addressed to Fauche-Borel, who is referred to in the third person in both. It is quite likely that the first was addressed to Hammond and the second to Flint. The first is recorded as reaching the foreign office on London on 3 July. No date of receipt is given for the second, but Danican wrote that he was sending four letters by the same 'courier', so it is reasonable to assume that the second arrived at the same time. The two letters range widely, but one point above all others caught Canning's attention, and it related to Denmark.

Before leaving Altona Danican had written to a 'correspondent' in Paris, announcing his arrival, and he found two letters waiting for him when he landed at Le Havre. This mysterious correspondent cannot have been Perlet, because Danican describes him as 'an old friend' and as an Irishman who had provided Flint with reliable information in the past. The two letters from Danican's correspondent declared that Napoleon was attempting to detach Russia from Britain through 'seductive' peace offers. As soon as peace had been concluded, Napoleon would induce his Spanish ally to declare war on Denmark and would use Spanish troops based in Hamburg area to occupy Holstein and Schleswig. Once these two duchies were in his hands, Napoleon would demand the surrender of the Danish navy and undertake 'a desperate endeavour' against the north of Ireland, while the French troops stationed between Bordeaux and Brest attempted to land in Ireland from the south. Danican lent credence to his report about Denmark by adding that there was great activity in all the ports and that the United Irishmen were assembling in great numbers on the coasts of Brittany.

This information features in both the letters Danican wrote on 7 June, and in both cases the section on Denmark has been specially marked out on Canning's copy, presumably by the foreign secretary himself. This piece of intelligence was to play a large role in shaping Canning's thinking about Denmark over the next few weeks – but was it true?

The spectre of a French descent on Ireland touched a very raw nerve. A French squadron from Brest had twice, in 1796 and 1798, evaded the

Royal Navy and reached Ireland, and on the second occasion had landed troops to support an uprising by the United Irishmen movement. With the benefit of hindsight, we now know that after 1803, the United Irishmen in France were weak and riven by factionalism, sometimes to a ludicrous extent, and that there were discontent and agrarian disturbances in Ireland and an expectation that the French would come one day, but no real republican organisation within the country. That did not stop the British authorities from fearing that such an organisation did exist or from being extremely edgy in response to any supposed threat to their position in Ireland. In 1807, it was less than nine years since the United Irishmen had risen in rebellion and the French had landed on Irish soil. Between 1803 and 1805, when Napoleon had been making his great preparations at Boulogne to invade England, he had also entertained plans for a secondary or diversionary landing in Ireland from Brest.[41] In the 1790s and again between 1803 and 1805, these projects had sometimes involved sending part of the invasion force for Ireland from Dutch ports rather than Brittany, so the suggestion that the northern route, around Scotland, might be used was not a novel one.[42]

Against this background, it is no great surprise that Canning took Danican's report to heart, but he was in fact the victim of deliberate strategic deception. There is nothing in Napoleon's correspondence to suggest that he had any plans for invading Ireland in 1807, but it suited his purposes that the British should believe that he did. Throughout the early months of 1807, locked in his desperate struggle with the Russians, Napoleon had remained anxious about a possible British diversion, a British landing somewhere between France and northern Germany to relieve the pressure on their hard-pressed allies. The French emperor sent a constant stream of orders from his headquarters in Poland to ensure that the troops guarding his lines of his communication were well placed to repel a British landing on the coast of western Europe.[43] On 29 April 1807 he wrote to his minister of the marine, Denis Decrès, from the castle of Finkenstein in East Prussia, instructing him to undertake preparations at Brest which would give the impression that an expedition to Ireland was planned. At the same time, the minister should speak to the United Irishmen and ensure that this piece of news was widely disseminated.[44]

The ploy was a fairly obvious one, but the British government could hardly fail to take it seriously, and Danican's report provided the final nail

for the Danish coffin. Danish protests about the British Orders in Council
and the detention of Danish merchant ships had already made Canning
deeply suspicious. Pembroke's letter about the state of the Danish navy
had suggested that the Danes were preparing to act on their veiled
hostility when the time was ripe. But while the war in eastern Prussia
remained in the balance, it had been possible to follow a policy of wait-
and-see. All changed, utterly changed, by Tilsit. For the British, the
accumulating indications of a separate peace between France and Russia
placed Denmark's position in international affairs in a new light. Such a
peace would give Napoleon the freedom to act, and the reports from
Altona and Normandy highlighted the areas where action was likely to
occur. Napoleon would seek to deny British shipping access to the ports of
Jutland and to the Baltic, and to mobilise the Danish fleet against Britain.
And if Prince Fredrick was secretly hostile to Britain, Napoleon would do
so with Danish cooperation. By 10 July 1807, Canning had decided, as
Thornton had already recommended, that the time had come for pre-
emptive action.

Chapter 6

THE DECISION TO STRIKE AGAINST DENMARK: LONDON, 10–21 JULY 1807

A FLEET FOR THE BALTIC

O ver a twelve-day period, between 10 and 21 July 1807 inclusive, the British cabinet came to a grim resolution – to make war on Denmark. It was not put as baldly as that, of course, but the let-out clauses depended on a level of Danish submissiveness to British will that could never realistically be expected. By 21 July the thinking of the British government was permeated by the assumption that the Danes were so hostile to Britain or so submissive to France as to render war virtually inescapable. The decision did not leap into life fully formed on 10 July. It evolved incrementally as what began with a proposal to send a powerful squadron to Danish waters with no more than a watching brief, ostensibly at least, turned into a plan for a combined operation of land and sea forces to seize Copenhagen and capture the Danish fleet. The men who took this decision were the twelve members of the cabinet, and there is nothing to suggest that there was ever the slightest disagreement or dissent within the cabinet over the line that was adopted towards Denmark.

It is hard to follow the details of this escalation in ministerial ambitions with precision: the surviving evidence is too limited for that. We can identify some of the immediate developments that persuaded Canning to press the urgency of the problems presented by Denmark on his cabinet colleagues on 10 July. Danican's report on French plans to use the Danish fleet for a descent on Ireland reached the foreign office in London on 3 July 1807, and the first hard news that Russia had concluded an armistice with France arrived on 7 July. But the immediate catalyst that spurred Canning into action seems to have been the receipt on 9 July of

Cockburn's report that France had obtained permission from the Danish government to take possession of Holstein and that a French occupation of that province was imminent. After that, it is impossible to gauge the effect of incoming news. Little of it was good. Cockburn's alarmist rumour about Holstein was shown within a few days to be erroneous, or at any rate premature, by Thornton's subsequent reports, but the overall picture from the continent was bleak. Thornton's transcription of Alexander's letter to the hereditary prince of Mecklenburg-Schwerin arrived on 12 July, and a cluster of reports reached London on 16 July, which not only contained the first descriptions of the meeting in mid-river between Alexander and Napoleon at Tilsit but also Gower's account of how he had been excluded from all serious contact with the Russian government beforehand.[1]

It may be that this contributed to a hardening of attitudes that can first be discerned on 17 July, but it is more likely that ministers took an ever tougher line as a result of ongoing reflection and discussion about factors that remained unchanged throughout the decision-making process. The first was the simple calculation that after Napoleon had defeated and made peace with Russia, he would be free to turn his attention to Denmark and that Russia would not be able to protect her client from his encroachments. It had long been obvious that this would mean steps to close Tonningen and Husum to the British flag. But it might also involve a French advance across the Great Belt to gain control of Zealand so as to exclude British shipping from the Baltic and to use the Danish fleet for a descent on Ireland.

The second fundamental factor was British uncertainty about how the Danes would react to a French invasion or to French demands. Canning suspected that they were 'much more hostile than they have yet avowed' and that their behaviour over the Rist affair lent credibility to this suspicion.[2] Pembroke's letter from late May stating that the Danish fleet was being armed for active service suggested that the Danish government might well have already decided to side with France if it came to the crunch.

The two other underlying considerations were of a military nature. One was that a simple repetition of 1801 – a purely naval assault on Copenhagen – would not be possible. Since then, the sea defences of Copenhagen had been improved by the creation of a permanent sea fort called Prøvesten, which consisted of three superannuated ships of the line sunk in shallow water in 1802. It was located in a channel known as the King's Deep (*Kongedybet*), which ran along the north-eastern shore line of Copenhagen. The Danish defence line had made its stand against Nelson there in 1801 and after it had been broken, the bomb vessels of the British fleet had taken possession of the King's Deep, where their mortars had been within range of the Danish fleet moored inside Copenhagen harbour. Prøvesten had been created precisely in order to deny control of the King's Deep to a hostile fleet in the future. The fire from Prøvesten, combined with that from the older sea fort of Trekroner placed in the northern entrance to Copenhagen harbour, would make any venture into the King's Deep extremely hazardous.[3]

The second military factor was that, quite providentially, at the crucial moment in mid-July 1807, Britain was in a position to launch a combined operation against Denmark. By this time, the first contingent of the much-heralded British expedition to the continent, between 8,000 and 9,000 men from the King's German Legion, mainly Hanoverians from George III's ancestral electorate, had reached or were en route to Swedish Pomerania. The first division of these troops had sailed from England on 19 June and arrived at the island of Rügen in Swedish Pomerania on 8 July.[4] In addition, there was a disposable force of 16,000 men on British soil, originally also intended for service in Germany if the great struggle in eastern Prussia had continued. It did not require great powers of prophecy to grasp that a separate peace between France and Russia would quickly lead to the fall of Swedish Pomerania to the French and the evacuation of the British force in that province. This meant that over 25,000 men were immediately available for action against Zealand at a moment when the bulk of the Danish field army was absent in Jutland.

The discussions that culminated in the decision for military action against Denmark were initiated by Canning on 10 July, when he circulated a lengthy minute to his cabinet colleagues, backed up with a briefer supplementary one the following day, on the measures required to deal with the new situation that was emerging in northern Europe. The first contingent of the King's German Legion had sailed without any large naval escort and there was still no significant British naval presence in the Baltic. Canning was convinced that this position needed to be rectified, and that matters had been allowed to drift for too long.[5] He had already told Lord Mulgrave, the first lord of the admiralty, on 7 July that 'I cannot forbear *again* suggesting to you the expediency of taking measures for augmenting our naval force in the Baltic'.[6]

The cabinet discussed the question on 8 July, but without reaching any result, and on 10 July Canning could contain himself no longer. His minute expressed 'the clear and decisive opinion' that the fleet which had been collected for the Baltic since the spring but which had been held back until then should now 'be prepared for its destination, so as to be ready to sail with as little delay as possible'. While 'the fortune of war on the continent was balanced', this measure might not have been required, but now – 'with Bonaparte all-triumphant' – it was necessary that 'we should take a much higher tone than before, if we could not be supposed to sink to a much lower one'.[7]

The reasons that Canning gave for this step related almost entirely to Denmark. For more than a month, he had taken no action at all in response to Pembroke's letter from Copenhagen of 28 May concerning the Danish navy. Now Canning copied the letter to his colleagues and described it as 'one among many testimonies to the [naval] preparations of the Danish government and the disposition of the [Danish] people'. He would have been more accurate had he said that it was the *only* testimony to those preparations and to the alleged Anglophobia of the ordinary Dane. He placed equal or greater emphasis on Cockburn's report concerning 'the intended occupation of Holstein by the French'. Canning also circulated a note with snippets from various despatches and letters that underlined the need for vigilance and concern. This note included extracts from Danican's letter from Le Havre of 7 June about a two-pronged descent on Ireland; Gordon's report of 1 July about the assembly of an army of 50,000 men on the Elbe to enforce compliance with French demands on Denmark; and Thornton's letter of the same date on the need for a strong squadron in the Baltic able to act if required and to prevent the passage of hostile troops across the Great Belt to Zealand.[8]

Canning clearly expected resistance or at least reluctance among some of his colleagues and deployed a range of arguments to anticipate their objections. His trump card was the danger posed by the Danish navy to British interests. He asserted that there could be

no doubt that Bonaparte reckons up the Danish fleet at a fit time as an instrument of hostility against Great Britain. And if the court of

Denmark is not able to refuse him the occupation of Holstein, it is not probable that a more active or more effectual resistance would be opposed by them to a demand of their fleet.

As for the possible objection that the Danish fleet was 'not yet sufficiently manned', Canning claimed that Napoleon would have available to him all the unemployed Prussian seamen in the ports of northern Germany. In addition, there were French sailors in the Baltic area, as Thornton had reported,[9] who had been brought from France to operate in small vessels along the coast of eastern Prussia.

Canning also sought to anticipate the argument that the appearance of a British fleet in the Baltic would in itself constitute a virtual declaration of war against Denmark and turn Britain into the aggressor. On the contrary, it was far more probable, he argued, that the British squadron would effectively deter the Danish navy from putting to sea and would therefore prevent rather than provoke a new war. Cockburn's report suggested 'that a state of hostility with Denmark may not be far distant – and at least that nothing but a greater fear, counteracting their fear of France, can prevent it'. In any case, Britain had no need to make excuses to Denmark or to Europe generally for sending a squadron to Danish waters. Denmark's naval preparations, as reported by Pembroke, were quite sufficient in themselves to justify a demand for an explanation – 'and a counter-preparation'.

Even so, Canning thought it might be 'expedient' to notify the Danish government that Britain was equipping a fleet for the Baltic and to accompany this notification with a complaint over the occupation of Holstein (if the rumours proved well-founded) or over Denmark's own naval preparations. Alternatively, if 'a more pacific policy' proved 'practicable', the notification might be accompanied by a profession of Britain's peaceful intentions towards Denmark but also of her need to protect her merchant shipping in the Baltic and the possible retreat of her forces from Pomerania, to help her one remaining ally, Sweden, and to give Denmark a reason for rejecting 'the demands which Bonaparte is likely to make upon her'. But Canning did not believe it would be necessary to make excuses to the Danes – he thought it 'highly probable' that before the British fleet was ready to sail, Britain would learn of 'some actual compliance on the part of Denmark with the will of Bonaparte, which will justify us in accompanying our preparations with a remonstrance rather than an apology'.

Finally, Canning drew attention to the potential domestic political implications of a failure to act. The security of British merchant shipping currently in the Baltic was a genuine source of concern: if Denmark suddenly declared war on Britain, 'the Danish fleet could, in the present state of things, sweep the Baltic of our trade and of our smaller vessels before our fleet could come to their assistance'. It was by no means certain that a British fleet could give full protection to Britain's seaborne trade in the Baltic, but if any misfortune were to befall it, 'the absence of a British fleet would be, in the opinion of the public, and in parliamentary discussions, a circumstance of aggravation very difficult [for the government] to repel'.

There was also the point that the Grenville administration had prepared a fleet for the Baltic whose departure had been delayed by the Portland government. Canning therefore urged his colleagues to bear in mind that, 'of all points in the conduct of the war', where an act of omission by the present government 'would be judged most harshly, would be one on which their predecessors had most loudly boasted of their own promptitude and preparation'.[10] He made a similar point in a letter to his wife a few weeks later when he wrote that the government would greatly enhance its standing if it achieved something great and striking abroad after the inertia and incompetence of the Grenville administration.[11]

Canning was dead right about the line the opposition was likely to take about any laxity in the Baltic. On 12 July Lady Bessborough, whose social contacts were more with the Foxites than the Pittites, wrote to Gower that 'the opposition say they had prepared a fleet of 16 ships of the line, which had received sailing orders when they went out [of office], but that the newcomers countermanded them' and 'that it would have been wiser to *keep* the Sound open than to force it open when it was once closed'. She also passed on worrying rumours that the Sound had already been shut to British shipping and that 'the Danish fleet . . . will sail round the North of Scotland and make a descent on Ireland'[12] – a piece of gossip which suggests that the cabinet was applying a fairly lax news blackout in relation to London high society.

Canning urged that a quick decision was necessary, and asked his cabinet colleagues to consider the question on the coming Monday,

13 July. The hesitations that Canning seems to have feared failed to materialise. Three ministers added minutes of their own, endorsing his views. The prime minister threw his full weight behind him. Canning's arguments were too strong to require further support, Portland claimed, but he could not help reminding the cabinet of 'the invariable effects of that system of terror which has been adopted by the French from the commencement of their revolution down to the present day'. The Danes, in other words, were likely to yield to French demands. The home secretary, Lord Hawkesbury, and the lord chancellor, Lord Eldon, were also supportive. Hawkesbury placed somewhat more emphasis than Canning on protecting British trade in the Baltic and securing Britain's supply of naval stores for 1807, and both he and Eldon were concerned about weakening Britain's naval strength in home waters. As Eldon put it, the despatch of a fleet to the Baltic was 'a necessity, which can only be suspended by danger at home, if the absence of such a fleet from home would create it'. Even so, both ministers agreed with Canning that a strong squadron should be sent to Danish waters.[13]

We do not have any written evidence on the views of the other members of the cabinet, but there is nothing to suggest any dissent from the remainder. The cabinet met either on 13 or 14 July, because by the latter date the first lord of the admiralty, Lord Mulgrave, was able to write to the king with a concrete proposal. That proposal was entirely along the lines suggested by Canning. Mulgrave asked George III to agree that 20–22 ships of the line should be sent without delay to the Kattegat. It would have three tasks: to keep a watch on the movements of the Danish fleet; to 'counteract' the designs of France either in Zealand or Holstein; and, finally, 'to execute such prompt and vigorous operations as the circumstances of the moment may point out'.[14] George approved these measures and also Mulgrave's suggestion two days later, on 16 July, that Admiral Sir James Gambier, 'a man of tried talents and zeal for Your Majesty's service', be appointed to command the Baltic squadron.[15]

On the same day, Canning took a step that he believed would strengthen British diplomatic representation at Copenhagen by dismissing Garlike from his post. He kicked off by administering a string of reprimands. Canning was angry that Garlike had failed to provide information on events in the eastern Baltic – 'of which we hear through every channel but that of our own ministers'.[16] Nor had he received from

Garlike since becoming foreign secretary 'any account whatever of the state of preparation in the port of Copenhagen', even though Pembroke's letter of 28 May had presented 'those preparations as in great forwardness and acquiring strength every day', and Garlike was to rectify this omission without delay.[17] And to top it all, Canning was dissatisfied with the manner in which Garlike had conducted his discussions with Joachim Bernstorff over the Rist affair. The object had been to give the Danish government 'an opportunity of manifesting its real disposition towards this country' and Garlike had failed to obtain 'a precise and intelligible answer'.

Garlike's dismissal was outwardly disguised as a mark of confidence. Since late 1806 Britain had only been represented by a *chargé d'affaires* at the Prussian court, and Canning had decided to appoint one of his cronies, John Hookham Frere, a former envoy to Portugal and Spain, as a fully accredited minister. Frere, however, had just been prevented from setting out for Memel by the death of his father. This provided Canning with a neat means of removing Garlike from Copenhagen. Garlike had served at Berlin in the past, and Canning informed him that, in view of 'his long experience of the Prussian court, and acquaintance with many of the persons composing it' and his ability to reach Memel more quickly from Copenhagen than any new envoy sent out from England, Garlike was to go on a temporary mission to Prussia until Frere arrived. The Danish government was to be told that Garlike's absence would be temporary and 'of short duration'.[18] Canning was extraordinarily kind and tactful – not qualities for which he was generally noted. A further private letter declared effusively: 'I think myself peculiarly fortunate in having you at hand to relieve me from the embarrassment which Mr Frere's inability to proceed to Memel has occasioned.' But he left Garlike in no doubt that he was keen to see him on his way and the letter ended: 'I have only to add that you cannot be too soon at Memel: and cannot too soon let me hear from you from thence.'[19]

Whatever his attempts at disguise, the truth was, of course, that Canning had lost confidence in Garlike, suspecting that he had been negligent in failing to report the naval preparations at Copenhagen spotted by Pembroke and both dilatory and ineffectual in his handling of the Rist affair. As he wrote to Gower, 'between ourselves', he had wanted Garlike 'out of the way at Copenhagen, where I thought he had not been doing well'. Besides, Canning added cryptically, he had also learnt that Garlike was 'in the hands, or in the constant familiarity' of the new Prussian envoy to Denmark, a certain von Caesar, whom Canning regarded as 'a most frenchified raggamuffin'. Canning was 'not sorry therefore upon the whole to send somebody to look at things with a fresh eye'.[20] The fresh eye he had in mind turned out to be that of Brook Taylor, Britain's former envoy to Hesse-Cassel and Cologne, who was to stand in for Garlike during his absence at Memel. Canning was spoiled for choice when he turned over the rock and looked at the list of unemployed British diplomats, but Taylor, though inexperienced, had one strong advantage: his elder brother was the king's private secretary.[21]

The instructions that Canning drafted for Taylor on 16 July were entirely in line with what he had suggested the Danish government should be told in his long minute for the cabinet on 10 July. If asked, Taylor was to explain the presence of a British naval force in the Baltic by the need to cooperate with Sweden; to protect any reinforcements that might be sent to Pomerania or to cover the return of the troops already there if they were withdrawn; and thirdly, 'to secure against all annoyance the large mass of British property which is now afloat in the Baltic'. If Bernstorff responded that the fleet was larger than necessary to achieve these objects, Taylor was to reply that the size of the fleet had been influenced by Denmark's naval preparations and 'the avowed designs of Bonaparte'. Indeed, Taylor was to explain to Bernstorff that Britain was in fact acting in the best interests of Denmark herself in sending a fleet that was 'decidedly superior' to the Danish navy. This was because 'her safety is to be found, under the present circumstances of the world, only in a balance of opposite dangers'. The presence of a strong British fleet, and the consequent risk of British reprisals, would give the Danish government an excuse for refusing to agree to a French occupation of Holstein. The strong position France had now acquired in northern Europe would, 'unless balanced and controlled by the naval power of Great Britain, leave to Denmark no other option than that of compliance with the demands of Bonaparte, however extravagant in their nature, or however repugnant to the feelings and interests of the Danish government'.[22]

It is not easy to determine precisely what the cabinet had decided to do by 16 July beyond sending a powerful squadron to the Kattegat. Taylor's instructions set out a series of excuses for its presence that he was to convey to Joachim Bernstorff, but they contained no precise demands or proposals. A number of dangers had been identified, but it was not clear how Gambier was supposed to deal with them. Was he to prevent the passage of French or indeed Danish troops across the Great Belt to Zealand? And what was he meant to do if he found Danish ships of the line at sea or attempting to leave the port of Copenhagen, when he arrived? In principle, the commanding admiral had been given wide discretion to undertake 'vigorous operations' in response to 'the circumstances of the moment', but in practice ministers had no intention of leaving matters in Gambier's hands and everything depended on the further instructions that he received. The nature of those instructions became clear on 17 July when the cabinet submitted further proposals to the king. Those proposals represented a major escalation in Britain's strategic aims.

ESCALATION

Between 10 and 16 July, there had been no mention of anything beyond the use of sea power. On 17 July the whole nature of the precautionary measures against Denmark changed when the cabinet addressed a new letter to the king, which referred for the first time to a combined operation employing land as well as naval forces and spoke explicitly of military action to secure possession of the Danish fleet. The letter came not from Mulgrave but from Lord Castlereagh, the secretary for war, and began merely by reiterating the proposal, which George had already approved, that a strong fleet should be sent to the Baltic. Castlereagh then moved onto new ground. He explained that Copenhagen's defences towards the sea had been improved since 1801 and that a repetition of a purely naval attack on the Danish fleet along the lines undertaken by Nelson would now be 'an operation of much hazard'. It therefore seemed to the cabinet that, 'in the event of a rupture' with Denmark, 'a conjoint operation' of land and sea forces was more likely to obtain possession of the Danish fleet.

There were believed to be few Danish troops on Zealand at the present time, and so long as this remained the case, the island of Zealand and the Danish fleet would be 'within the power of Your Majesty's arms'. The cabinet consequently presented two further recommendations for the king's approval. One was that Gambier should be instructed to prevent the passage of troops onto Zealand across the Great Belt from any other part of Denmark until he received further instructions from home. The second was that 'the disposable force . . . now held in readiness at home' should be prepared for service abroad without loss of time, 'with a view to any eventual rupture with Denmark', while the troops in Pomerania were held in readiness to cooperate with any force that might be sent from Britain to act against Denmark.[23]

In a few brief paragraphs, Castlereagh had outlined the essential features of the British plan for war against Denmark that was put into execution in the following months. It represented a huge escalation in British objectives (the capture of the Danish fleet) and methods (a combined operation to seize Copenhagen) when compared with the proposals Mulgrave had put to the king only three days before. Now that the Baltic had become a combined operation, Mulgrave was pushed into the background and the more influential and perhaps also more effective figure of Lord Castlereagh came to the fore. For the next three months, it was Castlereagh who sent instructions to both the army and naval commanders, while Mulgrave dealt with more secondary naval matters. Canning was the initiator and driving force of the strike against Denmark, but Castlereagh became the minister who carried the burden of driving the operation on a day-to-day basis.

Over the next few days, Castlereagh moved quickly to follow up his letter to the king with a string of communications to the army and naval commanders. First he ordered the Admiralty to draw up instructions for the naval commander along the limited lines Mulgrave had proposed on 14 July and to tell him that he was to obey instructions from Castlereagh.[24] Second he wrote to Gambier with secret instructions to supplement those he received from the Admiralty. The reasons Castlereagh gave for the measures that were being taken are the clearest succinct summary of the cabinet's motives.

In the present predominant state of the power of France on the continent, and exposed as a principal part of the Danish dominions are to the grasp of the enemy, His Majesty cannot but entertain the most anxious apprehensions that the maritime power, position and resources of Denmark may shortly be made the instrument in the hands of France not only of excluding our commerce from the Baltic and of depriving us of the means of naval equipment, but also of multiplying the points from which an invasion of His Majesty's dominions may be attempted under the protection of a formidable naval force.

Precautionary measures were needed until proper assurances could be obtained that 'the power of Denmark' would not be made 'the means of inflicting a most fatal blow against the interests of this country', especially in view of recent Danish naval preparations, which could only have been undertaken 'in contemplation of being compelled by France . . . to adopt a course of conduct which must involve [Denmark] in hostilities with Great Britain'.

Gambier was therefore to prevent any military reinforcements being sent to Zealand, as it was of the utmost importance that the forces on the island were not strengthened to such a degree as to 'place it beyond the reach of a combined attack of His Majesty's sea and land forces'. Gambier was to leave smaller vessels unmolested, but if any Danish ships of the line attempted to put to sea, he was to ask them to return to port – 'in the first instance . . . in the most amicable manner' – but if they refused, he was to 'use your best exertions to capture or destroy them'.[25]

On the same day, 19 July, Castlereagh wrote to Major-General Lord Cathcart, who was in command of the forces in Pomerania, explaining the situation. In these circumstances, Britain had decided to enter into 'such explanations with the court of Denmark as the nature of the case may require'. However, if British representations were to carry 'their due weight', negotiations should not begin until they could be supported by 'an adequate naval and military force assembled on the spot'. Gambier had been ordered to proceed to Danish waters with a powerful fleet, and 16,700 troops from Britain would follow as soon as they could be embarked. The British force in Pomerania was also required, and Cathcart was therefore to re-embark it and proceed immediately to join Gambier. When he had done so, Cathcart would take command of the whole land force – both the King's German Legion from Pomerania and the troops that would arrive from Britain. Castlereagh expressed the hope that the whole force in Britain, including the ordnance, would be in a position to sail within seven or eight days.[26]

Castlereagh's instructions spoke of negotiations with the Danish government to secure adequate assurances of Danish good conduct – negotiations that would be facilitated by an overwhelming show of force. But what were the British demands to be – and how were they to be conveyed to the Danes? What guarantee could the Danish government give to Britain that would render an armed assault unnecessary? Canning's instructions to Taylor on 16 July say nothing about this. By 18 July at the latest, the cabinet had decided that the surrender of the Danish fleet into British hands was the only form of security that would suffice. This might be accompanied, as the Danes preferred, either by an alliance between the two countries or by continuing Danish neutrality, but British control of the Danish fleet was the sine qua non.[27] Once it was in British hands, the Danish fleet could be used neither to interfere with British access to the Baltic nor to carry a French invasion force to the north of Ireland. The French might still close the ports of the Jutlandic peninsula to the British flag, but there was nothing the cabinet could do to prevent that. The main point was that Denmark would have been neutered as a significant naval power.

How was this demand to be conveyed to the Danish government? In principle, it would have been possible to issue further instructions to Taylor, but he was clearly deemed too junior for the task of presenting such an offensive ultimatum and handling the awkward discussions that would follow. The solution hit upon was to send a special envoy to Denmark, and the choice fell on another currently unemployed British diplomat, Francis Jackson. Jackson was somewhat higher up the diplomatic food chain than Taylor – both older and more senior in that he had been British minister in Berlin between 1802 and 1806.[28] Jackson had angled for employment in the Baltic by writing on 14 July to Lord Malmesbury setting out his views on the crisis in northern Europe and suggesting that British naval forces should take control of the Sound and the Great Belt.[29]

The letter to Malmesbury was an oblique and clever means of approaching Canning. Malmesbury was sixty and more or less retired, perhaps because of his growing deafness, but he was Britain's most senior diplomat and had acted as Canning's mentor when he first held office in the 1790s as one of the two under-secretaries of state at the foreign office.[30] On becoming foreign secretary in 1807, Canning had returned

the compliment by appointing Malmesbury's son, Lord Fitzharris, as one
of his two under-secretaries to serve alongside George Hammond. Jackson
had been Malmesbury's private secretary in his younger days, and
nothing could seem more natural than that he should write to him about
the current crisis in the north.

Canning may not have been altogether delighted by Malmesbury's
shadowy presence in the background. Canning's own private secretary was
another of Malmesbury's men, James Tyrell Ross, who reported regularly
and sometimes indiscreetly to Malmesbury on what was going on at the
foreign office.[31] This may be why Canning asked his wife Joan to copy out
at least one highly confidential letter 'without putting it even into Ross's
hands'.[32] Even so, he liked the sound of Jackson when Malmesbury sent
him his letter with a recommendation that he was the best person to take
the Danes in hand, and on 17 July a messenger was sent to summon
Jackson with the greatest urgency to London from deepest
Northamptonshire. Jackson was woken at one in the morning on 18 July,
left ninety minutes later and reached the foreign office in Downing Street
by early afternoon. He had a long meeting with Canning the same day,
agreed to undertake a mission to Denmark and was shown his draft
instructions. These have not survived, but Jackson saw immediately that
their 'object . . . was to get possession of the Danish fleet'.

Jackson also received an apology for the haste with which he had been
fetched to London. Taylor would leave for Copenhagen that evening to
replace Garlike, but the original intention of also sending Jackson to
Denmark immediately had been rescinded because the military
preparations were 'not . . . quite ready'.[33] Jackson was not, however, told
why the preparations had been delayed and he would have been surprised
had he known the reason. It was that the plan to attack Denmark had
encountered opposition from an unexpected but influential quarter, the
king himself.

Castlereagh's letter to the king outlining the plan for a combined
operation against Copenhagen went off to Windsor on 17 July, the same
day as a messenger had been sent to fetch Jackson. The king's reply on
18 July gave the cabinet a jolt. George was happy to repeat the approval
he had already given for sending a strong squadron to Danish waters and
to endorse all the measures of *preparation* proposed to him, but there was
a sting in the tail. The king was

confident that his ministers will see with him the necessity of proceeding with temper and caution and of avoiding any violent step adopted towards Denmark, which may appear unprovoked, to force that power into the arms of France and give weight to the attempts of France to induce Russia to join with her in a league of northern powers against this country.[34]

This was not what 'Your Majesty's confidential servants' wanted to hear and it put the cat among the pigeons. The cabinet met the next day, a Sunday, and afterwards the prime minister wrote to King George just before midnight. Portland said that ministers were disturbed that the measures proposed by Castlereagh to him 'had not been so fortunate as to have obtained the unqualified approbation of Your Majesty'. The prime minister therefore requested permission to visit George the next day 'to explain more fully the motives and object' behind them. Portland signed off by saying that it was 'the humble but most deliberate and serious opinion of Your Majesty's servants that the nearest and dearest interests of Your Majesty's empire are essentially and indissolubly involved' in this question.[35]

The king saw the prime minister at 12.45 p.m. on 20 July.[36] We do not know what passed between them, but we must presume that Portland laid all the secret intelligence that had been received before the king. At all events, he obtained George's acquiescence but it was a grudging one. When the instructions that Castlereagh had written for Gambier and Cathcart on 19 July were sent to the king, George did not quite express approval – he merely replied to Castlereagh that the instructions 'appear to His Majesty to be in conformity to the measure which has been submitted by his ministers'.[37] This was not exactly a ringing endorsement, and George remained opposed to the assault on Denmark. In late August he had a long conversation with Canning on the subject, and afterwards the foreign secretary reported to his wife:

Good knobs! He is really very respectable with all his scruples. 'I am afraid Your Majesty is still shocked at the immorality of the measure.' 'Yes – yes – I have not altered my opinion. It is a very immoral act. So immoral that I won't ask who originated it. I have determined not to ask that question.' But all this in the most perfect good humour, laughing even at his own difficulties – but determined honestly to declare his opinion.[38]

Whatever George's private reservations, Portland's visit to Windsor on 20 July had done the trick. The king was squared and the machinery for embarking troops in England could be set in motion. The first orders to this effect left the Admiralty and the War Office on 21 July.[39] The countdown to war had begun.

And there was no doubt that war was envisaged. A fortnight later, Canning professed to believe that the massive show of force by Britain would produce Danish acquiescence in the British ultimatum – 'a very cheerful one certainly not – but an acquiescence that will save extremities'.[40] But this was a polite fiction: no state would surrender its navy, in the Danish case a potent symbol of national pride and honour, to another power. Jackson was closer to the mark when he later recalled that neither Canning nor any other minister ever supposed that the Danes would yield to the demand for their fleet. 'Nobody ever ventured even to suspect that [my mission] could [succeed]. And in fact there was not from the first to the last a single one in which there appeared the slightest glimmering of hope that it would succeed'.[41] This was a decision for war and everyone knew it.

THE RUSSIAN DIMENSION

When King George expressed his reservations about the Danish venture on 18 July, he gave two reasons for caution. The first was the obvious one that Denmark would be turned into an enemy by British aggression, but the other was that high-handed action against Denmark might provoke Russia into joining France in a league of northern powers directed against Britain. This is a rare mention of Russia in the documents relating to the days when the decision for war against Denmark was taken. This silence is surprising since Friedland, Russia's defection from her alliance with Britain and Tilsit were quite fundamental to the transformation of the international situation that made it possible for France to threaten Holstein and the Danish fleet, even if there was still no suggestion that Russia would play an active part in mobilising Denmark as an enemy of Britain.

This does not mean that Russia was absent from the thoughts of British ministers. The only evidence we have for the British government's attitude towards Russia during the eleven days when the decision to strike at Denmark was taken is provided by some remarks made by Canning to Maksim Alopeus on 18 July and by a series of despatches and letters that Canning sent to Gower on 21 July, just as the king had been brought into line and the first military orders were being issued. They are suffused with a spirit of moderation and sweet reason entirely lacking in Canning's approach to the Danes.

Canning asked Alopeus to pass on to Alexander directly and in the strictest confidence that the British government accepted he had felt compelled to conclude a separate peace, but that this should not be allowed to loosen the ties that bound Britain and Russia together. The disaster at Friedland was largely to be blamed on the inertia of the Grenville government – an observation Canning would never have made in writing. Now the previous government and certain newspapers that had always opposed continental alliances had joined forces to deflect the blame onto Russia. Alexander should pay no attention. Such outbursts were merely the 'effusions of party' and did not reflect the views of the present government, which was committed to 'a system of continental union'.[42]

By 21 July Canning had not written to Gower for three weeks, and in the meantime the news of the Franco-Russian armistice and the meetings at Tilsit had reached London. Indeed, there had even been reports from French agents and 'news-writers' that a preliminary peace had been signed. The same sources contained accounts of 'the disgusting details . . . of the constant intercourse of the emperor and Bonaparte', but Canning pretended to disbelieve them on the grounds that they 'exceed all reasonable belief'. He also pretended to hope that Alexander might have insisted in his discussions with Napoleon on including his British ally in a negotiation for a general (not just a separate) peace. In that event, King George remained willing to participate, 'in concert with his ally', in such negotiations for a European settlement.[43]

All this was pure baloney. Canning was perfectly aware by then that what was afoot at Tilsit was a separate peace from which Britain was excluded. In principle, that could have prompted a sense of grievance and hostility towards Russia, but that was not at all how Canning reacted. Instead, he remained convinced of the vital importance of 'keeping well' with Alexander and that 'a union whether in war or peace between [Britain and Russia] is the only chance of good to either'. But he feared that a 'much more likely' scenario was that Britain would remain at war, while Russia was at peace, and then the question would be whether it would still be possible to maintain 'a good understanding' between the two states. The answer would depend on Russia as much as on Britain, but – he declared – 'we are ready to do our part'.

What that meant in practice was set out in an extraordinary passage in Canning's private letter (not his official despatch) to Gower on 21 July.

> My notion is . . . that the Emperor has been dragged into this business against his *taste* and *feeling*, if not against his opinion; that the very violence with which he gives into it now, and out-does all that it was necessary or becoming for him to do in affecting a friendly intercourse with Bonaparte, proceeds from an attempt to disguise from others, and to hide even from himself, the disgust which he really feels at the part which he has determined to act; that he will go through with it, however; that he will even be elated for a time with the peace-popularity which he will suppose himself to have acquired; that he will for a time at least be ashamed of his old feelings and fancy that he has got the better of them . . .
>
> But that the time will come when this popularity will grow distasteful; when he will reflect in bitterness upon the humiliations to which he has submitted; and when, if we in the meantime have behaved ourselves to him like friends, have not reproached, or dealt unkindly with him, he will turn thankfully to us again, and may be again won to good politics, with perhaps less chance of a relapse than before. It is with this in view that you are directed to abstain from recrimination, and to mix the expressions of regret and disappointment which are unavoidable with expressions of personal regard to the Emperor. It is upon his *personal* feelings, and them only that I found any hopes of political improvement.

Accordingly, once he was in St Petersburg, Gower was to cultivate Alexander assiduously. 'He must be unhappy – and must therefore be sensible to kindness, even to pity, if delicately administered, after the fervour of his first exultation of shabbiness has once subsided.'

In a nutshell, Gower was to play the part of an avuncular therapist until Alexander saw the error of his recent ways. Canning's letter must rank among the more eccentric instructions sent by a foreign minister to an ambassador, but it reveals very clearly the basis of Canning's thinking about Russia at this time. Alexander had betrayed Britain and himself at Tilsit, but he intended no real harm to Britain and might in time be drawn back into closer association with her. To that end, British policy towards Russia was to be conciliatory and ingratiating. This was, in fact, a perfectly sensible approach, despite the faintly ludicrous psychobabble in which Canning indulged. We know now that Tilsit involved an alliance directed against Britain, but that was not yet clear to Canning and there was nothing to be gained by following a more aggressive path while there was still a possibility that Tilsit involved no more than a separate peace.

But of course on 21 July British policy in the Baltic did not consist merely of conciliation towards Russia. It also involved an attack on Denmark, and we may ask how Canning thought that this would impact upon Britain's relations with Russia. In his letter to Gower, Canning brushed the point aside. He did not, of course, admit that an attack was imminent. He merely said that a strong British squadron was to be expected in the Baltic and that Gower was to explain its presence, if asked by the Russians, along the same lines as Taylor employed to Joachim Bernstorff. However, he claimed to expect 'no disposition in Russia to question the propriety' of British action against Denmark. This was because the Russians had been concerned in the months before Friedland about 'the conduct and designs of Denmark'[44] and Alexander had made representations to the Danish government on the subject.

This was quite true. Back in February 1807, Alopeus, the newly appointed Russian ambassador to London, had been told at his first meeting with Howick about British discontent at the Danish withdrawal from Holstein and Danish attempts to dissuade the British from sending their packet boats to Husum. As a result, Alopeus had written both to the Russian minister in Copenhagen and to Budberg to convey these concerns. The wheels of bureaucracy turned ponderously at the Russian foreign ministry, but eventually – in June 1807 – the Danes were presented with a note backing up the British on these points and complaining generally about Denmark's failure to play her proper part in the great crusade against Napoleon.[45]

It must have occurred to Canning that even if Alexander had chosen to reprimand the Danes over their weak-kneed attitude to France *before* Friedland and Tilsit, he would no longer care about that once he had made peace with France himself. Yet the tenor of Canning's letter to Gower was that Alexander was still fundamentally antagonistic to French expansionism and ashamed of his own recent conduct. It was a short step from that to assuming that Alexander would be glad to see French designs on Denmark thwarted. Indeed, he might even be pleased to see Britain's position in the Baltic and her ability to act within that region strengthened as a counter-weight to French power.

Even so, Canning's blithe unconcern about the Russian reaction does not quite hold water. He must have realised the risk that Alexander would be aggrieved by brutal British action against a state which he regarded as under Russian protection. More than two months later, Canning claimed in a letter to one of his private friends on 30 September that 'one of the recommendations' of the attack on Denmark had been that it was certain 'to stun Russia into her senses again'.[46] By then, Canning had reason to take a far more suspicious view of Russian intentions and he may have been extrapolating backwards sentiments that he did not feel between 10 and 21 July. But it is more likely that this was a strong, if unspoken, consideration on 21 July and that in relation to Russia the assault on Denmark was intended to have a dual effect. Yes, it was expected to encourage Alexander by showing that Britain was still able and willing to act against French interests. But it was also meant to send him a warning that Britain was still a force to be reckoned with.

Canning's private letter to Gower on 21 July demonstrates his belief that Russia could not possibly have become a real ally of Napoleon. Instead, Canning looked to a withdrawal into sullen but still fundamentally benevolent neutrality, which might lead eventually to a renewal of close ties with Britain. He wrote to Gower late in the evening. As he finished it at two o'clock in the morning, a letter was placed in his hands that challenged all the assumptions he had just expressed about Alexander's state of mind. The communication he had just received contained the celebrated 'secret intelligence from Tilsit'.

Chapter 7

THE SECRET INTELLIGENCE
FROM TILSIT, JULY–AUGUST 1807

COUNT D'ANTRAIGUES IN ENGLAND

The letter that Canning received in the witching hours was dated 'Richmond, 21 July', and its author was Count d'Antraigues. The count had spent the day at his country house along the riverside of the Thames at Barnes, which he evidently regarded as part of Richmond. He had a home in London too, but like many other French émigrés – and well-heeled native Britons too – he liked to maintain a second residence in the fashionable swathe of countryside between London and the king's palace at Windsor.

As émigrés went, Louis-Emmanuel-Henri-Alexandre de Launay, Count d'Antraigues, was a more substantial figure than Fauche-Borel or Danican and was more skilled at persuading others of his importance. He was an implacable foe first of the French republic and then of the Napoleonic empire and a man of passionate enthusiasms and hatreds.[1] D'Antraigues emigrated from France in 1790. Over the following years, he devoted himself to writing royalist propaganda and, above all, to producing intelligence reports on the basis of information he received from various agents inside France. He had links both with the Pretender to the French throne, the future Louis XVIII, and with many European governments hostile to the French republic. The reliability of his reports has been debated endlessly by historians. It seems indisputable that, to put it charitably, he enjoyed a rich imaginative life and that there were elements of distortion and fabrication in much of the intelligence material that emanated from his tireless pen. It does not, however, follow that all the intelligence transmitted by d'Antraigues was valueless. Indeed, it is perfectly possible that the greater part of these reports is essentially authentic. As one of his more hostile biographers lets slip, some of d'Antraigues's reports contain summaries or extracts, rapidly and often badly copied to be sure, of documents that can still be found in public archives.[2]

A great turning point in his life was his arrest at Trieste by the French in 1797, his imprisonment and interrogation at Milan by General Bonaparte, the commander of the French army in Italy, and his subsequent escape. The episode destroyed d'Antraigues's relations with the royalist court in exile and delivered a blow to his reputation from which it never fully recovered. This tangled affair hinged on a document, purportedly found in d'Antraigues's possession when he was arrested, which the French government in Paris used to damage the royalist cause. It was easy to suspect – and many did – that d'Antraigues had produced or doctored it at Bonaparte's dictation in order to save his own life and had been allowed to escape in return.

After Milan, d'Antraigues spent several years in Austria, where he worked for a number of European governments, though his relations with most of them were troubled. His life assumed a more stable pattern between 1802 and 1806, when he resided at Dresden attached to the Russian legation to the Saxon court. His main task was to pass on intelligence reports and analyses of the international situation to St Petersburg, but he also engaged in propaganda activities. Under this second heading, he published an erudite and allegorical anti-Napoleonic tract in 1805, which caused a great stir in Germany and beyond. D'Antraigues had many Russian enemies, but he also had one powerful protector, Prince Adam Czartoryski, a close friend of Emperor Alexander I and acting foreign minister since 1804. It was Czartoryski who arranged for d'Antraigues's removal to London in the summer of 1806.

The suggestion came from d'Antraigues himself, who feared a renewal of the pressure Napoleon had exerted in the past on the Saxon government for his expulsion from Dresden. Even worse, one of his informants in Paris had warned that if he ever fell into the hands of the French army a second time, he would most assuredly be shot. When it became clear to Czartoryski early in 1806 that his increasing inability to work with Emperor Alexander would necessitate his resignation from the foreign ministry, he took care to safeguard the futures of a number of his protégés, among them d'Antraigues. He arranged for d'Antraigues to move to England, where he would receive an increased Russian pension but without being officially attached to the Russian embassy. In return, d'Antraigues would continue to produce anti-Napoleonic propaganda and would write regular memoranda for the Russian government – one each month on the situation in Britain and another on that in Europe.[3]

This was an agreeable and safe posting for a man in his early fifties, and he led a comfortable existence in London with his wife, Anne Antoinette Saint-Huberty, a celebrated opera singer in Paris before the revolution. As a commoner, Saint-Huberty had not attracted the approbation of d'Antraigues's mother, and it had taken him seven years to tell her that Saint-Huberty was his wife rather than his mistress. Saint-Huberty had been a tigress in her husband's defence at Milan in 1797, but by the time they got to London, the marriage was less than harmonious, and d'Antraigues's main consolation in his domestic life seems to have been their only child, Jules, born in 1792 – 'my son and my friend', as he called him.[4]

D'Antraigues did not get much joy out of the Russian embassy in London. Count Simon Vorontsov had just retired earlier in 1806 after twenty-two years as ambassador to London, but had opted to remain in Britain and was kept informed of events at the embassy by his henchman and former deputy, Baron Paul Nicolai, who was *chargé d'affaires* pending the arrival of a new ambassador. Czartoryski wrote to Vorontsov, asking him to receive d'Antraigues kindly. He had certain faults and his 'moral character was not generally the object of praise', Czartoryski conceded, but d'Antraigues had great knowledge and intelligence and had shown himself sincerely attached to Czartoryski himself.[5] This cut no ice with Vorontsov, who urged Nicolai to have as little as possible to do with d'Antraigues[6] – an indication of his dubious reputation. As a result, Nicolai dutifully transmitted d'Antraigues's memoranda to the new Russian foreign minister, General Budberg, but refused d'Antraigues's request to be presented at court 'as a Russian gentleman' unless and until he received explicit instructions from Budberg to do so.[7] Such instructions were ultimately forthcoming,[8] and d'Antraigues was eventually presented at court, not by Nicolai but by the new ambassador, Maksim Alopeus, on 4 June 1807.[9] This was a kindness on Budberg's part, but he spared little time for d'Antraigues. In August 1806 Budberg wrote to d'Antraigues confirming Czartoryski's previous instructions, and urging d'Antraigues to place the same confidence in him as he had done in his predecessor. After that, it was not until early April 1807 that d'Antraigues at last received a second letter from Budberg.[10]

The coolness of his reception in official Russian circles in London and Budberg's silence doubtless added to d'Antraigues's awareness that his role in Russian service had been diminished,[11] but that does not mean that either he or Czartoryski regarded the tasks which he was to perform in London as unimportant. We should take care against regarding d'Antraigues exclusively, or even primarily, as a spy. When Czartoryski proposed to Alexander that d'Antraigues be sent to London, he wrote that d'Antraigues was one of those well-informed and perceptive writers on political affairs who could not only exert a salutary influence on public opinion but also sometimes present ideas that might be helpful to the Russian government in formulating its own policies.[12] D'Antraigues would doubtless have agreed. He did not wish merely to provide secret intelligence. He also wanted to sit at the right hand of princes and ministers and to exert an influence on policy. Indeed, he probably saw little difference between the two activities. And on top of that there was his insatiable appetite for money, and he was accomplished at getting it – he had lost everything in France, yet when he died, he left £15,000,[13] a small fortune in those days. In his eyes, London was not a place where he could enjoy the honourable semi-retirement that Czartoryski had secured for him – it was a new world to conquer.

D'Antraigues prepared the way by cultivating Henry Watkin Williams Wynn, the British minister at Dresden. Wynn was young, naive and inexperienced, but he had important connections. Above all, he was the nephew of Lord Grenville with whom he corresponded, largely about his efforts at self-improvement through historical reading. One typical letter gives the flavour: 'My dear Uncle – If I require any incitement to study, your letter would certainly be the greatest I could have'.[14] Wynn was a little frightened of d'Antraigues at first, describing him as 'of a very dangerous character'. Nor was Wynn so green that he failed to realise that it was 'excessively difficult to distinguish the true intelligence from that which he creates himself'.[15] In the long run, however, Wynn was easy meat for an old hand like d'Antraigues – he was 'a nice boy' (*un bon enfant*), but 'the nephew lacks the talents of the uncle'.[16] By the summer of 1806, on the eve of d'Antraigues's departure for London, Wynn had succumbed and now saw him as 'one of my most intimate friends . . . [and] as the man whom I should point out above all others as having the clearest insight into the affairs of the continent'. He was therefore more than happy to accede to d'Antraigues's request for a letter of introduction to Grenville.[17]

D'Antraigues made rapid use of this letter of introduction. On 3 September, the same day he reached London, he sent Wynn's letter to Grenville, and he had his first interview with Grenville on 15 September.[18] He had made it through the prime minister's door. Grenville rapidly tired of d'Antraigues's often atrocious handwriting.[19] Within a few weeks, the prime minister had delegated the task of dealing with d'Antraigues to Nicholas Vansittart, a subordinate minister at the Treasury, but he was in no sense brushed aside. By the time the Grenville government fell in March 1807, d'Antraigues had developed a good relationship with Vansittart – and with Lord Howick, the foreign secretary. He had also been accorded an annual pension of £600 from the foreign office's secret service fund, backdated to 1 October 1806[20] on the grounds that his 'connections and correspondence abroad [might] afford important service to the Government'.[21] What had d'Antraigues done to earn the friendship of ministers and the generosity of the British taxpayer?

On the personal level, d'Antraigues clearly had a certain presence. His letters give no sign of it – they are invariably self-important and devoid of the slightest hint of humour – but his charm is attested to by none other than Jane Austen, who met him some years later. She found him 'a very fine looking man, with quiet manners, good enough for an Englishman – and I believe [he] is a man of great information and taste . . . If he would but speak English, I would take to him'.[22] And Wynn predicted that Grenville would 'be much pleased by his conversation; he is equally well informed both in modern and ancient literature'.[23] According to his bitter enemy, Fauche-Borel, d'Antraigues 'captivated' Lord Howick 'by the charm of his conversation and the forcefulness of his writing'.[24] Charm was allied to exceptional gifts of sycophancy. In October 1806, he told Grenville that he had in this moment of supreme crisis become 'not only the prime minister of England but, properly speaking, that of all Europe'.[25] Just after the Talents had fallen, d'Antraigues asked to see Howick in order to 'assure you of the high esteem both your talents and your character have inspired in me'.[26] That was no obstacle for writing to Howick's bitter rival Canning some months later that 'the crisis is cruel and could intimidate a minister of the ordinary mettle (*un ministre vulgaire*), but I flatter myself that it cannot have that effect on the pupil and friend of Mr Pitt'.[27]

But obviously flattery, educated conversation and a familiarity with the great world were not enough to secure continuing access to the British political elite. In addition, d'Antraigues supplied a series of real or supposed political services. First of all, he produced anti-Napoleonic propaganda. Within weeks of his arrival in England, he was writing articles for the *Courier d'Angleterre*, a French-language newspaper financed by the British government for dissemination on the continent. He had soon become the middleman between its editor and the British government.[28] Secondly, because of his long experience and wide contacts, he was able to provide information and analysis on the situation in France and the rest of western Europe.[29] Thirdly, there was his most obliging willingness to be guided by what British ministers told him in the reports about British policy that he sent to St Petersburg. On 29 December 1806, he reminded Vansittart that he had promised d'Antraigues a note which he could transmit to Emperor Alexander 'as coming from myself' and which would demonstrate that Britain had the financial resources to continue the war alongside her Russian ally for another twenty years, if necessary, without accepting 'a perfidious and infamous peace'.[30]

All this was helpful, but by far his strongest card was his connection to Czartoryski. The line he peddled was that he was in London on an unofficial mission charged with reporting to Czartoryski and Alexander on the nature of British policy in Europe. It was essential that the object of d'Antraigues's mission should remain secret, even from the Russian ambassador in London. Czartoryski's resignation had no relevance to d'Antraigues's mission. Czartoryski, though out of office, was still the friend and favourite of the Russian emperor, and would continue to direct Russian foreign policy behind the scenes.[31] It was a nice story, but the claim that d'Antraigues was a sort of parallel ambassador on a secret mission was doubly fictional. In the first place, it is clear from his frequent, though unanswered, letters to Czartoryski during his first ten months in London that Czartoryski had told him to send all his memoranda to the new Russian foreign minister and that Czartoryski addressed no communications at all to d'Antraigues between 6 September 1806 and 2 June 1807.[32]

The story was also fictional in a second and more fundamental sense in that it rested on a profound misreading of the political situation at St Petersburg. In the first couple of years after Alexander I came to the throne in 1801, Czartoryski had been one of the emperor's four 'young friends', a group that met regularly with Alexander to discuss ideas of internal reform. The other members of this 'unofficial committee' were Victor Kochubey, Nicholas Novosiltsov and Paul Stroganov. They were all anglophile in outlook and – with the partial exception of Kochubey, who leaned towards a more isolationist stand – they all came to be strong partisans of the war against Napoleonic France. In Britain, they were seen as reliable allies in Russia, none more so than Czartoryski, one of the architects of the third coalition against France in 1805.

But by 1806 their star was on the wane. The unofficial committee had long since ceased to meet, and all of the young friends felt increasingly sidelined by the emperor. Their eclipse was not apparent to the naked eye – it was not Alexander's style to dismiss advisers who had fallen out of favour; he merely stopped listening and saw them less frequently. It had taken months of prolonged and agonising discussion before Alexander accepted Czartoryski's resignation. But even if the withdrawal of the young friends from official positions was slow and gradual, they no longer exerted real influence.[33] As Novosiltsov put it, they were only consulted occasionally and on isolated aspects of policy.[34] Far from being the hidden hand guiding Russian foreign policy, Czartoryski was not even selected at first to be included among those who would form Alexander's entourage when he set off in March 1807 to visit the army in eastern Prussia. Instead, Czartoryski had to ask to be allowed to accompany the emperor so as to be close to his person while he was in danger and 'without the slightest pretension to involvement in political affairs'.[35]

None of this was obvious to British ministers, who did not understand the political situation at the Russian court and lacked any unembarrassing means of verifying d'Antraigues's claims. If indeed Czartoryski retained a powerful role behind the scenes and d'Antraigues was a subterranean channel of communication to him and the emperor, d'Antraigues simply could not be ignored. The niche that d'Antraigues had established for himself also reflected the primitive administrative structure of the age. Czartoryski's words to Alexander about the role 'right-thinking writers' (les écrivains bien pensants) like d'Antraigues could play both in the field of propaganda and in giving advice to governments could have been echoed by British ministers.[36] When the British government wanted to produce propaganda in the French language, it subcontracted the job to émigrés, and d'Antraigues was not the only émigré paid to provide information and advice to the British authorities.[37] In an age when Britain possessed no ministry of propaganda and when the officials who worked in the foreign office were scribes not foreign-policy experts, there was a place in the system for a freelance intelligence-gatherer, political analyst and journalist like d'Antraigues.

Canning inherited the relationship with d'Antraigues from the Grenville administration when he became foreign secretary in late March 1807. He seems to have taken an instant dislike to the Frenchman. His misdemeanours were several. D'Antraigues was distressed by the fall of the Grenville government in that it removed from office men with whom he had already established a rapport, and he did not conceal his displeasure. Canning was also irritated by the incessant flow of letters from d'Antraigues and by his request for an increase in his British pension from £600 to £1,000 a year, citing the high cost of living in London (some things do not change). On this last point, Canning fobbed him off by claiming that he was unable to give an immediate response.[38]

More fundamentally, Canning was quickly on a good footing with Maksim Alopeus, the new Russian ambassador, and he was irritated that Alopeus was inhibited by 'the consciousness (which I know him to feel) that he is under the constant and watchful supervision of a person who carries on a secret correspondence with the Russian government'.[39] What was more, d'Antraigues was 'very, very importunate' in his requests to see Canning to discuss 'points already decided' with the ambassador 'for the purpose of enabling him [d'Antraigues] to write a private memoir . . . to Prince Czartoryski or the Emperor'. Canning saw d'Antraigues as an able man who might also be 'a very honest one'. But he was 'very indiscreet' and this made him 'somewhat dangerous'.

For all these reasons, Canning wanted to be 'well rid of him' and wished to see d'Antraigues 'working in the [foreign] office at St Petersburg, instead of collecting material for his memoirs here'. Unlike the Grenville government, Canning had a means of tackling d'Antraigues's presence in London discreetly. Gower had come to know Czartoryski well on his previous tour of duty in Russia, so Canning asked him to approach Czartoryski privately and confidentially to request d'Antraigues's recall – regardless of 'whether (as we agree in hoping most anxiously) you find him restored to his former situation [i.e. as foreign minister] or whether he be still only a private individual attached to the person of the emperor'.[40]

In the meantime, however, Canning did not dare ignore d'Antraigues, because he too, like the ministers of the Grenville government, could not disregard the fairy story that d'Antraigues was on a special mission to London. Canning therefore granted d'Antraigues a regular interview once a week, even if many of these meetings seem to have occurred *al fresco* as Canning walked from his home in Stanhope Street in Euston to the foreign office in Downing Street. Jackson often received similar treatment when he wanted a private word while waiting to depart on his special mission to Kiel[41] – like many of those driven by their love of power, Canning enjoyed making the point that he was an exceedingly busy man.

When he got to Tilsit on the eve of the battle of Friedland, Gower found time among his stressful interviews with Alexander and Budberg for a discreet talk with Czartoryski about d'Antraigues. Czartoryski's response cut the ground from under d'Antraigues's feet, but was unhelpful over his removal from London. 'Czartoryski lamented extremely that his protégé should have acted so foolishly, but expressed a strong wish that you [Canning] would not insist upon his recall saying that there was really no other asylum for him than England.' When Gower suggested that d'Antraigues might be employed in the foreign ministry at St Petersburg, Czartoryski dismissed the idea on the grounds that d'Antraigues was too 'restless' (*remuant*) to work there. He assured Gower that

[D'Antraigues] possessed in no degree the confidence either of the emperor or of any person of influence in the Russian government, that he was instructed to attend more to literary than political subjects, and that if you would only repress his forwardness by refusing to see him so frequently as you had done he might, he hoped, be permitted to continue in England.[42]

Gower's report on Czartoryski's remarks reached London on 10 July, the very day that Canning was writing his first minute about the urgent need for action against Denmark. In normal circumstances, those remarks would presumably have put an end to d'Antraigues's regular meetings with Canning and would possibly also have led to his removal from

Britain. But circumstances were not normal. We have no evidence to suggest that Canning said a word to d'Antraigues. He was too preoccupied with Denmark and the crisis in Britain's international position to bother with the importunate émigré – d'Antraigues was a fly who could be swatted at leisure when he had a spare moment. It was against this background that d'Antraigues produced what, on the assumption it were true, was the greatest intelligence coup of his career.

PRINCE TROUBETZKOI AND THE SECRET INTELLIGENCE FROM TILSIT

The letter that d'Antraigues sent to Canning was headed portentously, 'For your eyes only' (*Pour vous seul*), and concluded with similar portentousness, 'Burn this letter, not for my sake but for the sake of my friends' – an injunction that Canning failed to follow. Its contents were dynamite. D'Antraigues claimed that he had that evening received a letter from Tilsit dated 27 June, two days after Napoleon and Alexander held their first meeting in mid-river on the Niemen. It came from a man whom d'Antraigues would name when he next met Canning. In the meantime, he would only say in writing that it was not Czartoryski, but a Russian general who held a position close to the emperor. As such, he had accompanied Alexander to Tilsit and had been present at the interviews between the two emperors on 26 and 27 June. At these meetings, there had been much discussion – and here we reach the key passage –

about combining against England, a country with which our emperor is displeased and not without reason. Napoleon . . . has proposed a maritime league of this country [i.e. Russia] against England and the unification of the Russian squadrons with those of Sweden and Denmark, being certain, he says, of the forces of Spain and Portugal in order to attack England at close quarters (*corps à corps*). This proposal was heard with surprise and without objection, and although Bonaparte reverted to it twice, the emperor did not reply. *This is quite certain*, because I was there. [d'Antraigues's emphasis]

D'Antraigues's correspondent was emphatic that no comfort was to be derived from this silence, because Alexander was well aware of his sentiments and would not have wished to respond in front of him or others in his entourage who were hostile to France.

> This silence therefore proves nothing at all. I was no longer in attendance at subsequent conferences . . . and I must warn you that my opinion . . . is that Bonaparte will win him over. The emperor has lost his head and . . . will commit a grievous fault.[43]

If this intelligence were reliable, it had enormous implications for Britain's foreign relations. It suggested that Britain had to fear not only the use of the Danish fleet for a descent on the north of Ireland, but also 'a maritime league' of all the naval powers of the continent to challenge British supremacy at sea. Perilous stuff, but – as must be the case with any piece of intelligence coming from d'Antraigues – was it reliable? Was this one of the occasions when he had recourse to distortion or even complete fabrication?

On one point at least, d'Antraigues was and remains on plausible ground. The name that he gave to Canning as the author of the letter from Tilsit can only have been that of Prince Vassili Troubetzkoi.[44] And Troubetzkoi was certainly in correspondence with d'Antraigues and in a position to furnish information about the first meetings at Tilsit. The two men had become close friends in 1805 when they both lived in apartments located in the same large house in Dresden – d'Antraigues with his family, Troubetzkoi with his new wife, Wilhelmine, Princess of Sagan[45] (later better known as the mistress of the Austrian statesman Metternich). The marriage was dissolved after only one year, and d'Antraigues provided a sympathetic ear and avuncular advice to the young couple before and after their estrangement.[46] Needless to say, this did not prevent d'Antraigues from treating the 'tragicomedy of our unhappy princess' as a piece of ripe gossip when reporting to a mutual acquaintance. Troubetzkoi's willingness to be paid off with a handsome *douceur* from the wealthy princess attracted his particular derision.[47] Some friend.

After he left Dresden, Troubetzkoi kept in touch with d'Antraigues in letters that frequently affirm his undying friendship and his violent hatred of Napoleon – 'this Corsican devil' (*ce diable de Corse*).[48] By July 1806 Troubetzkoi was back in St Petersburg, where he was appointed as one of

Emperor Alexander's aides de camp. He was also commander of a guards cavalry squadron and served with distinction during the hard-fought winter campaign of 1806–7, including the battle of Friedland – he was twice decorated, given the title of general aide de camp and promoted to the rank of major-general. As one of Alexander's aides de camp, he accompanied him to Tilsit in June 1807 to meet Napoleon.[49]

So Troubetzkoi clearly could have written to d'Antraigues in the terms described, but two further questions remain – did he in fact write to d'Antraigues at all and, if so, did d'Antraigues tamper with the contents of the letter? D'Antraigues certainly had good reason for doing so. He cannot have known Czartoryski's remarks about him, as reported by Gower, but the instinctive cunning, innate to a conman of his stature, may have alerted him to some alteration in Canning's demeanour towards him. But if he simply invented the whole of Troubetzkoi's letter, a more likely explanation is that he read accurately the direction in which Russian policy was moving and decided that the time had come to establish himself more securely in the British camp.

The second half of his letter to Canning is devoted to his own affairs, not the great arena of high politics. He claimed, still purportedly quoting Troubetzkoi, that Napoleon would demand that d'Antraigues be recalled to St Petersburg. But he should resist any attempt to lure him to Russia. Troubetzkoi implored him to remain in England at all costs, because it was essential that there should be someone in London who enjoyed the confidence of those Russians opposed to Alexander's new policy of alliance with France. If the British government failed to provide him with an adequate pension, his Russian friends would club together to ensure that he was not destitute. After putting these words in the mouth of Troubetzkoi, d'Antraigues went on to assure Canning that he would never accept charity, even from his friends, but that he would be proud to accept money from Britain, if his Russian pension were stopped, 'because I shall serve her with all my energies and devote to her such little talent as I possess'. If the British government were not inclined to employ him, he would not go to Russia; he would merely leave London and 'bury' himself in the English countryside, where he could survive on the limited funds he possessed in his own right.

This second section of d'Antraigues's letter is largely hogwash (it contains one sentence that is clearly fabricated[50]), designed to underpin his plea for permanent refuge in Britain and an enhanced British pension.

Fear as well as greed lurked behind such aspirations – fear that the reversal of Russian policy might lead to his dismissal from Russian service and the loss of his Russian pension or that he might indeed be summoned to St Petersburg, perhaps even handed over to the French. What he offered Canning in return was that the friends of Britain in Russia wanted him to remain in London to serve as an intermediary between them and the British government. This was a variation on what he had claimed was his previous role – an unofficial channel to Czartoryski and Emperor Alexander. The alleged discussions between Alexander and Napoleon about a maritime league served as a sample of the kind of high-quality intelligence he could supply in the future.

This is the case for fabrication,[51] and it is a case that has to be made as d'Antraigues has no credibility as a source. But there is also an argument to be presented in his favour. For a start, the ultimatum eventually presented to Portugal by France included the demand that the Portuguese 'unite their squadrons to those of the continent'[52] – a form of words that has some parallels with the central passage in d'Antraigues's letter to Canning. That letter to Canning contains many details about the summit conference at Tilsit other than the passage about a maritime league against Britain. Some of those details are demonstrably false, added – we can only assume – to embellish the tale, to make the scene depicted more colourful and more plausible. But d'Antraigues also provides information that it would have been difficult for him to know *unless* he had received some kind of communication from Tilsit. He was aware of the Russian courier who had carried Alexander's letter to the hereditary prince of Mecklenburg-Schwerin at Altona[53] – indeed he claimed this courier was also the bearer of the letter he himself received from Troubetzkoi.

More significantly, d'Antraigues knew that the actual text of the treaties of Tilsit was negotiated on the Russian side primarily by Prince Alexander Kourakin and also that Kourakin had been summoned to Tilsit expressly for this purpose. Budberg was part of Alexander's entourage when he met Napoleon for the first time on 25 June, and he would have been the natural choice, as foreign minister, to conduct these negotiations. But Budberg did not become involved in them at all, though he remained at Tilsit writing shifty or rude letters to Gower. Kourakin was not at Tilsit on 25 June, but he was nearby at the village of Schawel on his way to Vienna on a special mission to the Austrian government. He was sent for in haste, and he held his first round of discussions with the French on 28 June. Kourakin's role was not publicly announced at this stage. It was not until 2 July that Gower was able to report to Canning from Memel that Kourakin was 'said' to have been appointed as one of the Russian plenipotentiaries in the peace negotiations with France, and this despatch did not reach London until 23 July.[54]

On the balance of probabilities, we have to conclude that d'Antraigues did receive a letter from Troubetzkoi which transmitted some information about what was happening at Tilsit. But was the central piece of intelligence it allegedly contained true? Did Alexander and Napoleon discuss the formation of a maritime league against Britain at Tilsit? There is not a hint of it in any of the treaties, public or secret, signed at Tilsit or in the related correspondence between Alexander and Napoleon.[55] The treaties merely stipulate that Russia would make common cause with France if Britain had failed to accept peace under Russian mediation by 1 December 1807. In that event, Denmark, Portugal and Sweden would be coerced by concerted French and Russian demands to close their ports to British navigation and to declare war on Britain. It might be argued that once four new states (Denmark, Portugal, Russia and Sweden), which all possessed significant naval forces, joined France in her war against Britain, a maritime league would in practice exist and that its formation was therefore implicit in the Tilsit treaties. But in that case, why is there no mention, not the slightest hint, of concerted naval action against Britain in the treaties?

Instead, the emphasis of the Tilsit treaties is on closing the mainland of Europe to British trade, on enforcing Napoleon's 'continental system'. In Germany, the dukes of Oldenburg and Mecklenburg-Schwerin were to be restored to their duchies, but their ports were to be held by French garrisons until the conclusion of peace between Britain and France. A clause in the secret treaty of alliance between France and Russia stipulated that strong pressure would be applied to Austria to induce her to close her ports to British navigation and to declare war on Britain. The peace treaty between France and Prussia signed at Tilsit on 9 July 1807 also obliged Prussia to close her ports to the British flag.[56] The cardinal point is always the same: the exclusion of British trade from the continent. The whole thrust of Napoleon's endeavours at Tilsit was the elimination of all gaps in his campaign of economic warfare against Britain, not the creation of a maritime league.

The *only* direct evidence that a maritime league was on the agenda at Tilsit is what Troubetzkoi allegedly wrote to d'Antraigues, and d'Antraigues's unsupported testimony can never be good enough. It does not necessarily follow that on this occasion his testimony was false. There were many private conversations at Tilsit between Alexander and Napoleon in which future possibilities were discussed, often in vague terms and without finding their way into the text of the actual treaties.[57] The two Russian memoranda drawn up in the days just before Alexander's first meeting with Napoleon at Tilsit refer to the possibility of reviving something like the armed neutralities of 1780 and 1800 between Russia, Denmark and Sweden with the aim of excluding Britain from the Baltic.[58] This idea did not appear in the final treaties, but the fundamental principle behind the old armed neutralities – that Britain should recognise that the flags of all states were to enjoy 'an equal and complete independence at sea' – does feature in the secret alliance treaty as a central element in the peace terms that were to be imposed on Britain.

It is not inherently implausible that there was some vague and nebulous discussion at Tilsit about the prospects of creating a maritime league against Britain, but in the absence of further evidence, the question has to be left open.[59] Either way, whether the words ascribed to Troubetzkoi about a maritime league were true or false, in a looser but more profound sense 'the secret intelligence from Tilsit' was accurate – the atmosphere between Alexander and Napoleon and the spirit of the Tilsit alliance were fundamentally inimical to Britain. And in that sense, d'Antraigues did Canning a service by starting to disperse the cloud of illusions that the foreign secretary still entertained about Alexander.

Canning reacted swiftly to d'Antraigues's communication. He immediately added what he regarded as its central core as a postscript to the private letter he had just written to Gower. As he scribbled hurriedly by candlelight, his normally confident and well-formed handwriting became a scrawl.

Since I finished my letter to you at two o'clock this morning I have received intelligence which appears to rest on good authority, coming directly from Tilsit, that, at a conference between the Emperor of Russia and Bonaparte, the latter proposed a maritime league against Great Britain to which Denmark and Sweden and Portugal should be invited or forced to accede. The Emperor of Russia is represented not indeed to have agreed to the proposition but not to have said anything against it. He preserved a profound silence which is attributed in the report made to me to the presence at the conference of persons before whom he probably would not like to open himself. I think it right to give notice to you [of] this information; but it is strictly in confidence for Your Excellency alone, as the knowledge of it would infallibly compromise my informer. If this be true our fleet in the Baltic may have more business than we expected. Ascertain the facts, if possible, and write by the quickest mode; and by more than one.[60]

Despite all his reservations about d'Antraigues and all he had come to learn about him, it does not seem to have crossed Canning's mind that Troubetzkoi's letter, as quoted by d'Antraigues, might be a fabrication. It was, of course, a highly convenient piece of information, and Canning the politician would instantly have realised its usefulness in justifying the attack on Denmark. But even if he were content to believe what it suited him to believe, there is nothing to cast doubt on the sincerity of his belief. Canning asked Gower to obtain confirmation if he could, but he stated that the 'intelligence . . . appears to rest on good authority', and he never wavered in that view. Over the specific case of Denmark, he was willing to concede that Alexander might not have been made aware of Napoleon's plan of employing the Danish fleet for a descent on Ireland and had merely agreed to coerce Denmark into joining a confederacy to enforce the principles of the old maritime neutralities on Britain.[61] This was in no way an expression of scepticism about d'Antraigues's letter (which made no mention of the invasion of Ireland), and two months after its receipt Canning reiterated his belief in its accuracy. On 27 September he again told Gower that 'it was well known that Bonaparte's intention to unite Denmark in the confederacy against this country had been openly avowed [at Tilsit], and had not been resisted by the Emperor [Alexander]'.[62]

THE SECRET INTELLIGENCE AND RUSSIA

If it were true, the secret intelligence which Canning received from d'Antraigues in the early hours of 22 July undermined the assumptions underpinning British policy towards Russia. It suggested that Alexander was not well-disposed towards Britain and liable to revert to his true allegiances if treated with benevolent patience. He might instead be Napoleon's accomplice in a design to destroy the foundations of British power. In principle, this could have prompted pre-emptive British action to seek out and destroy Russian warships wherever they might be found in the Baltic or the Mediterranean. Suspicion and uncorroborated intelligence had been enough to damn the Danes. That was not, however, the line that the British government followed towards Russia. The rules that applied to a minor state like Denmark did not hold good for a great power like Russia, and British policy towards her mighty erstwhile ally remained circumspect.

Circumspect, but not wilfully blind, and over the three or four weeks following receipt of d'Antraigues's letter of 21 July, certain precautions were taken. France's peace treaty with Prussia closed the ports of that country to British trade and shipping, and its published text reached the foreign office in London on 2 August. Canning knew of the terms of the *public* treaty of Tilsit between France and Russia by 12 August. Even though it contained no similar stipulation, Canning was sure that Alexander had agreed to close Russian ports against Britain.[63] The next natural step (it was what Emperor Paul had done in 1801) was that the Russian government might forcibly detain the British merchant ships in its ports and seize the property (and indeed the persons) of British subjects in Russia. Canning also felt some anxiety that the British attack on Denmark had been foreseen at Tilsit, and that the Russian navy might intervene against the British operations at Copenhagen.[64] Precise figures for the number of operational Russian warships in the Baltic in the summer of 1807 are unavailable, but on paper there were 18 Russian ships of the line at Cronstadt or Reval, though it is likely that some of them were unseaworthy or under repair.[65] The Russians would have been crazy to tangle with Gambier's fleet, but even so, the Russian naval forces in the Baltic needed to be kept in mind.

The use of force to meet such threats was not ruled out. When transmitting the secret intelligence from Tilsit to Gower, Canning had added the ominous words: 'if this be true our fleet in the Baltic may have more business than we expected.' The precautions taken were veiled in discretion. When Castlereagh included a reference to Russia in some draft instructions to the two military commanders of the Copenhagen

expedition, Canning reminded him: 'The policy observed by us hitherto
. . . has been to avoid all mention of Russia one way or other in this
business. I think it highly advisable to continue to avoid it.'[66] Instead of
formal instructions, Canning and Mulgrave wrote private letters to
Gambier on 12 and 13 August that Gower might request him to detach
part of his force and send it to Russian waters. If that happened, the
success of the Copenhagen operation was not to be jeopardised, and
Gambier had absolute discretion to refuse.[67] What Canning had in mind
was the appearance of a British squadron off Reval or Cronstadt to lend
weight to Gower's remonstrances in the event of 'any flagrant outrage
against this country', but he did not exclude 'hostile operations' against
the Russians in these circumstances if a show of strength proved
insufficient.[68]

Canning's overriding fear was for Britain's supply of naval stores for
1807 from Russia, and he also acted to accelerate its safe arrival on
British shores. In the summer of 1807, Sir Stephen Shairp, the British
consul-general at St Petersburg, was in Britain while his brother deputised
for him in Russia. On 13 August Shairp was ordered to return
immediately to St Petersburg. Once he was there, he was to take steps to
ensure 'the speedy departure of all British vessels which may still be
loading in the Russian ports but most especially of such as may be loaded
with hemp, iron or other articles required for naval purposes'. On his way
to Russia, Shairp was to stop in the Sound and give Gambier all the
information he possessed about the condition of the Russian Baltic fleet,
the defences of Russia's Baltic ports and the ability of the Russian
government to engage in 'the speedy equipment of any naval force on that
station'.[69]

These measures of precaution were part of a dual-track strategy. Its
second component was conciliation and delay. On 23 July Canning finally
received a report from Gower at Memel enclosing Budberg's offensive note
of 30 June, which had confirmed the conclusion of a separate peace and
offered Alexander's mediation between Britain and France.[70] Just over a
week later, on 1 August, the offer of Russian mediation was repeated in
more formal and solemn terms in a communication from Alopeus to
Canning. The note affirmed Alexander's conviction that Napoleon was
'sincerely desirous of the re-establishment of a maritime peace, upon
equitable and honourable principles'.[71] The British reaction was to stall.

Canning replied to Alopeus on 5 August with an eloquent statement of Britain's desire 'to contribute to the restoration of a general peace, such as may ensure the repose of Europe'. The British government therefore waited with eager anticipation to learn the terms of the peace treaty of Tilsit and a statement of 'those equitable and honourable principles' which Alexander claimed that France wanted to make the basis of a settlement with Britain. Britain would happily accept the offer of mediation in principle, but could not 'return a more specific answer' until this information had been supplied.[72]

Canning instructed Gower to follow the same line. In his dealings with Alexander, Gower was to 'abstain, as much as possible, from the language of reproach', but he was to make it clear that no reply could be given to the Russian mediation offer until the whole treaty of Tilsit had been communicated to Britain. This demand for full disclosure was 'an indispensable preliminary' to a British acceptance of Russian mediation.[73] If the Russians did communicate their peace treaty with France to Gower and it contained no article affecting the rights and interests of Britain, Gower was then to demand the communication of any secret articles that might have been concluded 'or a formal disclaimer of their existence'.[74]

Canning also tried half-heartedly to link the mediation offer to the renewal of the treaty of commerce concluded by Britain and Russia in 1797. The treaty had given a favourable position to British merchants in Russia, but it had expired on 25 March 1807. What was worse, even before that, in January 1807, Alexander had issued a decree, an *ukaz*, introducing a variety of restrictions on British traders operating in Russia, partly at least in retaliation for the British failure to mount a diversion on the European continent.[75] Trade had continued at its normal level through 1807, but the British were naturally anxious to reverse these restrictions and to secure a new treaty of commerce on the same or better terms than the old. The Russians were not averse to negotiating, and Alopeus had been instructed in May 1807 to invite Canning to submit the draft of a new treaty of commerce.[76]

On the face of it, the new situation created by Tilsit did not offer an auspicious moment to pursue this ticklish problem, but that is not how Alopeus saw things. He still hoped that a breach between Britain and Russia could be avoided (how right Canning had been to see him as a friend) and was keen to send the draft home to his government before his existing instructions were countermanded. Canning accordingly gave him a draft treaty, drawn up by Sir Stephen Shairp, and Alopeus sent it to St Petersburg on 31 July recommending it strongly as mutually advantageous to both countries.[77] Canning did not have high hopes that the treaty would get a warm welcome from the Russian government in the current circumstances, but he still instructed Gower to tell Budberg that a 'favourable reception' would do much to counteract the impression that Russia had turned against Britain and would make her more disposed to accept the offer of mediation.[78] Canning warmed to this theme over the following weeks and told Gower that Russian acceptance of the draft treaty of commerce could serve as 'a token of friendship and impartiality'.[79]

This temporising policy was obviously well-advised. Britain had nothing to gain from an unprovoked rupture with Russia – and certainly not before the Danish fleet and the year's supply of Russian naval stores were safely in British hands. But there was more to it than that. Canning (and presumably other ministers) still could not bring themselves to believe that the reconversion of Alexander to sound principles was a hopelessly lost cause. It was impossible to accept the Russian mediation offer unconditionally without asking questions or displaying any signs of wariness. That would be 'like a confession that we are beaten'. The reference not just to peace but specifically to 'a *maritime* peace' in the Russian note was a clear signal that the powers which Britain exercised on the oceans would be on the negotiating table. The mediation offer was really 'only a contrivance to bring the maritime question into discussion with two against one'.

Even so, Canning was desperate to maintain a good understanding with Russia and still saw it as the only hope of Europe's salvation. The eventual acceptance of the Russian offer, 'though probably useless and perhaps in other respects detrimental to us', might be 'a price worth paying' to maintain that good understanding. If Alexander denied that the Tilsit treaty contained secret articles, 'even though we not believe it, [that] might take away the *shame* at least of submitting ourselves to so partial a tribunal'. Above all, Canning looked to a change in Alexander's attitude, that he might 'recover from his intoxication' when separated from his daily intimacy with Napoleon. Perhaps there would be a misunderstanding over one of 'the many abominable stipulations' that had doubtless been agreed at Tilsit.[80] Canning simply could not divest himself of the hope that the Russian government would seek to 'defer, and, if possible, elude the execution of any stipulations hostile to this country into which [Alexander] may have been betrayed in a moment of alarm or infatuation'.[81]

THE SECRET INTELLIGENCE AND DENMARK

In other words, the secret intelligence from Tilsit did not lead to a fundamental change in British policy towards Russia. Canning accepted it as an accurate snapshot of Alexander's state of mind at Tilsit, but not as an expression of his fixed and unalterable intentions. As for Denmark, the secret intelligence from Tilsit had no discernible effect on British policy towards that country. It could hardly have done so – the decision for war had already been taken, and d'Antraigues's letter of 21 July could only reinforce the conviction that the decision was the right one. In the long run, it exerted a strong influence on the way the British government defended its policy towards Denmark against subsequent criticism, but for the moment it could only serve more limited presentational functions. The intelligence from Troubetzkoi merely enabled the foreign secretary to employ somewhat different arguments with the Danish government to justify the British ultimatum. It did not necessitate any alteration in the terms of that ultimatum.

Taylor was already on his way to Copenhagen to replace Garlike. His original instructions of 16 July had been designed to soothe the Danes by explaining the impending arrival of a British fleet in Danish waters as a precautionary measure that would also help Denmark to stand up to French pressure.[82] D'Antraigues's letter prompted Canning to think that Taylor should take a more forceful line, which paved the way for the ultimatum Jackson would soon present. On 22 July Canning wrote to Taylor, summarising the secret intelligence in so far as it related to Denmark, and ordered him to demand from Joachim Bernstorff a formal assurance that no French demand for Denmark's adherence to 'a maritime league against Great Britain' had been made or, if made, that it had been rejected. Taylor was also to make it clear – and here was the sting – that Britain required 'some sufficient security' that such a demand would be rejected in the future.[83]

Taylor was not to say (and indeed at this stage was not even told) what this adequate but unspecified 'security' consisted of – that was Jackson's job. Despite frenetic activity, the task of assembling the warships and troops for the Danish expedition took time, and Jackson's departure for Kiel was put back day by day. It was not until 28 July that Jackson received his instructions in their final form. They were quite unequivocal: it was essential that the Danish fleet – 'upon which Bonaparte is known to calculate as the principal element of a maritime league to be concerted for the destruction of Great Britain' – should not fall into French hands. In the present circumstances, 'the possession of the Danish fleet itself is the only security which in the nature of things can be adequate'. Britain was not unaware of 'the apparent harshness of the demand' and would do all she could 'to soften and reconcile it to the feelings' of Denmark. Jackson was therefore authorised to agree to all stipulations that might do this and was furnished with two draft treaties, one for an alliance between the two countries, and the other for continuing Danish neutrality. Both contained a solemn British assurance that the Danish fleet would be restored at the end of the war, and a promise to pay an annual subsidy of £100,000 a year for its use.

Canning was happy to go along with a number of wheezes to secure Danish cooperation. If the Danes opted for neutrality rather than alliance and feared that compliance with the British demand would hasten a French attack, then Britain would connive in giving the surrender of the fleet the appearance of 'force and restraint' – the overwhelming strength of the British land and sea forces in the Sound would render this charade plausible.[84] Or if they preferred, the Danes could sell their fleet to Britain either permanently or until the peace at whatever price Gambier considered acceptable.[85] There was also the possibility that the Danes would reject the British ultimatum but become willing to negotiate once British troops had actually landed on Zealand. In that event, they were to be offered the same terms as before operations began, provided hostilities had not been 'pushed to the last extremities'.[86] The extensive overseas conquests Britain had made in the present war had placed in her hands the means of gratifying any Danish desires for more extensive colonial possessions – perhaps the Danes might care to avail themselves of the conquered Dutch colony of Surinam in South America?[87] They could also keep their frigates and smaller vessels – only ships of the line were to be handed over.[88]

George Canning. After he assumed office as foreign secretary in March 1807, Canning would be the driving force behind British policy towards Russia and Denmark. (*National Portrait Gallery, London*)

ENTREVUE DES DEUX EMPERÉURS.

The first meeting of the two emperors in mid-river at Tilsit, 25 June 1807. This French print gives the official version. The two emperors exchange a cordial embrace, each accompanied by a boat crammed with his simpering entourage. (© *Copyright the Trustees of The British Museum*)

A British satirical print provides a less pious take on the same event. Alexander finds that his side of the raft is sinking and that the force of Napoleon's embrace has dislodged his crown. The King of Prussia is already in the water and is scrabbling to climb aboard and to retrieve his crown. (© Copyright the Trustees of *The British Museum*)

Lord Granville Leveson Gower. A close friend of Canning, Gower agreed to become ambassador to Russia for a second time at the new foreign secretary's pressing request. Gower derived little pleasure from his mission to Russia in 1807. (*National Portrait Gallery, London*)

King George III. In 1807 George III had been on the throne for almost fifty years. He was Prince Fredrick of Denmark's maternal uncle. In July 1807 he favoured a more moderate policy towards Denmark than the one adopted by his ministers. (*National Portrait Gallery, London*)

Crown Prince Fredrick of Denmark. Although he did not become king as Fredrick VI until 1808, Prince Fredrick had already been *de facto* regent of Denmark for his mentally unstable father for more than twenty years. (*Rosenborg Castle, Copenhagen*)

Robert Stewart, Lord Castlereagh. As war secretary, Castlereagh played the major role in coordinating the naval and military measures taken against Denmark in 1807. (*National Portrait Gallery, London*)

Charles Grey, Lord Howick. As foreign secretary in the Grenville government during the winter of 1806–7, Howick was the first British minister to become alarmed about the risk that the Danish navy might pose to Britain. As the second Earl Grey, he returned to office as prime minister between 1830 and 1834 after a lifetime largely spent in opposition. (*National Portrait Gallery, London*)

A model showing the Danish fleet moored in its central naval base in the heart of Copenhagen. The fleet had been decommissioned and stationary since 1801, but was kept in good repair. (*Royal Danish Naval Museum, Copenhagen*)

A panoramic view of central Copenhagen, painted by Lieutenant George Lawrance of HMS *Centaur* in August 1807. The spires of the city can be seen on the left, and the masts of the Danish fleet to the right of his watercolour. (*Royal Danish Naval Museum, Copenhagen*)

A model of the unimaginatively named 'floating battery no. 1'. It had formed part of the Danish defensive line which fought Nelson in April 1801 and had survived to perform further service in 1807. (*Royal Danish Naval Museum, Copenhagen*)

A model of one of the Danish gunboats that held their own against the smaller vessels of the British fleet in 1807. Without its sails, it would not have looked very different from 'floating battery no. 1', and it is understandable that some British visitors to Copenhagen confused the two types of craft. (*Royal Danish Naval Museum, Copenhagen*)

Francis Jackson. Previously British envoy to Berlin between 1802 and 1806, Jackson was selected by Canning to undertake a special mission to Denmark in 1807 to present the British ultimatum to Prince Fredrick. (*Bristol Art Gallery*)

Lieutenant-General William Schaw Cathcart, Baron Cathcart. An experienced soldier who had first seen action during the American War of Independence, Cathcart was chosen to command the British land forces employed in the Baltic in 1807. (*National Portrait Gallery, London*)

Major-General Sir Arthur Wellesley. As commander of the reserve, Wellesley defeated the Danes in the only pitched battle of the campaign at Køge, and Cathcart later employed him as the army's principal representative in the negotiations for the surrender of Copenhagen. (*National Portrait Gallery, London*)

Admiral Sir James Gambier. As Cathcart's naval counterpart, Gambier ultimately had 65 warships under his command in Danish waters in 1807. In retirement he became the first president of the Church Missionary Society. (*National Portrait Gallery, London*)

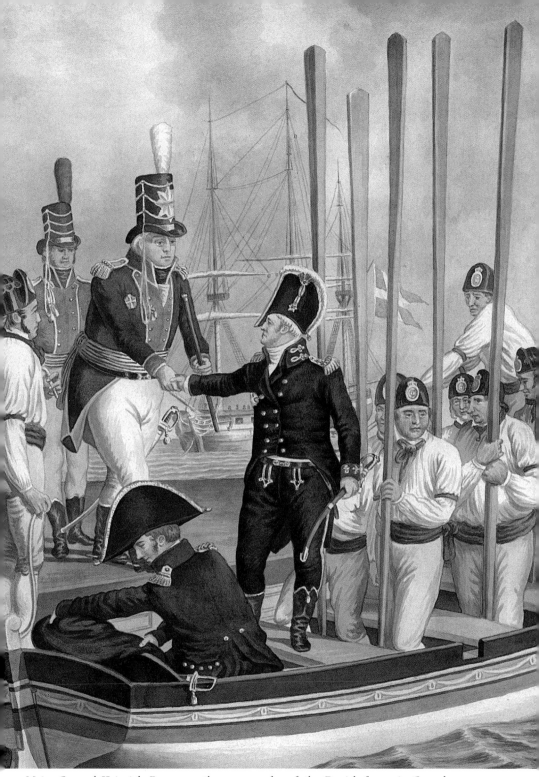

Major-General Heinrich Peymann, the commander of the Danish forces in Copenhagen, shakes hands with Commander Steen Bille, who was in charge of the naval forces in the city under Peymann's overall responsibility. This idealised representation of comradeship bore little relation to reality. (*Owner of the picture: Copenhagen City Museum*)

The sea fort of Trekroner barred the entrance to Copenhagen harbour. This section from Lawrance's watercolour shows an artillery duel between the Danish gunboats to the left of Trekroner and the British advanced squadron to the right of the fort. Swan Mill is visible on the shore behind Trekroner. (*Royal Danish Naval Museum, Copenhagen*)

A rare picture of the sea fort of Prøvesten, which was created in 1802 by sinking three superannuated ships of the line in the shallows in order to deny control of the waters closest to central Copenhagen to a hostile fleet. In August 1807 it was reinforced by 'floating battery no. 1' (visible to the left of Prøvesten) and an armed barge. (*Royal Danish Naval Museum, Copenhagen*)

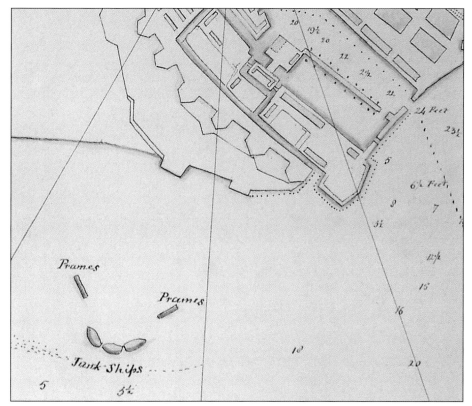

This detail from a chart of the waters around Copenhagen prepared by Edward Strode, the master of HMS *Centaur*, in August 1807, shows the precise position of Prøvesten (which Strode calls 'junk ships'). 'Floating battery no. 1' and the armed barge are described as 'prames'. The naval base where the Danish fleet was moored and the entrance to Copenhagen harbour appear on the upper right of the detail. (*Royal Danish Naval Museum, Copenhagen*)

A view taking in part of central Copenhagen and the countryside to the south of the city. The royal summer palace of Frederiksberg can be seen towards the left on top of a low hill. In 1807 the British forces established artillery batteries on the terraces below the palace. (*Royal Danish Naval Museum, Copenhagen*)

Copenhagen seen from the north on the third and final night of the bombardment (4–5 September 1807). One British naval officer, watching from out to sea, described the bombardment as 'the most tremendous sight that can well be conceived'. (Owner of the picture: Copenhagen City Museum)

William Congreve. Trained as a lawyer, Congreve never practised, and turned his hand to 'inventions'. The rocket named after him was first used on active service during a naval raid on Boulogne in 1806. It was employed again on a larger scale under his personal supervision at Copenhagen in 1807. (*National Portrait Gallery, London*)

Two examples of a 'Congreve rocket'. The upper type was intended to embed itself in buildings, while the lower type was designed to explode just above roof level. Copenhagen is often remembered as the first occasion when this novel weapon of war was employed against a major European city, but only 300 of them were used during the bombardment of Copenhagen, a mere 5 per cent of the 6,000 British projectiles that rained down on the city. They did, however, cause terror and shock, and their impact cannot be measured in purely numerical terms. (*Royal Danish Naval Museum, Copenhagen*)

A view of central Copenhagen during the bombardment. The Church of Our Lady, already in flames, is visible in the centre of the picture. Its spire was a target throughout the bombardment and finally collapsed during the third night. (*Owner of the picture: Copenhagen City Museum*)

One of the major squares in Copenhagen, Kongens Nytorv, during the bombardment. Many of the inhabitants fled to the eastern part of the city on the island of Amager with whatever possessions they could carry in search of safety. (*Owner of the picture: Copenhagen City Museum*)

The British occupying forces removed the entire Danish navy from Copenhagen down to the smallest vessel. Some of the Danish ships, however, were deemed too old or too unseaworthy for the journey to Britain and were destroyed in the dockyard at Copenhagen. Three ships of the line (including one under construction), two frigates and a few smaller vessels suffered this fate. (*Owner of the picture: Copenhagen City Museum*)

British Tars, towing the Danish Fleet into Harbour; – the Broadbottom Leviathan trying to swamp Billy's old Boat, & the little Corsican tottering on the Clouds of

A satirical print by Gilray, published on 1 October 1807, celebrates the British success at Copenhagen. A dinghy called the *Billy Pitt* heads for the coast of Britain, where John Bull adorns the shore singing *Rule Britannia*, foaming tankard in hand. Hawkesbury and Castlereagh are rowing the dinghy, while Canning sits in the stern holding the ropes attached to the Danish navy. In the background, Napoleon hovers in the air in impotent rage. A three-headed sea monster showers the *Billy Pitt* in jets of water entitled 'opposition clamour', 'detraction' and 'envy'. The head to the right is Grenville and the balding, scrawny-necked one in the centre is Howick. (For further information, see Mary Dorothy George, *Catalogue of the Political and Personal Satires Preserved in the Department of Prints and Drawings in the British Museum*, vol. 8, 1801–1810 (London, 1947), plate 10762.)

But all such dodges and sweeteners could not conceal that this was an ultimatum: it would cause 'sincere and painful regret' to Britain if the sword were drawn, but drawn it would be unless the Danes gave way.[89] And Jackson was left in no doubt on the crucial point – 'you will carefully bear in mind that the possession of the Danish fleet is the one main and indispensable object to which the whole of your negotiation is to be directed, and without which no other stipulation or concession can be considered as of any value or importance'. Even if the Danish government agreed to enter into an alliance with Britain, the delivery of the Danish fleet had to take place immediately and without waiting for the formal ratification of the treaty.[90]

By this time, Gambier had sailed from Yarmouth for the Kattegat on 26 July with an imposing but at this stage purely naval force – 16 ships of the line, 7 frigates and 16 smaller vessels. The troops from Britain were already assembling at four embarkation points – Hull, Harwich, the Nore and the Downs – and the first convoys of transports left for Danish waters on 30 July.[91] Efforts to whip up public hostility towards Denmark had been in full swing for some time. As early as the weekend of 11 and 12 July, the newspapers were full of reports that the British expedition bound for Swedish Pomerania had been halted in the Sound by the Danish government. The rumour was entirely without foundation, but in the following week the press and in particular the *Morning Post*, the ministry's leading mouthpiece, continued to speak of the closure of Danish ports to the British flag and of a probable rupture with Denmark. Lady Bessborough reflected the prevailing atmosphere when she wrote to Gower that the Danish fleet was to be employed 'to forward the long threatened invasion, and . . . will sail round the North of Scotland and make a descent on Ireland', and urged her husband to liquidate the family assets in Ireland before it was too late. The departure of Gambier's fleet and the assembly of troops attracted much attention and fevered speculation about its destination. Some thought in terms of a sudden descent on the Pas de Calais or the Low Countries, but most believed – correctly – that an attack on Zealand was intended. On this point at least, Canning and his colleagues remained silent.[92]

The government considered speed to be crucial, and elaborate arrangements were put in place to ensure that the Danes were unable to prepare for war or to drag out the negotiations with Jackson. On 29 July

Canning ordered Taylor to inform Joachim Bernstorff of the ultimatum
Jackson was presenting to Prince Fredrick and to demand that the Danes
should undertake no military preparations on Zealand until the outcome
of the negotiations at Kiel was known. If the Danes failed to abide by this
demand, Taylor was to ask Cathcart to disembark his troops at once.[93] On
the same day, Castlereagh wrote to Cathcart to confirm these instructions
and to add a timetable for action. Jackson would be accompanied to
Tonningen by a ship that would carry on to the coast of Zealand and
inform Gambier and Cathcart of the date of his landing on Danish
territory. If after eight days of his landing, no word had been received
from Jackson, Cathcart was to disembark his army on Zealand but not yet
to engage in active hostilities. But if there were still no word from Jackson
within twelve days of his landing, Cathcart was to initiate operations
against Copenhagen unless the Danish authorities in that city agreed to
the immediate surrender of the Danish fleet.[94]

The cabinet calculated that eight days was enough for Jackson to get
from Tonningen to Kiel, negotiate with Fredrick and communicate the
outcome to Gambier and Cathcart, but some leeway was permitted.
Canning conceded that unforeseen delays might occur or that Fredrick
might have gone from Kiel to Copenhagen, forcing Jackson to chase after
him. Jackson was therefore authorised to extend the timetable by writing
to Gambier and Cathcart, provided the delay did not arise from 'wilful
procrastination or a determined unwillingness to treat on the part of the
Danish government'. If necessary, Jackson was to tell Fredrick and
Christian Bernstorff of the timetable and to say that the military
commanders had orders to consider silence on his part as proof that the
Danes were refusing to negotiate or that he, Jackson, had been placed
under 'constraint'.[95]

On paper, it was all very tidy. In practice, the best-laid plans were
subject – as ever – to the jealousies and resentments within and between
different branches of government. Jackson left London for Yarmouth on
the morning of 31 July with three secretaries or clerks and four servants
or messengers. As in the case of Taylor, the customary practice of
formally taking leave of the king was omitted 'to avoid calling the public
attention to his mission'.[96] When Jackson reached Yarmouth twenty-four
hours later, he found that the warship which he expected would carry
him to Tonningen was not available. Frigates and other smaller warships

were in short supply, and Mulgrave was even unable to meet Gambier's requests for more in full.[97] The admiralty had also dragged its feet over taking steps to provide a ship for Jackson – perhaps out of mere inefficiency, perhaps for the pleasure of irritating the foreign office – and orders to do so only reached Yarmouth the day before his arrival.

To make matters worse, the three admirals at Yarmouth appeared to be at war with each other as much as with the French. Essington, who commanded the warships that were to reinforce Gambier, was sympathetic to Jackson's plight and so too was Douglas, but not so Russel, the only admiral with a sloop at his disposal, who was on board his flagship in the Yarmouth roads. Jackson, noticing that 'there seemed to be some sort of misunderstanding or professional jealousy between these admirals', sent his principal secretary, Edward Nicholas, out to Russel with a letter. Russel was 'already very much out of humour' and told Nicholas, 'I want that sloop and I'll be damned if Mr. Jackson shall have her'. Nicholas returned to shore 'very justly offended', as Jackson put it, 'both on his own account as well as on mine'. There was nothing for it but to travel in the modest gun brig Admiral Douglas could offer, but it was the early evening of 2 August – 36 hours after reaching Yarmouth – before Jackson was able to embark.[98] It was to this muffled drumbeat of farce that Jackson set out on a mission that would determine the question of war or peace.

Chapter 8

THE BRITISH ULTIMATUM TO DENMARK, AUGUST 1807

ADMIRAL GAMBIER IN THE SOUND

Gambier's fleet reached the beacon of Vinga at the western extremity of the archipelago outside Gothenburg on 2 August. In the course of the same afternoon, Gambier detached a squadron under Commodore Keats with the crucial task of isolating Zealand and its adjacent islands from the rest of the Danish state. Keats had four ships of the line, three frigates and ten smaller warships at his disposal, and his orders were to work his way down through the Great Belt, leaving the frigates and sloops at key points on the route. The strategic object was to create a cordon between the islands east of the Great Belt – Zealand, Lolland, Falster and Møn – and the islands to the west of it. Keats's ships were to stop and search all vessels they encountered in the Great Belt and to turn back any that were carrying troops from the west to the east of the Great Belt.[1]

Richard Goodwin Keats was fifty, an able and enterprising officer well regarded by such towering naval figures of his age as Nelson and Earl St Vincent. He was a natural choice to command a semi-independent, subsidiary operation that was absolutely central to the larger success of any attack on Copenhagen, and his services in the Great Belt clinched his promotion to the rank of rear-admiral in October 1807.[2] His task was not without difficulty and called for great qualities of seamanship. The Danes had long tried to keep foreigners in ignorance of the navigational secrets of the Great Belt. A start had been made on breaking down that ignorance by the British fleet sent to the Baltic in 1801. When it returned home, it had chosen to leave the Baltic via the Great Belt rather than the Sound. The British had used the opportunity to take bearings and measure the depth of the waters and to mark the many shoals on their charts.[3]

Despite the work done six years earlier, Keats's squadron often found the going hard. A sloop, the *Mosquito*, led the way sounding the channels and marking the banks and shallows. There were strong underwater currents in the Great Belt, subject to sudden changes of direction, and the ships of the line often had difficulty in keeping to their course. Despite these obstacles, on 9 August Keats reached the southern end of the Great Belt. He took up a position off the island of Møn on his own flagship, the *Ganges*, with the other ships of the line under his command along with the *Mosquito* and two gun-brigs. The British fleet had sailed for the Kattegat uncertain of whether it would find the Danish navy equipped for service or perhaps even at sea, and off Møn Keats could oppose any attempt by Danish naval forces to enter the Great Belt from the south and interfere with the work of the frigates and smaller warships he had left there.[4]

As for Gambier, after detaching Keats's squadron, he headed for the Sound, which he entered on 3 August after a polite exchange of gun salutes with the fortress of Kronborg at Elsinore. The passage of the Sound at its narrowest point between Elsinore and Helsingborg on the Swedish side was a potential hazard, but less so than all those who spoke blithely of 'closing the Sound' imagined. The artillery range of the time did not allow effective fire against vessels steering a course down the centre of the channel separating Elsinore and Helsingborg, and in 1801 the British fleet had forced its way through without being hit by a single cannon ball from the guns of Kronborg.[5]

On 3 August, the point was purely hypothetical. The Danes were still blissfully ignorant of what was afoot and allowed Gambier to pass without any attempt at molestation. Gambier's force remained anchored in the roads of Elsinore for a fortnight, taking no hostile action and merely watching out for any attempt by all or part of the Danish fleet to leave Copenhagen. In reality, of course, there could be no such attempt, since virtually the whole fleet was unrigged. Every year the Danes stationed a single frigate in the Sound as a guard ship during the sailing season, and the only commissioned Danish warship in home waters was a 32-gun frigate, the *Frederiksværn*, which lay at anchor off Elsinore peacefully alongside Gambier's fleet.[6]

On his flagship, the *Prince of Wales*, one of the great beasts of the Royal Navy with its 98 guns, Gambier had space for a large staff and eclipsed the other ships of the line under his command, which all carried 74 or 64 guns. Like Keats, James Gambier had just turned fifty and was an experienced and competent officer. He had distinguished himself for bravery on the 'Glorious First of June' in 1794, when the British had gained a great victory over the French fleet based at Brest, but his subsequent career suggests that he was a cautious commander with a liking and aptitude for administration. The depth of his Christian faith was unusual in the Royal Navy of that time and he was among a small band of evangelical officers. He supported the distribution of religious tracts and the Bible among ordinary seaman, and in retirement he would become the first president of the Church Missionary Society.[7]

The cautious side of Gambier's nature would have been heartened by the strong reinforcements that soon joined him in the Sound. Within six days of dropping anchor in the Elsinore roads, Gambier had been strengthened by another seven ships of the line under Rear-Admiral Essington, though he detached one to reinforce Keats's squadron in the Great Belt. Of the land forces, about 18,000 men had sailed from England by the time Gambier reached Elsinore. The great bulk of these troops arrived at Elsinore in two large convoys of transport vessels on 7 and 8 August. A few more warships and transports reached the Sound over the next week or two, and Gambier ultimately had a total force of about 65 warships under his command (including Keats's detached squadron) – 25 ships of the line and 40 frigates, sloops, bomb-vessels and gun-brigs. There were also a huge number of transport vessels for carrying the troops – 377 in total.[8]

Paradoxically, the troops from England were quicker to arrive than the 8,500 or so soldiers of the King's German Legion who were much closer in Swedish Pomerania. It was not until 3 August, the same day as Gambier anchored off Elsinore, that Lord Cathcart received Castlereagh's orders to re-embark his troops and take command of any land operations on Zealand. For Cathcart, these orders came like a gift from heaven, because his position in Pomerania was an awkward one. On 2 July Gustavus IV had denounced the armistice covering Pomerania, which had been in force since late April 1807. His motives for renewing military operations just as he received news that Emperor Alexander had signed an armistice of his own with the French have defied attempts at rational analysis,[9] but must have been connected with the impending arrival of a British auxiliary corps, which reached the island of Rügen on 8 July.

Things had gone inauspiciously for the legion from the start – it took a week to disembark the cavalry because the shallowness of the water forced most of the transports to anchor two miles from the shore[10] – and when Cathcart arrived on 16 July, he found a situation that was already verging on the catastrophic. When the ten days' notice required for cancelling the armistice elapsed, the French resumed hostilities on 13 July and within days the fortress of Stralsund, the last outpost of the Swedes on the continental mainland, was under siege. Cathcart immediately concluded that it was 'very doubtful' if Stralsund could hold out for long and was concerned for the safety of the men under his command. It was also obvious to him – as to everyone else apart from King Gustavus – that once Russia had made peace with France, a campaign in Pomerania could serve no purpose. Cathcart wrote home asking for fresh instructions, and in the meantime made discreet arrangements for re-embarkation.[11] His language was restrained, but the subtext screamed with a monarch's voice – 'get me out of here!'

His following reports were equally gloomy about the growing strength of the French before Stralsund and the 'apparent ease and indifference' of its defenders.[12] He was evidently delighted by Castlereagh's orders to withdraw his forces from Pomerania. As soon as the three token battalions that had been sent to Stralsund were safely reunited with the rest of his forces on Rügen, Cathcart set sail with most of his staff officers, leaving his second-in-command, Lieutenant-General Lord Rosslyn, to deal with the re-embarkation.[13] Cathcart joined Gambier off Elsinore on 12 August, and the last soldiers of the King's German Legion left Rügen, bound for the Sound, on the following day. By 14 August the first contingent of the troops from Rügen had reached Møn.[14]

As for Stralsund, the fortress surrendered to the French on 20 August. The Swedish army had successfully pulled back to Rügen before the town fell and held out on the island until 7 September, when a convention for their peaceful evacuation to Sweden by the end of the month was signed with the French commander, Marshal Brune.[15] Pomerania was lost, but the King's German Legion had been extricated with minimal losses and was available for the Danish operation. Its three regiments of light dragoons, the only cavalry earmarked for Zealand, were to prove invaluable.

Within three weeks of the first orders being issued on 21 July, Zealand had been isolated by Keats's squadron policing the Great Belt and an overwhelming combination of land and sea forces had been assembled in the Sound. The Danish battle fleet lay unrigged and bottled up in Copenhagen harbour, while the Danish field army was deployed, equally incapable of intervention, to the west of the Great Belt. In purely military terms, it was a logistical triumph, and the credit must rest with the organisational skills and tireless energy of Castlereagh. The means for the military coercion of Denmark lay at anchor off Elsinore like a coiled snake ready to strike. But first the diplomats had to be given their chance to secure the surrender of Denmark by peaceful means.

BROOK TAYLOR AT COPENHAGEN

On the diplomatic front, the main act of the drama was played out at Kiel, but it was preceded by a muddled prologue at Copenhagen. Benjamin Garlike was shattered by his dismissal. He did not see the writing on the wall when he received Canning's stinging reprimands on 23 July. He complained to his protector, Thomas Grenville (now of course in opposition), that Canning's remarks 'were of the most unpleasant sort possible',[16] but they spurred him into a burst of frenzied activity to repair his standing with the foreign secretary. He protested to Canning with sincere self-regard that 'no point of public business was ever one instant neglected under [my] direction',[17] and set about proving the point.

There had been a fresh spate of rumours in late July of an impending French occupation of Holstein with or without Danish consent. They provided Garlike with an opportunity to demonstrate his attention to 'public business'. On his own initiative, he sought from Joachim Bernstorff a renewed assurance that Denmark would reject any French demands to close Tonningen and Husum to the British flag and resist by force any French occupation of Holstein and these ports. A little wearily, Joachim repeated the promises he had made on these points 'during the last two years'.[18] Joachim found Garlike on this occasion 'unusually difficult and stubborn', and had trouble in dissuading him from presenting a formal note setting out his concerns. Joachim ascribed Garlike's conduct to a fear that his government might think him excessively passive.[19] How right he was on that score.

To underline his zeal, Garlike also hinted heavily to Canning that he should receive instructions to go to Kiel to obtain further assurances from

Prince Fredrick himself.[20] Above all, he insisted persistently and at length that no unusual naval preparations were afoot at Copenhagen. The only reason he had sent no reports on the subject of the Danish navy was that 'no alteration has taken place' since Dunbar had visited the dockyard in December 1806.[21] With a cruel ignorance of his impending fate, he ventured to add that 'if I were capable of inattention to such a point you ought not to let me remain here an hour'.[22]

To lend weight to his protestations, it was now that Garlike sent Lieutenant Hanchett's report of 2 May 1807 to Canning and commissioned another from Captain Beauman, whose ship happened to be at Elsinore at the time. In combination, these documents and in particular Beauman's conclusion – 'I may venture to assert there is not at present the shadow of appearance for the equipment of a fleet, as it is impossible it could be hid from the eye of any naval officer' – were a devastating refutation of the claims made by Pembroke and one of the central pillars of the cabinet's decision to strike at Denmark.[23]

They reached Canning on 9 August, far too late to lead to a reconsideration of existing policy. Besides, Pembroke's mistaken report about the state of the Danish navy had only been one of Canning's original reasons for action against Denmark, and since then the secret intelligence from Tilsit had provided him with more. Hanchett and Beauman's reports could have no effect. Nor could these reports – or any other of his exertions – save Garlike. On the evening of 31 July Taylor arrived in Copenhagen bearing Garlike's relegation to Memel in his baggage.

Canning had removed Garlike from his post with great tact, and Garlike's response was equally urbane on the surface. In his official despatch, he feigned gratitude for his temporary appointment at Memel and, adopting the customary formula, asked Canning 'to lay me at the King's feet for this most gracious mark of His Majesty's favour'.[24] His humiliation and bitterness poured forth in the private letters he addressed to Canning and Thomas Grenville. He expressed gratitude to the foreign secretary for 'all the pains you have taken to disguise the real disgrace of my retreat'. But his removal was 'grounded on a supposition of unpardonable neglect', and he owed his appointment to Memel 'so much to my disgrace rather than to favour that I am sure I cannot undertake it with the confidence and cheerfulness which I think indispensable'. He therefore begged Canning to grant him leave of absence or, if that were impossible, his open recall from Copenhagen.[25]

Garlike handed over the ciphers and correspondence of the legation to Taylor on 2 August, but lingered in Copenhagen. The clause in the public peace treaty between France and Prussia closing all Prussian ports to the British flag had become known and furnished the excuse for delaying his departure for Memel. He claimed that this new development made it necessary to await further instructions.[26] In reality, he must have hoped that Canning would allow him to return to England. Either way, he remained a ghostly figure in the background throughout Taylor's brief stay in Copenhagen.

The Bernstorff brothers were as little pleased to see Taylor as Garlike was. Taylor was young and inexperienced, but he still managed to have a past. During his stint as British minister to Hesse-Cassel, he had corresponded – or so at least the French government publicly alleged – with two brothers who claimed to be preparing an attempt on the life of Napoleon.[27] It was likely that France would protest if the Danish government accepted him as Britain's envoy at Copenhagen, and for Joachim Bernstorff his sudden arrival was an unpleasant turn of events. He could not, however, see any reason for refusing Taylor an audience with the king to present his credentials. But what he could do was to refuse to have any official dealings with Taylor until that audience had taken place, and that was the line he took when Garlike introduced Taylor to him on 2 August. This bought some time for obtaining instructions from Kiel. Joachim said he would arrange such an audience for 7 August and suggested that in the meantime he should continue to transact business with Garlike.

At this point, Joachim's evasive manoeuvres broke down. Garlike replied that from that very moment his mission to Copenhagen was suspended and withdrew, leaving Taylor alone with Joachim. Taylor seized the opportunity to bring up the secret intelligence from Tilsit, as Canning had instructed him to do. Napoleon had suggested the formation of a maritime league against Britain to Alexander, he declared, and had presented Denmark's adherence to this league as a certainty. Had any such proposal been made to the Danish government? Joachim laughed off the question. No suggestion of this kind had been made to Denmark by France or any other power. He brushed aside Taylor's objections that this was more than 'a mere idle rumour', and expressed surprise that the British cabinet was so prone to believe every report that cast doubt on Denmark's determination to maintain 'the most perfect neutrality'.[28]

And that was it. The interview was over. Taylor never got a chance to carry out his elaborate instructions explaining the presence of a British fleet in the Sound or to have another meeting with Joachim until 11 August, when the main drama at Kiel was already over. Nor was he ever able to present his credentials to the Danish king. The audience on 7 August was postponed on a transparently specious pretext. Christian Bernstorff and Prince Fredrick were angered by the embarrassment with France that Taylor's appointment would cause, but shared Joachim's view that it was impossible to refuse to receive him.[29] Joachim blocked the audience on his own initiative, largely because he thought that would enable him to talk to Garlike instead. His personal distaste for Taylor was probably another factor – his dislike for the new British envoy oozes from the pages of every report to his brother. Garlike, however, evaded Joachim's attempts to see him, and the end result was that there were no discussions at all between Joachim and any British representative between 2 and 11 August.[30] A curious state of affairs as a great British armada gathered in the Sound.

As a diplomatic holding operation for Jackson's mission to Kiel, Taylor's stay in Copenhagen was a wash-out, but Taylor was able to provide Gambier with useful information about the military situation on Zealand. On 2 August he sent Gambier a copy of Beauman's report on the Danish navy.[31] At a stroke, this removed what must have been Gambier's main anxiety – the risk of encountering fully equipped Danish ships of the line at sea. Taylor was also able to report on 8 August that there was not yet 'the slightest appearance' of military or naval preparations for the defence of Copenhagen itself.[32]

FRANCIS JACKSON AT KIEL

After the obstacles that had delayed his departure from Yarmouth, a fair wind carried Jackson quickly across the North Sea and he reached Tonningen around midday on 5 August. Jackson is at the centre of our story for the nine days he remained on Danish soil. What sort of a man was he? One young British diplomat at Memel claimed that 'all reports' held Jackson to be 'a vulgar, disagreeable man'.[33] That may be so, but what is certain is that he was full of himself. Jackson didn't do laconic and he left a mass of written material behind him – not only his private and official correspondence but also a long memoir written in October 1807 in his own hand to justify his conduct in Denmark. We can deduce from its 400 pages that he was determined to vindicate his own actions down to the smallest detail and quick to find fault in others. Thornton, Taylor, Cathcart and even Canning all felt the lash of his pen.

As soon as he landed at Tonningen, Jackson sent his secretary overland to Elsinore with letters for Gambier and Cathcart, informing them of his arrival and asking them to calculate the eight days allowed for the success or failure of his negotiations from 6 a.m. on 6 August. For his own part, he set off the same evening for Kiel, where he arrived at 10 p.m. on 6 August. Despite the lateness of the hour, he wrote at once to Christian Bernstorff to say that he was charged with a commission of the greatest importance from his government and to request both an interview with the foreign minister and a subsequent audience with Prince Fredrick. Christian replied the next morning, agreeing to see Jackson, and they met at 11.30 a.m. on 7 August.[34]

It is difficult to assess how far Christian Bernstorff was prepared for the storm about to break over his head or how he viewed Denmark's position in general at that time. In their conversations with Jackson, both he and Fredrick dismissed the very idea that the French might move into Holstein and Schleswig on the grounds that this would throw the most important parts of the Danish monarchy – Zealand, Norway and the Danish colonies – into the arms of Britain. This was play-acting. The Danish envoy at Hamburg sent the same reports and rumours to Kiel that Thornton was transmitting to London.[35] Fredrick and Christian knew that the French threat was real, but they did not regard it as immediate. They hoped the Russian mediation might bring about a general European peace or would at least delay the execution of French measures against Holstein and Schleswig.[36] In the meantime, there was nothing to be gained by admitting that such measures were on the cards.

When and if the blow fell, the Danes expected it to come from the south. They were less prepared psychologically for a British attack. From a Danish perspective, there was no crisis in relations between the two countries, no acute dispute that might lead to armed conflict, and they were slow to react to the danger signals. In London, Rist was both deceived and self-deceiving. He had not seen Canning since their falling out in early June, but he was so perturbed by the anti-Danish tone of the ministerial press that he steeled himself to call at the foreign office on 14 July to discover what was going on. Canning was unavailable (no surprise perhaps), but Rist was able to see Fitzharris, who conveyed the impression that the fleet assembling in the North Sea was intended to observe the movements of France and Russia in the Baltic and that Britain would act with all possible consideration towards Denmark.[37] It was a tradition among his descendants that Fitzharris found the lies he had been obliged to tell Rist so distasteful that he left the government.[38] Unlike many family traditions, this one may be true: Fitzharris resigned as under-secretary at the foreign office just over a month later.[39]

But there was more to it than deliberate deception. Rist also proved astonishingly unwilling to believe that an attack on Denmark was in preparation. His reports for the second half of July are full of detail on the troops and ships that were being assembled and on the rumours that Denmark was the intended target of the forthcoming British expedition. But he clung to the hope that it was destined for northern France or the Low Countries or would only be used in the Baltic in the event of a breach with Russia.[40] It was not before early August that the scales dropped from his eyes and he admitted the fault of having been unable to persuade himself that Britain had been planning such 'an atrocity' as an attack on Zealand.[41]

Rist was not alone. After he had seen Garlike and Taylor on 3 August, Joachim Bernstorff learnt in the course of the afternoon that Gambier's fleet had anchored off Elsinore. The report he wrote to his brother at ten o'clock that night gives no impression of immediate alarm. The tone was petulant rather than frightened. He was irked that the British had adopted such a threatening posture towards Denmark before the eyes of all Europe, and thought it 'an extremely ill-considered measure'. But he professed himself unable to fathom its purpose.[42] Prince Fredrick also reacted with remarkable calm. On 7 August he wrote to General Peymann, the military commander of Copenhagen and Kronborg, and ordered him to strengthen the batteries protecting both places. But Fredrick emphasised that he did not believe Denmark had anything to fear from the British. Vigilance yes, but Peymann should remember that 'we are not at war with England and do not expect to be'.[43]

There is some substance in Jackson's accusation that 'the appearance of the fleet in the Kattegat had not even created the sensation which it ought in reason and common sense to have done'.[44] But Christian Bernstorff was more perturbed than his master and than his brother. In a despatch he wrote to Rist on the morning of 7 August, just hours before he met Jackson, he admitted that the arrival of a British fleet in Danish waters had placed Denmark in 'an extraordinary and difficult position'. He had expected from the first that Tilsit would give rise to 'embarrassments of more than one kind', but not that 'the first disagreement, the first mortification' would be caused by Britain. It might be that the 'peevish credulity' of British ministers had made them the dupes of ill-founded rumours. Perhaps it was no worse than that. But Christian conceded the alternative possibility – that the British were seeking a quarrel with Denmark so as to seize the island of Zealand and use it as a base for a war in the Baltic.[45] He did not therefore meet Jackson with an entirely unsuspecting and complacent mind.

There are some contradictions between Jackson's accounts of his conversations with Christian Bernstorff and Fredrick and what the Danish sources say. It seems pretty clear from the Danish material that Jackson adopted a strategy of indirect approach and held back his central demand, the surrender of the Danish fleet, until late in the day – without, of course, admitting this in his reports to Canning.[46] This makes for an occasionally murky picture, but we still have a vivid portrait of a series of extraordinary encounters.

The waves ran high during Jackson's first two-hour interview with Christian Bernstorff on 7 August. Jackson claims he 'remained calm and temperate' since if he had 'given way in the manner Count Bernstorff did to passion and reproach, our meeting would have exhibited a scene for a mad house rather than for a statesman's closet'. But as Jackson also tells us that he resented the absence of 'that decorum which as the representative of the most powerful party I was most entitled to expect at his hands', we may perhaps take this assertion of self-possession with a pinch of salt.

As he had been instructed to do, Jackson rehearsed British grievances and the suspicions of Danish hostility that they had prompted – Danish protests at the British Orders in Council, Rist's tone in his letters to Canning and the alleged Danish naval preparations at Copenhagen.

Christian responded by denouncing the oppressive and arbitrary treatment that neutral trade received at British hands and by laughing off the suggestion of naval preparations.

This was merely a preliminary skirmish. Jackson began to approach the heart of the matter when he claimed that Napoleon intended to close the ports of Denmark to the British flag and to employ the resources of Denmark against Britain. It was impossible to believe that Denmark would be able to resist his demands, and Britain therefore had to take steps to obtain 'an infallible pledge' that the Danish fleet would not fall into the enemy's hands. At his point, according to Jackson, Christian jumped from his seat and 'moved in hasty strides from one end to the other of a large room, holding his hand against his forehead, with an impetuosity of steps and gesticulation that upon any less important occasion would have afforded an ample subject of ridicule'.

Christian's account of the conversation confirms the demand for a pledge, but gives no indication that Jackson directly linked it to the Danish navy. Indeed, it states quite categorically that Jackson did not specify the nature of the pledge and merely calls it 'a necessary pledge for [Britain's] security'. It is likely that Christian's testimony is more reliable on this point as Jackson only intended to present the British ultimatum in its full extent when he saw Prince Fredrick. At the end of this rancorous and lengthy meeting Jackson repeated his request for an audience with the prince, and Christian said that he would inform Jackson of the prince's wishes on this point.[47]

The interview left both men with much food for thought. Christian went straight to Fredrick and found him in a state of great agitation over whether he should or should not go to Copenhagen to give instructions on the spot for the defence of Zealand. Either way, he was willing to see Jackson the following day, but the next step was less certain. Christian was inclined to think that Fredrick ought to go to Copenhagen, while he (Christian) entered into further discussions with Jackson. He would play for time and try to postpone the execution of any actual acts of violence until it was clear whether the British government would accept the Russian mediation offer and open the way for a general European peace settlement. These were precisely the sort of delaying tactics that Canning's eight-day deadline was designed to avoid. Christian was not optimistic that this approach would work. Even though he did not know yet of this deadline, he doubted that Jackson was authorised to grant such a reprieve, but he could think of no other way of proceeding.[48]

After his stormy interview with Christian Bernstorff and a largely sleepless night, Jackson received letters from Canning and Thornton on the morning of 8 August. Canning's letter was dated 2 August and contained a veiled but savage rebuke: 'I hear that you are at Yarmouth, refusing to embark.' Canning was sure the Admiralty was at fault for the absence of any vessel other than a gun-brig, but observed with a drip of acid 'at a moment such as this, I can hardly imagine that any person as zealous for the public service as yourself would decline any conveyance, however incommodious'. It was essential that Jackson should press on to Kiel and present his ultimatum to the Danish government without delay – 'for God's sake, embark and lose no time'.[49]

It might have been expected that Thornton would have urged an equally robust line, but in fact he had subtly changed his tune. He still expected a French occupation of Holstein and Schleswig, but thought it would be delayed until more troops arrived around Hamburg in mid to late August and perhaps also until the British response to the Russian mediation offer was known.[50] Jackson had written to Thornton on his arrival at Tonningen to inform him confidentially of the purpose of his mission, and Thornton's reply from Altona gave him a jolt. Far from approving of the British ultimatum, Thornton deplored the nature of 'the terrible pledge' demanded of the Danes, the eight-day time limit placed on Jackson's negotiations and his lack of discretionary powers.

If he had possessed such discretion, Thornton would have implored him to hold back from demanding the surrender of the Danish fleet and to seek to clothe it in the appearance of a junction of naval forces. He was convinced the French would ultimately invade Holstein and did not want the blame for striking the first blow against Danish neutrality to fall on Britain. It was inconceivable that Denmark would yield to the British demand without some amelioration of its rigour and, if it were pursued, 'it is impossible that . . . we can have in Denmark any other than a bitter and implacable enemy, though subdued, eager to invite our national enemy to drive us out of the country at any risk'.

He claimed that what he himself had proposed in his private letter to Canning on 31 July was to send a substantial force to the Baltic that could assist in the defence of the Danish islands in the event of a French attack. This force would also have been able to compel the Danes to cooperate, if necessary, but he was 'entirely persuaded that [British assistance] would have been gratefully accepted in the actual event of a French invasion of Holstein'. He was sure France would never have succeeded in forcing Denmark into an alliance against Britain, 'and certainly never, while we have so great a force present in the Baltic'. But 'the positive, naked demand' for the surrender of the fleet was a different matter – it 'must ruin all'.[51]

Thornton was not being entirely frank when he implied that there was no discrepancy between his letter of 1 July and his current letter to Jackson. He was either deceiving himself or he was deceiving Jackson. His earlier letter had manifested a far less trusting attitude towards the Danish government and a far greater readiness to take unilateral action against Denmark.[52] What he now wrote to Jackson was suffused with moderation and restraint, and it prompted Lord Malmesbury to remark that Thornton had 'acted more like a Dane than an Englishman'. Malmesbury thought it a great injustice that Jackson 'got no credit' in London, while Thornton was praised because of Jackson's 'forbearance' in not showing this letter to anyone – except, of course, for his patron, Malmesbury.[53] There is some force in this observation – Canning would doubtless have been much enraged if Thornton's letter to Jackson had fallen into his hands.

Jackson already had other reasons for doubt. Since his arrival at Tonningen, he had ascertained both from direct observation and from what he was told by various subordinate British agents on the spot – like the officer in charge of recruitment for the King's German Legion – that many of the fears and assumptions entertained in London were false. The French had not moved into Holstein, and there was not the slightest sign that the Danes were in league with the French to take up arms against Britain. The Danish troops on the Jutlandic peninsula 'were all quiet in their respective garrisons and cantonments' and had made no move to cross onto Funen or Zealand. Above all, it was clear that the Danish navy at Copenhagen was not being fitted out for sea. In his knockabout interview with Christian Bernstorff, Jackson had been savaged on this point and had concluded that this argument was not 'tenable ground' and 'could not be too soon abandoned'. All Jackson had left was the perfectly justifiable conviction that France intended at some point to move against Denmark, though even here he acknowledged to himself that the French forces would then face the problem of how they were to cross the Great Belt to Zealand.

Against the background of these misgivings, the first thought that occurred 'very forcibly' to Jackson on reading Thornton's letters was whether he should carry out his instructions to the full, whether 'it was advisable to proceed in my original intention and persist in the demand of the navy'.[54] That was all very well, but Jackson also appreciated that his career was on the line. He had written to Canning from Yarmouth on 1 August acknowledging the importance of his mission and the confidence that had been placed in him. 'If I fail in doing justice to the ample and excellent instructions you have given me, I will never ask you to give me any more.' The letter from Canning, which he received at the same time as Thornton's, 'showed how little mercy, the slightest hesitation, the least even involuntary or unavoidable delay would meet with'. The outcome of Jackson's ruminations could hardly be in doubt – he chose to obey his orders.[55] But when he saw Prince Fredrick later that day, he took Thornton's advice to the extent of not stating explicitly that Britain demanded the surrender of the Danish fleet.

Jackson got his audience with Fredrick at four in the afternoon on 8 August. He was struck by the soldierly simplicity of the prince's antechamber and by the absence of 'the appearance of art or preparation' in his conversation – 'his sentences were often abrupt and unconnected: nothing of method or of elegance appeared in what he said'. There was, however, a certain artifice in the prince's remarks. He deployed all the arguments that Christian Bernstorff had already used. The British government was misled by false rumours, he said, there was no reason to expect a French invasion of Holstein and Schleswig. Above all, he laid great weight on the probability that the Russian mediation offer would rapidly lead to a general peace settlement, and urged Jackson to suspend his negotiations with Denmark until he could obtain new instructions from London.

All this sounds perfectly plausible, but it is less clear what Jackson actually said to the prince. Jackson had deliberately held back the outright demand for the surrender of the Danish fleet until he saw Fredrick. In his report to Canning, he claimed that he stopped talking about a 'pledge' and did now explicitly demand 'the immediate junction of the Danish fleet to that of His Majesty' (not quite the same as the surrender of the fleet, but getting close). According to Fredrick, however, Jackson did not even raise the question of 'a pledge' during the audience. Fredrick was not perhaps the sharpest blade in the knife rack, but it is difficult to see how he could have missed the point if Jackson had really been as explicit as he claimed. Perhaps Fredrick was misled by Jackson's additional remark that the form and appearance given to this 'junction' of British and Danish naval forces was for the Danes to decide.

There is no real discrepancy over how the meeting ended – Jackson employed the language of menace and Fredrick threw him out. The way Jackson tells it, he reiterated his demand over the Danish fleet and said that, if Fredrick refused, the British warships and troops assembled around Zealand would be used to enforce it. Fredrick puts it slightly differently: Jackson told him that Denmark had to choose between alliance or war with Britain. Either way, Fredrick 'assumed an angry look' and told Jackson that he was unwilling, 'as a prince and as a general', to listen to threats and that Jackson would have to present his proposals to Christian Bernstorff. Jackson tried to mitigate the impression he had created 'by saying that I should consider it as the happiest moment of my life could I be the successful instrument of restoring perfect harmony between our two countries. With these words I looked for his bow of dismissal, received it and retired.'[56]

His conversation with Jackson convinced Fredrick that his immediate departure for Copenhagen was indispensably necessary, and he set off the same night to organise the defences of Zealand. Jackson had suspected that the prince might try to give him the slip and had placed the palace under observation, but Fredrick got away undetected. The next morning, Christian Bernstorff coolly informed Jackson by letter that 'circumstances of the moment' had obliged Fredrick to depart for Copenhagen, but that he, Christian, was authorised to listen to Jackson's proposals.[57]

This may sound as if he hoped he could detain Jackson in Kiel with endless negotiations, but in fact Christian had no such expectation. He was sure that Jackson would chase after Prince Fredrick and that if there were any further negotiations, they would be conducted by his brother Joachim in Copenhagen. In that case, he advised Joachim to try and use Garlike as a channel for urging moderation on Jackson. But Christian was clutching at straws and he knew it. As he wrote to his brother: 'The more I consider the difficulty of our position the less I can see a way out of it.

A war with England would be ruinous for us and . . . any compliance with her demands must infallibly lead to a breach with France.'[58] He knew that the sands of time were running out for Danish neutrality.

This fatalism somehow transmitted itself to Jackson when the two met for the last time on 9 August. Jackson thought he saw in Christian 'the first decisive symptom of a determination to abide by the consequences of resistance'. When Christian made it clear that he was authorised to negotiate with Jackson but not to conclude an agreement without reference to Prince Fredrick, Jackson divulged for the first time the deadline for the success or failure of his mission. Military operations would commence on 14 August, he said, if no amicable arrangement had been reached before that time. It was therefore impossible for him to remain at Kiel since Christian did not have the power to take a final decision, and he would follow Fredrick to Copenhagen in a last-ditch effort to prevent 'the shedding of blood'.

It was also at this final interview that Jackson divulged that the pledge he had so often referred to was, in Christian's words, 'nothing less than the delivery of our fleet' to Britain. The tone in which Christian passed this piece of information on to his brother shows that this was the first time that Christian heard the crucial element in the British ultimatum. There was not really much more to say, and Jackson took his leave.[59]

THE LAST ACT IN COPENHAGEN

Fredrick reached Copenhagen at midday on 11 August and immediately summoned a conclave of the leading military and naval commanders, ministers and senior officials in Copenhagen. He stayed in Copenhagen for less than 24 hours, but issued a stream of orders for the defence of Copenhagen and Zealand before he left. Apart from that, his main concern was to make sure that his aged and deranged father, Christian VII, did not fall into British hands. The old king was dislodged from his summer residence outside Copenhagen, Frederiksberg Castle, and set off with his son during the night of 11 to 12 August. Fredrick had intended that the Danish crown jewels should be brought to Holstein, but the risk of taking them over the Great Belt was deemed excessive and they were concealed in a coffin in Sorø church in western Zealand. They were never found by the British.[60]

Fredrick and his father reached Korsør, the main port for the passage across the Great Belt to Nyborg on Funen, in the mid-afternoon of 12 August. They crossed the same evening on an ordinary civilian sloop that plied the route, but had an anxious moment when they were detained by a British warship for 45 minutes. Fredrick hid in the bowels of the ship, while the king was successfully passed off as an ailing Swedish baron on his way to take the waters in Germany.[61] The subterfuge probably made little difference. The British cabinet had decided when Gambier was sent to Danish waters that it would be 'indecorous' to obstruct the passage of George III's nephew, as Prince Fredrick was, 'from one part of his dominions to another', but the necessary instructions to this effect had not reached Keats in the Great Belt.[62] Even so, it is unlikely that a British naval commander would have seized the king and crown prince of Denmark before war had broken out. It was only on 14 August, the day fixed for the commencement of hostilities, that Keats asked Gambier how Fredrick should be treated 'in case of intercepting him'.[63]

Fredrick was back in Kiel by the evening of 15 August, while his father was lodged at Kolding in central Jutland. All members of the council of state and the most senior officials and some of the clerks in the various ministries were evacuated to Kolding, and left Copenhagen on 12 and 13 August. The greater part of the diplomatic corps also decamped for Kolding. Only Joachim Bernstorff remained for the time being to receive Jackson on his arrival in Copenhagen.[64] Before that, he had a second and last encounter with Brook Taylor.

Taylor had instructions from Canning, as soon as the British fleet and expeditionary corps had arrived in the Sound and he knew that Jackson had landed at Tonningen, to tell Joachim that Britain would not tolerate any Danish military preparations on Zealand before the negotiations at Kiel were concluded.[65] On 10 August the limited precautionary measures that Fredrick had ordered on 7 August began to be implemented, and Taylor requested an interview with Joachim. Even though Taylor had still not had his audience with the king, Joachim decided to see him and they met early in the afternoon of the following day. By now, Joachim was aware of the nature of the British ultimatum, which he described to Taylor as 'the most extraordinary and most insulting that had ever been proposed by one nation to another'. That set the tone, and the interview largely consisted of mutual recrimination and point-scoring. It ended when Taylor demanded that the Danes immediately suspend their military preparations at Copenhagen and Joachim refused.

Taylor withdrew with the whole of the British mission to the *Cambrian* frigate off Copenhagen the following day.[66] Canning had intended that a Danish refusal to desist from military preparations at Copenhagen should be followed at once by the disembarkation of the British army onto Zealand, even if the eight-day deadline for the completion of Jackson's mission had not elapsed, but that proved impossible. Cathcart did not even arrive until 12 August, and the preparations for a landing were not complete until a couple of days after that.[67] From start to finish, Taylor's mission to Copenhagen had achieved virtually nothing. That did not prevent a pat on the head from Canning, who wrote to him a month later to express King George's 'gracious approbation of your conduct'.[68]

As for Jackson, his final days in Denmark were equally futile. He had no success in his attempts to catch up with the crown prince. Fredrick held most of the cards. He had a head start and he gave instructions that Jackson should be detained for two hours at each posting station when he stopped to change the horses for his carriage.[69] Jackson's only chance of overtaking the prince was by sea and a couple of smaller British warships had been stationed in the bay of Kiel throughout the summer. Their original purpose was to accelerate the delivery of despatches between London and Memel, which passed across the North Sea and then overland from Tonningen to Kiel, but they were available to carry Jackson to Copenhagen. He embarked on the *Fearless* gun-brig late in the evening of 9 August. The wind and the weather were against him, and he eventually abandoned the attempt and returned to Kiel the next day and set off in Fredrick's footsteps. He was now hopelessly delayed and by the time he reached Copenhagen at 5 p.m. on 13 August, Fredrick had already been and gone.[70]

Jackson was furious to find that Taylor had departed and was unavailable to brief him on the situation in Copenhagen. When he went to the inn where Taylor had been staying, Jackson was told 'by the master of the house that Mr Taylor . . . had absconded the preceding day, without giving any notice whatever of his intention, leaving all his clothes and other effects in the rooms which he had occupied'. Undaunted by this 'curious specimen of diplomatic courage', Jackson announced his arrival to Joachim Bernstorff, who saw him at 8 p.m. for the final act of the diplomatic prelude to war.[71]

There was no prospect of a positive outcome from their interview. While in Copenhagen, Fredrick had authorised Joachim to promise, if necessary in writing, that Denmark would not shut her ports to the British flag. He could even, as a last resort, agree to suspend the military preparations at Copenhagen, if the British would also refrain from hostilities, until the outcome of the Russian attempt at mediation was known.[72] The chasm between such limited concessions and the surrender of the Danish fleet was unbridgeable. By now, Jackson had just about had enough. He was justifiably angry that he had chased Fredrick to Copenhagen only to find him gone and by the way the Danish government had played him for a fool by 'referring me backwards and forwards to different places for a decision'.

Now he wanted an unequivocal answer. For Jackson, the surrender of the Danish fleet was the only question that mattered. When he asked Joachim if he was authorised to conclude an agreement on this basis, Joachim could only admit that he was not in a position to do so. That brought down the curtain. Jackson said he had no choice in that case but to request a passport so that he could leave Danish territory. Joachim remarked, 'then you are come to declare war against us; you should at least inform me at what period hostilities will commence'. Jackson merely replied that this was a question for the military commanders. He went aboard the *Cambrian* the same night.[73] Negotiations were at an end, and the outcome now rested on the test of war.

THE EMPEROR AT SAINT-CLOUD

When Napoleon left Tilsit on 9 July 1807, it was the hour of his greatest triumph. He bestrode the European continent like a colossus. He remained three days at Königsberg, and then went straight to Dresden, where he arrived on 17 July after spending 100 hours without leaving his carriage. After some days at Dresden, he was on the road again and reached Paris in the early hours of 27 July. He had been absent for ten months – ten months in which he had crushed Prussia and brought Russia to terms. After that, he spent over a fortnight at the palace of Saint-Cloud, his main summer residence a few kilometres outside the capital. The heat was stifling around Paris in the first half of August 1807, but nothing could enervate his restless spirit or stem the stream of orders on the most diverse subjects that poured from his secretariat.

His immediate concern was to gather in the remaining fruits of victory. At Königsberg, his negotiator signed a convention with the Prussians regulating the evacuation of their country. On paper, it was all very neat. The French troops were to be pulled back in stages to the Elbe by 1 November 1807. In practice, their withdrawal depended on the payment of indemnities, and when the French presented the final bill, the amount came to more than seven times the sum the Prussians had anticipated. They could not pay. As a result, French troops only evacuated the city of Königsberg, while the *Grande Armée* remained deployed across the remaining territories of the truncated Prussian kingdom – a guarantor of Prussia's continuing subjugation and a potent reminder to both Russia and Austria of French military might. At Dresden, Napoleon dictated a constitution for the new duchy of Warsaw, which among other things abolished serfdom in its lands, and signed a convention with the king of Saxony. That lucky sovereign was granted the duchy of Warsaw and agreed that 30,000 French troops should be stationed on its territory.[74]

Napoleon had no intention of loosening his grip on the lands he had conquered since the battle of Jena in October 1806. Nor was he inclined to abide patiently by the timetable agreed at Tilsit when it came to enforcing his continental system on the neutral powers of Europe. The secret treaty of alliance at Tilsit stipulated that if Britain had not accepted peace under Russian mediation by 1 December 1807, then France and Russia would in concert and simultaneously demand that Denmark, Portugal and Sweden should close their ports to the British and declare war on Britain.[75] The Swedes were still allied to Britain and at war with France, so nothing could be done about them for the moment, but the two neutral states of Denmark and Portugal were a different matter.

Napoleon paid no heed to the 1 December deadline or the idea of acting in concert with Russia. At Dresden on 19 July he ordered that an ultimatum be presented to the Portuguese government, insisting on the closure of their ports to Britain by 1 September on pain of an invasion of their country by France and her Spanish allies. Ten days later, at Saint-Cloud, he issued the first instructions for assembling a French army of 20,000 men (later increased to 30,000) under General Junot at Bayonne for the conquest of Portugal. On 29 July the Portuguese ambassador in Paris was informed of the demands that would be presented to his government, and a courier left Paris for Lisbon the following day with a note containing the French ultimatum. Its demands were savage. Not only was Portugal required to close her ports and declare war against Britain. She was also to seize British citizens and merchandise on Portuguese territory and to 'unite her squadrons with those of the continent'.[76]

Napoleon moved somewhat more slowly in the case of Denmark, and it was only on 31 July that he issued the first instructions designed to bring Denmark to heel. The Danes were to be softened up by drawing attention to Napoleon's displeasure at the continuing flow of British merchandise and correspondence through Tonningen and Husum and their failure to prevent the entry of British warships into the Baltic. But the cardinal point that he wanted his foreign minister, Charles-Maurice de Talleyrand, to raise with the Danish envoy in Paris, Christopher Vilhelm Dreyer, was what Denmark intended to do if Britain refused to make peace on reasonable terms. In that event, it was 'possible' that all the ports of the continent would be closed to the British flag and that the continental powers would declare war on Britain. And if that happened, despite the emperor's desire to treat Denmark with consideration, she would have to choose between war with Britain and war with France. There was no reference at all to the Danish navy.[77] Compared with Portugal, the approach was less brutal and the timetable less hurried, but the bottom line was the same.

When Talleyrand saw Dreyer on 6 August, he watered down Napoleon's communication by omitting any direct threat of war. The emperor, he said, was now in agreement with the main powers of Europe to prevent all contact between Britain and the continent as the only means of forcing the British to make peace. What did the Danish government intend to do in these circumstances? The closest he came to menace was when he claimed that the risk of British reprisals was hypothetical, whereas the dangers Denmark would face if she failed to adhere to the measures adopted by the other continental powers against Britain were all too real – a remark that Dreyer chose to interpret as reasoned argument rather than a threat.[78] Talleyrand (or the Prince of Benevento, to use the grand title Napoleon had conferred on him as a reward for his services) reinforced the omission a week later by telling Dreyer off the record that he did not foresee any danger to Denmark 'at the present time' provided the Danes responded with their 'usual wisdom and moderation' when rejecting Napoleon's demands.[79]

Talleyrand's behaviour is puzzling. He was notoriously urbane, devious and slippery – Napoleon memorably described him as 'shit in a silk stocking' – and it is often difficult to fathom what he was up to. The departure of Gambier's fleet for northern waters was known in Paris at this time, and maybe he thought it portended British measures against Denmark that would of themselves bring the Danes into the French camp without any offensive pressure on his part.[80] It is also possible that Talleyrand was simply disinclined to do Napoleon's dirty work just as he was on the point of leaving his service. He had acted as Napoleon's foreign minister ever since 1799. Now he had reached the conclusion – belatedly and imperfectly, some might say – that he no longer wanted to bear responsibility for the emperor's inability to set any limits to his ambition, and at Tilsit he had told him that he wished to leave the foreign ministry. He submitted his formal resignation at Saint-Cloud on 9 August.[81] His replacement was another member of the old nobility, Jean-Baptiste Nompère, Count de Champagny, a former naval officer before the revolution and an old school friend of d'Antraigues – which goes to show how small the world can be.

Whatever Talleyrand's motives, the upshot was that Dreyer was left with the impression that there was not all that much to worry about. He was even tempted to believe that the French approaches to Denmark and Portugal (he had learnt from the Portuguese ambassador in Paris of the impending ultimatum in Lisbon) were intended to become known in London and to put pressure on the British to accept the Russian mediation.[82] If his own account is to be believed, Dreyer even felt able to strike a high tone with Talleyrand at their formal interview on 6 August. Dreyer had a long career behind him.[83] He had been in Paris since 1796 and seems to have been held in a certain personal regard both by Talleyrand and even by the emperor himself. He was seventy now, independent-minded and prone to act on his own initiative. This occasion proved a case in point. He told Talleyrand quite bluntly that the danger that France posed to Denmark's continental possessions was merely 'transient'. Britain in contrast could destroy Denmark as a maritime and commercial power, and she would never, could never, take unprovoked measures that would prompt an open breach with the British.[84] Robust, not to say defiant, words – if only Rist and Joachim Bernstorff could have given a similar impression in their discussions with Canning and Garlike.

Not that any of it mattered. The negotiation that Talleyrand had initiated when he saw Dreyer on 6 August proved entirely abortive because it was overtaken by events. By mid-August Paris was abuzz with rumours that Gambier's expedition was directed at Denmark, and on 16 August, at the fortnightly audience he granted to the diplomatic corps, Napoleon asked Dreyer about them and took a great interest in the whereabouts of the Danish army and how quickly it could be moved to Zealand. Dreyer was sceptical that a British attack on Denmark was imminent, but Napoleon was not persuaded. The British could no longer have in mind a landing on the continent, he said, and he could see no purpose for the expedition other than the seizure of Copenhagen, the Danish fleet and the island of Zealand.[85] This was an entirely accurate assessment of the situation.

The reports of an impending British attack on Denmark prompted Napoleon to put his forces on alert for military action in Denmark. That had not formed part of his original plan. The approaches to Portugal and Denmark were intended as diplomatic pressure, a preliminary that might be followed at a later stage by the use of force. In the first weeks of August, what was to become the 'Army of Portugal' had only begun to assemble, and no immediate military steps were intended in the case of Denmark either. For the moment, the emperor's military priority in northern Germany was to drive the Swedes out of Pomerania, and it was not until the end of September that the Swedish forces were evacuated back to Sweden. The outcome was never in doubt, but while they lasted, the operations in Pomerania tied down 50,000 French troops and served as a disincentive to direct measures against Denmark.[86]

On 2 August Napoleon wrote to his new governor of the Hanseatic Towns, Marshal Jean-Baptiste Bernadotte, Prince of Ponte Corvo (Napoleon had a partiality for comic-opera titles), who had arrived at Hamburg on 23 July to take up this position. Bernadotte was very gung-ho and was soon requesting orders to occupy Holstein,[87] but that is not what Napoleon had in mind for the moment. He repeated what he had written to Talleyrand – if Britain declined the Russian mediation, Denmark would have to declare war on her or he would declare war on Denmark. If that happened, it would be Bernadotte's task to seize the continental possessions of the Danish state (once again there was no mention of the Danish islands or the Danish fleet). But for the time being,

Bernadotte was to do nothing. He had 15,000 Spanish troops under his command at Hamburg and 12,000 to 14,000 Dutch troops were available in case of need around Emden, and Napoleon told him he would be reinforced by 20,000 French troops in the course of August,[88] presumably as the need for troops in the Pomeranian theatre declined.

As his words to Dreyer on 16 August demonstrate, the arrival of the British fleet in the Sound obliged Napoleon to focus his attention on Denmark with a new and unexpected urgency. The emperor must have been uncomfortably aware that, on this occasion, he had been caught napping.

The interviews between Talleyrand and Dreyer in Paris on 6 August and between Christian Bernstorff and Jackson at Kiel the following day highlight the crumbling foundations of Danish neutrality in the late summer of 1807. But they do not lend much support to the notion that things could have turned out differently if the British ultimatum had been presented a few days *after* Prince Fredrick had learnt of Talleyrand's remarks to Dreyer.[89] It is hard to see how this could have changed the outcome. Fredrick and Christian Bernstorff would have immediately realised, despite Dreyer's soothing commentary, that the French overture was an ultimatum in the making. But it was not an ultimatum *yet*, and it was clothed in a form that did not wound Fredrick's self-regard and sense of his own dignity.

In contrast, the British demands were humiliating in the extreme and such as no sovereign state would ever accept. Not only would Jackson have needed to arrive two weeks later in Kiel. As Thornton realised, Jackson would also have needed authority to drop the demand for the outright surrender of the Danish fleet and to negotiate an alliance on some other basis, and this authority he did not have. If he had possessed this authority, then Denmark might well have sided with Britain rather than France, but this presupposes a degree of willingness among Canning and his colleagues to trust the Danes that did not exist. The cold, hard reality was that, in the absence of a preceding French invasion of Holstein, Jackson's mission was doomed to failure. Jackson recognised this himself when he wrote that 'there was no prospect or probability that argument would produce what could only be the effect of force'.[90]

Chapter 9

THE STRUGGLE FOR ZEALAND, AUGUST 1807

COPENHAGEN BESIEGED

Jackson reached a British warship around midnight on 13 August and had his first meeting with Cathcart and Gambier the following morning aboard the admiral's flagship, the *Prince of Wales*. He told them that his diplomatic mission had failed, and 14 August was also, as it happened, the deadline for the commencement of military operations. But the fleet was still off Elsinore and unfavourable winds slowed its progress towards Vedbæk, a fishing village about 19 kilometres north of Copenhagen, which had been chosen as the army's initial disembarkation point. This gave time for Jackson to send a proclamation addressed to the local population of Zealand from Cathcart and Gambier to the university town of Lund in Sweden for printing after it had been translated into a hybrid of Swedish and Danish.[1]

The proclamation affirmed, predictably enough, that 'we come . . . to your shores, inhabitants of Zealand, not as enemies, but in self-defence, to prevent those who have for so long disturbed the peace of Europe [the French, needless to say] from compelling the force of your navy to be employed against us'. It renewed 'the most solemn pledge' already offered to the Danish government that every ship would be restored to Denmark when a general peace was concluded if the navy were amicably surrendered, and promised that property would be respected and strict discipline enforced among the British troops. 'But if these offers are rejected . . . the innocent blood that will be shed, and the horrors of a besieged and bombarded capital, must fall on your heads.'[2]

Armed with this pious but menacing document, the first units of the British army went ashore at Vedbæk at dawn on Sunday, 16 August. They met no resistance, more perhaps by accident than design. Peymann did send out a reconnaissance force of 500 to 600 men, accompanied by no less than 16 cannon, but Fredrick had ordered him on 11 August to avoid appearing as the aggressor and Peymann took this to heart. His men were instructed to proceed with caution and to refrain from firing the first shot. They returned with news of the British landing, but without doing any mischief to the invader.[3] By the end of the first day, the bulk of the British forces were ashore and marching towards Copenhagen in three columns.

On the morning of 17 August Copenhagen was invested. The British line ran just over 2 kilometres from the ramparts of the city and arched from Swan Mill in the north through Emdrup, Gladsaxe and Vanløse to the area just beyond the royal palace of Frederiksberg, so recently vacated by Christian VII. It touched the sea at both ends. Frederiksberg Castle itself fell within the section of the line held by two Guards battalions – the royal apartments were kept locked, but troops were quartered in the rest of the building and cannon mounted on the terraces below it. When Jackson visited Swan Mill on 18 August, he thought that the British line stretching southwards through the cornfields offered 'a very picturesque appearance'. He noted that the corn had provided good material for the improvised beds and huts constructed by the soldiers, who had left England in such a hurry that they were without tents.[4]

The British kept their promise in the proclamation that discipline would be enforced. The troops generally behaved well, and those who did not received harsh treatment. Four death sentences were passed (though for technical legal reasons they were not carried out), one gunner was condemned to transportation, and a number of men received no less than 100 lashes.[5] But some damage to the buildings and fields around Copenhagen was inevitable. Two weeks after the siege commenced, Captain William Bowles of the navy wrote after a visit ashore that 'the country is very pretty and more like England than most places I have seen, but the mischief we are doing is of course great, and would make one melancholy if war did not harden one's heart'.[6] The ever patriotic Jackson claimed that most of the damage done to the farms and houses around Copenhagen was caused by Danish artillery fire, but even he conceded that 'much consideration was not to be expected . . . from an invading army'.[7] Quite so. As Bowles had remarked, it was wartime.

Cathcart's headquarters were established in the country residence of an unfortunate merchant called Ericksen at Hellerup, a little behind the front line at Swan Mill and convenient for communication with Gambier. Two other seaside villages on the Sound, Charlottenlund and Skovshoved, which were closer to the British lines than Vedbæk, provided landing posts for the artillery, horses and supplies. The numerous transport vessels were also anchored off Skovshoved. Within a week, Cathcart's force was complete once all the troops from Pomerania and the last contingent from England were ashore. It numbered about 27,000 men. The King's German Legion provided the army's entire cavalry force, three regiments of light dragoons and almost half its infantry – ten battalions as against eleven battalions and five companies of British troops. Castlereagh had also ordered Gambier to send ashore a 'naval brigade' to cooperate with the army and 2,800 marines and sailors were made available for this purpose.[8]

The three cavalry regiments were based at Charlottenlund, Jægersborg and Vanløse[9] and had the task of protecting the backs of the besieging army by guarding the main roads from Roskilde and Køge in the west and south and from Elsinore in the north. It was not a particularly large exclusion zone, but it was enough. From 17 August, Copenhagen was cut off from news and learnt virtually nothing during the remainder of the siege about what was happening in the rest of Zealand and Denmark as a whole.[10] Cathcart had decided to ignore Kronborg Castle at Elsinore and any approach from that direction would have been spotted by the cavalry in time for a blocking force to be drawn from the siege lines.

So far the operations on land had been almost non-violent, but in fact the first blood had already been spilled far to the north on the appointed day, 14 August. The *Frederiksværn*, the Danish watch ship in the Sound, had coexisted peacefully with the British armada off Elsinore for more than a week, but after Fredrick's visit to Copenhagen on 11 August its master, Captain Henrik Gerner, was ordered either to return to Copenhagen or, if that were impossible, to burn his ship (though not its crew). But when Gerner surreptiously slipped his cable on the night of 12 to 13 August, he found the wind was from the south-east and he decided instead to make a break for the Kattegat and sail for Norway.

If the *Frederiksværn* had made for Copenhagen, Gambier would have let her go since Jackson's negotiations were not yet at an end, but he could not allow the frigate to slip beyond his reach and when her departure was detected at dawn on 13 August he sent one ship of the line and a frigate, the *Comus*, in hot pursuit. The *Comus* caught up with the *Frederiksværn* on

14 August off the Swedish port of Marstrand. Just before midnight, there was a short but vicious battle between them, which cost the Danes 12 dead and 20 wounded against only one injury on the British side. The *Comus* was outgunned but carried the day, and the *Frederiksværn* surrendered and was brought back to the Sound.[11]

As military operations commenced, there were three former British envoys afloat in the Sound, but only Garlike finally slipped from the stage. He had left Copenhagen with Taylor on 12 August and concluded that he could no longer disregard Canning's instructions to proceed to Memel. But he remained bitter, and before he left the Copenhagen roads, he called on Jackson to grumble at his treatment from Canning. Even Jackson, who was not prone to sympathy for fellow British diplomats, conceded in his journal that 'there are circumstances of peculiar hardship in the judgement that was formed in Downing Street of his official conduct'.[12] Garlike sailed on one of Gambier's brigs, the *Pelican*, on 16 August, and arrived there eight days later.[13]

Jackson remained in the Sound as a guest of Gambier on board the *Prince of Wales* in the vain hope that the Danes might show an inclination to reopen negotiations. He sent a letter to Joachim Bernstorff through the lines, but received no reply. Joachim was long gone – he had left Copenhagen on 16 August as soon as he learnt the British had landed and was in Kiel a few days later.[14] Taylor also stayed around, but on a frigate, the *Cambrian*, as befitted his lower place in the pecking order. Jackson paid occasional visits to terra firma to observe (and, as a patriotic Englishman, invariably to admire) the actions of the troops, but he was so surplus to requirements that he and Taylor indulged in a spot of tourism and spent six days in late August on a jaunt through southern Sweden.[15] Jackson had evidently put aside his resentment at Taylor's abrupt departure from Copenhagen. For the time being, diplomacy had played its part, and the military men moved to the centre of the stage.

The commander of the land forces, Lieutenant-General William Schaw Cathcart, the tenth Baron Cathcart, was a Scot approaching his fifty-second birthday. He was an experienced soldier who had seen action during the American War of Independence and in the Netherlands in the early stages of the conflict with revolutionary France. But he was rather more than a plain army man. As a teenager, he had spent some years at St Petersburg where his father was ambassador to Russia and later studied at the university of Dresden. Cathcart had found favour at court and was politically engaged as a supporter of Pitt. His previous experience of Russia and Germany, along with his political connections, are presumably why Castlereagh saw him as a good man to employ in northern Europe. Cathcart was appointed to command first a short-lived British landing in north-western Germany in late 1805 and then the expeditions to Pomerania and Zealand in 1807.[16]

Jackson instantly took against Cathcart, and his journal of his mission to Denmark is scathing about his conduct and demeanour. In fact, Jackson describes a man virtually on the verge of a breakdown. He claimed that the first thing that struck him when they met on 14 August was

> the wavering undetermined language, but still more the dejected downcast looks of Lord Cathcart. . . He had the appearance of a general already half beaten and reflecting only how he should retrieve a shattered condition. This was visible in the half sentences, inconclusive opinions and ominous forebodings which formed the substance of his confidential conversations.

Jackson also asserts that Gambier shared his anxiety at Cathcart's inertia and that they both had to intervene to chivvy Cathcart along.[17]

It makes for amusing reading, but there is little corroborating evidence. Cathcart's actions and correspondence show a cautious and methodical commander, averse to taking risks and with a tendency to dwell on worst-case scenarios. He was clearly not a man inclined to walk on the sunny side of the street, but the evidence does not bear out Jackson's assertion that he was gripped by lethargic depression.[18] It is difficult to see how he could have proceeded more quickly when stores and artillery were still being landed as late as 28 August, and Captain Bowles, while clearly impatient for more to happen, still conceded that the construction and mounting of batteries 'naturally takes up some time, which, to us lookers on, seems to be passed in inactivity'.[19] It seems safe to conclude that Cathcart's leadership was perfectly competent, even if not bold or inspirational.

Gambier, in contrast, escaped Jackson's criticism. He put Jackson up aboard his flagship and discussed his 'plans and ideas' with him in an

'open and confidential manner'. 'Nothing', Jackson wrote, 'could exceed
the Admiral's attentions.'[20] This may give us the key. Jackson was not a
man who suffered from low self-esteem, and the explanation for his
strictures is probably that Cathcart failed to show a due regard for his
opinions and importance.

THE FIGHTING AROUND COPENHAGEN

The target of the British operations, Copenhagen, was a sizeable city of
about 100,000 inhabitants, by far the largest within the Danish
monarchy. It was the heart of the Danish state – the seat of government,
the residence of the king and the focal point of Danish overseas trade. The
larger, western part of the city lay on the island of Zealand and was
separated from its eastern portion, known as Christianshavn, on the much
smaller island of Amager, by a narrow channel, which ran like a canal
between them. Both the eastern and western sections of the city were
surrounded by strong earth ramparts with numerous bastions, protected
by deep, flooded ditches.

Amager was flat as a pancake, and even the main, western part of
Copenhagen was situated on low-lying, open country, but its land defences
were not derisory. The real weakness of its defenders was a shortage of
trained manpower. The Danish regular army consisted of about 35,000
men, but the bulk of them had been stationed to the west of the Great
Belt since 1805 and their return was blocked by Keats's squadron. As a
result, there were only about 5,500 regular troops in Copenhagen in
August 1807. The second line of defence was the militia (the *landeværn*).
There were nineteen locally based battalions of militia on Zealand and its
three adjacent islands, and six of them had been assembled in
Copenhagen before the city was sealed by the British. There were about
2,300 militiamen in Copenhagen, but their military value was doubtful. A
more numerous force was provided by the so-called burgher militia of
Copenhagen itself, which raised around 4,000 men from among the city's
inhabitants. Along with several bodies of volunteers, including about 800
students from the university of Copenhagen, the total force manning the
land defences of the city came to about 13,000 men. It was thrown
together from disparate elements, many of which lacked much by way of
training. It was also not a particularly mobile force as many were tied

down to manning fixed positions on the ramparts. Despite orders to desist, the artillerymen of the burgher militia fired off their cannon from the city's ramparts with more enthusiasm than discretion, occasionally taking aim at a single British soldier.[21]

The commander of this motley force was an ageing Hanoverian, Major-General Heinrich Ernst Peymann, who had crossed the border into Holstein and taken service in the Danish army at an early age. The church records of his birthplace suggest that he was seventy in August 1807, but – reversing the usual trend – he claimed to be seventy-two. He enjoyed a long and comfortable career, which was drawing to a natural close in the spring of 1807, when the military commander of Copenhagen and Kronborg fell ill. Peymann was appointed to replace him. This would have been fine in peacetime, less so in the circumstances of August 1807. Peymann was popular as a gentle and likeable man, but he had never commanded troops in battle and could not physically bear riding a horse.[22]

Commander Steen Andersen Bille, who was in charge of the city's naval defences under Peymann's overall responsibility, was a very different kettle of fish. The son of an admiral, he had joined the navy as a cadet at the age of eleven and had never looked back. In 1807 he was in his mid-fifties with a long record of distinguished service, most notably as the commander of the small squadron that had protected Danish trade in the Mediterranean in the late 1790s. He was probably Denmark's ablest naval officer – even if the principle of Buggins's turn delayed his promotion to rear-admiral until 1825.[23]

The Danes were much better placed against assault from the sea than they were on land. The base where the navy was moored, the dockyard and the naval arsenal were all located in the far north-eastern corner of the city, on Amager. The immediate approaches to the naval base were shielded by batteries mounted on the Citadel, the town's main fortress, and by another battery on the northern tip of Amager called Sixtus. But the first line of defence against any attempt to reach the naval base by sea was the Trekroner Battery, which was located about 1,300 metres north-east of the harbour's mouth at the end of a shoal that projected from the channel that ran through Copenhagen. These and other, smaller batteries rendered any naval attack from the north straight into the heart of Copenhagen extremely hazardous, and the construction in 1802 of the

Prøvesten Battery about 900 metres off the eastern shore of Amager, a little to the south of the naval base, had also made an approach from that direction an unappealing option.

Fredrick's instructions to the Admiralty and Peymann from Kiel on 7 August had ordered that all the batteries should be fully manned and placed on full alert. In the days after Fredrick's flying visit to the capital on 11 August, the batteries were reinforced by floating defences. The seagoing fleet was immobilised, but three of its warships – one ship of the line, one frigate and one brig – were turned into blockships. 'Floating battery no 1' and the four armed barges that had excited Pembroke back in May were also available. The floating battery and one of the armed barges were towed next to Prøvesten on 13 and 14 August. They proved an effective deterrent. Prøvesten mounted 89 guns, while the armed barge had 20 and the floating battery 24.[24] Gambier placed three ships of the line close to Prøvesten and its two mobile batteries, but no serious attack was ever made, and throughout the siege of Copenhagen the British fleet stayed out of the King's Deep, the stretch of water where the naval base and the city would have been vulnerable to bombardment from the sea.[25] Gambier's caution shows that the British cabinet had been right in its assumption that a repeat of 1801 was not on the cards and that a combined operation involving large land forces was required.

Around the mouth of the harbour, two blockships were stationed between the Trekroner Battery and the shore of Zealand on 14 and 15 August while two armed barges were placed to the east of Trekroner on 16 August.[26] The Danes also had quite a large flotilla of gunboats. The naval plan of 1806 envisaged the eventual construction of hundreds of gunboats, and ten new ones were launched between 25 May and 2 July 1807,[27] providing a total force of 26 available at Copenhagen in August. The gunboats had sails, but they were also flat-bottomed rowing vessels with thirty oars and sixty rowers, which could operate in shallow water close to the shore. Each of them carried two long cannons and between four and six howitzers. The gunboat flotilla was backed up by five smaller vessels, armed with mortars or howitzers, and Bille laid his hands on another sixteen launches, which were each armed with a single mortar.

The flotilla and its supporting vessels were stationed around the Trekroner Battery. In this case, manpower was not a problem. As the great ships of the line were decommissioned, there was enough manpower to provide the 3,500 or so men for the floating defences and a similar number for the fixed defences.[28] Large warships could only enter and leave Copenhagen harbour in the north – the channel separating Zealand and Amager was too narrow and shallow for this purpose in the south. Even so, the third and smallest blockship was stationed by the southernmost of the two bridges that linked Zealand and Amager as a precaution. Later, on 24 August, as the British forces approached the ramparts more closely, one gunboat and two smaller vessels were sent beyond the bridge to fire on the British lines.[29]

The Danish gunboats were a threat to the store ships and transports at Charlottenlund and Skovshoved and to the line of communications between those villages and the British army. It was to protect the left flank of the besieging forces against attack from the sea that Cathcart ordered the construction of an artillery battery at Swan Mill, and Gambier also took precautionary measures. On 17 August Gambier moved his main fleet further down the Sound and anchored off Taarbæk, a fishing village about 6.5 kilometres north of the harbour entrance. But his great warships could not operate close to the shore, and on the same day, he ordered Captain Peter Puget to take command of an advanced squadron of smaller vessels and to station them in the shallow waters closer to the shore so as to cover the left wing of the army.[30] Puget's squadron was an improvised force, made up of three sloops, seven gun-brigs, five bomb vessels, three armed transport ships, one 'armed ship' and ten launches fitted with a mortar.

The British commanders were right to be concerned. Bille and Captain Krieger, the officer in charge of the gunboat flotilla, were aggressive and enterprising. They did hope at first that some of the gunboats might slip through and wreak havoc among the British transports. They were never able to do that, but they kept up a sustained naval duel with Puget's squadron in the waters off Swan Mill for over a fortnight. There were numerous sharp encounters between 17 August (when Bille led his gunboats in person) and 31 August. Bille and Gambier both tended to claim in their reports that the enemy had withdrawn at the end of the battle, so it is difficult to know who gained the upper hand on each particular occasion. But the Danes clearly held their own, partly because they enjoyed a slight technological edge. The Danish gunboats could manoeuvre closer to the shore and had longer and heavier artillery than their British opponents. What they could not do was to knock out or cope with the battery at Swan Mill and other British artillery positions on land. Krieger and his crews had far more difficulty with fire from the shore than from Puget's squadron.

Captain Bowles, who formed part of that squadron as the master of the *Zebra* bomb vessel, was more frank than Gambier. Writing home, he conceded that 'those confounded [gunboats] are so small that we may fire all day without being able to touch them, while they hit us every time', and that their cannon 'have proved more than a match' for the guns mounted on the British squadron. But he also hit the nail on the head when he noted that, although the Danish gunboats 'have continued very troublesome, a battery of heavy guns, which has been mounted [on land] so as to flank them as they advance, keeps them in order'.[31]

Neither the British nor the Danes suffered heavy casualties in their naval duel, but there were several incidents that highlight the pity of war. On 17 August two merchantmen leaving the Baltic went aground off Copenhagen as the buoys marking out the channels had been removed by the Danes. One was found to be American and was released, but the other was British, laden with timber, and was burnt in the water. The Danes removed the crew first but rowed them around 'the ship in flames with expressions of joy and exultation. Cruel to the suffering individuals but not unnatural on the part of those from whom they proceeded'.[32] The ship was still burning at 11 p.m. and made 'a very brilliant appearance' in the night.[33] On 26 August one Danish gunboat, the *Stubbekiöbing*, was hit by a British mortar on land and exploded. Over half the crew of 59 were killed.[34] Five days later it was the turn of the British, when one of their armed transports, the *Charles of Kirkaldy*, exploded and sank with 11 men lost and 20 wounded to jubilant cheers from the Danes. On 27 August, the three Danish vessels operating to the south of Copenhagen harbour took a heavy battering from the British artillery onshore and the largest of them, the *Nakskov* gunboat, went aground and had to be evacuated. The report that reached Cathcart stated that 'shocking screams were heard, and she seemed to have no hands to work her'.[36]

Bille and his crews performed well, but they were an irritant rather than a fundamental threat to the British. On land, the build-up of troops and artillery around Copenhagen proceeded inexorably, and on 24 August the British hand was immeasurably strengthened by a successful general advance across the whole front facing the western ramparts of Copenhagen. The so-called suburbs of Copenhagen lying just beyond the water-filled ditches that protected the ramparts had not been burnt by the Danes and it did not prove difficult to eject the light screen of Danish skirmishers holding them when the British attacked at three in the morning. A Danish sortie was repulsed and, as Cathcart put it, 'the works intended and begun by us were abandoned, and a new line was taken within about 800 yards of [the city], and nearer to it on the flanks'. This led to the construction of new artillery batteries much closer to the city. Danish attempts to set fire to the suburbs after they fell back from them largely failed, and the besiegers were shielded from view by the surviving houses.

As the British advance on 24 August and its consequences demonstrate, Danish resistance on land was ineffective. There were five sorties between 17 and 31 August, mostly in the direction of Swan Mill, but only the last of them achieved its very limited objectives of burning some houses and cutting down some trees north of the Citadel. The others were all driven back without much difficulty. Peymann participated personally in the last sortie and received a bullet wound in the leg for his trouble. According to Jackson, there was 'a general feeling of contempt among our troops for the enemy', partly because they had 'the look of peasants in uniform' rather than soldiers. Even though he had no military or naval expertise, Jackson felt constrained to put in a word for the enemy – they usually fought 'with considerable bravery but without method or judgement . . . The Danes are in general a strong but clumsy race of men.'[37] The lack of any extended training among the bulk of the defenders was probably a more pertinent factor. By 1 September the last artillery battery west of the ramparts was completed. The noose was tightening around Copenhagen's neck. Only external forces could save the city now.

SIR ARTHUR WELLESLEY AND THE BATTLE OF KØGE

Cathcart's subordinate commanders included one who would go on to much greater things, Sir Arthur Wellesley, the future Duke of Wellington and the conqueror of Napoleon at Waterloo. Wellesley was an unusual and potentially awkward lieutenant. He was only thirty-eight and his promotion to the rank of major-general was relatively recent, but – as ever – connections were king. He served in India from 1797 to 1805 while his elder brother, Marquess Wellesley, was governor-general in Calcutta and able to give him more important commands than his seniority might have warranted. Young Arthur had risen superbly to the challenge and had won great victories over various Indian princes. This gave him both substantial prize money and a reputation in London – a great compensation for the torments of 'the distressing skin complaint known as the Malabar itch' that he contracted in India.

After his return to England, his brother's contacts both with Lord Grenville and the Pittites as well as his own abilities had put Wellesley in the house of commons for a succession of seats, and when the Portland government was formed in the spring of 1807 he received office as chief secretary for Ireland. But the main object of his intense ambition was still military glory, and he only accepted the post on the condition that it would not hamper his army career.[38] It was this let-out clause that got him to Zealand in August 1807 as one of several major-generals under Cathcart's command.

His position was anomalous. He was a member of the government on leave of absence and while on Zealand he wrote at least one letter a week to Lord Hawkesbury, and he sometimes wrote to Castlereagh as well. He was never overtly disloyal to Cathcart, but he was providing ministers with an alternative source of news and opinion to Cathcart's official despatches. For his part, Cathcart treated him with courteous caution. He gave Wellesley the honour of landing with his division first at Vedbæk on 16 August to cover the debarkation of the rest of the army, and his reports to Castlereagh contain only praise of Wellesley. But he also kept him at arm's length. Towards the end of the campaign, Wellesley wrote to one of his younger brothers that 'you are quite mistaken if you suppose that either [Lord Cathcart or Admiral Gambier] ever consults my opinion, excepting on points in which I am to act'.[38]

In practical terms, this meant placing Wellesley in command of a division called 'the reserve', a force stationed first in the centre of the British lines facing Copenhagen and then just behind them with the task of countering any Danish relieving force that might appear on the scene. In both places, Wellesley was well away from headquarters at Hellerup. Cathcart was a political general too. It was as commander of the reserve that Wellesley got his one chance of adding to his reputation while on

Zealand, when news arrived that what looked like a Danish military force bent on assisting the defenders of Copenhagen was approaching the city.

The Danish militia was the only potential source of assistance for the defenders of Copenhagen. The militia was made up of former regular soldiers who had returned to the plough. On paper, it was all very neat. There were nineteen locally based battalions of militia on Zealand and its three adjacent islands. Each battalion was 600 strong, and there was also a complement of artillery and cavalry.[40] Six of the battalions had been brought into Copenhagen before the city was sealed by the British and another two had been placed at Elsinore. That left 11 battalions at large beyond the British lines and supposedly able to do mischief to the invader.

In practice, the raising of the militia was a shambles. The peasant-soldiers of the militia had only been exercised for six days a year at best, and everything was in short supply from weaponry to uniforms. Many wore wooden clogs rather than boots. Additional volunteers of various kinds, including vagrants, were recruited from the countryside but they generally carried homemade weapons, mostly pikes. The officers were too few and badly trained. There were only 13 artillery pieces and about 100 cavalrymen from the regular army supplemented by 500 peasant volunteers riding plough horses.[41] It was a sorry spectacle.

While he was in Copenhagen on 11 August, Prince Fredrick conferred command of all the forces on Zealand outside Copenhagen and Elsinore on Lieutenant-General Joachim von Castenschiold, while Major-General Peter Oxholm was appointed as his deputy and put in charge of the four militia battalions on the adjacent islands to the south. Castenschiold was a cavalry officer in his mid-sixties, as much a courtier as a soldier. His deputy was ten years younger and had spent twenty years in the Danish West Indies, where he had made his fortune by marrying into a plantation-owning family.[42] Neither had ever seen active service, but both would display some spirit in the discharge of their duties over the coming weeks. Many Danish skippers were willing to run the British blockade of the Great Belt at night-time, and Fredrick had little trouble in communicating with his commanders on Zealand. They both received further orders from Fredrick on 16 August authorising them, once they had assembled a sufficiently large and effective force, to operate at their discretion, but while bearing in mind that the primary objective was to support Copenhagen and Kronborg.[43]

Oxholm had hurried south to muster the four battalions on the smaller islands, while Castenschiold assembled the remaining seven battalions from the north of Zealand. Castenschiold had little difficulty in collecting his forces in one place, but Oxholm experienced many tribulations on his journey to the south. Many of the militiamen of Falster, Lolland and Møn were reluctant to cross over to Zealand, claiming that the law only obliged them to defend their own 'province'. They were concerned over getting the harvest in and about the risk of attack on their own islands by British landing parties. Patriotic exhortations from Oxholm got a mixed reception, and there were several instances of mutiny, but all four battalions were eventually coaxed onto Zealand.

Castenschiold had initially stationed his seven battalions around Roskilde, incautiously close to the British army, but pulled them back to wooded, rolling country to the west of that town after a brush with the Hanoverian cavalry on 21 August. Over the following few days Castenschiold worked tirelessly to pull his ill-trained, ill-equipped force into some sort of shape, but on 26 August, in response to a new order from Fredrick to unite his forces with those of Oxholm, he marched his force to the more vulnerable position of Køge. It was to prove a fatal move. On the morning of 29 August it was exposed to the British army in open battle, just as the last of Oxholm's battalions was arriving from the south.[44]

The British were aware of the existence of Castenschiold's force, and on 23 August Wellesley, as commander of the reserve, drew up a plan to attack and destroy Castenschiold with the troops under his command and part of the Hanoverian cavalry. Cathcart approved the plan and on 26 August, as soon as the last troops from Pomerania had replaced Wellesley's soldiers in the lines around Copenhagen, Wellesley set off after his prey. He headed for Roskilde, but wheeled south when he realised that Castenschiold was moving towards Køge. Some of his troops had marched a long way and needed rest, and it was not until first light on 29 August that Wellesley was ready to move forward and engage the enemy.[45]

The Danes were encamped in and around Køge, a small coastal town of 1,600 inhabitants. A stream or rivulet, also called the Køge, ran towards the sea from the west of the town. Wellesley decided to divide his forces in two so as to mount an enveloping movement, which might entrap the whole Danish force ranged against him. Colonel von Linsingen, of the

King's German Legion, was placed in charge of a column that would march inland, cross the rivulet well away from the sea and then advance on Køge from the west.[46] Von Linsingen had about 2,000 infantry (both British and Hanoverian) and 6 squadrons of cavalry (just over 1,000 men) and 4 light cannon under his command. Wellesley's main column moving down the main road from Copenhagen closer to the sea was larger – 3,000 infantry (all British), 2 squadrons of cavalry (about 350 men) and 6 light cannon. The Danish forces at Køge were slightly more numerous, around 7,500 men, but they were up against trained regular troops. It was a case of lambs to the slaughter.

By 9 a.m. Wellesley had reached a favourable position on the main road 5 kilometres north of Køge. The terrain sloped gently down to the town over open countryside, and he deployed his troops in line to wait for news from von Linsingen. But no word came as von Linsingen was finding it more difficult to get over the rivulet than anticipated, and by the time his column was south of the stream and advancing on Køge, battle had already been joined.

Reports of the British approach had been sent, but had not reached Castenschiold and he only realised what was up when Wellesley suddenly appeared on the scene. He responded immediately by pushing forward his cavalry, two artillery pieces and three militia battalions to confront Wellesley's troops. It was a bizarre decision – this was definitely an occasion when discretion would have been the better part of valour. Retribution was swift. At ten o'clock Wellesley had still heard nothing from von Linsingen and resolved to attack the Danes with his own forces alone. The Danish cavalry and two of the militia battalions simply fled. Only the third fired a few rounds first and retreated in good order.

Castenschiold tried to form a new line with four fresh battalions in front of Køge, but the story repeated itself. Wellesley advanced in echelon with a battalion of the Gordon Highlanders in the lead. As the Scots approached and lowered their bayonets, the Danes broke and fled heedlessly back into the town. There were ugly scenes in the narrow streets of Køge: a few of the Danes took refuge in houses and fired on their pursuers, the Hanoverian dragoons sabred militiamen caught in the open and some of the highlanders indulged in a spot of quick looting.

With commendable tenacity if little sense, Castenschiold attempted to form a third line behind the bridge at the southern end of the town with his remaining units and what could be rallied from the battalions that had already broken. They put up a fair resistance at first, but by now von Linsingen's men were emerging from the wooded terrain to the west of Køge and fell on the left flank and rear of the defenders. Once again, the Danes fled and this time the rout became complete. The road was strewn with the clogs and weapons that the peasant-soldiers had discarded to speed their getaway.

Even now, their commanders attempted to salvage something from the wreckage. Oxholm tried to hold up the British at the churchyard in the village of Herfølge just south of Køge with just over a hundred men, while Castenschiold rallied such troops as he could further south. The church was on high ground and the walls of the churchyard were thick and tall, but when two cannon of the British horse artillery arrived and occupied a higher position by the village windmill, Oxholm realised that the game was up. At 4 p.m. he surrendered along with all his men. The Hanoverian dragoons relieved him of all his possessions, but they were returned later once a certain Colonel von Alten arrived and took him under his protection.

Castenschiold, however, slipped the net. Wellesley halted his own men, who had been marching and fighting all day, at Herfølge, while further pursuit was entrusted to the horse artillery and von Linsingen's cavalry. They never caught up with Castenschiold, who eventually managed to assemble the equivalent of about two militia battalions along with 350 or so cavalry and four cannon. But there were insufficient weapons and ammunition for them all, and Castenschiold decided to discharge the infantrymen from Zealand so that they might return home. With the cavalry, the artillery and the infantrymen from the three southern islands, he withdrew to Vordingborg on the southern shores of Zealand. When he learnt on the night of 1 to 2 September that the enemy were drawing close, he crossed to Møn and Falster with his remaining forces. Von Linsingen entered Vordingborg on 3 September to find that the bird had flown. The Danish militia on Zealand had ceased to exist as a fighting force. In the following days, von Linsingen's detached corps ranged over southern and south-western Zealand, to ensure that no pockets of resistance remained. It reached Korsør, the main port on the western coast of Zealand for communications across the Great Belt, on 5 September. The commander of the fort at Korsør and his men –

22 'invalides . . . old and infirm, without arms' – surrendered without a struggle.[47]

As might be expected, British casualties at the battle of Køge were extremely light – 29 dead, 121 wounded and 21 missing. Danish losses were also limited – about 150 dead and around 200 wounded. But there were many prisoners – 58 officers and about 1,100 ordinary soldiers along with nine cannon and great quantities of ammunition and supplies. Oxholm persuaded Cathcart to release the officers on condition that they returned to their homes and took no further part in the campaign, but the ordinary soldiers were imprisoned aboard Gambier's fleet.[48] Wellesley's triumph was overwhelming and he could bask in the glow of Cathcart's approbation. During the short campaign against the Danish militia Wellesley had, Cathcart told Castlereagh, 'distinguished himself in a manner so honourable to himself, and so advantageous to the public'.[49]

Destroying Castenschiold's army of peasant-soldiers does not add much to Wellesley's military glory, but it was certainly advantageous to the public interest of his country. The battle of Køge on 29 August completed what the naval blockade of the Great Belt had begun. It left Copenhagen without any hope at all of external assistance. The city and its garrison were on their own now. Small wonder that Cathcart graciously permitted Oxholm to write to Peymann from his captivity to inform him of the outcome of the battle.[50] The letter would have done little for Peymann's morale as he lay on his sick bed recovering from the leg wound he had received during the last Danish sortie from Copenhagen on 31 August.

THE VIEW FROM KIEL

As the battle for Copenhagen and Zealand raged, the Danish and British governments waited anxiously for news of the outcome. Prince Fredrick had admonished Peymann to avoid firing the first shot, but he did not himself bother to wait for confirmation that Cathcart's forces had actually landed on Zealand. On 16 August he issued a declaration of war against Britain, citing Jackson's statement to Joachim Bernstorff three days earlier that the British intended to commence hostilities against Denmark. The declaration ordered the seizure of all British property in Denmark and called on all Danish subjects to take up arms against the invader.[51] It was followed by feverish activity to place the defences of the Danish territories west of the Great Belt, particularly those on the coast, in good order.[52]

Small bodies of regular troops were also assembled on the islands of Funen, Langeland and Fehmarn in the hope that they might evade the British blockade and link up with Castenschiold's army on Zealand. The first shipment of 350 men, sailing in small boats at night, crossed from Fehmarn to Lolland on 4 September. They got across safely, and in fact none of the small parties who sailed later was ever caught by Keats's squadron. But it was of no real significance. By 4 September Castenschiold's army had already been defeated and von Linsingen's cavalry had brought virtually the whole of Zealand under control. In any case, the number of Danish troops – no more than about 2,500 all told – who were intended to cross the Great Belt was so small that they could hardly have affected the outcome if they had arrived in time.[53]

These efforts were no more than a gesture. The Danish government knew the score, and Christian Bernstorff spelled it out with brutal clarity when writing to Dreyer on 16 August.

> There is no room for hiding from ourselves that the inequality of the forces engaged will be such that we hardly dare indulge in the hope of retaining Zealand for any length of time. The island was taken off guard, practically denuded of troops, and is so surrounded by the English, that it is virtually impossible to elude their vigilance and pass reinforcements to it.

Christian placed his hopes in the coming of winter, which would drive the British warships out of the Great Belt. Then, a new set of rules would apply and it would become practicable to reconquer the island from the British.[54]

In the meantime, the Danes sought to mobilise international support for their cause, and on 21 August issued a public declaration presenting themselves as the victims of an atrocious outrage. It was written in French and addressed to the governments of Europe,[55] but in reality there were only two foreign powers that counted – Russia and France. Traditionally, Russia was Denmark's great patron. But for the moment Russia was, technically at least, neutral in the war between Britain and France and was indeed trying to mediate a peace settlement between them. Christian Bernstorff therefore felt unable to do more than express confidence that Alexander would always be 'disposed' to intervene to deflect or reverse the evils to which Denmark had been exposed.[56]

That was all very well and good, but the only realistic source of immediate assistance was France, and in the short term the Danes saw France more as a threat than a lifeline. They were fearful that Napoleon might suspect the Danes of secret collusion with Britain, of putting up no more than token resistance. Their nightmare scenario, the one that caused them 'to tremble', was that Napoleon would declare he could no longer respect a neutrality that had been violated by his enemies and would invade the Jutlandic peninsula. In that event, Denmark would then be 'crushed' between the British hammer and the French anvil.[57] Less drastically, the French might insist on moving troops into Holstein and Schleswig under the guise of providing assistance. The Danish government had no desire to see Bernadotte's troops living off the fat of the land in the two duchies at a time when they could be of no military use to Denmark.

But in the longer run the Danish government needed and wanted French help both in regaining Zealand and in looking after Danish interests in any peace that Napoleon might conclude with Britain. Christian Bernstorff's solution was to emphasise the impossibility of crossing the Great Belt at the present time of year. Bernadotte's army around Hamburg should therefore remain where it was, ready to provide an auxiliary force to assist in the recapture of Zealand once the change in the season had driven Keats's squadron out of the Great Belt. Napoleon could also help Denmark by assembling troops around the ports of the English Channel to make the British fearful for their own safety and by sending flat-bottomed boats from Holland to Denmark, which could later be used in transporting Danish and French troops to Zealand.[58]

As for Talleyrand's unfortunate remarks to Dreyer on 6 August about Danish participation in the closure of continental Europe to Britain, the least said the better. Christian told Dreyer that they should be regarded as 'null and void'. At another time, they would have caused the Danish government 'as much embarrassment as sorrow', but the British by their own actions had now produced the outcome that Talleyrand had requested. In the circumstances, it was best that this 'overture' should remain strictly secret so as not to furnish the British with a pretext for their assault on Denmark.[59]

Christian Bernstorff awaited the French reaction to the Danish suggestions with unease,[60] and he was right to do so. Bernadotte was dubious that the Danes were sincere in their claims to be resisting the British and was keen to occupy Holstein and Schleswig with or without Danish agreement. Napoleon had only to give the word, and Bernadotte was sure that the operation could be successfully and quickly accomplished. And once it had been carried out, Bernadotte was confident that the two duchies could sustain an army of 50,000 men for six months – precisely the line of thinking the Danes were frightened of.[61]

Napoleon shared these suspicions, but proceeded with more caution than his man on the spot wished to observe. The British assault on Zealand had given him the moral high ground, a position he was not used to occupying, and he did not want to throw it away gratuitously. On 18 August orders were sent to Bernadotte that he should hold himself ready to march with the Spanish and Dutch troops currently at his disposal, without waiting for the promised reinforcements, either to the assistance of Denmark or, depending on the turn taken by events, against Denmark. Napoleon clearly hoped the first alternative would apply and ordered Bernadotte to write to Prince Fredrick, offering all the help he needed to resist 'the unjust aggression' of Britain.[62]

In early September the emperor even acted on the Danish requests that flat-bottomed boats should be sent from Holland to Denmark and that a show of strength should be made around the Channel ports.[63] In particular, Bernadotte was held, panting and growling, on his leash. Through diplomacy, Christian Bernstorff and Dreyer had bought time. Above all, during the first vital weeks after the British landing in Zealand, they had avoided simultaneous French and British invasions that might have wiped the Danish monarchy off the map – perhaps forever. It was a significant achievement, but in the longer term Denmark was now committed and there would be no escaping the close Napoleonic embrace.

THE VIEW FROM LONDON

For British ministers, August was a month of agonised waiting. On 31 July Canning wrote to his wife Joan that 'the anxious interval' until the outcome was known would be long and painful indeed . . . I think we have made success almost certain. I am sure if we succeed we do a most essential service to the country. But the measure is a bold one and if it fails – why we must be impeached I suppose and dearest dear will have a box at the trial.[64]

The reference to impeachment was a joke, no doubt, but the political price of failure would certainly be high. Sadly for Canning's peace of mind, the prevailing winds delayed the arrival of news from Denmark throughout August. Jackson's reports and private letters describing the ultimate failure of the negotiations, and news that military operations had begun around Copenhagen did not reach London until 2 September. Canning was left dangling on his hook, bewailing the weather – 'It is the wind and nothing else that has prevented our hearing,' he complained on 16 August.[65] He had difficulty in sleeping and woke on one occasion 'with the noise of disembarkation in my head'.[66]

The absence of hard news did not prevent the cabinet from developing a growing appetite as the month of August progressed. On 3 August Castlereagh wrote to Cathcart that, if hostilities commenced, the promise to restore the Danish fleet at a general peace should not be renewed in any subsequent discussions with the Danes. The British government would prefer to have the freedom to hang on to the Danish navy or not, depending on the political circumstances at the end of the war. But he allowed Cathcart the discretion to renew the promise of restoration if military prudence made it important 'to terminate promptly an operation which if protracted might be exposed to failure'.[67]

Castlereagh's ambitions flew higher than that. On the same day, he asked Gambier in a letter, which was also copied to Cathcart, about the practicality of retaining the island of Zealand on a permanent basis. Could a naval force be kept in the Great Belt during the winter, and what land and naval forces would be needed to hold Zealand if the French were in possession of 'the adjacent ports'? Castlereagh wanted an answer under three possible scenarios. The first was if the Danes cooperated in the defence of Zealand (Jackson's negotiations at Kiel had not even begun, let alone failed, when Castlereagh wrote this letter, so the question is not as strange as it seems). The second scenario was if a Swedish army were placed in possession of Zealand, and the third was if Britain herself should attempt to hold the island 'as a position commanding the entrance to the Baltic'.[68]

Castlereagh's enquiries reveal that, beyond the anxiety and the eagerness for news, ministers were beginning to turn their minds to reaping greater benefits from the great armada they had sent to Danish waters than the immediate but temporary possession of the Danish navy. They were like hungry street urchins with their noses pressed against the panes of the bakery window. The attractions of retaining Zealand as a permanent base would play an important role in their thinking over the coming months, but it was briefly pushed aside in late August by a sudden turn of events. On 25 August reports reached the foreign office from Lord Strangford, the British minister in Lisbon, of new and alarming developments affecting Portugal.

On 13 August the French and Spanish envoys in Lisbon had presented the ultimatum despatched from Paris on 30 July. It demanded the closure of Portuguese ports to British shipping, the detention of British subjects in Portugal and the seizure of all British property on Portuguese soil. And that was just for starters. Portugal was also required to declare war on Britain and to join her naval forces to those of the continent. Refusal would lead to a combined French and Spanish invasion of the country.[69] The Portuguese government informed Strangford and said that the country's regent, Prince John, would play for time until he learnt British views. But it was clear that the Portuguese hoped that Britain would relieve them of their terrible dilemma by accepting the Russian mediation and making peace with France.[70]

Portugal had a navy of 12 ships of the line,[71] and Troubetzkoi's alleged letter from Tilsit, which d'Antraigues had passed on to Canning on 21 July, had placed Portugal as much as Denmark at the centre of Napoleon's secret schemes. Canning cannot have been surprised by the news from Lisbon. It was precisely what he would have expected, and he reacted with typical aggression. 'We have more work on our hands,' he declared. 'Lisbon *ought* to be another Copenhagen. Would that our fleet and army were come back and ready to start again!'[72] Some British ministers were pessimistic about the chances of intervening effectively in Portugal. But the cabinet as a whole thought that Britain's naval supremacy and the ability this conferred of mounting amphibious operations provided an opportunity of forestalling Napoleon at Lisbon no less than at Copenhagen.

Intelligence reports from Jersey suggested that south-western France was so denuded of troops that it would take Napoleon 100 days to get an army to Lisbon, and this gave Britain a window of opportunity for a quick strike to seize the Portuguese fleet. About 7,000 men, just under half the British garrison on Sicily, had already been ordered to Gibraltar for service wherever circumstances might demand,[73] but that was not enough. On 27 August Castlereagh instructed Cathcart to prepare to send back to England 10,000 or more of the troops under his command in Zealand. Gambier was to detach six or seven ships of the line and as many frigates as he could spare. These orders were, however, 'conditional'. They were not to interfere with the successful completion of any operations against Copenhagen that might have begun or with the removal of the Danish fleet.[74] Lisbon was important, but Copenhagen retained priority.

Castlereagh's instructions were obsolete within days of being written. On 1 September a letter from Prince John of Portugal to George III was delivered, containing an appeal for British understanding and restraint. It set out the French demands in full and frankly stated that Prince John would agree to the closure of Portuguese ports to the British flag in order to avoid war with France. But he would reject all Napoleon's other demands, and if the French invaded, he would embark for Brazil, the jewel of the Portuguese overseas empire. If Napoleon was satisfied with this one concession, and the British connived in their exclusion from the ports of mainland Portugal, Prince John would compensate them with trading concessions in Brazil and by allowing them an unopposed occupation of the island of Madeira. In the meantime, until the outcome of the Portuguese negotiations with France was known, he appealed to Britain to take no measures against his country.

It was a remarkable diplomatic approach, and – even more remarkably perhaps – the British cabinet accepted it. Canning was stern in his warnings that Napoleon would never accept the mere closure of ports as the limit of Portuguese concessions and that the Prince Regent had to prepare to sail for Brazil with the Portuguese fleet under British naval escort. But he accepted that if, against expectation, France could be induced to acquiesce in the closure of Portuguese ports 'as the sole and extreme measure of its [Portugal's] hostility to us', then Portugal would find Britain prepared to show a 'disposition to forbearance'.[75] Canning was astonished by his own moderation and the fear that he had been duped niggled at him. He confessed in a private letter that 'I am not quite without an apprehension, that passes over my mind now and then, lest we should have been deceived'.[76]

He was right to be suspicious, and the Portuguese crisis would follow many tortuous twists and turns before it was resolved in late November 1807. But in the short term thoughts of immediate British military action were shelved, and the potential for a direct link between events at Lisbon and on Zealand was removed. In any case, when the news that a full-scale military campaign was in progress on Zealand reached London in the first days of September, the extreme unlikelihood that Cathcart and Gambier would be in a position to detach any part of their forces for service in Portugal was immediately apparent to ministers. Castlereagh was quick to reassure Cathcart that the cabinet had grasped this point as the siege of Copenhagen reached its climax.[77]

Chapter 10

THE FLAMES OF COPENHAGEN, SEPTEMBER 1807

THE STRATEGY OF BOMBARDMENT

By 1 September the western section of Copenhagen was closely invested and the batteries clustered around it were all complete. Wellesley had destroyed the only Danish force on Zealand that might interfere with the activities of the besiegers. The question now was how the surrender of the Danish navy was to be achieved.

Cathcart's siege of Copenhagen is best remembered for the indiscriminate bombardment of civilian targets within the city, and if blame has been apportioned, it has generally been placed on the shoulders of the British government. There is no mistaking the ruthless urgency of Castlereagh's instructions to Cathcart and Gambier, but the cabinet never ordered them to secure their objectives by means of a terror bombardment. How they did it was left to them. Ultimate responsibility rests with the two commanders on the spot, particularly Cathcart, since it was he who assumed the lead as the operation became predominantly land-based, even if all major decisions were in principle taken jointly.

The method Cathcart and Gambier ultimately adopted grew out of the demands of the situation that confronted them. Before that, the question of ways and means prompted much discussion among the military men involved in the Danish operation and some inter-service rivalry. Some naval officers were put out that the army might gain all the glory. We get a glimpse of this sort of thinking from a report by Captain Paget, the master of the *Cambrian* frigate. After he arrived off Elsinore on 3 August, Gambier sent the *Cambrian* further south to take up a station off Copenhagen for the sake of better communications with the British legation in that city. He also asked Paget to reconnoitre the defences of Copenhagen before the landing of British forces on Zealand, and Paget obliged with a report that exaggerated the number of its defenders and the strength of its fortifications.

He also laid great weight on all the difficulties and dangers of a landing on Zealand or Amager or both. His predictable conclusion was that the best approach was to rely on naval strength. The Trekroner Battery would be seized by a surprise attack from the sea and turned into a site for bombarding the Danish fleet at close quarters. The combined fire from this battery and the British bomb-vessels that could be stationed close to it would destroy the Danish navy at its moorings. By this means, 'the operation of disembarking and re-embarking the army and the stores would be avoided'.[1] How very convenient – at least for the navy's glory boys.

Paget was moved by the same feelings that Captain Bowles articulated more openly in a letter to his kinsman, Lord Fitzharris, on 25 August – 'between you and me I think we ought not to be idle, and see the army take the town by themselves'.[2] The army was quick to hit back. Cathcart arrived off Elsinore on 12 August, and two days later he received a 'plan of attack on Copenhagen' from one of his staff officers, Lieutenant-Colonel George Murray, the deputy quartermaster-general of the expedition. Murray was in his mid-thirties and a new breed of professional soldier, who sought to transcend the quartermaster-general's traditional, unglamorous role of ensuring that the troops were well-encamped and properly equipped with rations, ammunition and other necessities. Drawing on the example of some continental armies, he believed quartermaster-generals should also act as 'expert operational consultants to their commanders',[3] and he put this belief into practice in the detailed plan he submitted to Cathcart.

Murray dismissed the suggestion that operations should commence with, and perhaps be confined to, an attack from the sea on the Trekroner Battery. The outcome of any such attempt was very doubtful and the most he would say for it was that this hazardous undertaking might perhaps be undertaken if a favourable opportunity presented itself *after* the army had established itself on land. He was equally opposed to another suggestion that had been floated – that the army should disembark on the island of Amager alone. That would leave the troops cooped up in a confined area and vulnerable to attack from the whole garrison of Copenhagen. A third plan, the one Murray favoured, was to land on both Zealand and Amager and to invest Copenhagen on all sides. The initial disembarkation should take place on the coast north of Copenhagen, and once the city was surrounded on the side of Zealand, a second landing could be carried out on Amager to secure a complete investment of the Danish capital.

But what to do next? The army was not strong enough both to operate against Copenhagen and to cope with any Danish or French forces that might succeed in crossing to Zealand. Everything depended on the ability of Keats's squadron to police the Great Belt effectively, and here time was the enemy. The navy could not remain at sea in these northern waters much beyond October, and the 'lateness of the season' meant that there was insufficient time to conduct 'a regular siege' of Copenhagen. That was the traditional method of capturing a city, a laborious process of digging trenches parallel to the walls that would creep closer and closer to the fortress by means of zigzag trenches. Murray's conclusion was clear-cut: 'that our principal reliance must be upon the effect of a bombardment, and that we must either endeavour by that means to destroy the Danish fleet, or force the government to surrender it into our hands'.

Murray conceded that there were 'different opinions . . . as to the efficacy of a bombardment towards destroying the fleet', and he drew a further, unsentimental conclusion from the uncertainty that swirled around this point.

If it is found by experience that the destruction of the fleet is actually not within the power of our mortar batteries, we must then of necessity resort to the harsh measure of forcing the town into our terms, by the sufferings of the inhabitants themselves. But to give this mode of attack its fullest effect, it is necessary completely to invest the place, and oblige by that means, all persons of whatever description, to undergo the same hardships and dangers.

A large part of the city's garrison was made up of the burgher militia and other residents of Copenhagen, and Murray thought it 'not improbable' that a bombardment of the city itself might prove 'the speediest means' of bringing the garrison to terms.[4]

Murray's report was an impressive document – it was rapidly produced and cogently argued. It largely set out the plan of operations that

Cathcart was to follow over the coming weeks. But on one point he had misunderstood the situation and on another he proved too optimistic. Like Paget, he did not know that Cathcart's instructions were to capture the Danish fleet, not to destroy it. Wellesley, who was more aware of government thinking, realised that ministers, like himself, would be 'much disappointed' if 'our operations are confined to the seizure of the [Trekroner] Battery, and other posts which will best enable us to injure the fleet by the fire of mortars'.[5]

The landing at Vedbæk and the investment of Copenhagen on the side of Zealand were carried out entirely in line with Murray's suggestion, but it proved impossible to surround the city completely by a second landing on Amager. Cathcart initially held most of the troops arriving from Pomerania on ship so that they could be disembarked on Amager. But the landing never took place. The unexpected ferocity of the Danish gunboats put paid to the idea. It was the one significant strategic result that Steen Bille's flotilla achieved. On 19 August Cathcart wrote that the landing on Amager had been 'postponed' because of the difficulty of protecting the troops from the gunboats. Instead, the troops were landed in the northern part of Køge Bay on 21 August and simply joined the troops in the lines that had already been established around the western perimeter of Copenhagen. Cathcart never referred to the possibility of a landing on Amager again and all talk of a surprise assault on the Trekroner Battery also ceased.

In all other respects, Cathcart acted on Murray's plan – and that included the idea of a terror bombardment of the city. Moral qualms were widespread, and Murray acknowledged that among the British army officers attached to the expedition, 'the bombardment of the town itself was generally held to be improper'.[6] Arthur Wellesley for one expressed reservations, and wrote to Hawkesbury on 28 August that 'I think it behoves us to do as little mischief to the town as possible, and to adopt any mode of reducing it, rather than bombardment'.[7]

In Wellesley's case, it is difficult to disentangle his humanitarian objections from his hopes of self-aggrandisement. He had come to Zealand to enhance his military reputation and was reluctant to accept that a landing on Amager was no longer viable. On the contrary, he submitted a plan for such a landing to Cathcart and seems to have hoped that he would be put in charge of it himself. His plan, if put into execution, would totally invest Copenhagen and make it impossible for any provisions to get through. A British move onto Amager was 'a more certain mode of forcing a capitulation than a bombardment [since] no city . . . can be expected to hold out when cut off from all supplies'.[8] Wellesley was whistling in the wind. A landing on Amager was off the agenda, and dispersing the Danish militia at Køge was to prove his one stab at military glory on Zealand.

Cathcart himself was deeply unhappy at the prospect of a terror bombardment, and in his private journal Jackson mocked him for speaking of 'the horror of knocking down the houses and of the chance of a shell falling upon a girls' boarding school'.[9] Jackson was missing the point. However much Cathcart may have hated the idea, as early as 22 August, in his first report to Castlereagh after landing on Zealand, he had already accepted Murray's argument that an indiscriminate bombardment of the city might be the most effective way forward.[10] But his preferred solution was to achieve the surrender of the Danish fleet through negotiation with Peymann, and since the investment of Copenhagen he had written to the Danish commander on 20 August to appeal – in vain – for a peaceful settlement.[11] It may well be that an ethical revulsion against a terror bombardment coloured his thinking, but when writing to Castlereagh he could only give military reasons, and he produced a formidable list of them.

First of all, he claimed to be uncertain whether Copenhagen would necessarily surrender if subjected to indiscriminate bombardment. He regarded an attempt to storm the ramparts behind their flooded ditches as a difficult operation, and the lateness of the season argued against a regular siege, which would inevitably be a protracted affair. He did not have enough equipment to open trenches and to batter a breach in the ramparts in more than a few places, and this might enable the Danes to slow down progress. The coming of cold weather and dark nights might cause sickness among the British troops and undermine the effectiveness of Keats's blockade of the Great Belt. Finally, he knew from intercepted communications that Peymann had been ordered to defend the city to the last ditch and to destroy the Danish fleet before any capitulation.[12]

Cathcart believed that all these considerations argued in favour of a final attempt to win Peymann over. In this respect, the supplementary orders and enquiries that Castlereagh had sent to Cathcart and Gambier in early August were very unhelpful. Their original instructions had given them the task of going in, obtaining possession of the Danish fleet and getting out of Zealand again. The despatches that Castlereagh addressed to them on 3 August placed the operation in a different light. The cabinet was now looking for the permanent and unconditional, not the temporary, surrender of the Danish fleet, and it seemed also to be interested in retaining a long-term foothold on Zealand.

If these two new objectives were seriously pursued, a smooth handover of the Danish navy without further violence would become impossible. Cathcart needed to offer the ultimate return of the navy and a rapid evacuation of Zealand to have any chance of coming to terms with Peymann. Both military commanders also regarded the idea of holding on to Zealand as utterly unrealistic. Gambier fired off an immediate reply, declaring that it was 'altogether impracticable' to keep warships in the Great Belt during the winter because it was 'so liable to be filled with large masses of ice'. Moreover, in his opinion, he did not believe it was possible 'by any means that Great Britain possesses to defend the island against the immense bodies of troops which France might bring against it'.[13]

Cathcart was more subtle in his dismissal. He restricted himself to a straight-faced enumeration of the practical obstacles. Zealand could be held if the Danes were allies (hardly a condition likely to be fulfilled), though even then they would need the assistance of substantial British forces. The same applied even more strongly if Zealand were handed over to the Swedes, since Cathcart doubted that they could provide more than 10,000 men for the defence of the island. And if Britain tried to hold Zealand with her own resources, an army of 30,000 infantry and 6,000 cavalry would be required to do the job.

Castlereagh's new instructions allowed Cathcart to renew the offer of an ultimate restoration of the fleet, provided 'on grounds of military prudence', it might 'terminate operations, which, if protracted, might fail'. This left the final decision to Cathcart's discretion and he used it. On 31 August he wrote to Castlereagh that there were indeed good reasons of military prudence for renewing the offer to restore the Danish navy when the war was over, and that he proposed to do so.[14]

This did not mean that Cathcart was prepared to accept failure if Peymann rejected his final appeal. In that event, the bombardment of the city would begin, and if that failed to secure the surrender of the fleet, the ramparts would be stormed. Despite his reservations about attempting to take the city by storm, Cathcart ordered preparations to be made for crossing the water-filled ditches, and Gambier contributed a battalion of seamen and marines to assist.[15] The siege of Copenhagen was approaching its climax.

On 1 September, with the last batteries completed, Cathcart and Gambier made their final appeal to Peymann. They repeated their previous promise that if the Danish fleet were surrendered, it would be restored at the conclusion of a general peace, but the offer was accompanied by a threat. If it were now rejected again, it would not be renewed and the fleet would belong to its captors 'and the city, when taken, must share the fate of conquered places'. Peymann was given until 4 p.m. the same day to respond. Peymann tried to play for time. The offer was 'unbecoming an independent power' and 'honour and duty' obliged him to reject it, but he suggested that he might refer it to his king for a final decision.[16] Peymann's motive was utterly transparent, and the way was clear for the bombardment to commence.

THE BOMBARDMENT

The bombardment began at 7.30 p.m. on 2 September along the whole British line facing the western ramparts of Copenhagen and continued for about twelve hours through the night. The Danes replied with artillery fire from the ramparts and their gunboats drove back the British bomb-vessels that approached from the sea, but they could do nothing against the hail of projectiles that descended on the city. The British concentrated their fire on the northern part of Copenhagen, using the spires or towers of several prominent churches or public buildings as their targets. Fires broke out in thirty-eight places. They were all extinguished by the volunteer fire corps or ordinary people, but the morning revealed extensive damage and the flight of refugees began. Whole families carrying their most valuable possessions poured across the two bridges from the districts that had been bombarded into Christianshavn, the eastern part of Copenhagen, and further afield onto the open flatlands of Amager.

The British guns remained silent during the day, but the bombardment resumed around 6 p.m. on 3 September, and the story repeated itself.

Once again, the British bomb-vessels were driven off, but there were twenty fires, including one which destroyed Copenhagen's main timber-yard, and most of those inhabitants of the western part of the city who had remained in their homes joined the flood of refugees crossing the two bridges to Christianshavn. The bombardment ceased between seven and eight in the morning, though lighter, sporadic firing continued until the late afternoon.

A respite of three hours followed, but the bombardment began again at 7 p.m. on 4 September. It was heavy and unrelenting until around noon on 5 September, and this time the defenders proved unable to contain its effects. Much of the fire corps' equipment was damaged by now and many of its men were dead or injured. Fire caught hold in several places and raged out of control. On the ramparts, members of the burgher militia abandoned their posts to try and save their families and property. The destruction reached its most dramatic point when the venerable *Frue Kirke* (the Church of Our Lady), which had been a target throughout the two preceding nights, was finally brought down. Captain Bowles, watching from his warship out to sea, described the bombardment as 'the most tremendous sight that can well be conceived' and noted that the third night 'surpassed all rest, particularly when the largest church caught fire, and the spire (which was a remarkably beautiful one) fell in'.[17]

When the British artillery fell silent at noon on 5 September, the inhabitants of Copenhagen were stunned and terrified, and the city bore witness, as Cathcart and Gambier had warned in the proclamation they issued when British troops landed on Zealand, to 'the horrors of a besieged and bombarded capital'. One-fifth of Copenhagen's population – 20,000 people – had fled their homes to Christianshavn or Amager and two thousand of them (2 per cent of the total population) had been killed. Many of the British bombs and shells had penetrated right to the cellars of houses, the natural place of refuge, and this had increased the number of fatalities. It took several more days to bring the fires under control, and the flames in the ruins of *Frue Kirke* were not entirely extinguished until the end of September. About one-twelfth of central Copenhagen was burnt to the ground and buildings over a much larger area of the city had sustained lesser or greater degrees of damage.[18]

Excluding the ordnance kept in reserve, Cathcart carried out the bombardment with the forty mortars and ten howitzers of different kinds along with thirty 24-pound cannon actually mounted on the batteries that ringed the western perimeter of Copenhagen. The flat-trajectory artillery closest to the city was mainly used to engage the Danish guns on the ramparts and prepare the ground for storming the city, if that should prove necessary. The remainder was held further back and carried out the actual bombardment by lobbing shells into Copenhagen itself.[19] Gambier sent in his bomb-vessels to add their weight to the onslaught, but they were kept in check by the Danish gunboats and the bombardment was overwhelmingly a land-based operation.

Copenhagen is often remembered as the first occasion when a new weapon of war, the 'Congreve rocket', was employed against a major European city. William Congreve had trained in the law, but never practised, and became engaged first with various abortive business ventures and then with 'inventions'. He turned his hand to rockets in 1804. He may have been an enthusiastic amateur, but he also proved persuasive and effective. Congreve had soon designed incendiary projectiles with a sharp warhead, which adhered and ignited wherever the rocket struck. Thanks to the influence of his father, an artillery general, and the good impression made on leading ministers during a trial of Congreve's novel invention in September 1805, his rockets were quickly under production at Woolwich Arsenal near London. They were first used on active service during a naval raid on Boulogne in October 1806. The French claimed that they had little effect, but the British government thought otherwise and Congreve was given a second outing, this time to Copenhagen, in August 1807.

Congreve's rockets were designed to be launched from frames that could fire two projectiles at the same time. As he had done at Boulogne, Congreve directed their use in person with the assistance of sixteen civilians from the ordnance department.[20] He was something of a showman parading around in a white coat and white hat, and he does not appear to have been universally popular with the navy at Copenhagen. Charles Chambers, the surgeon of the *Prometheus* fireship, gleefully recorded in his journal, after the rockets had been used without effect in a duel with the Danish gunboat flotilla on 23 August, that Congreve had 'become the jest of the whole Fleet' and carried the nickname 'Commodore Squib'. Chambers thought him a self-important fellow, as well he might be since he was paid a handsome salary 'for an invention which hitherto has proved futile'.[21] This was a misjudgement. Congreve's rockets lacked precision except at very short range, but for an indiscriminate attack on a large target like a city they proved perfectly effective.

The bombardment of Copenhagen in 1807 marks a milestone in the history of the rocket, but the number actually employed was limited. Some of Congreve's rockets were fired from three of Cathcart's batteries on land, others from small boats, but only 300 were used during the bombardment, a mere 5 per cent of the 6,000 British projectiles that rained down on Copenhagen during the three nights of bombardment. It was conventional artillery, particularly the mortars, which inflicted the lion's share of the damage.[22] But the whining hiss of the rockets and the flames trailing behind them as they traversed the sky made a huge impression on the inhabitants of Copenhagen. A British soldier who observed the bombardment had no doubt about their psychological impact – 'as they rushed through the air in the dark, they looked like so many fiery serpents, which must have dismayed the besieged terribly'.[23] And it suited the Danes (not to mention Napoleon and other enemies of Britain) in their propaganda after the event to exaggerate the extent of the rocket bombardment.

TERMS OF SURRENDER

By the morning of 5 September, Peymann, who had been bedridden since the leg wound he had sustained on 31 August but who retained command, could see that the game was up. Reports from officers on the spot told him that many of the burgher militia had abandoned their posts on the ramparts the previous night and that the British could have mounted them without much resistance if they had only known the true state of affairs. There was, in other words, no longer any realistic prospect of withstanding a storm, and Peymann also came under pressure from some prominent burghers to capitulate. He too could see no other way. On the afternoon of 5 September he wrote to Cathcart proposing a 24-hour armistice so that the terms of the city's capitulation could be negotiated between the two sides.[24]

Cathcart smelled a rat. Was this yet another attempt at prevarication? In practice, he called a ceasefire in that the British artillery did not fire a single shot after he received Peymann's letter, but he was not yet willing to grant a formal armistice. He sent Lieutenant-Colonel Murray into Copenhagen with a letter asking Peymann to specify the conditions of the capitulation that he had in mind. Only then would Cathcart be able to decide whether he could agree to an armistice. He ordered Murray to explain orally that he would not listen to any proposal that failed to include the surrender of the Danish fleet.[25]

Cathcart's demand confronted Peymann with the ultimate, fearful decision and it was one he felt unable to take alone, even if the final responsibility was exclusively his. He replied to Cathcart that, in the absence of the king and the crown prince, he needed to confer with the leading civil and military authorities in Copenhagen, but he did promise an answer by noon the next day.[26]

At ten o'clock on the morning of 6 September a council of war was held at Peymann's headquarters. Generals, admirals, leading officials from the government ministries and a few representatives of the municipal authorities took part – twenty-three men in all. Peymann painted a bleak picture. The city's fortifications would be unable to withstand an attempted British storm – an opinion confirmed by the commander of the engineering corps. Some of the food stores had been consumed by the flames and more would be lost if the bombardment resumed. It was very difficult to contain the fires that were already raging, and a renewal of the bombardment would produce ever greater terror and devastation. Against this background, Peymann asked the assembled men if he should negotiate a capitulation on the basis demanded by Cathcart or continue the struggle. The decision was unanimous – everyone agreed that it was unavoidable to begin negotiations on the basis that the fleet would be surrendered.[27] Peymann's letter informing Cathcart that he accepted the delivery of the fleet 'as the fundamental basis of negotiations' reached the British commander just before noon on 6 September.[28]

Once he had received Peymann's letter conceding the essential point, Cathcart had to determine what other terms to demand, and he conferred with Gambier over this point on the afternoon of 6 September. According to Jackson, who was present for part of the time, Cathcart initially envisaged a total capitulation of the conventional sort – the Danish garrison would march out of the city, lay down their arms and become prisoners of war.[29] If so, the two British commanders-in-chief quickly abandoned any such thought after Jackson had left and proceeded on the principle that 'the object of securing the fleet having been attained, every other provision of a tendency to wound the feelings or irritate the [Danish] nation [should be] avoided'.[30]

Jackson was enraged when he learnt the next day that Cathcart had chosen the path of magnanimity. He had heard from Gambier (though not from Canning) of Castlereagh's enquiry about the prospects of retaining Zealand on a long-term basis and realised that only the unconditional and complete surrender of Copenhagen would leave the British government with a free hand over the permanent occupation of Zealand. Cathcart and Gambier chose instead to settle for what was in effect a partial and temporary surrender of the city.

Their antipathy to the idea of trying to hold on to Zealand may have had something to do with it, but they also believed there were good military reasons for a soft touch. It was clear to the Danes that their defences were on the verge of collapse, but this was not obvious to the British military, who also had to bear in mind Castlereagh's second enquiry about the possible recall of a large part of the British forces on Zealand for an expedition to Portugal. In addition, there was the risk of disturbances among the inhabitants of the city and particularly the personnel of the Danish navy in outrage at the loss of the fleet.[31]

All this suggested a cautious and lenient approach, but the final shape of the capitulation depended on the three officers chosen to negotiate with the Danes and the terms they thought they could get. Sir Home Popham, the captain of Gambier's own flagship, was chosen from the navy's side, while Cathcart picked Murray and Wellesley to represent the army. The selection of Wellesley caused a little delay as he had to be sent for from his command in central Zealand, but Cathcart clearly thought it expedient to include in the team a general who stood so well with ministers and who was indeed himself a junior member of the government.

Popham was to prove the most aggressive of the British negotiators. He was a controversial figure. He was a bold officer who had just been court-martialled and reprimanded for launching an unauthorised and ultimately unsuccessful attack on Spanish territory in South America. But he was also a Pittite member of parliament, and his trial and the protests of more senior captains in Gambier's fleet (including Keats) had not prevented his appointment as captain of the *Prince of Wales*.[32] As his previous conduct indicated, he was a man prepared to take an enterprising line.

The three officers appointed to draw up and sign the articles of capitulation met their Danish counterparts outside the eastern gate of Copenhagen around eight o'clock on the evening of 6 September. The British team insisted that the two sides should set to work immediately and the negotiations went on through the night at Peymann's headquarters in central Copenhagen. Wellesley was entirely of Cathcart's way of thinking and as the senior army man present took the lead in granting generous terms. The garrison was not required to surrender and only a small proportion of Copenhagen would be occupied. British troops would take possession of the Citadel and the dockyard, but nothing else.

For bargaining purposes, the British initially demanded the Trekroner Battery as well, but Wellesley did not press the point – 'we have no claim to this work', as he put it, 'not having, I believe, fired one shot into it from the moment we approached [Copenhagen]'.[33] And after six weeks, the period estimated as necessary to prepare the Danish fleet for removal, the British would withdraw from Copenhagen and all other parts of Zealand and re-embark. During this period, there would be a complete ceasefire on the island of Zealand, all prisoners would be returned and the persons and property of all Danish subjects would be respected.

In contrast, the final terms concerning the navy were by no means lenient. Cathcart and Gambier had authorised Wellesley to accept the Danish fleet in deposit for return at the conclusion of a general peace if that were necessary to clinch a deal. This was the offer they had made to Peymann on 1 September on the basis that it would never be repeated, but they clearly did not quite mean it. This ultimate concession was never offered because the Danes did not hold out for it with sufficient tenacity. They allowed their mutterings about a temporary surrender of the fleet in deposit to be brushed aside and accepted the unconditional and complete delivery of the navy by right of conquest. What is more, once this point had been conceded, Popham made it clear that the surrender of the navy included not just the ships of the line but every naval vessel at Copenhagen ('everything afloat', as he phrased it) and all the stores in its arsenal.[34] Popham was pretty pleased with himself afterwards. There had been 'much discussion [but] I would not cede one iota' and he had achieved 'a proud day for England'.[35]

At two in the morning on 7 September, the articles of capitulation were placed before Peymann. They were put to the same twenty-three men who had agreed to negotiate the previous day. They had reassembled on the floor beneath Peymann's sickroom at 6 p.m. and were still there in the witching hours. The minutes of the meeting capture the anguish expressed during the two hours of discussion that followed, but in the end, at four in the morning, the previous decision was reaffirmed and the terms of the capitulation were accepted.

It was a moment of national humiliation. As General Walterstorff, one of the Danish representatives who negotiated the capitulation said, in a vain appeal to soften British hearts, the navy was the nation's 'soul, which every Dane has always been accustomed to regard with pride and as Denmark's greatest adornment and source of strength'.[36] At Kiel, the Danish government assumed it was a humiliation that would be avoided through the destruction of the Danish fleet. On 16 August, Christian Bernstorff assured Dreyer that, although the navy might perish, it would never 'add to the trophies of our enemies'.[37] Prince Fredrick made the same point more prosaically when he wrote to Peymann from Kiel on 18 August ordering him, if Copenhagen was obliged to surrender, 'which God forbid', to ensure that before this happened the Danish fleet was burnt. It was better, Fredrick wrote, to choose the lesser of two evils and to see the navy in flames than in enemy hands.[38]

The letter was entrusted to Lieutenant Peter Steffens, who managed to evade Keats's squadron in the Great Belt and get close to Copenhagen before he was captured by the British. Steffens was allowed to write to his brother inside Copenhagen with the news that he was now a prisoner and had been carrying despatches, but Peymann never learnt what was in them.[39] In this respect, Cathcart was better informed than Peymann. The Danish sources relate that Steffens managed to get rid of the despatches before he was captured,[40] but this cannot be true since Cathcart knew from intercepted communications that Peymann had been ordered to destroy the fleet before any capitulation.[41]

Inexplicably, Fredrick failed to communicate his instructions over the fleet when he spoke to Peymann during his flying visit to Copenhagen on 11 August, but he did mention them that day to Admiral Lütken, one of several admirals whom the prince had disregarded when he entrusted the highest naval command to Bille. What happened next is a murky business. Just as inexplicably, Lütken failed to pass on Fredrick's words to Peymann, but he did tell Bille. On 21 August Bille ordered Commander Ole Andreas Kierulff, who was in charge of the dockyard and the ships located in it, to draw up a plan for the destruction of the fleet.

Burning it was deemed too great a hazard to the city, and preparations were made instead to sink the fleet where it was moored and to cut up all its masts and sails. Because of the shallowness of the water, the ships could be raised, but the British would find it infinitely more difficult and time-consuming to remove them from Copenhagen. By 2 September Bille had signed, but not dated or despatched, an order to carry out this plan, which it was estimated would take five or six hours to execute, and the carpenters required were on board the ships.[42] It was a bizarre state of affairs. A group of naval officers was aware of Fredrick's instructions, but the commander-in-chief in Copenhagen, General Peymann, remained in ignorance of them.

This was the position when the first council of war met on the morning of 6 September. Once again, what happened next is murky. Neither Bille nor any other of the naval officers who knew of the preparations that had been made to sink the fleet and the wishes that Prince Fredrick had expressed appears to have mentioned them with a single word. Accounts diverge as to what was said when the council of war reconvened at 2 a.m. on 7 September to consider the final terms of the capitulation. According to the official minutes, Lütken and Kierulff made a passing reference to the desirability of destroying the fleet if there was still time to do so, but the suggestion was not discussed further. Bille claimed, however, in a letter he wrote the next day to Prince Fredrick that he explicitly proposed the destruction of the fleet at the meeting, but that he received no support. Everyone else thought damaging the fleet would only lead to less favourable terms of capitulation.

There is no discrepancy between Bille's letter and the minutes over one very striking intervention he made in the discussion. He had changed his mind and now believed that the capitulation should be rejected. Every armed man in the city, he proclaimed, should launch a sortie against the British troops who were at the gates, while all the gunboats and the rest of the floating defences attacked the British fleet. The minutes record his concluding rhetorical flourish: 'when we then fight for our honour like desperate men, we can die a tranquil death'. Rousing stuff, but it was hardly practical politics or practical strategy, and Bille remained a lone, dissenting voice. At 9 a.m. Peymann signed the capitulation once it had been translated into French and copied out in good secretarial hand.

What was Bille's game? It would be charitable but implausible to ascribe his words to a paroxysm of patriotic despair. He can hardly have believed that the council of war would accept his proposal for a last, desperate sortie. He recanted the next day when he wrote to Prince Fredrick that although he had strongly opposed the capitulation, he did not wish to say that those who had taken a different view had 'acted unwisely'. His own proposal would have served no purpose but to give him and those who followed him 'an honourable death' and to gain time to destroy the fleet. Bille's letter achieved a masterful treble whammy. He endorsed the capitulation while avoiding responsibility for it and made Fredrick aware of how ardently he had shared the prince's wishes over the destruction of the navy. His whole performance would stand him in good stead when warding off the prince's wrath.

With such conflicting evidence, we cannot know for sure whether the council of war meeting in the early hours of 7 September gave serious consideration to sinking the Danish navy at its moorings. But it is clear that the destruction of the fleet was incompatible with signing the capitulation, which predicated its surrender to the British. And what would have happened then? Copenhagen could not hold out. It was very possible that the British would conquer the whole of Zealand, including all its fortresses, and might prove difficult to dislodge. This anxiety was expressed several times at the meeting, and even Bille in his letter to Fredrick conceded that, without the capitulation, the British might have turned Kronborg into 'a second Gibraltar'. The capitulation, after all, only involved a partial occupation of Copenhagen and committed the British to evacuate Zealand after six weeks.[43]

The truth was that if the fleet were to be destroyed, it needed to be done before negotiations for capitulation were initiated. It is likely that what held the Danes back was not only the fear of a complete and prolonged British occupation of Zealand but also a hope that something could be rescued from the jaws of disaster. Perhaps the British would allow them to keep a few of their ships of the line for defence against neighbouring powers or at least their frigates and other smaller warships? Perhaps the British would agree, even now, to the eventual return of the navy after the war? The Danish negotiators raised all these points in their discussions with Wellesley, Murray and Popham.[44] They secured none of these concessions, but it was simply too late by the early hours of 7 September, when the articles of capitulation were drawn up and ready for signature, to expose Copenhagen and its people to the risk of infinitely greater devastation and death.

Ratification of the armistice was exchanged in the course of the morning of 7 September and at four in the afternoon British soldiers took possession of the Citadel. At the same time, another detachment of British troops were embarked from a position halfway between the Swan Mill battery and the Citadel and landed in the naval dockyard. As they took possession of the arsenal and each of the Danish ships of the line in turn, the Danish guards successively withdrew.[45] It was a most civilised handover. Seven weeks after the cabinet had decided to strike against Denmark, the Danish fleet was in British hands.

Chapter 11

ENDGAMES, SEPTEMBER–NOVEMBER 1807

THE BRITISH ON ZEALAND: PULLING OUT OR HOLDING ON?

The British achieved another success against Denmark on 5 September, when the governor of Heligoland with his garrison of twenty-six invalids surrendered the island to a British naval force commanded by Vice-Admiral Russel – the same man who had refused Jackson a sloop at Yarmouth a month earlier. Heligoland was a good vantage point for observing the mouths of nearby rivers like the Ejder and the Elbe. Above all, it provided an excellent base for clandestine British trade with Germany now that Tonningen was closed, and it proved invaluable to the British over the following years.[1]

Prince Fredrick was put out by the loss of Heligoland, but his irritation paled into insignificance compared to the unbounded rage and grief he experienced when he learnt on 11 September that Copenhagen had surrendered and that the Danish navy had not been destroyed beforehand. He refused to respond to the reports that Peymann and others sent him from Copenhagen, and when General Walterstorff, one of the signatories of the capitulation, arrived in Kiel, he was placed under arrest. Only Bille, who had so cleverly covered his back, basked in the prince's favour and was summoned to Kiel to report in person.

Fredrick took the line that Peymann, as commander of Copenhagen and Elsinore only, had not been entitled to enter into a ceasefire covering the whole island of Zealand. In practice, however, he tacitly accepted the armistice and plans for shipping troops to Zealand were suspended. Fredrick restricted himself to slipping forces past Keats's squadron from Langeland and Fehmarn to the three islands south of Zealand where Castenschiold had taken refuge with the remnants of the Danish militia.[2] By 19 October, when the armistice expired, close to 9,000 men were assembled on Møn, Falster and Lolland, and were in a position to cross to Zealand.[3]

In Copenhagen itself and on Zealand as a whole, relations between the British and the Danes were tolerably good, both at an official and a private level. Tensions and disagreements were inescapable, but there were no serious incidents throughout the six weeks of the ceasefire.[4] In the dockyard, the British set to work with gusto on the task of preparing the Danish navy for removal to England, employing strong working parties from the army as well as sailors from the fleet. Within nine days, fourteen of the seventeen Danish ships of the line had been equipped for sea and towed out of the harbour into the Copenhagen roads. By the expiry of the six weeks appointed for the task, the whole Danish navy at Copenhagen, down to and including the gunboats, was ready to sail.

The store-houses of the arsenal were also stripped of all their naval materials – masts, spars, timber, hemp and so on. Apart from what was placed aboard warships, ninety-two of the transports were fully loaded with material of this kind. The total value of the naval stores seized at Copenhagen was eventually put at over £320,000.[5] Some of the Danish ships were deemed too old and rotten or too unseaworthy for the journey to England and were simply destroyed. Three ships of the line (including one under construction), two frigates and a few smaller vessels suffered this fate.[6]

As well as preparing the Danish navy for removal, Cathcart and Gambier also had to fend off the British cabinet's importunate interest in retaining Zealand on a long-term basis. Castlereagh had first put this idea to the military commanders in early August, but in a tentative form. Ministers returned to the charge a month later in response to the news that the Danes had declared war on Britain, and this time there was nothing tentative about their enquiries. Canning neatly summed up the intensity of their concern: 'we feel our work to be but half done, if we get the fleet only, and have not the option of keeping possession of Zealand . . . The declaration of war completely changes our situation.'[7]

British ministers feared the evacuation of Zealand would be followed by the arrival not only of Danish but also of French troops on the island. Ostensibly, they were mainly anxious for the security of their ally, the king of Sweden, but they were also attracted by 'the immense control [the retention of Zealand] would give us over the Baltic powers and interests during the remainder of the war'.[8] Holding onto Zealand, while Sweden remained an ally, would also enable British merchant shipping to use the Sound freely for entering and leaving the Baltic.

The benefits were tempting, but the obstacles were huge. For a start, there was the small matter of the capitulation, which committed Britain to the evacuation of Zealand after six weeks. Ministers were furious when they learnt that Cathcart and Gambier had agreed to this stipulation, and hunted in vain for pretexts that might enable them to evade it. The most far-fetched idea was the suggestion that the Danes by boring scuttle-holes in the hulls of their warships, even though they had not used them, might have furnished 'a sufficient cause of declaring the capitulation to be void'.[9] Mulgrave was sure the government would 'have the country with us in any specious ground we may take for retaining Zealand'.[10]

But in the end, the cabinet concluded that 'we are, above all things, anxious to preserve our character for good faith untainted'[11] and reluctantly resolved to abide by the capitulation. The most ministers felt able to do was to send eager exhortations to the military commanders to seize on any infringement of the capitulation by the Danes to pronounce it invalidated. Cathcart and Gambier did not prove helpful: they persistently reported that Peymann was keeping to his side of the bargain.

The terms of the capitulation were not, however, the fundamental problem. In the last resort, it was possible to get round them by evacuating Zealand and then reinvading the island a few days later. The intractable difficulties were manpower and the northern winter. Cathcart kept saying that 35,000 men were needed to hold Zealand, and Gambier was equally insistent that the Great Belt could not be effectively policed in wintertime. There was also the problem that Gambier estimated he would need at least 12,000 troops to help navigate the Danish fleet to Britain. Cathcart was able to enlist the support of Wellesley, who was eager to return to Britain now that the fighting was over. Wellesley was entirely of Cathcart's way of thinking on this subject, and they had a long confidential conversation before Wellesley set out for home on 18 September. Wellesley worked on Castlereagh and probably played an important part in persuading ministers that an attempt to retain Zealand would be an operation of great risk and difficulty.

Castlereagh did on one occasion write that 20,000 men could at a pinch be spared for Zealand on a long-term basis, but this would have gobbled up a fair chunk of Britain's disposable land forces. In any case, it came nowhere near the numbers Cathcart and Wellesley believed were required for the job, and from the outset the British government thought of involving Swedish troops. There was much blithe talk of employing as many as 20,000 Swedish soldiers on Zealand. But there was a large element of wishful thinking about this apparently neat solution. Henry Pierrepont, the British envoy to Sweden, put the total strength of the Swedish army at no more than 45,000–50,000 men.[12] There must have been doubts about just how many Swedish troops could be found for Zealand in practice, and Cathcart claimed that he could 'have no confidence in the exertions of Sweden as a military power'.[13]

But in the last resort ministers threw in the towel not because of uncertainties about Swedish involvement but because of the arguments against trying to hold Zealand, with or without Swedish assistance, which the military commanders had set out so graphically. Canning suspected that those arguments had been influenced by 'the prospect of an uncomfortable service', but he acknowledged that 'the opinions of our officers both by land and sea were so peremptory that no government could publicly have taken upon itself to act in contradiction to them'.[14]

But the government still hoped to keep a foothold in Scandinavia. When it met on 8 October, the cabinet resolved that there would be no immediate attempt to reoccupy Zealand when the island was evacuated on 19 October. Instead, 15,000 British and Hanoverian troops would spend the winter in Scania, which would leave open the option of a renewed invasion of Zealand in cooperation with Swedish forces in the spring of 1808.[15] Castlereagh conveyed the decision to Cathcart on 9 October in the following terms: 'The difficulties you have stated to belong to the retention of Zealand against the Danes and the French . . . are such as to determine His Majesty's ministers to defend Sweden in Scania rather than in Zealand.'[16]

The cabinet always assumed that Swedish cooperation would be forthcoming, and this was a reasonable assumption. The Swedes had just signed a convention with the French for the evacuation of Rügen by the end of September, and southern Sweden was indeed vulnerable to attack through Denmark. A foothold on Zealand would be a valuable bargaining counter for regaining Pomerania and perhaps even for pursuing Gustavus IV's long-standing ambitions for acquiring Norway from Denmark. When Gustavus was first approached about Swedish participation in a permanent occupation of Zealand, he indicated that he would be 'inclined to accede to any more formal proposal on the subject', but also that it might create problems for Sweden. It would probably have provoked a declaration of war from Denmark and that might lead to hostilities on the frontier between Norway and Sweden.[17] Gustavus also needed to keep substantial forces in Finland to protect his border with Russia.

In the end, the British government solved the problem for him by deciding that there would be no immediate attempt to reoccupy Zealand. The cabinet's fallback position that 15,000 British troops should spend the winter in Scania ought to have appealed to Gustavus as a measure that would enhance the security of Sweden. But from the start he was worried about the problems of supply, and his advisers, who were a good deal less committed to the idea of an unending crusade against Napoleon than the king, eventually persuaded him that the presence of British troops during the coming winter would be economically ruinous for Scania. And maybe Gustavus himself was a little wary of the British. Pierrepont suspected that 'perhaps even with the king himself some little jealousy might exist at the idea of our getting a footing at the entrance of the Baltic'.[18] Whatever the motive, Gustavus declined the offer of 15,000 British troops stationed on Swedish soil.[19]

The embarkation of the British army began on 13 October and at the same time the advanced posts in outlying parts of Zealand like Vordingborg and Korsør were withdrawn. By the afternoon of 18 October the whole army was afloat except for detachments at Hellerup, the Citadel and the dockyard. That evening a strong gale blew up and lasted for twenty-four hours. This made the final evacuation impossible on the appointed day, 19 October, but the Danes did not initiate hostilities. On the morning of 20 October, the weather was calm again and the final troops were embarked.[20] The following day the fleet set sail up the Sound and as it passed Elsinore, keeping to the Swedish side of the water, King Gustavus, his queen and his court stood on the pier at Helsingborg to witness the spectacle. Cathcart and Gambier went ashore to pay their respects to the king and were graciously received.[21]

The British brought away with them 16 Danish ships of the line, 9 frigates, 14 sloops and brigs and 31 smaller vessels. One was lost almost immediately, when an 80-gun ship of the line went aground on a sandbank in the Sound and was burnt. Bad weather in the Kattegat wreaked havoc among the smaller Danish ships and most were either sunk by the storm or abandoned. The Danes were later able to rescue six gunboats and two armed barges.²² Gambier's fleet had been scattered by the storm, but all the remaining ships were back in British ports by the end of October.

The spoils of victory were substantial for the individuals who had participated in the expedition to Zealand. There were knighthoods for some of the subordinate officers, while Cathcart and Gambier were both raised to the United Kingdom peerage (Cathcart's previous title derived from a purely Scottish barony). The two men also split an estimated £300,000 in prize money. And everyone else got his cut. As a subaltern, Thomas Browne's share of the prize money was £97.²³

By the time Gambier's ships reached Britain, the Danes had resumed military control over Zealand and on 6 November Prince Fredrick returned to his ravaged capital. He found that the British had left one vessel behind in the dockyard. It was a pleasure yacht, a gift from George III to his nephew Fredrick in 1785. The prince ordered that it should be manned by sixteen British prisoners of war under the command of a British merchant captain and sent back to England.²⁴

CONCILIATING THE DANES

This was not the first indication that the British government received of the depths of Fredrick's bitterness. When Castlereagh first raised the possibility of retaining Zealand in early August, he mentioned a third scenario in addition to a British or a Swedish occupation of the island. This was that Zealand might be held jointly by Britain and Denmark. Castlereagh mentioned this option before he knew that Jackson's negotiations had failed or that Cathcart's forces had landed on Zealand, and once he learnt that hostilities had commenced, he immediately acknowledged that the prospect of keeping the French out of Zealand by 'a concert with Denmark . . . now appears almost hopeless'.²⁵ A long shot indeed, but one which the British government pursued with astonishing tenacity, if little optimism, in September and October 1807. The cabinet had little to lose beyond the risk of a slap in the face.

Jackson set the ball rolling on his own initiative by writing to Peymann on 7 September, the very day the capitulation was signed, to request a passport so that he might return to Britain by way of Holstein. Jackson suffered from something of a sensitivity bypass, but even he recognised that 'it is not a very gracious thing to show oneself so soon among the Danes after what has passed'.[26] Even so, he thought he would be able to hold useful conversations that might lay the foundation for a restoration of peace between the two countries.

Peymann's passport got him nowhere. Jackson spent almost a week on a British warship off Nyborg, but the governor of that town was quite adamant that 'no person whatever would be allowed to land'. On 14 September Jackson sailed for England in a huff that the Danes 'appear rather to give way to their feelings of resentment than to any sense of interest which might lead them to avert the further calamities of protracted war'. He landed at Yarmouth on 22 September and reported in person to Canning at the foreign office two days later.[27]

By then, ministers had already decided to send a different envoy to seek a peaceful settlement with Prince Fredrick.[28] The man chosen for this task was Anthony Merry, who had served as *chargé d'affaires* at Copenhagen for over a year between 1799 and 1800, and Canning imagined he was fondly remembered by the Danes because of his 'moderate and conciliatory manners'.[29]

When they learnt of Jackson's frosty reception at Nyborg, ministers were naturally anxious to avoid the humiliation of a repeat performance in Merry's case. Their solution was to send Merry to join the fleet in the Sound to await developments, while Canning made an informal approach to Rist in London to ascertain whether the Danes were prepared to negotiate. He would set out the British terms for a settlement, and offer the Danes a choice of authorising Rist to conduct the discussions in London or of sending Merry a passport so that he might go to Kiel.

This set the scene for a renewal of personal relations between Canning and Rist after their quarrel in early June. Rist had been in an uncomfortable position since August. Communications with Tonningen were broken and he had not received any instructions from Christian Bernstorff dated later than 7 August. At the same time, the British press left him in no doubt about what was happening on Zealand. On the surface, correspondence with the British government continued as normal, but Rist made no attempt to see ministers as he knew they would tell him nothing. He also discreetly arranged that Danish merchant ships in British ports should be advised to sail for Norway. Despite this tip, 335 Danish vessels had been detained by 25 September. Finally, when the news of Copenhagen's capitulation arrived on 16 September and was announced to the public by the firing of cannon in St James's Park and at the Tower of London,[30] Rist broke off all contact with the British government and withdrew to the countryside just outside London.

It was there, in his rural retreat, that Rist received a note on 23 September from Edward Thornton, who had left Altona and returned to England at the outbreak of hostilities. Thornton was the bearer of a message that Canning wished to see Rist, and this led to a series of daily and often prolonged meetings between 24 and 27 September. They all took place at Canning's home, not the foreign office. Canning laid on the charm, and any awkwardness arising from their earlier quarrel was quickly washed away. Canning, Rist cooed, was the embodiment of frankness, courtesy and studied consideration for Rist's wounded national feelings.[31] It doubtless helped that Rist decided from the outset to avoid recrimination and to focus exclusively on the situation as it now was.

What emerged from their confabulations was a document written by Rist, and approved as accurate by Canning, setting out the substance of the British proposals and a shorter minute by Canning in English giving more detail about the British offer to Denmark. A Danish courier was allowed and indeed helped by the British authorities to carry this overture to Tonningen and to return with the Danish reply.

If Canning did a grease job on Rist personally, he regarded a carrot and stick approach as suitable for the Danish government. The stick consisted of an enumeration of the disadvantages Denmark would suffer if she failed to come to terms with Britain. Her overseas trade would be destroyed, her colonies would be seized and her detained merchant shipping would be confiscated. That was all fairly predictable, but the *pièce de resistance* was the big bad Swede. Canning observed that he knew nothing could be more repugnant to the Danish government than Swedish involvement. In the absence of an agreement with Denmark, Britain might be obliged to invite Swedish troops to occupy Copenhagen and perhaps even to 'reward and compensate' King Gustavus by giving him Norway.

The carrot was a fairly gnarled and mouldy object. If Denmark would make peace, Britain offered her a choice between alliance and neutrality. In either case, the Danish colonies and Danish merchant shipping would be spared and there would be compensation for the Danish navy three years after the conclusion of a general peace in Europe. At that time, Britain would either restore all or some of the warships to Denmark or she would pay 'the fair value' of any that were not returned. In the meantime, she would have the free use of the ships. Heligoland would not be returned, but Britain would pay 'such valuable consideration as shall be agreed upon' for permanent possession of the island. In the case of alliance, there were additional inducements. Britain would provide military and naval assistance to Denmark, would hand over one or more of the colonial possessions she had conquered from the enemy and would guarantee the territorial integrity of the Danish state or an equivalent for any provinces that might be lost during the war.

There was an additional sweetener that was not transmitted to Rist and that never reached the Danish government. Instead, Merry carried it in his back pocket for use if he ever got to Kiel. It would not have made a difference, but it is very interesting. Merry was instructed on arrival at Copenhagen to make discreet enquiries about the extent of the losses caused by the British military operations. In the event of an amicable arrangement with Denmark, Merry was authorised to say that 'His Majesty would not be unwilling to afford some pecuniary aid for the alleviation of the sufferings of the poorer classes of those who have suffered in the siege', provided that this was not a formal part of any agreement.[32]

Canning told Rist that the British government preferred the option of an alliance, but recognised that the recent attack on Copenhagen might make that unpalatable to Denmark. In that case, he believed that neutrality was a realistic option, since the British seizure of the Danish fleet had removed the principal French motive for invading Denmark. In addition, Russia was likely to sustain Danish neutrality against French encroachments. It was, as Canning declared, 'indispensable to invite and obtain the guarantee of Russia to such a state of neutrality'. Finally, the British government regarded an immediate preliminary convention suspending the evacuation of Zealand by 19 October until the negotiations had been concluded as an essential step towards an amicable arrangement. Otherwise, Denmark might be subjected to importunate French demands to admit troops onto the island or – and here the stick was glimpsed again – the risk of a reinvasion by British forces.[33]

The Danish government naturally smelled a rat and saw the suspension of the evacuation as the primary purpose of the British approach, but in fact the British were prepared in principle to withdraw from Zealand. Wellesley hit the nail on the head after he had returned to England and spoken with Castlereagh, when he wrote privately to Cathcart on 1 October that 'I think the government feel very little anxiety to continue in the occupation of Zealand, excepting to keep the French out; and if they thought they were secure of that, I believe they would prefer to see Zealand again in the hands of the Danes'.[34]

Even if Rist praised Canning's manners, he described the British overture as 'degrading' and 'humiliating' to Denmark, and warned the foreign secretary that there was little chance that his government would react favourably to it. This was the general opinion in London. Figures as diverse as King George and Wellesley expressed strong scepticism that the British approach would obtain a favourable reception from the Danes. Canning himself admitted to Rist that the Danish government was likely to feel a strong aversion to a reconciliation with Britain and might already have entered into engagements with France that made such a reconciliation impossible.[35]

Canning was absolutely right both about the feelings of the Danish government and the recent course taken by its relations with France. One Danish diplomat predicted in early October 1807 that 'the barbaric policy' of Britain towards Denmark would force Fredrick 'to throw himself into the arms of a government which he detests from the bottom of his heart',[36] and this is precisely what was happening. The Danes were still fearful of a unilateral French occupation of the Jutlandic peninsula, and felt they had no choice but to draw closer to France after Copenhagen's capitulation and the surrender of the Danish fleet. Prince Fredrick was terrified at how Napoleon would react to this news, and hurried to mollify him.

On 12 September he sent a senior adjutant to Paris with a letter, written in his own hand, to the French emperor. Fredrick assured Napoleon that, if his intentions had been fulfilled, the navy would have been destroyed rather than handed over to the British, and that he would never negotiate with their common enemy. On the same day, Christian Bernstorff set off on the shorter journey to Hamburg to see Bernadotte. Christian's task was to signal that the time was drawing closer when his government would welcome the arrival of French troops. Could Fredrick count, he asked, on the assistance of a French auxiliary corps stationed on Funen to act as a reserve once the bulk of the Danish army was able to cross the Great Belt to Zealand? Bernadotte was effusive in his promises of whatever assistance Fredrick might request. But he dryly remarked (though not to Christian's face) that the presence of French troops on Danish territory was a question the Danes had hitherto evaded with 'a dexterity worthy of Machiavelli'.[37]

In the event, Napoleon let the Danes off pretty lightly with reproaches about the lack of trust in France which had caused them to station their army in Holstein instead of on Zealand where it could have resisted the machinations of perfidious Albion. But he also took steps to bind Denmark more closely to him. Jackson's attempt to land at Nyborg was noted with suspicion and the Danes were left in no doubt that France would not tolerate any negotiations between Denmark and Britain. The emperor also indicated that the circumstances of the hour required the conclusion of a formal alliance between Denmark and France, and an official suggestion to that effect reached Kiel just as the Danes were considering the British proposals that Rist had sent them.[38]

Against this background, the Danish government had no leeway at all for entering into discussions with Britain, even if it had been inclined to do so. Rist's courier reached Kiel on 7 October, but Christian Bernstorff took a week to send a reply. He and Prince Fredrick regarded the document as exceptionally important and took the trouble of obtaining the old king's formal approbation. Most unusually for a foreign ministry despatch, it bears the endorsement 'approved Christian R'. That may have caused some delay, but the main reason was that the Danish response should not reach London before 19 October, the date set for the evacuation of Zealand. The Danish government doubted that the British were going to pull out at all, but it certainly did not want its negative reply to serve as a pretext for evading this stipulation in the capitulation.

The Danish response was a ferocious raspberry. Christian Bernstorff had a predilection for rhetorical hyperbole, and this gave him a chance to indulge it. Even if the Danes could draw a veil over what had just happened and 'accept gratuities from the bloody hand which has torn the entrails from our innocent and peaceful country', the British offers could provide no real and solid advantage to them. An alliance with Britain could give Denmark no security for the future and no shelter against the wrath of France. The offer relating to the Danish fleet was 'insulting', and it was absurd to suggest that France would now allow Denmark a neutrality that her British enemies had already violated. Britain had by her own actions irrevocably associated Denmark with the cause of her enemies, and Denmark's only hope lay in the ultimate 'humiliation' of Britain.

Rist was consequently instructed to tell Canning that the Danish government had received the British offers and threats with the same indignation. British aggression had made Denmark the natural and necessary ally of her enemies, and there could be no question of a separate arrangement between the two countries. At the same time, Rist was to demand his passports and leave Britain as soon as he could.[39]

There was nothing more to say. Rist left England on 21 November after an exquisitely courteous correspondence with Canning concerning his mode of departure. Canning expressed his 'regrets and good wishes' and the hope that Rist would enjoy 'a safe passage'.[40] It was a fitting end to the comedy of their personal relationship.

By then, the alliance treaty between Denmark and France had already been signed by Dreyer and Champagny on 31 October 1807 at Fontainebleau, one of Napoleon's favourite palaces in the vicinity of Paris. Given the weakness of their bargaining position, the Danes got a reasonably good deal. The treaty contained the usual provision that neither party would make a separate peace, and Napoleon undertook to use his influence in any future peace negotiations with Britain to secure the return of all Danish property or compensation for it. Napoleon also promised in general terms to support Denmark in her war against Britain. The Danes avoided any stipulation for the immediate entry of French troops onto Danish territory, but had to accept an article that committed them to join any war against Sweden initiated by France and Russia. This was the worst aspect of a treaty that created the foundation for a relationship of subordination that would tie Denmark to France for years to come.[41]

THE RUSSIAN BREACH WITH BRITAIN

The final act of the Anglo-Russian *pas de deux* was also nearing its end. Gower had not been having a great time of it since he reached

St Petersburg from Memel in late July 'after a tiresome journey of six days during which the heat of the weather and the dust were intolerable'. Within days he was complaining to Lady Bessborough that 'I feel very uncomfortable here altogether, and curse the hour in which I accepted this . . . mission'.[42] His personal affairs did not prosper. Princess Galitzin intimated from their first encounter that marriage was no longer on the agenda. They continued to meet, but their relations were on a downward slope and Gower's letters to Lady Bessborough on the subject are a sorry tale of tiffs and jealousies.[43]

Things were no better in Gower's official dealings with the Russian government. He reached St Petersburg around the same time as General Savary, Napoleon's aide de camp, whom Napoleon had appointed as his personal representative to Alexander until France and Russia could exchange fully accredited ambassadors. Savary got a cool reception from St Petersburg high society, where Gower was far more welcome. But Alexander saw Savary frequently and invited him to dinner several times a week.[44] For his part, Gower was never granted another audience with the emperor, and informed Canning grumpily that 'I have it not in my power to follow your advice of cultivating personally the emperor; the opportunities of meeting him are rare indeed'.[45]

Gower was convinced that Alexander had become deeply hostile towards Britain and was only playing for time until the coming of winter would enable him to risk a state of hostilities without fear of immediate reprisals. Gower noted the attention the Russian government paid to the defences of Cronstadt and its alarm at the arrival of Gambier's squadron in the Sound. He was right on all counts. Alexander cannot have seriously expected Britain to accept his mediation, and the offer was never much more than a device for deferring war until 1 December, the date stipulated in the secret alliance treaty of Tilsit. It also enabled Alexander to cut a *bella figura* as the would-be peacemaker while he made the transition from a British to a French alliance.

Gower did see Budberg three times between 8 and 20 August, but their discussions led to nothing of substance and often degenerated into recrimination. Gower complained of 'the irksomeness of discussing matters with him – his perseverance in repeating the same thing over and over again, his foolish pride . . . his stupid silence, put my patience to a high trial every time I confer with him'. Gower's only source of political comfort were the emperor's 'young friends', particularly Czartoryski, who accepted that Russia had needed to end her war against France but detested the new intimacy with Napoleon and the anti-British thrust of Russian policy. On every level, both personal and professional, it was proving an unpleasant posting and Gower frankly admitted to Canning that 'I detest this place'.[46]

The arrival of Canning's instructions about the Russian offer of mediation on 29 August finally gave Gower something concrete to say and he immediately hurried to say it. Budberg was 'extremely unwell' but received him on the evening of 31 August. The British line, as already communicated to Alopeus, was to accept the mediation offer on condition that Russia divulged the secret articles attached to the peace of Tilsit.[47] In addition, Gower was instructed to request discussions on the draft treaty of commerce which Canning had given to Alopeus as a token of goodwill that demonstrated Russian impartiality. Budberg admitted the existence of secret articles, but denied that any of them affected the interests of Britain. Gower could not accept this as a satisfactory answer and asked Budberg to seek Alexander's authority for acceding to the British request.[48]

During this meeting, Gower found Budberg much changed in 'tone and temper' from their earlier interviews, and at its end Budberg went off the record to say that he did not believe the peace with France could last long. Both the government and the people of France retained 'too much of their revolutionary restlessness' for that, but it was impossible for Russia at the very moment of making a peace with Napoleon, however temporary, to enter into contingency arrangements with Britain for a future war against France.[49] This was indeed a change of tone and it was also replicated at the very highest level, by the emperor himself, the following day. The reason lay in the outbreak of hostilities between Britain and Denmark.

The British landing on Zealand had a paradoxical effect. On the one hand, it persuaded Gambier of the unlikelihood that he could spare any naval forces at all from the waters around Zealand for operations off the shores of Russia, and he said so to both Canning and Gower. On 5 September Canning wrote to assure the admiral that his point had been taken and that he would not be called on to divide his forces for operations against Russia.[50] But on the other hand, it deepened the alarm of the Russian government about British intentions, and led to placatory signals designed to keep the British at bay for a few months more. Budberg's off-the-record remarks were one such overture, but Alexander himself was the source of the main one.

The medium chosen by Alexander to convey his conciliatory overture to the British government was Sir Robert Wilson, a lieutenant-colonel in the British army, who had arrived at Memel in January 1807 as part of a special military mission to Prussia. Wilson was a brave soldier and distinguished himself at the battle of Eylau. As a result, Alexander had conferred the cross of St George on him. In the brief summer campaign before Tilsit, Wilson fought at Heilsberg and Friedland as well, and then passed a few months of recreation in St Petersburg.[51] He was just about to return home, when he was summoned to a private audience with the emperor on 2 September. Here was an Englishman who had risked his life for Russia and whom Alexander could pretend to respect. What was more natural than that he should prefer to speak man-to-man with a gallant soldier rather than a polished diplomat?

As ever, much of what the emperor said was short on precision. One sentence in Wilson's oral report to Canning illustrates Alexander's technique – Wilson described Alexander as making it clear that he wished to avoid an immediate quarrel with France but also as 'having shown the most evident anxiety to create an impression on [Wilson's] mind (though without distinctly expressing the idea) that the present state of things could not last'.[52] This led on naturally to saying that, although he lamented the British attack on Copenhagen and feared that it was a prelude for an assault on Cronstadt, he was also frightened of the degree of control over Russia that Napoleon would acquire if Zealand were occupied by the French.

Alexander claimed he was resolved to stay at peace with Britain, provided Gambier's fleet refrained from hostilities against Russia. He also indicated that as a preliminary to reconciliation he would welcome an explanation from Britain of the aims and intentions behind the Danish expedition which also contained some mark of respect for himself, some 'evidence that he was not treated with indifference by the British government'. After the audience, Wilson saw Budberg, 'whom I found dying, in his opinion and mine'. The foreign minister may have felt dreadful, but he rose to the occasion and assured Wilson that he had placed the correct construction on the emperor's words – Russia would welcome a continuing occupation of Zealand by Britain, provided she were assured of Britain's friendly intentions.[53]

Wilson set out for home immediately with his hot news and with Gower's most recent despatches, and reached London on 19 September after almost three weeks of hard travelling. He also carried messages from Czartoryski and another of the emperor's 'young friends', Count Paul Stroganov, expressing the hope that Britain would retain control of Zealand. Otherwise, the French would enter the island and become complete masters of the Baltic and Russian commerce, creating yet another bond that tied Russia to the Tilsit alliance.[54]

Naturally enough, all these reports from St Petersburg made a powerful impression on the British government. On the face of it, they seemed to confirm everything Canning had been saying about Russia since Tilsit. As recently as 29 August Canning had reiterated that 'the course which I [have] taken with Russia, that of *managing* the emperor's feelings, but at the same time showing that we are not afraid of him, is the most likely to succeed in bringing him to reason'.[55] Here at last might be the long-awaited sign that the prodigal son was about to return. But in fact the government's reaction was not starry-eyed, and British policy remained a wary mixture of conciliation and suspicion.

Caution was entirely natural. For a start, it was blindingly obvious that Alexander's change of tone was to be attributed to the British landing on Zealand and the threat to Cronstadt that it implied. Canning was convinced that the secret intelligence from Tilsit was accurate and the French ultimatum to Portugal seemed to corroborate it. In that case, Alexander had been prepared at Tilsit to connive in hostile measures against Britain. It might be that he had now repented, but perhaps he had not. Yes, there were good reasons for Russia to avoid a new war with France in the short term, but equally Alexander might simply be trying to buy time in relation to Britain until the winter set in.

These doubts and suspicions coloured the series of long despatches and private letters that Canning wrote to Gower between 27 September and 2 October. There were no concessions at all in the line taken towards the Russian mediation offer. Gower was to renew in an official note the demand for the disclosure of the secret articles of the peace of Tilsit. In addition, Gower was to request, though not as a precondition for accepting the mediation, a gesture of goodwill in the form of a renewal of the commercial treaty between Britain and Russia.[56]

This continuing preoccupation with the secret articles is perfectly understandable but it failed to hit the bull's-eye. What neither the British government nor Gower suspected was the existence not only of a public peace treaty of Tilsit with attached secret articles but also of a secret treaty of alliance. The clauses directed at Britain – the Russian promise to go to war on Britain by 1 December and to assist France in forcing Denmark, Portugal and Sweden to do the same – were embodied in the alliance treaty. In comparison, the secret articles of the peace treaty were of lesser importance, though it was quite untrue – as Budberg had asserted – that British interests were untouched by them. Two clauses concerned the handover by Russia of Cattaro and the Ionian Islands to Napoleon and would have a strong impact on Britain's strategic position in the central Mediterranean.

Even if Canning had no inkling of the existence of the alliance treaty, he did suspect that there might be agreements additional to the secret articles. On 22 August, d'Antraigues handed him the deciphered transcript of a letter he claimed to have received from Czartoryski. The letter was dated 20 July, just five days after Alexander's return to St Petersburg from Tilsit, and purported to describe several confidential conversations between Czartoryski and Alexander since the emperor's return to St Petersburg five days earlier.[57] Like Troubetzkoi's letter from Tilsit, Czartoryski's may have been one of d'Antraigues's concoctions entirely or in part, but Canning was very impressed by it. So impressed in fact that he confessed to his wife: 'Lucky that I did not get my will in having d'Antraigues recalled. Such a letter as this is worth all the bore, and all the pensions, that he can give and take.'

Czartoryski portrayed the emperor as unhappy and confused, and Canning summarised the thrust of his account as being that in addition to the formal secret articles, there were other agreements reached between him and Napoleon in their one-to-one discussions. In these cases, either nothing had been put in writing or Napoleon had retained the only copy. Alexander had confessed that he had only 'a confused and imperfect recollection' of 'the substance' of some of these additional agreements. This is why Canning now instructed Gower to press not only for access to the secret articles but also for 'a full disclosure of all that passed at Tilsit' and to place no 'implicit reliance' in anything said about the secret articles without an admission of the existence of such informal agreements.[58]

A stern tone indeed, but what if Alexander had been genuine when he said that he wanted better relations with Britain? The cabinet had to explore this possibility, and the instrument chosen was the future of Denmark. Budberg, Czartoryski and Stroganov explicitly, the emperor more obliquely, had all emphasised the need to keep the French out of Zealand. By now, the problems inherent in holding on to Zealand were beginning to sink in among ministers, but the more important object of excluding the French could be achieved by the restoration of Danish neutrality. It is here that we find the origins of the proposal put to the Danes at the very same time that their neutrality might not only be resurrected but also guaranteed by Russia.

This proposal also provided the cabinet with a means of making a conciliatory gesture towards Russia and giving Alexander, as he had demanded, some 'evidence that he was not treated with indifference by the British government'. Gower should tell Budberg that Britain would welcome Russian assistance in re-establishing peace with Denmark. Indeed, the British government would be happy if the negotiations with Denmark appeared to the outside world as being conducted under Alexander's auspices. An alliance between Britain and Denmark was the best solution, but if that were impossible, a restored Danish neutrality guaranteed by Russia was perfectly acceptable.

To reinforce the point, Wilson was sent back to St Petersburg to seek a second audience with the emperor where he would present these proposals in person at the same time as Gower put them to the Russian foreign minister.[59] It was a pretty construction, but it had feet of clay, because Alexander was stringing the British along, as the cabinet suspected he might be.

While Wilson was racing back and forth between St Petersburg and London, Gower had been deluged with mounting evidence that Alexander had no genuine interest in improving relations with Britain. On 3 September Budberg asked to be relieved of his duties until his health had recovered. Six days later, his deputy, Count Alexander Saltykov, informed Gower that the emperor did not think it 'proper' to divulge the secret articles of the Tilsit peace treaty to Britain. When Gower lamented that this would make it impossible for his government to accept the Russian mediation offer, Saltykov merely replied that British mistreatment of Denmark had 'made a very strong impression on the mind of the emperor'.[60]

On 13 September Gower was informed that Count Nikolai Rumiantsev had been appointed acting foreign minister until Budberg's health had improved. Gower suspected that Budberg would never return to the foreign ministry, and he was right – though the general did not die as quickly as he and Wilson had expected and hung on until 1812. The change was significant. Gower had not found Budberg easy to work with, but he was no great friend of France and on the eve of his retirement from the foreign ministry described Britain in a letter to the emperor as 'an old ally who may still be useful to us in the future'.[61] Rumiantsev in contrast supported the French alliance because he thought it would confer opportunities for expansion in the Balkans.[62]

On 23 September Rumiantsev wrote to Gower complaining of Britain's failure to give Russia any warning of her plans about Denmark. British actions against Denmark were directly contrary to Russian interests, and Alexander did not believe he could remain 'insensible' to that fact. The remonstrance about lack of prior notification was a bit rich in the light of Russian behaviour towards Britain over the past few months, and Gower was able to have some fun in his reply by pointing to the Russian refusal to communicate the secret articles of the Tilsit treaty – 'is it, then, for Russia to complain of secrecy?'[63]

On 30 September Rumiantsev finally delivered the emperor's reply to the British request for a renewal of the treaty of commerce. Alexander did not regard the present time, 'when our fleets and armies were in a menacing position at the entrance to the Baltic', as 'a fit moment' to enter into negotiations of this subject. Gower had picked up rumours that an embargo would be placed on British ships in Russian ports. Rumiantsev dismissed them as baseless, but he would give no guarantee about Alexander's future intentions in this respect, and Gower urged Sir Stephen Shairp to expedite the departure of British ships from Russia as far as he could.[64]

Wilson got back to St Petersburg on 17 October, armed with Canning's new instructions for Gower about seeking to involve Russia in bringing about peace between Britain and Denmark. But Gower knew that they were already a dead letter. Russian behaviour during Wilson's absence had 'dissipated' the hopes created by Wilson's audience with the emperor and Gower's last meeting with Budberg. Even so, Gower put Canning's proposals about Denmark to Rumiantsev, who promised to consult the emperor.[65] On 23 October Gower also sent Rumiantsev a formal note, as he had been instructed to do, requesting a written explanation of why Russia would not divulge the secret articles of Tilsit to Britain. He never received an answer, and he never saw Rumiantsev again. His requests for an interview were evaded,[66] and by 5 November he was convinced that war between Britain and Russia was now 'unavoidable'.

Gower found it difficult to persuade Wilson on his return that 'the state of things was such as to afford but little hopes of succeeding in the execution of the instructions of which he was the bearer'. But there was no keeping a good man down, and Wilson possessed 'a very sanguine temper' and had been 'flattered with the personal civility of the emperor'.[67] At all events, Wilson wrote to Alexander on 18 October requesting an audience so that he might, on behalf of the British government, 'explain the past and with candour . . . represent future objects'. Wilson did not get his audience, but he was received by Rumiantsev on 29 October and was allowed to make a plea for more harmonious relations between Britain and Russia and for Russian cooperation over Denmark. Rumiantsev seems to have been perfectly civil and they parted on the basis that an audience with the emperor would be arranged.[68]

But it was all just a hoax. The axe fell on 8 November, when Gower received a note from Rumiantsev along with a printed proclamation, which was circulated to all diplomatic missions at St Petersburg. Both documents essentially made the same points and they amounted to a declaration of war on Britain. They expressed Alexander's outrage at Britain's treatment of Denmark and her attempts to inveigle him into trying to convince Prince Fredrick to submit to the injustices he had experienced. In more concrete terms, Alexander declared that he annulled forever the Anglo-Russian convention of 17 June 1801, which had largely recognised Britain's maritime rights, and instead proclaimed anew the principles of the armed neutralities of 1780 and 1800.

Alexander would never renew friendly relations with Britain until she had given satisfaction to Denmark for the wrongs that had been inflicted and until Britain made peace with France 'without which no part of Europe can promise itself real tranquillity'.[69] On 9 November an embargo was placed on all British vessels in Russian ports. Gower did not reply beyond acknowledging receipt and demanding his passports. He left St Petersburg on 15 November and had reached the Swedish frontier in Finland two days later.[70]

It was a bitter end to a brief and unhappy mission. But Britain gained something too from all the evasions and chicaneries of Russian policy and the delay in the declaration of war. Sir Stephen Shairp was ordered first by Canning and later by Gower to accelerate the departure of British exports from Russia, but British merchants needed little encouragement. They too feared the closure of Russian ports, and many were keen to make a killing while the going was good. In September and October the tempo of British trade with Russia reached feverish levels, and in the end the level of British exports from Russia's Baltic ports in 1807 was more or less the same as it had been in 1806. Indeed, the quantity of naval stores like hemp and flax obtained in 1807 was higher than the previous year. What is more, the British merchants got away in time. Only four British ships were still at Cronstadt when the embargo was imposed and were sequestered.[71]

It was a good outcome for the British, and things also went their way at the other end of Europe over Portugal. The Portuguese crisis rumbled on until the end of November 1807 as the government of Prince John twisted and turned between the competing pressure from France and Britain. In the end, it was Napoleon's implacability that tipped the balance. On 12 October he ordered Junot's army at Bayonne to march on Lisbon through Spain, and the news that his forces had crossed the Portuguese frontier reached Lisbon on 21 November. The regent hesitated to the end, but on 29 November he – along with his government, most of the Portuguese aristocracy and the Portuguese navy, 36 warships in all – sailed for Brazil under British naval escort. The advanced guard of Junot's army entered Lisbon the following morning.[72] Canning reacted with predictable glee. 'Huzza! Huzza! Huzza! We have saved the Portuguese royal family and the Portuguese navy . . . Denmark was saucy and we were obliged to *take her* fleet. Portugal had confidence, and we have rescued hers.'[73]

Canning's tone is a tad too self-righteous to be endearing, but Copenhagen and Lisbon were indisputably great triumphs for Britain in the dark months after Tilsit. Nothing could compensate, of course, for the loss of Russia, and Canning would have felt that keenly when Sir Robert Wilson, come hotfoot from St Petersburg, woke him at four o'clock in the morning on 2 December with news of the Russian declaration of war. And, as a man who revelled in his own cleverness, he would have felt humiliated by the appearance that he had been outwitted by the Russian government. Canning had written to Gower on 2 October.

> We could strike a blow against [Russia] which would humble her in the eyes of Europe, and the emperor personally in the eyes of his subjects. We abstain from doing so, in consideration of the hopes held out to us of a change of policy. But these hopes may be delusive . . . Now if this should turn out to be the case, if we should find Russia after all arrayed against us in the spring, we shall appear to have been duped – which I do not like.[74]

Canning was wrong on both counts. Once Gambier had declared that he had insufficient resources both for the operations in Danish waters and for an attack on Cronstadt, Britain no longer possessed the option of striking a blow that 'humbled' Russia in the eyes of Europe. And even if Britain could have done so, would it have been wise? The damage to Russia's coastal defences and the destruction of Russian warships would have been helpful when military operations began in the spring of 1808, but could only have been achieved at the cost of initiating hostilities, of appearing the aggressor. As for being duped, Canning and his colleagues had been well aware that Alexander might be essentially hostile at the very least since the receipt of the secret intelligence from Tilsit on 22 July.

In truth, Canning was really concerned with appearances and prestige, with looking like a fool rather than being one. So long as any hope remained of a reasonably benevolent neutrality on the part of Russia after Tilsit, that goal had to be pursued in preference to all other policy options. Where the British cabinet wandered into the realms of fantasy was over Zealand. It was absurd to believe that 20,000 Swedish troops could be made available for the permanent occupation of Zealand. It was absurd to imagine that the Danes could be persuaded to make peace with Britain. And most of all it was absurd to think that Napoleon would ever have accepted a restoration of Danish neutrality. It was over Zealand, not Russia, that British policy was permeated by a fundamental lack of realism in the autumn of 1807.

THE BALANCE SHEET

The assault on Zealand produced a bitter post-mortem in both Britain and Denmark. In Britain, the event was received with mixed feelings. There was certainly support for the attack on Copenhagen as a great triumph and as a necessary act of self-defence, but Jackson complained of 'a disposition to commiserate with the Danes' and the opposition press launched a 'violent attack on . . . the Copenhagen expedition'.[1] The most intense discussion took place in parliament, which reassembled on 21 January 1808 after it had been adjourned for over five months.

Copenhagen was the subject of recurring debate until early April 1808, and the waves often ran high. The government relied initially on the secret intelligence from Tilsit, claiming that it proved France and Russia had agreed to force the two neutral states of Denmark and Portugal to join a maritime league against Britain. The king's proclamation of 18 December 1807 replying to the Russian declaration of war had already set out the thrust of this argument.

His Majesty feels himself under no obligation to offer any atonement or apology to the emperor of Russia for the expedition against Copenhagen. It is not for those who were parties to the secret arrangements of Tilsit, to demand satisfaction for a measure to which those measures gave rise, and by which one of the objects of them has been happily defeated.[2]

The difficulty with this argument was that ministers could not disclose their source or give any details. Canning posed the classic rhetorical question in the commons: 'was this country to say to the agents, who served it from fidelity, or from less worthy motives, you shall never serve us but once, and your life shall be the forfeit?'[3] And young Lord Palmerston, then a junior minister at the outset of his career making his maiden speech, chipped in with the equally classic observation that disclosure would destroy 'the future sources of information'.[4] This was good enough for government loyalists, who pronounced themselves happy to accept the government's word without divulging the source of its secret information 'to the curiosity of [the] house or to the vengeance of Bonaparte'.[5]

But the opposition was less trusting, and several of its spokesmen claimed that the secret intelligence from Tilsit did not exist at all. Both the former prime minister, Lord Grenville, and the former foreign secretary, Lord Howick – or the second Earl Grey as he had become since his father's death in November 1807 – were among those who made this allegation.[6] The opposition also raised the time factor. How could secret intelligence from Tilsit have reached the government in time to influence policy towards Denmark?[7] This was a shrewd thrust. The government was lying to parliament over this point, since the decision to attack Denmark had been taken *before* receipt of the secret intelligence from Tilsit. Ministers soon became uncomfortable with the whole subject and shifted their ground onto the misdemeanours of the Danish government.

They were given their chance in the first debate devoted solely to the expedition against Copenhagen on 3 February 1808, when the lead spokesman for the opposition in the commons, George Ponsonby, delivered a robust defence of Denmark. The Danes would have chosen war with France rather than with Britain, he claimed, if 'the rashness and precipitation' of the British government in presenting Jackson's insulting ultimatum had not forced them to take the contrary path. And he raised the question of Danish naval preparations.

Prussia had been forced to declare war on Britain on 1 December 1807, and this had abruptly terminated Garlike's diplomatic career. Garlike was now back in London and he was out for revenge. We know that he was in touch with the opposition through Thomas Grenville.[8] He must have been behind Ponsonby's demand that the government lay before the house all the reports received from Garlike or British naval officers passing through Copenhagen on any steps that had been taken to place the Danish navy on a higher level of preparedness and to assemble seamen for the purpose of manning it.[9]

This was another shrewd thrust because Pembroke's letter to Canning about the Danish navy in late May had played such a large part in the decision to attack Denmark. The government knew by now that Pembroke's claims were erroneous and had already taken steps to avoid all mention of them. When Gambier's report to the Admiralty on taking possession of the dockyard at Copenhagen on 7 September was published in the official gazette, one passage was carefully deleted. It read: 'as few of the ships are in any considerable progress of equipment, it will require some time to complete them for sea.'[10]

Needless to say, Canning never produced the reports Ponsonby had requested and consistently evaded detailed discussion of the level of Danish naval preparedness. But by focusing the debate on Danish conduct, Ponsonby enabled Canning to move away from the secret intelligence from Tilsit as a justification for the Copenhagen expedition. Canning spoke for three hours and hardly mentioned it. Instead, he was much more interested in talking about the Danish government's long-standing hostility to Britain and weakness towards France. The Danish withdrawal from Holstein in November 1806, the failure to protest at the Berlin Decree and Rist's note attacking the British Orders in Council of January 1807 all featured at length in his speech. Ponsonby was therefore mistaken: Prince Fredrick's conduct showed that from necessity or inclination Denmark would have sided with France if it came to the crunch.[11]

The debates rumbled on, under one guise or another, for some months more. They were often acrimonious and spiteful. Opposition spokesmen had some telling points to make, but it did them no good. The government had a secure majority in both houses and never won a vote with a margin of less than two to one.[12] By early April, the arguments had been exhausted, if not resolved, and the expedition to Zealand began to drift out of the realms of topical debate.

There could be no public debate in an absolute monarchy like Denmark, and the post-mortem took a more brutal form. The day after Prince Fredrick's return to Copenhagen in November 1807, Peymann along with some of his senior officers and the three men who had negotiated the capitulation were placed under arrest. They were to be tried by a court martial for dereliction of duty. Fredrick drew up a list of eighteen questions for the court to investigate. Some of the questions dealt with fairly secondary matters, but the main ones were aimed at Peymann. Had he obeyed his orders to resist to the last extremity and had capitulation been a necessity? And if capitulation could not be avoided, why had the fleet not been destroyed rather than surrendered?

The wheels of the legal machinery turned slowly, and it was not until more than a year later, on 16 November 1808, that judgment and sentence were pronounced. Peymann was found guilty and condemned to death. There were also death sentences for two of his subordinate commanders and minor punishments for some of the junior officers, but the men who had negotiated the capitulation were cleared of blame. Steen Bille, of course, was not among those charged and only played a role in the legal proceedings as a witness.

The old king Christian VII had died in March 1808, and by this time the crown prince had become King Fredrick VI. He had made his point and chose to exercise his prerogative of mercy. When the sentences were officially promulgated on 18 January 1809, the death sentences were all commuted to dismissal from the army without a pension. Peymann retired to Holstein to live with his brother. In 1816, his pension and his right to wear uniform were restored. He died in 1823, aged eighty-five.[13]

THE LONGER TERM

The war between Britain and Russia declared in November 1807 lasted almost five years, but never amounted to much. Its most striking event was the capture of the Russian Mediterranean fleet by Britain. As agreed under the terms of the Tilsit treaties, Russia handed over Corfu to French troops who slipped across from the Italian coast opposite in late August 1807. This left the Russian fleet that had been operating in the eastern Mediterranean without a base of its own. Some of its warships found refuge at Trieste, but the bulk of it – seven ships of the line and five frigates – headed for the Baltic. The British admiral blockading Cadiz allowed them to pass, but they got no further than Lisbon, where they fell into British hands in the summer of 1808 as a result of Wellesley's first campaign in Portugal and victory over Junot at Vimiero.[14] There was also some fighting between British and Russian warships in the Baltic, but neither side felt an interest in pushing matters to extremities and the conflict remained a low-key affair.

In his speech to the commons on 3 February 1808, George Ponsonby ended by suggesting that 'Divine Providence' punished states no less than individuals when they departed from the rules of justice and morality. The three powers which had formed 'that detestable confederacy' to partition Poland had now all suffered retribution. Prussia had been reduced to 'the most abject and deplorable state', while Austria and Russia were 'crouching at the feet of Bonaparte'.[15] High-minded stuff, but Ponsonby was wrong. If the British assault on Copenhagen in 1807 was a departure from justice and morality, it went unpunished. Denmark, not Britain, was the loser in the long term as well as the short. The events of 1807 were an unalloyed disaster for Denmark, which the future did nothing to repair, and Britain suffered no evil consequences from it.

The capture of the Danish fleet destroyed Denmark as a significant naval power forever. The Danes lacked the time and resources to rebuild a large battle fleet of ships of the line and poured their energies into constructing the sort of gunboats that had been so effective at Copenhagen against Puget's advanced squadron. In narrow waters like the Sound and the Great Belt they could be highly effective on windless days. The Danes also licensed a large number of privateers who attacked British trade not only in the two Danish straits but also from southern Norway and from the island of Bornholm.

It was to little avail. The Danish gunboats and privateers inflicted some damage and pulled off some morale-boosting coups, but they could not prevail against British naval might and the Baltic proved the largest gap in Napoleon's continental system between 1808 and 1813. For each of these six years, huge convoys of merchant vessels sailing on the British account were regularly escorted in and out of the Baltic during the sailing season by a powerful British naval squadron. In the spring of 1808 the Sound was favoured as the familiar route, but the ships proved vulnerable in calm weather to Danish gunboats in the narrow channel off Malmö just south of Copenhagen, and the convoys were switched to the Great Belt. It often took four days or more to get through, but the passage was wider and the six British ships of the line stationed there were able to provide ample protection.

Once well past Bornholm, the merchantmen scattered to trade in ports that were nominally closed to British commerce. They came equipped with forged papers, customs officials could generally be bribed and so too could many French consuls. Systematic smuggling also played a large role. The problem for Napoleon was enforcement of the continental system on the ground, and it proved an intractable one. In the event, the Danish war effort against Britain achieved very limited results.[16]

But the supreme catastrophe of 1807 for Denmark was that it placed her on the wrong side in the final phase of the Napoleonic Wars. As so many had eagerly predicted in the last months of 1807, the Tilsit alliance was a fragile creation and ended in tears with Napoleon's disastrous invasion of Russia in 1812. For five years, it made Napoleon virtually invulnerable in the heartlands of Europe, but it had few lasting consequences. The Ottoman Empire was not partitioned between France and Russia, and after Napoleon's downfall Prussia rose like a phoenix restored and strengthened. The kingdom of Westphalia was swept away, and the duchy of Warsaw was largely transformed into 'Congress Poland' under Russian control.

It was only in Scandinavia that Tilsit had direct and durable effects. The secret alliance treaty envisaged that not only Denmark and Portugal but also Sweden would be forced to adhere to Napoleon's continental system. It is a well-worn myth that Napoleon offered the eastern portion of the Swedish kingdom, Finland, to Alexander at Tilsit as a reward for bringing Sweden into the continental system, but there is no hard evidence that this was so. It was rather the case that bringing Sweden into line, by force if necessary, was a service that Alexander would render to Napoleon. Finland would indeed have been an important sweetener: in the hands of Sweden, it represented a threat to the security of the Russian capital, St Petersburg, and the Russian government had considered a war against Sweden to conquer Finland as recently as 1803.[17]

But at Tilsit and for many months afterwards Alexander's eyes were fixed on the south, on the spoils of the Ottoman Empire. Besides, it was not yet certain at Tilsit that Gustavus IV would prove impervious to reason and choose to remain Britain's sole ally in northern Europe. It was only when this did become clear that Napoleon began to dangle Finland in the autumn of 1807 as an incentive for Alexander to take military action against the recalcitrant king of Sweden. Napoleon was keen not only to bring Sweden into the continental system but also to divert Alexander's persistent interest in the Balkans. And for Alexander, it had become important to obtain a tangible gain from the Tilsit alliance – if not in the south, as he preferred, then in the north. Russian troops crossed the frontier without a declaration of war on 21 February 1808, and six weeks later Alexander informed foreign governments that Finland had been incorporated into the Russian empire.[18]

It was the first step in a territorial revolution that would tear the old kingdoms of Denmark and Sweden asunder.[19] Finland and Norway had been integral parts of the Danish and Swedish monarchies since the middle ages. Now, Alexander had pronounced Finland annexed to Russia and he followed this up by granting Finland autonomy as a grand duchy within the Russian empire. In 1809 Gustavus IV was deposed by a conspiracy organised by senior army officers and officials, and the new regime was obliged to accept the loss of Finland and, nominally at least, to join the continental system. The throne passed to Gustavus's elderly uncle, Charles XIII. The new king was childless and the Swedish parliament needed to elect a successor. The choice ultimately fell on none other than Marshal Bernadotte, the former French proconsul in Hamburg who had been so eager to coerce the Danes in 1807.

As crown prince, Bernadotte was the effective leader of Swedish foreign policy from 1810 and did not decide, as might have been expected, to lead Sweden in the direction of alliance with Napoleonic France and an eventual war of revenge against Russia to regain Finland. Bernadotte chose instead to take up Gustavus IV's darling project, the conquest of Norway. Out of this was born what Swedish historians call 'the policy of 1812', which involved renouncing Finland forever in return for Russian support in acquiring Norway from Denmark. In fact, Bernadotte's manoeuvres were more opportunistic and less single-minded than this implies, but this description of his policy encapsulates the outcome.

By January 1814 Bernadotte was allied to the victorious great-power coalition that was on the verge of defeating Napoleon and was able to dictate peace terms to the Danes at Kiel. Norway was surrendered to Sweden – a shattering blow to Fredrick VI, even if resistance by the Norwegians themselves eventually forced Bernadotte to grant them extensive autonomy within their new union with Sweden. There was a second treaty of Kiel signed at the same time – a peace between Britain and Denmark. The chief British negotiator – another old acquaintance, Edward Thornton – rejected all pleas for the return of the Danish navy and insisted that Britain should retain the island of Heligoland, but the Danish overseas colonies were given back.[20] By itself, this treaty would have been a bitter pill for the Danes to swallow, but in the circumstances of January 1814, the terms of the peace with Britain were entirely overshadowed by the loss of Norway.

INDIVIDUAL DESTINIES

Among the four British politicians who formed the core of the Portland government in the summer of 1807, three went on to become prime minister.[21] Spencer Perceval held the office after the Portland cabinet collapsed under the weight of its internal rivalries in 1809 until his own assassination in 1812, and Hawkesbury (under the title of Lord Liverpool) then served as prime minister for fifteen years from 1812 to 1827. Castlereagh missed the highest office but was foreign secretary for ten years after 1812 and played a major role in the reshaping of Europe in the Vienna peace settlement that followed the downfall of Napoleon.

As for George Canning, he was essentially sidelined in political terms for thirteen long years after 1809. But in his case, the old adage applies – in politics, where there is death, there is hope. Castlereagh's suicide in 1822 enabled Canning to step centre stage again and serve a second stint as foreign secretary. At last, in 1827 he landed the supreme prize, but it was on the edge of the grave and he died after only four months as prime minister at the age of fifty-seven. It was a paltry outcome for a man so driven by the furies of ambition and an awareness of his own gifts.

The British military men who had taken a prominent role in the expedition to Zealand in 1807 all prospered, and none more so than Wellesley. He went on to lead the British forces to victory in the Peninsular War and at Waterloo and to be heaped with honours. He also served fairly briefly as prime minister. Gambier almost came a cropper in 1809, accused of the one sin the navy could not forgive – cowardice or at least excessive caution in the face of the enemy (cowardice towards superior officers was entirely acceptable). But he was honourably acquitted by the court martial he demanded and went on to become admiral of the fleet in 1830. Cathcart never received another command in the field, but was a successful British ambassador to Russia from 1812 until 1820. George Murray had a distinguished army career and then served as a cabinet minister in various Tory governments between 1828 and 1846. They all lived to a great age.

The fortunes of the British diplomats active in the Baltic in 1807 were more mixed. It is perhaps no great surprise that Garlike was never employed again in the diplomatic service. He died, aged forty-nine, in 1815 after a short illness brought on by an unspecified 'act of goodness'.[22] Francis Jackson did get another posting, as envoy in Washington from 1809 to 1811, but was equally unlucky with his health. He died in 1814 after a lingering illness while still only forty-three. Edward Thornton did better. He had a long life and a long career as minister first to Sweden and then to Portugal. He was made a count in the Portuguese nobility and knighted by George IV.

Gower achieved a glittering prize, but he had to wait for it. After Canning returned to the foreign office in 1822, Gower gained the greatest posting of all, the embassy at Paris. He served there from 1824 to 1828 and again from 1830 to 1841. He was made Earl Granville in 1833. His matrimonial affairs were resolved by his marriage to Lady Bessborough's niece in 1809. Bessborough gave her blessing, but the new wife was not tolerant of the long-standing mistress. Relations became awkward, and by 1812 Bessborough had concluded that Gower was 'the man who has probably loved me least of all those who have professed to do so'.[23] She died in 1821, Gower in 1846.

Count d'Antraigues had secured his position in Britain. In fact, Canning had begun to believe his own propaganda and in October 1808 told Hawkesbury '(as you probably already more than suspect) that we owe Copenhagen in a great degree to his intelligence'.[24] In 1812 d'Antraigues and his wife were murdered by a domestic servant at their home in Barnes, the very house where d'Antraigues wrote to Canning on 21 July 1807.

After his return from London, Johan Rist was appointed as the Danish representative in Hamburg in 1808, but resigned in 1813 because he thought Fredrick VI's policies were excessively pro-French – which is a little ironical in the light of what Canning said about him in June 1807. After that, Rist was employed in a variety of posts in the administration of Schleswig-Holstein. He died in 1847.

Fredrick VI reigned until 1839. He preserved the absolute monarchy intact, but it is unlikely that anything could compensate for the consequences of Denmark's disastrous involvement in the Napoleonic Wars between 1807 and 1814. The Bernstorff brothers left their posts in the Danish foreign ministry in 1810, to King Fredrick's displeasure, but within a few years both were serving as Danish envoys abroad. Joachim was Danish minister at Vienna from 1816 to 1835, the year of his death.

Christian's career followed a rather different path. He made such a good impression as Danish envoy in Berlin that in 1818 the king of Prussia invited him to become foreign minister of Prussia. Christian accepted and served in that post until 1832. He died in the same year as his brother. That Christian could serve both Denmark and Prussia as foreign minister is a remarkable comment on the cosmopolitan aristocratic world of diplomacy in the early nineteenth century.

Of the individuals who played a large part in the events of 1807, he who had reached the highest fell the lowest. Napoleon ended his life in 1822 confined to the remote island of St Helena, all his power and glory dissipated – though not his legend. The other man who had done the deal at Tilsit, Alexander I, died three years later after having led his country to a position of unparalleled prestige and greatness in Europe. It was a triumph of slipperiness and nebulous ambitions over genius and the will to power. It is hard to tell what conclusion a moralist would draw from the contrast.

REASON OF STATE AND PRE-EMPTIVE WAR

It is easy to find fault with the British decision to attack Denmark. Pre-emptive war is never attractive, especially when it is launched by a major state against a far less powerful one, and the same applies to the terror bombardment of a civilian population.

Matters are not improved when we take into account that some of the intelligence on which decisions were taken was inaccurate and that its reliability was assessed with a frivolity that bordered on the irresponsible. Most of the blame in this respect falls on Canning. There is no defending his uncritical reading of Danican's reports about a descent on Ireland or his failure to obtain verification of Pembroke's claims about the Danish navy *before* unleashing an attack against Denmark. But there were other reasons why the dogs of war were unleashed on Denmark, and it is perfectly possible that the decision would have been the same without Danican's and Pembroke's reports, so we should not focus too strongly on the role of flawed intelligence.

The argument for pre-emptive war rested, as it generally does, on reason of state. Gower put the point neatly:

> The measure is rigorous, and perhaps scarcely reconcilable to the strict rules of justice, but there are questions upon which depend the existence of nations which justify a deviation from the common rules of action.[25]

Well, one or two cheers for that, perhaps, but reason of state only works if pre-emptive war was in reality the option that served British interests best. It was not the only option available to the cabinet. It could instead have chosen to proceed against the Danes with moderation by treating Denmark in the same way as it treated Portugal a couple of months later. What might have happened then?

The only thing that was certain in the summer of 1807 was that Danish neutrality had no chance of survival. As Napoleon said, Denmark merely faced a choice between war with Britain and war with France. Even if the British government had remained entirely passive in relation to Denmark, French pressure would within months have forced the Danes to make that choice.

All the evidence we have about the attitudes of the Danish government in the nine months before Jackson's arrival at Kiel in August 1807 indicates that the ultimate choice between the belligerents would have depended on the identity of the aggressor. Leaving aside the question of national honour and sovereignty, cold calculation did not suggest that war with France was more of a catastrophe for Denmark than war with Britain. In that case, the likely outcome of a British policy of restraint was a Denmark allied to Britain and holding Zealand against the French with British assistance.

But it is impossible to be certain that the Danish government would indeed have been guided solely by the identity of the aggressor when it became clear that the choice was not between Britain and France but rather between Britain on the one side and France allied to Russia on the other. Russia was Denmark's traditional protector and the ultimate guarantor of the Danish hold on Norway. For Denmark, war against both France and Russia would have been a fearsome prospect, and no one can be sure what the Danes would have done if faced with that scenario. In this case, as in so many others, all bets were off after Tilsit.

A different British policy towards Denmark might have produced a better outcome for British interests, but pre-emptive war was the policy that involved least risk. It is not for the historian to mark the past out of ten and to instruct the dead on how they ought to have behaved. That is why I prefer to leave it to readers to assess for themselves whether the British cabinet made the right decision about Denmark in July 1807. I also believe it is more important to understand than to judge.

The decision of the British cabinet in July 1807 to attack Denmark and seize the Danish fleet was no more ruthless than many of the actions by other powers during the Napoleonic era – or indeed during other periods of history. But it is not enough to say that boys will be boys. The decision still needs to be explained in more specific terms than merely by reference to a predatory mindset created by fifteen years of war, bad faith and unprovoked aggression.

The fundamental reason why the cabinet chose to attack Denmark was, of course, that the Danes possessed in the form of their navy a means of inflicting serious injury on British interests. Quite apart from the risk that the Danish fleet might be hijacked to convey an invasion force to Ireland or conscripted into some continental maritime confederacy against Britain, it could also be used on a more down-to-earth level to bar British access to the Baltic. In that event, the Royal Navy would have needed to divert substantial resources to hunting down the Danish ships of the line or, if they would not put to sea, to blockading them in the harbour at Copenhagen.

Beyond that, we can identify three clusters of motivation that influenced Canning and his colleagues. The first was connected with the erosion of British confidence in the Danish government over the eight months before July 1807. It started with the evacuation of the Danish army from Holstein in November 1806. After the initial shock, this had little impact on British thinking, even if it was used for propaganda purposes to present the Danes in a bad light on many later occasions. Danish protests against the British Orders in Council of January 1807 and the detention of Danish shipping were far more important. They were the fundamental reason, not to say the only real reason, why British ministers came to suspect that the Danish government was essentially ill-disposed towards Britain.

But these altercations were not sufficient by themselves to provoke war. No one would have recommended war because Rist had been writing rude notes to the foreign secretary. Under normal circumstances, the Rist affair would have blown over. The additional and vital ingredient was the sudden transformation of the European political scene by the extraordinary reconciliation of Alexander and Napoleon at Tilsit. It was entirely reasonable to surmise that Tilsit had created a situation where the previous French policy of restraint towards Denmark would be abandoned. That the French might now move against Holstein and Schleswig and that Napoleon would attempt to force Denmark onto his side simply lay in the nature of things as they now were.

The third cluster of motivation related to political and psychological factors. The evidence is more scattered, but we should never forget the role of domestic politics in shaping foreign-policy decisions. The leading members of the Portland government were determined to demonstrate that they were committed to a more aggressive and effective prosecution of the war than the Grenville government had been. Canning made this point explicitly when commending strong measures against Denmark to his cabinet colleagues. That does not mean Canning was insincere in professing to believe those measures in the national interest. When he claimed that whether the Danish operation succeeded or not, 'I am satisfied that we should have deserved to lose our heads, if we had not attempted it', he may well have meant it.[26]

And there was also the question of Britain's standing and prestige in Europe. Canning was anxious to avoid giving any impression that 'we were half-beaten already'.[27] He made a similar point more graphically when he wrote 'we must not disguise the fact from ourselves – we *are* hated throughout Europe, and that hate must be cured by *fear*.'[28] This sort of thinking was reinforced by a gut feeling that it was only by imitating Napoleon that Britain could hope to defeat him or to secure an honourable peace.

As usual, Canning made the point most vividly – 'to do by him as nearly as possible what he has been so long doing by others, is the best chance of bringing him to reason in the end'.[29] Mulgrave made the same point when writing to Canning.

I do fear some of our colleagues have too much of the milk of human nature to catch the nearest way. . . . I have so often expressed my opinion that Bonaparte is to be checked and suppressed only by the adoption of his own system, by the full exercise of power for the attainment of the object to which it can be applied. And that the old course of proceeding which we still value in morals and have hitherto adhered to must give way, when a question of power and means between France and Great Britain is at issue.[30]

Unlike Lord Mulgrave, we need to possess enough of 'the milk of human nature' to understand the mentality of feverish decision-making, isolation and paranoia that gripped the British cabinet in July 1807. Understanding is not the same as endorsement.

NOTES

ABBREVIATIONS

AAE, FB	Archives du Ministère des Affaires Étrangères, Fonds Bourbons, Paris
BL	British Library
DBL	*Dansk biografisk Lexikon*
DRA	Rigsarkivet (Danish National Archives)
DUA	Departementet for de Udenlandske Anliggender (Archives of the Danish Foreign Ministry)
DUL	Durham University Library
GskA	Gesandtskabsarkivet (Archives of Danish missions abroad)
LDA	Leeds District Archive
NLS	National Library of Scotland
ODNB	*Oxford Dictionary of National Biography* (2004)
Parl. Deb.	*The Parliamentary Debates from the Year 1803 to the Present Time* (London, 1812)
SRA	Riksarkivet (Swedish National Archives)
TNA: PRO	The National Archives: Public Record Office

CURTAIN-RAISER

1. There are good English-language accounts of the battle of Friedland in Harold T. Parker, *Three Napoleonic Battles* (Durham, NC, 1983); F. Loraine Petre, *Napoleon's Campaign in Poland, 1806–1807* (reprinted edn, London, 1989); David Chandler (ed.), *Napoleon's Marshals* (London, 1987), pp. 150–5; and David Gates, *The Napoleonic Wars 1803–1815* (reprinted edn, London, 2003), pp. 77–80. Petre and Gates also cover the preceding campaign in eastern Prussia.
2. Alistair Horne, *How Far from Austerlitz? Napoleon 1805–1815* (London, 1996), p. 216.
3. Nicholas Mikhailovitch Romanov, *Portraits Russes*, 5 vols (St Petersburg, 1905–9), vol. 4, no. 5.
4. Petre, *Napoleon's Campaign*, pp. 224–5.
5. Herbert Butterfield, *The Peace Tactics of Napoleon 1806–1808* (Cambridge, 1929), pp. 188, 212–13.

6. Petre, *Napoleon's Campaign*, pp. 230, 275–6; Gates, *Napoleonic Wars*, p. 76.
7. *Mémoires du Général Bennigsen*, vol. 2 (Paris, 1906), p. 196.
8. *Ibid.*, p. 194.
9. Parker, *Three Napoleonic Battles*, p. 6.
10. *Sbornik imperatorskogo russkogo istoricheskogo obshchestva* (St Petersburg, 1893), vol. 89, p. 5; see also p. 7.
11. *The Memoirs of Baron de Marbot* (London, 1892), p. 278.
12. Petre, *Napoleon's Campaign*, p. 321.
13. Parker, *Three Napoleonic Battles*, p. 14.
14. *Mémoires du Général Bennigsen*, pp. 200–1.
15. J. David Markham, *Imperial Glory: The Bulletins of Napoleon's Grande Armée 1805–1814* (London, 2003), p. 169.

CHAPTER 1

1. For Gower's life and background, see Castalia Countess Granville, *Lord Granville Leveson Gower: Private Correspondence*, 2 vols (London, 1916), vol. 1, pp. xxi–xxviii; the entry on Gower by K.D. Reynolds in *ODNB*; and Jane Aiken Hodge, *Passion & Principle: The Loves and Lives of Regency Women* (London, 1996), pp. 46–51.
2. Granville, *Correspondence*, vol. 1, p. xxvii.
3. Entry on Gower in *ODNB*.
4. Frances Wilson, *The Courtesan's Revenge: Harriette Wilson, the Woman who Blackmailed the King* (London, 2003), p. 108.
5. Granville, *Correspondence*, vol. 2, pp. 245–8.
6. For good recent accounts of European international relations in the eighteenth century and the Revolutionary and Napoleonic era, see Paul W. Schroeder, *The Transformation of European Politics 1763–1848* (Oxford, 1994), and Jeremy Black, *European International Relations 1648–1815* (Basingstoke, 2002).
7. James J. Sheehan, *German History 1770–1866* (Oxford, 1989), p. 249.
8. For good accounts of Britain during the Revolutionary and Napoleonic Wars, see H.T. Dickinson (ed.), *Britain and the French Revolution, 1789–1815* (Basingstoke, 1989); Christopher D. Hall, *British Strategy in the Napoleonic War 1803–15* (Manchester, 1992); Rory Muir, *Britain and the Defeat of Napoleon 1807–1815* (London, 1996); and N.A.M. Rodger, *The Command of the Ocean: A Naval History of Britain, 1649–1815* (London, 2004), pp. 408–574.
9. Richard Glover, *Britain at Bay: Defence against Bonaparte 1803–14* (London, 1973), p. 19. See also Tom Pocock, *The Terror before Trafalgar: Nelson, Napoleon and the Secret War* (London, 2002).
10. Elmo E. Roach, 'Anglo-Russian Relations from Austerlitz to Tilsit', *International History Review*, vol. 5 (1989), p. 187.

11. Schroeder, *Transformation*, p. 325; see also Butterfield, *Peace Tactics*, pp. 107–78.
12. Roach, 'Anglo-Russian Relations', p. 188.
13. *Ibid.*, pp. 189–92; Schroeder, *Transformation*, p. 313.
14. Petre, *Napoleon's Campaign*, pp. 229–33.
15. Schroeder, *Transformation*, pp. 313–14.
16. Granville, *Correspondence*, vol. 2, pp. 245–6.
17. TNA: PRO FO 65/69, desp. 1, Canning to Gower, 16 May 1807.
18. TNA: PRO FO 65/69, desp. 4, Canning to Gower, 16 May 1807.
19. Hall, *British Strategy*, p. 154.
20. TNA: PRO FO 65/69, desp. 5, Canning to Gower, 16 May 1807.
21. Granville, *Correspondence*, vol. 2, p. 257.
22. TNA: PRO FO 65/69, desp. 1, Gower to Canning, 17 June 1807.
23. *Sbornik*, vol. 89, pp. 8, 12–13.
24. LDA, George Canning Papers, HAR/GC/57, Gower to Canning, 19 June 1807.
25. *Sbornik*, vol. 89, pp. 9–11.
26. *Ibid.*, p. 16.
27. Serge Tatistcheff, *Alexandre 1er et Napoléon d'après leur correspondance inédite* (Paris, 1894), pp. 120–1.
28. *Ibid.*, pp. 125–7, 129–34; Butterfield, *Peace Tactics*, pp. 214–23.
29. Tatistcheff, *Alexandre 1er et Napoléon*, pp. 135–6, 139–40.
30. *Ibid.*, pp. 148–9.
31. *Ibid.*, p. 150.
32. *Ibid.*, p. 149.
33. LDA, George Canning Papers, HAR/GC/57, Gower to Canning, 19 June 1807.
34. TNA: PRO FO 65/69, desp. 7, Gower to Canning, 25 June 1807.

CHAPTER 2

1. For accounts in English of the proceedings at Tilsit, see Butterfield, *Peace Tactics*, pp. 202–76; Alan Palmer, *Alexander I: Tsar of War and Peace* (London, 1974), pp. 135–44; and Janet M. Hartley, *Alexander I* (Harlow, 1994), pp. 75–8. There are good accounts in French in Tatistcheff, *Alexandre 1er et Napoléon*, pp. 150–87; Albert Vandal, *Napoléon et Alexandre 1er: L'Alliance russe sous le premier empire*, vol. 1, *De Tilsit à Erfurt* (Paris, 1911), pp. 56–111; and Édouard Driault, *Napoléon et l'Europe: Tilsit. France et Russie sous le premier empire. La Question de Pologne (1806–1809)* (Paris, 1917), pp. 171–98.
2. *Sbornik*, vol. 89, p. 39.
3. Palmer, *Alexander I*, pp. 134–5.
4. Driault, *Napoléon et l'Europe*, p. 173.

5. For a beguiling account of different interpretations of Napoleon, see Pieter Geyl, *Napoleon: For and Against* (reprinted edn, Harmondsworth, 1965), particularly the section on Napoleon's foreign policy, pp. 215–312.

6. Driault, *Napoléon et l'Europe*, quoted in Geyl, *Napoleon*, p. 284.

7. Paul W. Schroeder, 'Napoleon's Foreign Policy: A Criminal Enterprise', *Journal of Military History*, vol. 54, no. 2 (1990).

8. Driault, *Napoléon et l'Europe*, p. 174.

9. Isabel de Madriaga, *Russia in the Age of Catherine the Great* (reissued edn, London, 2002), pp. 383–4.

10. *Sbornik*, vol. 89, pp. 27–9.

11. TNA: PRO FO 65/69, Mackenzie to Gower, 23 June 1807.

12. Butterfield, *Peace Tactics*, p. 243; Palmer, *Alexander I*, p. 133.

13. Palmer, *Alexander I*, pp. xvii, 8, 136.

14. *Sbornik*, vol. 89, pp. 33–7.

15. Palmer, *Alexander I*, p. 94.

16. The texts of the three treaties of Tilsit are printed in *Sbornik*, vol. 89, pp. 51–62; Vandal, *Napoléon et Alexandre 1er*, pp. 499–507; and Soviet Foreign Ministry, *Vneshniaia Politika Rossii XIX i nachala XX veka: dokumenty rossiiskigo ministerstva inostrannykh del*, Series 1, *1801–1815* (Moscow, 1960 and ongoing), vol. 3, pp. 631–44.

17. *Correspondence de Napoléon 1er* (Paris, 1864), vol. 15, pp. 382–5.

18. Schroeder, *Transformation*, pp. 346–8.

19. Tatistcheff, *Alexandre 1er et Napoléon*, pp. 169, 619–23.

20. Driault, *Napoléon et l'Europe*, pp. 175, 177.

21. *Sbornik*, vol. 89, p. 35.

22. Brian Lavery, *Nelson's Navy: The Ships, Men and Organisation 1793–1815* (London, 1989), pp. 131, 277; Richard Hill, *The Prizes of War: The Naval Prize System in the Napoleonic Wars, 1793–1815* (Stroud, 1998).

23. A.D. Harvey, 'European Attitudes to Britain during the French Revolutionary and Napoleonic Era', *History*, vol. 63 (1978), pp. 356, 360–1.

24. Madriaga, *Russia*, pp. 381–7; Ole Feldbæk, 'The Foreign Policy of Tsar Paul I, 1800–1801: An Interpretation', *Jahrbücher für Geschichte Osteuropas*, NS vol. 30 (1982), pp. 16–36.

25. Ole Feldbæk, 'The Anglo-Russian Rapprochement of 1801', *Scandinavian Journal of History*, vol. 3, no. 3 (1978), pp. 205–27.

26. Schroeder, *Transformation*, pp. 249, 261.

27. *Sbornik*, vol. 89, p. 35.

28. Driault, *Napoléon et l'Europe*, pp. 186–7.

29. *Correspondence de Napoléon*, vol. 15, pp. 393, 395–6.

30. Driault, *Napoléon et l'Europe*, p. 196.

31. TNA: PRO FO 65/69, desp. 10, Gower to Canning, 12 July 1807.

32. Tatistcheff, *Alexandre 1er et Napoléon*, pp. 186–7; Vandal, *Napoléon et Alexandre 1er*, p. 109.

33. Palmer, *Alexander I*, p. 136.

34. Herbert Randolph (ed.), *The Life of General Sir Robert Wilson*, vol. 2 (London, 1862), p. 285.

35. Granville, *Correspondence*, vol. 2, pp. 265, 267–8, 270.

36. TNA: PRO FO 65/69, desp. 7, Gower to Canning, 25 June 1807; and LDA, George Canning Papers, HAR/GC/57, Gower to Canning, 26 June 1807.

37. TNA: PRO FO 65/69, desp. 2, Canning to Gower, 16 May 1807.

38. Gower to Budberg, 28 June 1807, enclosed in TNA: PRO FO 65/69, unnumbered desp., Gower to Canning, 26 June 1807.

39. *Sbornik*, vol. 89, pp. 44–5.

40. TNA: PRO FO 65/69, desp. 8, Gower to Canning, 2 July 1807.

41. LDA, George Canning Papers, HAR/GC/57, Gower to Canning, 7 July 1807.

42. TNA: PRO FO 65/69, desp. 9, Gower to Canning, 12 July 1807; LDA, George Canning Papers, HAR/GC/57, Gower to Canning, 12 July 1807.

43. Granville, *Correspondence*, vol. 2, p. 270.

44. LDA, George Canning Papers, HAR/GC/57, Gower to Canning, 12 July 1807.

45. LDA, George Canning Papers, HAR/GC/57, Gower to Canning, 15 July 1807.

46. Granville, *Correspondence*, vol. 2, p. 272.

CHAPTER 3

1. The phrase is Benjamin Garlike's: TNA: PRO FO 22/51, desp. 22, Garlike to Howick, 15 February 1807.

2. For general Danish history in this period, see [Gyldendals] *Danmarks historie*, Ole Feldbæk, vol. 4, *Tiden 1730–1814* (Copenhagen, 1982). For Fredrick and the Bernstorff brothers, see A. Lindvald, *Kronprins Frederik og hans Regering 1797–1807* (Copenhagen, 1923), pp. 22–55, 72, and the relevant entries in *DBL*. The fundamental works on Danish foreign policy in this period are E. Holm, *Danmark-Norges udenrigske Historie under den franske Revolution og Napoleons Krige fra 1791 til 1807*, vol. 2 (Copenhagen, 1875); E. Holm, *Danmark-Norges udenrigske Historie i Aarene 1800 til 1814*, vol. 7, pt 1, *1800–1807* (Copenhagen, 1912); Knud J.V. Jespersen and Ole Feldbæk, *Revanche og neutralitet, 1648–1814* (Copenhagen, 2002), vol. 2 of Carsten Due-Nielsen *et al.*, *Dansk udenrigspolitiks historie* (ongoing). For a recent summary in English, see Ole Feldbæk, 'Denmark in the Napoleonic Wars: A Foreign Policy Survey', *Scandinavian Journal of History*, vol. 26 (2001).

3. Jespersen and Feldbæk, *Revanche og neutralitet*, pp. 334–8; John Brooke, *King George III* (London, 1972), pp. 268–70.

4. Seved Johnson, *Sverige och stormakterna 1800–1804* (Lund, 1957), pp. 10–18.

5. Ole Feldbæk, 'Denmark and the Baltic, 1720–1864', in G. Rystad *et al.* (eds), *In Quest of Trade and Security: The Baltic in Power Politics, 1500–1990*, vol. 1, *1500–1890* (Stockholm, 1994), pp. 266–76.

6. Ole Feldbæk, *Denmark and the Armed Neutrality 1800–1801* (Copenhagen, 1980), *passim*; Feldbæk, 'The Anglo-Russian Rapprochement of 1801'.

7. Holm, *Danmark-Norges* (1912), pp. 120–1, 128–9, 150–1, 173–4.

8. *Ibid.*, pp. 125–7, 131–3, 135–41, 148–9, 163–4, 180–3.

9. *Ibid.*, pp. 137, 160–1, 180.

10. *Ibid.*, pp. 162–3.

11. DRA, Bernstorff family private papers, 5128/48, J. to C. Bernstorff, 31 January–8 August 1807.

12. For Garlike's career, see *Gentleman's Magazine*, January–June 1815, pp. 564–5; and the relevant entries in S.T. Bindoff *et al.*, *British Diplomatic Representatives, 1789–1852*, Camden Third Series, vol. 50 (London, 1934).

13. Lindvald, *Kronprins Frederik*, pp. 178–81.

14. TNA: PRO FO 22/47, desp. 1, Garlike to Mulgrave, 3 December 1805; Lindvald, *Kronprins Frederik*, pp. 173–4.

15. Lindvald, *Kronprins Frederik*, pp. 183–5.

16. F. Crouzet, *L'Économie Britannique et le Blocus Continental*, vol. 1 (Paris, 1958), pp. 131–4.

17. Lindvald, *Kronprins Frederik*, pp. 333–6; see also A. Lindvald, 'Bidrag til Oplysning om Danmark-Norges Handel og Skibsfart 1800–1807', (Danish) *Historisk Tidsskrift*, 8th series, vol. 6 (1917), pp. 448–52.

18. See, e.g., TNA: PRO FO 22/47, desp. 13, Garlike to Mulgrave, 1 July 1805; desp. 6, Hill to Mulgrave, 1 October 1805; desp. 3, Garlike to Mulgrave, 5 December 1805; and FO 22/48, desp. 2, Garlike to Mulgrave, 7 January 1806.

19. TNA: PRO FO 22/43, desp. 1, Hawkesbury to Liston, 23 June 1803.

20. Crouzet, *L'Économie Britannique*, pp. 127–9.

21. Feldbæk, *Tiden*, p. 132.

22. TNA: PRO FO 22/48, desp. 13, Garlike to Fox, 18 March 1806.

23. T. Munch-Petersen, 'A Prelude to the British Bombardment of Copenhagen: Viscount Howick and Denmark, 1806–1807', *Scandia*, vol. 65, no. 1 (1999), pp. 41–2.

24. C.T. Sørensen (ed.), *Meddelelser fra Krigarkiverne. Udgivne af Generalstaben*, vol. 2 (Copenhagen, 1885), pp. 280–1.

25. Holm, *Danmark-Norges* (1875), pp. 129–30; Sørensen (ed.), *Meddelelser*, vol. 2, pp. 292–5.

26. TNA: PRO FO 22/49, desp. 77, Garlike to Howick, 14 November 1806; extract printed in *Parl. Deb.*, vol. 10, pp. 762–5.

27. DRA, Crown Prince Fredrick's Archive, 1784–1808, Kabinets-sekretariatet/1474. Walterstorff to Fredrick, 25 November 1806.

28. Sørensen (ed.), *Meddelelser*, vol. 2, pp. 295, 404–5.

29. Holm, *Danmark-Norges* (1875), pp. 132–3.

30. TNA: PRO FO 33/35, unnumbered desp., Thornton to Howick, 31 December 1806.

31. TNA: PRO FO 22/49, desp. 77, Garlike to Howick, 14 November 1806; extract printed in *Parl. Deb.*, vol. 10, pp. 762–5.

32. TNA: PRO FO 22/49, desp. 81, Garlike to Howick, 24 November 1806; printed in *Parl. Deb.*, vol. 10, pp. 768–71.

33. For a concise life of Howick, see E.A. Smith, 'Grey, Charles, second Earl Grey (1764–1845)', in *ODNB*.

34. DRA, DUA/1988, desp. 102, Rist to C. Bernstorff, 16 December 1806.

35. DRA, DUA/1988, desps 4 and 8, Rist to C. Bernstorff, 13 and 27 January 1807.

36. A. Aspinall (ed.), *The Later Correspondence of George III, 1783–1810*, vol. 4 (Cambridge, 1968), pp. 493–4.

37. TNA: PRO FO 22/49, desp. 7, Howick to Garlike, 9 December 1806; printed in *Parl. Deb.*, vol. 10, p. 768.

38. TNA: PRO FO 73/36, desp. 8, Howick to Pierrepont, 26 December 1806.

39. TNA: PRO FO 22/49, desp. 6, Howick to Garlike, 3 December 1806; printed in *Parl. Deb.*, vol. 10, pp. 765–8; see also DUL, the second Earl Grey Papers, Howick to Pierrepont, 2 December 1806 (2 letters), B47/2/9–10.

40. Ole Feldbæk, *The Battle of Copenhagen, 1801* (Barnsley, 2002), pp. 70–86.

41. O.L. Frantzen, *Truslen fra øst: Dansk-norsk flådepolitik 1769–1807* (Copenhagen, 1980), pp. 126–32.

42. TNA: PRO FO 22/49, desp. 67, Garlike to Howick, 25 October 1806.

43. TNA: PRO FO 22/49, desp. 6, Howick to Garlike, 3 December 1806; printed in *Parl. Deb.*, vol. 10, pp. 765–8; see also DUL, the second Earl Grey Papers, Howick to Pierrepont, 2 December 1806 (2 letters), B47/2/9–10.

44. TNA: PRO FO 22/49, desp. 91, Garlike to Howick, 20 December 1806; printed in *Parl. Deb.*, vol. 10, pp. 775–7.

45. The personality and policies of Gustavus IV have been a classic subject of controversy among Swedish historians. Two recent English-language works with a lot to say about him are S.G. Trulsson, *British and Swedish Policies and Strategies in the Baltic after the Peace of Tilsit in 1807* (Lund, 1976), and Christer Jorgensen, *The Anglo-Swedish Alliance against Napoleonic France* (Basingstoke, 2004).

46. G. Björlin, *Sveriges krig i Tyskland åren 1805–1807* (Stockholm, 1882), p. 159.

47. Sørensen (ed.), *Meddelelser*, vol. 2, pp. 366–7, 376, 379, 380–1, 407–8; Holm, *Danmark-Norges* (1875), pp. 154–6.

48. TNA: PRO FO 22/49, desp. 9, Howick to Garlike, 30 December 1806; DUL, the second Earl Grey Papers, Howick to Thornton, 31 December 1806, GRE B54/12/27.

49. TNA: PRO FO 22/49, desp. 85, Garlike to Howick, 2 December 1806.

50. TNA: PRO FO 22/49, desp. 93, Garlike to Howick, 20 December 1806.
51. DUL, the second Earl Grey Papers, Howick to Garlike, 9 January 1807, GRE B15/11/13.
52. DUL, the second Earl Grey Papers, undated and unsigned note concerning the Baltic squadron, B1/5/22.
53. National Maritime Museum, Greenwich, Duckworth Papers, T. Grenville to Duckworth, 18 January 1807, DUC/13–38 MS 2002.
54. DUL, the second Earl Grey Papers, Garlike to Howick, 15 February 1807, GRE B15/11/24–24A.
55. SRA, Anglica/490, desp. 3, Rehausen to Gustavus, 13 January 1807.
56. DUL, the second Earl Grey Papers, Howick to Garlike, 22 January 1807, GRE B15/11/17.
57. DRA, DUA/1988, desps 12 and 23, Rist to Bernstorff, 10 February and 17 March 1807; TNA: PRO FO 22/51, desp. 31, Garlike to Howick, 23 March 1807.
58. Duke of Buckingham and Chandos, *Memoirs of the Court and Cabinets of George III*, vol. 1 (London, 1855), p. 124.
59. For Rist, see the entry on him in *DBL*.
60. Holm, *Danmark-Norges* (1875), pp. 138–42; Lindvald, *Kronprins Frederik*, pp. 210–12; see also H. Søby Andersen, *En lus mellem to negle: Dansk-norsk neutralitetspolitik 1801–1807* (Odense, 1991), pp. 80–2.
61. DUL, the second Earl Grey Papers, Garlike to Howick, 30 January 1807, GRE 15/11/20.
62. Holm, *Danmark-Norges* (1875), pp. 166–9; Lindvald, *Kronprins Frederik*, pp. 209–10, 216–20; Søby Andersen, *En lus mellem to negle*, pp. 86–9.
63. *Parl. Deb.*, vol. 8, pp. 620–56.
64. DRA, DUA/1988, desps 11 and 12 (quotation), Rist to C. Bernstorff, 6 and 10 February 1807.
65. TNA: PRO FO 22/51, desp. 14, Garlike to Howick, 30 January 1807.
66. DRA, GskA, England I, desp. 35, C. Bernstorff to Rist, 17 January 1807.
67. DUL, the second Earl Grey Papers, Garlike to Howick, 30 January 1807, GRE 15/11/20.
68. Lindvald, *Kronprins Frederik*, pp. 219–20.
69. Note from Rist to Howick, 9 March 1807, printed in *Parl. Deb.*, vol. 10, pp. 397–402.
70. Note from Howick to Rist, 17 March 1807, printed in *Parl. Deb.*, vol. 10, pp. 402–7.
71. DRA, DUA/1988, desp. 24, Rist to C. Bernstorff, 20 March 1807.
72. DRA, DUA/1988, desp. 34, Rist to C. Bernstorff, 21 April 1807.
73. SRA, Anglica/490, desp. 18, Rehausen to Gustavus, 17 March 1807.
74. TNA: PRO ADM 3/160, fos 7–8, Instructions from the admiralty to Keats, 1 April 1807.
75. DUL, the second Earl Grey Papers, Grenville to Grey, 29 December 1807, GRE B21/2/98.

76. Lindvald, *Kronprins Frederik*, pp. 183–5, 194–5; Crouzet, *L'Économie Britannique*, pp. 215, 219–25.

CHAPTER 4

1. DRA, DUA/1988, desp. 27, Rist to C. Bernstorff, 28 March 1807.
2. For Canning's background and early life, see the early chapters of Wendy Hinde, *George Canning* (London, 1973), Piers Dixon, *Canning: Politician and Statesman* (London, 1976), and, more concisely, the entry on Canning by Derek Beales in *ODNB*. There is interesting material on his friendships in A. Aspinall, 'The Canningite Party', *Transactions of the Royal Historical Society*, Fourth Series, vol. 17 (1984), and on his relations with Caroline of Brunswick in Flora Fraser, *The Unruly Queen: The Life of Queen Caroline* (London, 1996), pp. 123–6.
3. *Parl. Deb.*, vol. 9, p. 735.
4. Dixon, *Canning*, p. 66.
5. Lindvald, *Kronprins Frederik*, pp. 195–6. TNA: PRO FO 22/52, desps 1 and 3, Canning to Garlike, 17 April and 22 May 1807.
6. *Correspondence, Despatches, and Other Papers of Viscount Castlereagh, Second Marquess of Londonderry*, ed. C.W. Vane, Marquess of Londonderry (12 vols, London, 1848–53), 2nd series, vol. 6, p. 169.
7. TNA: PRO FO 65/69, desp. 8, Canning to Gower, 16 May 1807.
8. DRA, DUA/1989, desps 43, 44 and 46, Rist to C. Bernstorff, 22 May, 26 May and 2 June 1807.
9. Lindvald, *Kronprins Frederik*, p. 196.
10. TNA: PRO FO 22/57, Rist to Canning, 18 May 1807.
11. DRA, DUA/1989, desp. 43, Rist to C. Bernstorff, 22 May 1807.
12. TNA: PRO FO 22/57, Canning to Rist, 18 May 1807.
13. TNA: PRO FO 22/52, desp. 4, Canning to Garlike, 26 May 1807.
14. Lindvald, *Kronprins Frederik*, pp. 176, 188.
15. For the British prize system, see Hill, *The Prizes of War*, pp. 139–249.
16. Lindvald, *Kronprins Frederik*, pp. 198–9.
17. TNA: PRO FO 22/57, Rist to Canning, 8 May, 26 May and 5 June 1807.
18. TNA: PRO FO 22/57, Canning to Rist, 5 June 1807.
19. TNA: PRO FO 22/52, desp. 5, Canning to Garlike, 6 June 1807.
20. LDA, George Canning Papers, HAR/GC/42, Canning to Garlike, 7 June 1807. See also TNA: PRO FO 22/52, unnumbered desp., Canning to Garlike, 7 June 1807.
21. DRA, DUA/1989, Rist to C. Bernstorff, 26 May 1807.
22. TNA: PRO PRO 30/29/8/4, Canning to Gower, 9 June 1807.
23. TNA: PRO FO 22/57, Rist to Canning, 6 June 1807.
24. DRA, DUA/1179, Rist to the Ministry, 9 June 1807.

25. DRA, DUA/1989, desp. 48, Rist to C. Bernstorff, 9 June 1807; and DUA/1179, desp. 54, Rist to Ministry, 9 June 1807.
26. DRA, DUA/1179, J. to C. Bernstorff, 20 and 27 June 1807, C. to J. Bernstorff, 23 June 1807; Lindvald, *Kronprins Frederik*, pp. 202–5; LDA, George Canning Papers, HAR/GC/44, Garlike to Canning, 28 June 1807; TNA: PRO FO 22/52, desp. 71, Garlike to Canning, 27 June 1807.
27. DRA, DUA/1179, C. to J. Bernstorff, 28 July 1807.
28. Lindvald, *Kronprins Frederik*, pp. 212–16.
29. DUL, the second Earl Grey Papers, B15/11/24–24A, Garlike to Howick, 15 February 1807; Lindvald, *Kronprins Frederik*, pp. 221–2.
30. DUL, the second Earl Grey Papers, GRE 15/11/20, Garlike to Howick, 20 January 1807.
31. TNA: PRO FO 22/51, desp. 28, Garlike to Howick, 14 March 1807.
32. TNA: PRO FO 22/52, desp. 58, Garlike to Canning, 29 May 1807; see also LDA, George Canning Papers, HAR/GC/44, Garlike to Canning, 22 April 1807.
33. DRA, DUA/1944, C. to J. Bernstorff, undated (22 January 1807?).
34. TNA: PRO FO 22/51, desp. 22, Garlike to Howick, 15 February 1807.
35. TNA: PRO FO 22/51, desps 12 and 22, Garlike to Howick, 26 January and 14 March 1807; FO 22/52, desp. 45, Garlike to Canning, 22 April 1807.
36. LDA, George Canning Papers, HAR/GC/44, unnumbered desp., Garlike to Canning, 27 June 1807.
37. DRA, DUA/1988, desp. 24, Rist to C. Bernstorff, 20 March 1807.
38. TNA: PRO PRO/30/29/8/4, Canning to Gower, 21 July 1807; LDA, George Canning Papers, HAR/GC/41A, minute for the Cabinet by Canning, 11 July 1807.
39. DRA, GskA, Rusland I, desps 47 and 48, C. Bernstorff to Blome, 7 and 13 March 1807.
40. DRA, GskA, England I, desp. 40, C. Bernstorff to Rist, 13 March 1807.
41. DRA, GskA, Rusland I, desps 41 and 50, C. Bernstorff to Blome, 6 January and 3 April 1807.
42. DRA, GskA, Frankrig I, desps 33, 34 and 35, C. Bernstorff to Dreyer, 1 December, 15 December, 22 December 1806; Dreyer to Talleyrand, 30 December 1806, enclosed in DUA/2127, desp. 118, Dreyer to C. Bernstorff, 31 December 1806; DUA/2128, desp. 43, C. Bernstorff to Blome, 3 February 1807.
43. DRA, GskA, Rusland I, desp. 47, C. Bernstorff to Blome, 7 March 1807.
44. DRA, GskA, Rusland I, desps 45 and 50, C. Bernstorff to Blome, 20 February and 3 April 1807; DRA, GskA, England I, desps 35 and 41, C. Bernstorff to Rist, 27 January and 27 March 1807.
45. DRA, GskA, Rusland I, desps 51 and 53, C. Bernstorff to Blome, 10 April and 12 June 1807.

46. DRA, GskA, England I, desp. 43, C. Bernstorff to Rist, 10 April 1807; DRA, DUA 1989, desps 44 and 54, Rist to C. Bernstorff, 26 May and 30 June 1807.
47. DRA, GskA, Frankrig I, desp. 33, C. Bernstorff to Dreyer, 1 December 1806; GskA, England I, desp. 33, C. Bernstorff to Rist, 26 December 1806.
48. Hans Schulz (ed.), *Briefwechsel des Herzogs Friedrich Christian zu Schleswig-Holstein-Sonderburg-Augustenburg mit König Friedrich VI von Dänemark* (Leipzig, 1908), pp. 301, 311, 313, 314, 315, 320.
49. DRA, DUA 1989, desp. 54, Rist to C. Bernstorff, 30 June 1807.
50. LDA, George Canning Papers, HAR/GC/50, Pembroke to Canning, 28 May 1807.
51. LDA, George Canning Papers, HAR/GC/57, Gower to Canning, 29 May 1807.
52. DRA, Søkrigskancelliet, Kongens flådetabeller 1807, arkiv nr 509-E-17, sk 974.
53. DRA, GskA, Rusland I, desp. 52, C. Bernstorff to Blome, 21 April 1807.
54. DRA, Tillæg til søetatens arkiv-skibsjournaler 1675–1900 – år 1807 arkivnr 521-J-01 protokolnummer 832 [registratur 85 b2] (logbooks for the *Princesse Louisa Augusta*, *Prinds Christian Fredrick* and *Waldemar*, 1807); DRA, Admiral Hans Lindholms Arkiv, 5890, Fredrick to Lindholm, 17 April 1807.
55. Frantzen, *Truslen fra øst*, p. 23.
56. *Ibid.*, pp. 23, 27.
57. Feldbæk, *Copenhagen*, pp. 66, 87–97.
58. TNA: PRO FO 22/52, Hanchett to Garlike, 2 May 1807, enclosed in desp. 91, Garlike to Canning, 25 July 1807.
59. TNA: PRO FO 22/52, Beauman to Garlike, 25 July 1807, enclosed in desp. 91, Garlike to Canning, 25 July 1807 (emphasis added).
60. TNA: PRO FO 22/52, desp. 90, Garlike to Canning, 25 July 1807.
61. TNA: PRO FO 22/52, desp. 91, Garlike to Canning, 25 July 1807.
62. A.N. Ryan (ed.), 'Documents Relating to the Copenhagen Operation, 1807', *The Naval Miscellany*, vol. 5, *Publications of the Navy Records Society*, vol. 125 (1984), pp. 297–329, at p. 301.
63. LDA, George Canning Papers, HAR/GC/50, Canning to Pembroke, 9 June 1807.
64. TNA: PRO PRO 30/29/8/4, Canning to Gower, 9 June 1807.

CHAPTER 5

1. DRA, DUA 1989, desp. 54, Rist to C. Bernstorff, 30 June 1807; LDA, George Canning Papers, HAR/GC/31, Canning to Taylor, 29 June 1807.
2. TNA: PRO FO 65/69, desp. 21, Canning to Gower, 30 June 1807.

3. TNA: PRO FO 65/69, desp. 2, Canning to Gower, 16 May 1807.
4. See p. 68.
5. TNA: PRO FO 65/69, desp. 21, Canning to Gower, 30 June 1807; and TNA: PRO PRO 30/29/8/4, Canning to Gower, 30 June 1807.
6. TNA: PRO FO 33/38, desps 58 and 60, Thornton to Canning, 24 and 28 June 1807; DRA, DUA/1989, desps 55 and 56, Rist to C. Bernstorff, 3 and 7 July 1807.
7. Entry on Thornton by C.A. Harris, rev. H.C.G. Matthew, *ODNB*.
8. See Thornton's reports in TNA: PRO FO 33/35, FO 33/37, FO 33/38 and FO 933/16 for some of the intelligence he was receiving.
9. TNA: PRO FO 33/37, desp. 2, Canning to Thornton, 24 April 1807.
10. LDA, George Canning Papers, HAR/GC/44, Thomas to Edward Thornton, 1 August 1807.
11. Edward A. Whitcomb, *Napoleon's Diplomatic Service* (Durham, NC, 1979), pp. 81, 166.
12. Tatistcheff, *Alexandre 1er et Napoléon*, p. 157; *Sbornik*, vol. 89, Budberg to Saltykov, 16/28 June 1807, pp. 38–9.
13. TNA: PRO FO 33/38, desp. 65, Thornton to Canning, 5 July 1807. See also Elizabeth Sparrow, *Secret Service: British Agents in France 1792–1815* (Woodbridge, 1999), pp. 342–3, where Alexander's letter to the hereditary prince is printed in full.
14. TNA: PRO FO 33/38, Thornton to Fitzharris, 5 July 1807.
15. TNA: PRO FO 33/38, desp. 67, Thornton to Canning, 11 July 1807.
16. TNA: PRO FO 33/38, desp. 63, Thornton to Canning, 1 July 1807; also printed in Ryan (ed.), *Documents*, pp. 302–3.
17. TNA: PRO FO 22/52, desp. 8, Canning to Garlike, 10 July 1807.
18. Crouzet, *L'Économie Britannique*, p. 250.
19. Entry on Gordon by H.M. Chichester, rev. Jonathan Spain, in *ODNB*.
20. TNA: PRO FO 38/9, desp. 244, Gordon to the foreign office, 28 November 1806.
21. TNA: PRO FO 38/10, desp. 302, Gordon to the foreign office, 1 July 1807.
22. TNA: PRO FO 33/38, desp. 42, Thornton to Canning, 9 May 1807.
23. TNA: PRO FO 33/38, desps 51, 52, 53 (quotation), 55, unnumbered and 64, Thornton to Canning, 6, 10, 13, 17, 20 June and 4 July 1807.
24. TNA: PRO FO 33/39, Canning to Cockburn, 17 July 1807.
25. TNA: PRO FO 33/38, desp. 64, Thornton to Canning, 4 July 1807; Crouzet, *L'Économie Britannique*, p. 250.
26. LDA, George Canning Papers, HAR/GC/44, Thornton to Canning, 1 July 1807.
27. G. Lenotre, *Two Royalist Spies of the French Revolution* (London, 1924), pp. 158–60. This is a translation from French of G. Lenotre, *L'Affaire Perlet: Drames policiers* (Paris, 1923).
28. For Fauche-Borel and the early stages of the Perlet affair, see Lenotre, *Two Royalist Spies*, especially pp. 114–70.

29. Sparrow, *Secret Service*, pp. 317–20.

30. DUL, the second Earl Grey Papers, B9A/6/1, Howick to Canning, 1 April 1807.

31. Lenotre, *Two Royalist Spies*, p. 146; *Correspondence de Napoléon*, vol. 14, p. 510.

32. For Danican, see Lenotre, *Two Royalist Spies*, pp. 71–2, and Adolphe Robinet, *Dictionnaire historique et biographique de la Révolution et de l'Empire* (Paris, n.d.), p. 531.

33. DUL, the second Earl Grey Papers, B56/8/12–13, Danican to Vincent, 3 October 1806 and enclosed note by Danican for Hammond, 12 September 1803.

34. LDA, George Canning Papers, HAR/GC/44, two unsigned letters from Le Havre, 7 June 1807; two letters from D from Dondeville, 17 and 19 June 1807; undated letter from D, received in London on 29 July 1807; extract from unsigned letter to Fauche-Borel from Altona, 25 July 1807; extract from letter from Danican, 29 July 1807.

35. Sparrow, *Secret Service*, pp. 307–8.

36. [Louis Fauche-Borel], *Mémoires de Fauche-Borel*, vol. 4 (Paris, 1829), pp. 3–4.

37. Ernest d'Hauterive, *La Police secrète du premier empire: Bulletins quotidiens addressés par Fouché à l'Empereur*, vol. 3, *1806–1807* (Paris, 1922), pp. 365–6.

38. LDA, George Canning Papers, HAR/GC/44, unsigned and undated letter in the 'Secret Intelligence, Denmark' group of documents. See also Sparrow, *Secret Service*, pp. 338, 339–41, who argues that this agent was called Louis Bayard.

39. D'Hauterive, *La Police secrète*, vol. 3, p. 365.

40. Fauche-Borel, *Mémoires*, p. 5.

41. Marianne Elliott, *Partners in Revolution: The United Irishmen and France* (New Haven and London, 1982), pp. 324–49.

42. *Ibid.*, pp. 152, 155–61, 333–4, 338. See also Édouard Desbrière, *Projets et tentatives de débarquement aux îles britanniques*, 4 vols (Paris, 1900–2), who covers French plans of this kind between 1793 and 1805 in great detail.

43. Petre, *Napoleon's Campaign*, pp. 229–33.

44. *Correspondence de Napoléon*, vol. 15, p. 165.

CHAPTER 6

1. J. Holland Rose, 'A British Agent at Tilsit', *English Historical Review*, vol. 16 (1901), pp. 713–16; TNA: PRO FO 65/69, desp. 7, Gower to Canning, 25 June 1807; LDA, George Canning Papers, HAR/GC/57, Gower to Canning, 26 June 1807.

2. LDA, George Canning Papers, HAR/GC/42, Canning to Garlike, 18 July 1807.

3. Feldbæk, *Copenhagen*, pp. 70, 195–6, 208–9; Frantzen, *Truslen fra øst*, p. 124; Ole Feldbæk, 'Danmark og Øresund under revolutions- og Napoleonskrigene', in Johan Engström and Ole L. Frantzen (eds), *Øresunds strategiske rolle i et historisk perspektiv* (Lund, 1998), p. 119.

4. J.W. Fortescue, *A History of the British Army*, vol. 6, *1807–1809* (1910), p. 58.

5. TNA: PRO PRO/30/29/8/4, Canning to Gower, 21 July 1807.

6. LDA, George Canning Papers, HAR/GC/31, Canning to Mulgrave, 7 July 1807 (emphasis added).

7. LDA, George Canning Papers, HAR/GC/41A, minute for the Cabinet by Canning, 10 July 1807.

8. LDA, George Canning Papers, HAR/GC/44, 'Extract of a private letter from Lord G.L. Gower to Mr Canning dated Memel June 19th 1807', but including other extracts from private letters or secret intelligence from 7 June to 6 July.

9. TNA: PRO FO 33/35, desp. 161, Thornton to Howick, 20 December 1806; FO 33/37, desp. 6, Thornton to Walpole, 21 January 1807; and FO 33/38, desp. 49, Thornton to Canning, 20 May 1807.

10. LDA, George Canning Papers, HAR/GC/41A, minute for the Cabinet by Canning, 11 July 1807.

11. LDA, George Canning Papers, HAR/GC/22, George to Joan Canning, 1 August 1807.

12. Granville, *Correspondence*, vol. 2, p. 261.

13. LDA, George Canning Papers, HAR/GC/41A, minutes by Portland, 11 July 1807, Hawkesbury and Eldon (both undated).

14. *Correspondence George III*, p. 604.

15. *Ibid.*, pp. 604, 605.

16. TNA: PRO FO 22/52, desp. 8, Canning to Garlike, 10 July 1807.

17. TNA: PRO FO 22/52, desp. 9, Canning to Garlike, 10 July 1807.

18. LDA, George Canning Papers, HAR/GC/42, Canning to Garlike, 14 July 1807.

19. LDA, George Canning Papers, HAR/GC/42, Canning to Garlike, 18 July 1807.

20. TNA: PRO PRO 30/29/8/4, Canning to Gower, 21 July 1807.

21. Entry on Sir Herbert and Sir Brook Taylor by R.H. Vetch, rev. K.D. Reynolds, in *ODNB*.

22. TNA: PRO FO 22/53, desp. 2, Canning to Taylor, 16 July 1807; Rose, 'A British Agent', pp. 716–17.

23. *Correspondence George III*, pp. 606–7.

24. TNA: PRO WO 6/14, Castlereagh to the Lords Commissioners of the Admiralty, 18 July 1807, printed in Ryan (ed.), *Documents*, pp. 303–4.

25. TNA: PRO WO 6/14, Castlereagh to Gambier, 19 July 1807, printed in Ryan (ed.), *Documents*, pp. 304–5.

26. TNA: PRO WO 6/14, Castlereagh to Cathcart, 19 July 1807, partly printed in Ryan (ed.), *Documents*, pp. 306–7; see also LDA, George Canning Papers, HAR/GC/44, copy of Castlereagh to Cathcart, 19 July 1807.

27. TNA: PRO FO 353/56, Francis Jackson, 'A Review of the last two months of my Life written at Broadstairs in October 1807'.

28. Entry on Jackson by H.M Chichester, rev. H.C.G. Matthew, in *ODNB*. For a hostile portrait of Jackson, see William H. Masterson, *Tories and Democrats: British Diplomats in Pre-Jacksonian America* (College Station, Tex., 1985), pp. 121–3. The book also contains chapters on George Hammond, Anthony Merry and Edward Thornton.

29. TNA: PRO, Jackson, 'A Review'.

30. Entry on Malmesbury by H.M. Scott in *ODNB*.

31. *A Series of Letters of the First Earl of Malmesbury His Family and Friends from 1745 to 1820* (London, 1870), vol. 2, see, e.g., pp. 26–31, 32, 34–6, 43–4.

32. LDA, George Canning Papers, HAR/GC/22, George to Joan Canning, 22 August 1807.

33. *The Diaries and Letters of Sir George Jackson*, ed. Lady Jackson, 2 vols (London, 1872), vol. 2, pp. 187–8; and TNA: PRO, Jackson, 'A Review'.

34. *Correspondence George III*, p. 607.

35. *Ibid.*, pp. 607–8.

36. *Ibid.*, p. 608.

37. *Ibid.*, p. 610.

38. *Ibid.*, p. 607, n. 2.

39. Trulsson, *British and Swedish Policies*, pp. 27–8.

40. TNA: PRO PRO 30/29/8/4, Canning to Gower, 5 August 1807.

41. TNA: PRO, Jackson, 'A Review'.

42. Soviet Foreign Ministry, *Vneshniaia*, vol. 4, pp. 15–16.

43. TNA: PRO FO 65/69, desp. 22, Canning to Gower, 21 July 1807.

44. TNA: PRO PRO 30/29/8/4, Canning to Gower, 21 July 1807 (Canning's emphasis).

45. Soviet Foreign Ministry, *Vneshniaia*, vol. 3, pp. 508–19, 581–2, 618–19; Holm, *Danmark-Norges* (1875), pp. 176–8; TNA: PRO FO 22/52, desp. 82, Garlike to Canning, 17 July 1807.

46. Trulsson, *British and Swedish Policies*, p. 33.

CHAPTER 7

1. There are three biographies of d'Antraigues: Léonce Pingaud, *Un Agent secret sous la Révolution et l'Empire: Le Comte d'Antraigues* (2nd edn, Paris, 1894); Colin Duckworth, *The D'Antraigues Phenomenon* (Newcastle, 1986); and Jacques Godechot, *Le Comte d'Antraigues: Un espion dans l'Europe des émigrés* (Paris, 1986).

2. Godechot, *Le Comte d'Antraigues*, pp. 214–15. See also Pingaud, *Un agent*

secret, p. 231.

3. Pingaud, *Un agent secret*, pp. 317–20; *Sbornik*, vol. 82, pp. 332–3; AAE, FB, vol. 631, Czartoryski to d'Antraigues, 12 April 1806, fos 160–4.

4. DUL, the second Earl Grey Papers, GRE/2B/4/12, d'Antraigues to Grey, 18 July 1809.

5. *Arkhiv knyazya Vorontsova*, ed. P. Bartenev, 40 vols (Moscow, 1870–95), vol. 15, p. 419.

6. *Ibid.*, vol. 22, p. 327.

7. *Ibid.*, vol. 22, pp. 377–9.

8. TNA: PRO PRO 30/29/8/4, Canning to Gower, 16 May 1807.

9. DRA, DUA 1989, desp. 47, Rist to C. Bernstorff, 5 June 1807.

10. Czartoryski Library, Cracow, Czart. MS, vol. 5481, d'Antraigues to Czartoryski, 17 November 1806 and 7 April 1807.

11. *Ibid.*, d'Antraigues to Czartoryski, 15 May 1806, and 17 July 1807.

12. *Sbornik*, vol. 82, pp. 330–4.

13. DUL, the second Earl Grey Papers, GRE/B8/14/1, Butler to Grey, 25 July 1812.

14. BL Add. MS 58900, Wynn to Grenville, 23 May 1805, fos 92–3. Wynn's other letters to Grenville from Dresden are in the same volume and stretch from 19 July 1804 to 5 August 1806, fos 88–102.

15. TNA: PRO FO 353/85, Wynn to Jackson, 16 March 1804, fos 47–50.

16. DUL, the second Earl Grey Papers, GRE/B2/12/44, d'Antraigues to Grey, 4 July 1809.

17. BL Add. MS 58900, Wynn to Grenville, 1 August 1806, fos 100–1.

18. BL Add. MS 59035, d'Antraigues to Grenville, 16 September 1806, fos 5–6.

19. Grenville had legible copies of several of d'Antraigues's letters made by a secretary, BL Add. MS 59035, fos 7 and 10; and when sending Howick a letter from d'Antraigues, he gave a concise summary of its contents in a covering note, 'As the probability is that you [Howick] will not be able to read it', DUL, the second Earl Grey Papers, GRE/B21/2/59, Grenville to Howick, undated (but early November 1806).

20. LDA, George Canning Papers, HAR/GC/59, d'Antraigues to Canning, 29 April 1807.

21. TNA: PRO FO 27/76, note by Howick, 12 June 1807.

22. *Jane Austen's Letters*, coll. and ed. Deirdre Le Faye (3rd edn, Oxford, 1995), pp. 184–5.

23. BL Add. MS 58900, Wynn to Grenville, 1 August 1806, fos 100–1.

24. Fauche-Borel, *Mémoires*, vol. 3, p. 256.

25. BL Add. MS 59035, d'Antraigues to Grenville, 14 October 1806, fos 28–9.

26. DUL, the second Earl Grey Papers, GRE/2B/12/15, d'Antraigues to Howick, 29 March 1806.

27. LDA, George Canning Papers, HAR/GC/ 59b, d'Antraigues to Canning, 9 July 1807.

28. Simon Burrows, 'British Propaganda for Russia in the Napoleonic Wars: The

Courier d'Angleterre', *New Zealand Slavonic Journal* (1993), p. 87.

29. D'Antraigues's letters to Vansittart and Grenville between September and December 1806 are to be found in BL Add. MSS 31230, fos 154–85, and 59035, fos 1–39.

30. BL Add. MS 59035, d'Antraigues to Vansittart, 29 December 1806, fos 172–3.

31. DUL, the second Earl Grey Papers, GRE/B7/15/2 and 4, Boothby to Fox, 30 June and 20 July 1806.

32. Cracow 5481, d'Antraigues to Czartoryski, 17 November 1806–2 August 1807.

33. For the emergence and decline of the 'young friends', see Palmer, *Alexander I*, pp. 47–120, and Hartley, *Alexander I*, pp. 30–75. There is a good modern biography of Czartoryski: W.H. Zawadzki, *A Man of Honour: Adam Czartoryski as a Statesman of Russia and Poland 1795–1831* (Oxford, 1993).

34. *Arkhiv knyazya Vorontsova*, vol. 18, pp. 473–4.

35. *Ibid.*, vol. 15, p. 420.

36. *Sbornik*, vol. 82, pp. 330–4.

37. Simon Burrows, 'The Struggle for European Opinion in the Napoleonic Wars: British Francophone Propaganda, 1803–1814', *French History*, vol. 11, no. 1 (1997), especially pp. 37–9, 52–3. See also Simon Burrows, *French Exile Journalism and European Politics 1792–1815* (Woodbridge, 2000).

38. LDA, George Canning Papers, HAR/GC/59, Canning to d'Antraigues and d'Antraigues to Canning, both 29 April 1807, and Canning to d'Antraigues, 30 April 1807.

39. TNA: PRO FO 65/69, desp. 17, Canning to Gower, 20 June 1807.

40. TNA: PRO PRO 30/29/8/4, Canning to Gower, 16 May 1806, fo. 169.

41. LDA, George Canning Papers, HAR/GC/59B, d'Antraigues to Canning, 2 July 1807; TNA: PRO, Jackson, 'A Review'.

42. LDA, George Canning Papers, HAR/GC/57, Gower to Canning, 15 June 1807.

43. LDA, George Canning Papers, HAR/GC/59B, d'Antraigues to Canning, 21 July 1807. The letter is printed in full, both in the original French and in English translation in Thomas Munch-Petersen, 'The Secret Intelligence from Tilsit: New Light on the Events Surrounding the British Bombardment of Copenhagen in 1807', (Danish) *Historisk Tidsskrift*, vol. 102, pt 1 (2002), pp. 55–96, at pp. 77–83.

44. See Munch-Petersen, 'The Secret Intelligence from Tilsit', pp. 84–5, for the identification of Troubetzkoi.

45. Pingaud, *Un agent secret*, pp. 293–4.

46. See Troubetzkoi and Wilhelmine's letters to d'Antraigues between 1805 and 1807 in AAE, FB, vol. 643, fos 102–47.

47. Kansallisarkisto (National Archives of Finland), Helsinki, Armfelt archive,

d'Antraigues to Armfelt, 13 June 1806, microfilm PR 10. Carl von Bonsdorff, *Gustav Mauritz Armfelt: Levnadsskildring*, 4 vols (Helsingfors, 1930–4), vol. 2, p. 85.

48. AAE, FB, vol. 643, Troubetzkoi to d'Antraigues, 16 February 1805, fo. 103; undated, fo. 141 (quotation); 2 April 1806, fos 111–12; 15 May 1806, fos 113–14; 4/16 July 1806, fos 116–17; 11/23 April 1807, fos 128–9.

49. Romanov, *Portraits Russes*, vol. 5, no. 131.

50. Munch-Petersen, 'The Secret Intelligence from Tilsit', pp. 86–7, 89–90.

51. *Ibid.*, pp. 85–7.

52. André Fugier, *Napoléon et l'Espagne*, vol. 2 (Paris, 1930), p. 217.

53. See p. 85.

54. Munch-Petersen, 'The Secret Intelligence from Tilsit', pp. 87–90.

55. *Correspondence de Napoléon*, vol. 15, pp. 381–5, 389–91, 392, 400–3; Tatistcheff, *Alexandre 1er et Napoléon*, pp. 162–9.

56. Vandal, *Napoléon et Alexandre 1er*, pp. 99–100.

57. Tatistcheff, *Alexandre 1er et Napoléon*, pp. 181–3.

58. *Sbornik*, vol. 89, pp. 33–7.

59. Munch-Petersen, 'The Secret Intelligence from Tilsit', pp. 90–3.

60. Canning to Gower, 21 July 1807. The original of this letter, in Canning's hand, is in Gower's private papers, which are in TNA: PRO PRO 38/29/8/4. There is another copy in fine secretarial hand in Canning's private papers, LDA, George Canning Papers, HAR/GC/42; and the postscript is printed in Ryan (ed.), *Documents*, pp. 307–8.

61. TNA: PRO FO 65/70, desp. 30, Canning to Gower, 5 August 1807.

62. TNA: PRO FO 65/70, desp. 34, Canning to Gower, 27 September 1807.

63. LDA, George Canning Papers, HAR/GC/44, Thornton to Canning, 24 July 1807; TNA: PRO FO 65/70, desp. 32, and PRO 30/29/8/4, Canning to Gower, both 12 August 1807.

64. TNA: PRO FO 65/70, desps 33 and 34, Canning to Gower, 13 August and 27 September 1807.

65. Jan Glete, *Navies and Nations: Warships, Navies and State Building in Europe and America, 1500–1860*, 2 vols (Stockholm, 1993), vol. 2, pp. 398, 655; Bernhard Gomm, *Die Russischen Kriegschiffe 1856–1917*, 2 vols (Wiesbaden, 1991–2), vol. 2, pp. 106–7. I am grateful to Professor Glete for his invaluable advice on this subject.

66. LDA, George Canning Papers, HAR/GC/32, Canning to Castlereagh, 3 August 1807; Trulsson, *British and Swedish Policies*, p. 33.

67. *Memorials, Personal and Historical of Admiral Lord Gambier*, ed. Georgiana, Lady Chatterton (2nd edn, 2 vols, London, 1861), vol. 2, pp. 17–21.

68. TNA: PRO PRO 30/29/8/4, Canning to Gower, 5 August 1807; TNA: PRO FO 65/70, desp. 33, Canning to Gower, 13 August 1807.

69. TNA: PRO FO 65/71, unnumbered desp., Canning to Shairp, 13 August

1807.

70. See p. 36.

71. *Parl. Deb.*, vol. 10, pp. 113–14.

72. *Ibid.*, pp. 114–15.

73. TNA: PRO FO 65/69, desp. 27, Canning to Gower, 2 August 1807.

74. TNA: PRO FO 65/69, desp. 28, Canning to Gower, 4 August 1807.

75. David S. Macmillan, 'Russo-British Trade Relations under Alexander I', *Canadian–American Slavic Studies*, vol. 9, no. 4 (1975), pp. 439–41, 443; Roach, 'Anglo-Russian Relations', pp. 192–3.

76. TNA: PRO FO 65/71, Shairp to Fitzharris, 13 May 1807, and to Canning, 21 July 1807.

77. TNA: PRO PRO 38/29/8/4, Canning to Gower, 30 July 1807; Soviet Foreign Ministry, *Vneshniaia*, vol. 4, pp. 18–20.

78. TNA: PRO FO 65/70, desp. 29, Canning to Gower, 4 August 1807.

79. TNA: PRO FO 65/70, desp. 32, Canning to Gower, 12 August 1807.

80. TNA: PRO PRO 38/29/8/4, Canning to Gower, 5 and 13 August 1807.

81. TNA: PRO FO 65/70, desp. 33, Canning to Gower, 13 August 1807.

82. See p. 105.

83. TNA: PRO FO 22/53, desp. 3, Canning to Taylor, 22 July 1807, printed in Rose, 'A British Agent', p. 717.

84. TNA: PRO FO 22/54, desp. 1, Canning to Jackson, 28 July 1807 and two undated draft treaties, fos 20–3, 24–6.

85. LDA, George Canning Papers, HAR/GC/42, Canning to Taylor, 18 July 1807.

86. TNA: PRO FO 22/54, desp. 5, Canning to Jackson, 30 July 1807.

87. LDA, George Canning Papers, HAR/GC/42, Canning to Jackson, 30 July 1807.

88. *Ibid.*

89. TNA: PRO FO 22/54, desp. 1, Canning to Jackson, 28 July 1807.

90. TNA: PRO FO 22/54, desp. 2, Canning to Jackson, 29 July 1807.

91. A.N. Ryan, 'The Navy at Copenhagen in 1807', *Mariner's Mirror*, 39 (1953), p. 203; *Correspondence George III*, pp. 611, 613; Ryan (ed.), *Documents*, pp. 309–11.

92. Granville, *Correspondence*, vol. 2, pp. 261 (quotation), 273–4; DRA, DUA/1989, desps 58, 59, 60, 62 and 63, Rist to C. Bernstorff, 14, 17, 21, 28 and 31 July 1807.

93. TNA: PRO FO 22/53, desp. 4, Canning to Taylor, 29 July 1807.

94. TNA: PRO WO 6/14, Castlereagh to Cathcart, 19 July 1807; printed in Ryan (ed.), *Documents*, pp. 309–11.

95. TNA: PRO FO 22/54, desp. 3, Canning to Jackson, 29 July 1807.

96. *Correspondence George III*, p. 612.

97. *Gambier Memorials*, vol. 2, pp. 14, 21.

98. TNA: PRO, Jackson, 'A Review'.

CHAPTER 8

1. Ryan, 'The Navy', pp. 203–4; William James, *The Naval History of Great Britain, from the Declaration of War by France in 1793 to the Accession of George IV*, vol. 4 (London, 1886), p. 201.
2. Entry on Keats by A.B. Sainsbury in *ODNB*.
3. Feldbæk, *Øresund*, p. 125; Feldbæk, *Copenhagen*, p. 229.
4. Ryan, 'The Navy', p. 204.
5. Feldbæk, *Øresund*, p. 121; Feldbæk, *Copenhagen*, pp. 63–4.
6. Ryan, 'The Navy', p. 206; James, *Naval History*, vol. 4, p. 201.
7. Entry on Gambier by Richard C. Blake in *ODNB*.
8. James, *Naval History*, vol. 4, p. 201; Ryan, 'The Navy', p. 207.
9. Sten Carlsson and Torvald Höjer, *Den svenska utrikespolitikens historia*, vol. 3, pts 1–2 (Stockholm, 1954), pp. 110–11; Jorgensen, *The Anglo-Swedish Alliance*, pp. 97–8.
10. N. Ludlow Beamish, *History of the King's German Legion*, vol. 1 (London, 1832), p. 105.
11. TNA: PRO WO 1/188, Cathcart to Castlereagh, 16 July 1807.
12. TNA: PRO WO 1/188, Cathcart to Castlereagh, 20 July and 6 August 1807.
13. TNA: PRO WO 1/188, Cathcart to Castlereagh, 6 August 1807.
14. Fortescue, *A History*, p. 64; Beamish, *History*, p. 108.
15. For the final stage of the Pomeranian war, see Björlin, *Sveriges krig*, pp. 202–26.
16. Huntington Library MS STG, Garlike to T. Grenville, 2 August 1807.
17. TNA: PRO FO 22/52, desp. 88, Garlike to Canning, 23 July 1807.
18. TNA: PRO FO 22/52, desps. 93 and 94, Garlike to Canning, 28 July and 1 August 1807.
19. DRA, DUA/1919, J. to C. Bernstorff, 28 July 1807; Carl T. Sørensen, 'Den politiske Krise i 1807', (Danish) *Historisk Tidsskrift*, 6th series, vol. 1 (1887–8), pp. 8–13.
20. LDA, George Canning Papers, HAR/GC/44, Garlike to Canning, 24 July 1807.
21. LDA, George Canning Papers, HAR/GC/44, Garlike to Canning, 27 July 1807.
22. LDA, George Canning Papers, HAR/GC/44, Garlike to Canning, 24 July 1807.
23. TNA: PRO FO 22/52, desp. 91, Garlike to Canning, 25 July 1807, enclosing Hanchett and Beauman's reports.
24. TNA: PRO FO 22/52, desp. 95, Garlike to Canning, 1 August 1807.
25. LDA, George Canning Papers, HAR/GC/44, Garlike to Canning, 1 and 2 August 1807; see also Huntington Library MS STG, Garlike to T. Grenville, 2 and 18 August 1807.
26. TNA: PRO FO 22/52, desp. 95, Garlike to Canning, 1 August 1807.
27. Sørensen, 'Den politiske Krise i 1807', p. 16; *Gazette Nationale ou Le Moniteur Universel*, 27 Brumaire, An 13 (18 November 1804).

28. TNA: PRO FO 22/53, desp. 1, Taylor to Canning, 3 August 1807; DRA, DUA/1919, J. to C. Bernstorff, 1 and 3 August 1807; Sørensen, 'Den politiske Krise i 1807', pp. 17–19.

29. DRA, DUA/1919, C. to J. Bernstorff, 1 August (but clearly a slip of the pen for 2 or 3 August) 1807; Sørensen, 'Den politiske Krise i 1807', pp. 16–17.

30. DRA, DUA/1919, J. to C. Bernstorff, 7 August 1807; Sørensen, 'Den politiske Krise i 1807', p. 24; TNA: PRO FO 22/53, desp. 3, Taylor to Canning, 8 August 1807, enclosing J. Bernstorff to Garlike, 6 August 1807.

31. Ryan (ed.), *Documents*, p. 311; TNA: PRO FO 22/53, Taylor to Gambier, 2 August 1807.

32. TNA: PRO FO 22/53, desp. 4, Taylor to Canning, 8 August 1807.

33. Lord Ronald Gower (ed.), *Stafford House Letters* (London, 1891), p. 57.

34. TNA: PRO FO 353/29, Jackson to Cathcart and Gambier, 5 August 1807, Jackson to C. Bernstorff, 6 and 7 August 1807, C. Bernstorff to Jackson, 7 August 1807; TNA: PRO, Jackson, 'A Review'.

35. Holm, *Danmark-Norges* (1912), endnotes p. 15.

36. *Ibid.*, pp. 302–3.

37. Holm, *Danmark-Norges* (1875), pp. 190–1; DRA, DUA 1989, Rist to C. Bernstorff, 14 July 1807.

38. Earl of Malmesbury, *Memoirs of an Ex-Minister* (London, 1884), 2 vols, vol. 1, p. 2.

39. *Correspondence George III*, p. xlix.

40. Holm, *Danmark-Norges* (1875), pp. 217–21.

41. DRA, DUA/1989, Rist to C. Bernstorff, 11 August 1807.

42. DRA, DUA/1919, J. to C. Bernstorff, 3 August 1807; Sørensen, 'Den politiske Krise i 1807', pp. 20–1.

43. Sørensen (ed.), *Meddelelser*, vol. 2, pp. 42–3.

44. TNA: PRO, Jackson, 'A Review'.

45. DRA, DUA/1919, desp. 45, C. Bernstorff to Rist, 7 August 1807.

46. E. Møller, 'England og Danmark-Norge 1807', (Danish) *Historisk Tidsskrift*, 8th series, vol. 3 (1910–12), pp. 389–406; Jespersen and Feldbæk, *Revanche og neutralitet*, p. 495.

47. TNA: PRO FO 22/54, desp. 1, Jackson to Canning, 7 August 1807; TNA: PRO, Jackson, 'A Review'; DRA, DUA/1919, C. to J. Bernstorff, 7 August 1807.

48. DRA, DUA/1919, C. to J. Bernstorff, 7 August 1807.

49. TNA: PRO FO 353/29, Canning to Jackson, 2 August 1807.

50. TNA: PRO FO 33/38, desps 73 and 76, Thornton to Canning, 29 July and 5 August 1807.

51. TNA: PRO FO 353/77, Thornton to Jackson, 6 August 1807, 10 p.m.; Møller, 'England og Danmark-Norge 1807', pp. 401–2.

52. See pp. 87–8.

53. *Diaries and Correspondence of James Harris, First Earl of Malmesbury* (London, 1844), vol. 4, p. 392.

54. TNA: PRO, Jackson, 'A Review'.
55. TNA: PRO FO 353/29, Canning to Jackson, 1 August 1807; TNA: PRO, Jackson, 'A Review'.
56. TNA: PRO, Jackson, 'A Review'; TNA: PRO FO 22/54, desp. 4, Jackson to Canning, 9 August 1807; Sørensen, 'Den politiske Krise i 1807', p. 34; DRA, DUA/1919, C. to J. Bernstorff, 8 August 1807.
57. TNA: PRO, Jackson, 'A Review'; TNA: PRO FO 353/29, C. Bernstorff to Jackson, 9 August 1807.
58. DRA, DUA/1919, C. to J. Bernstorff, 8 August 1807.
59. TNA: PRO, Jackson, 'A Review'; TNA: PRO FO 22/54, desp. 5, Jackson to Canning, 9 August 1807; DRA, DUA/1919, C. to J. Bernstorff, 9 August 1807.
60. J. v. Raeder, *Danmarks Krigs- og Politiske Historie fra Krigens Udbrud 1807 til Freden in Jönkjöping den 10de December 1809*, vol. 1 (Copenhagen, 1845), pp. 55–61, 67. There is also a short book about the concealment of the crown jewels: H.G. Olrik, *Fra Rosenborg til Sorø Kirke: Kronjuvelernes Udflugt* (Copenhagen, 1945).
61. Raeder, *Danmarks Krigs- og Politiske Historie*, vol. 1, pp. 63–5.
62. TNA: PRO, Jackson, 'A Review'.
63. Henrik Saxtorph, 'Det britiske angreb og Københavns søforsvar 1807', *Marinehistorisk Tidsskrift*, vol. 23, no. 3 (1990), p. 6.
64. Raeder, *Danmarks Krigs- og Politiske Historie*, vol. 1, pp. 65–7.
65. TNA: PRO FO 22/53, desp. 4, Canning to Taylor, 29 July 1807.
66. TNA: PRO FO 22/53, desp. 5, Taylor to Canning, 11 August 1807. For Joachim's account of the interview, DRA, DUA/1919, J. to C. Bernstorff, 11 August 1807; and Sørensen, 'Den politiske Krise i 1807', pp. 43–7.
67. TNA: PRO, Jackson, 'A Review'.
68. TNA: PRO FO 22/53, desp. 6, Canning to Taylor, 5 September 1807.
69. C.T. Sørensen (ed.), *Meddelelser fra Krigarkiverne: Udgivne af Generalstaben*, vol. 3 (Copenhagen, 1888), p. 10; Raeder, *Danmarks Krigs- og Politiske Historie*, vol. 1, p. 55.
70. TNA: PRO, Jackson, 'A Review', and FO 22/54, desp. 7, Jackson to Canning, 15 August 1807.
71. TNA: PRO, Jackson, 'A Review'.
72. Sørensen, 'Den politiske Krise i 1807', pp. 51–2.
73. TNA: PRO FO 22/54, desp. 7, Jackson to Canning, 15 August 1807; DRA, DUA/1919, J. to C. Bernstorff, 13 August 1807; Sørensen, 'Den politiske Krise i 1807', pp. 53–7.
74. Schroeder, *Transformation*, pp. 346–7; Vandal, *Napoléon et Alexandre 1er*, pp. 180–1; Driault, *Napoléon et l'Europe*, pp. 199–205; *Correspondence de Napoléon*, vol. 15, pp. 407–14, 421–2, 428–9, 451–3, 484.
75. See pp. 31–2.
76. Fugier, *Napoléon*, pp. 202, 216–17; *Correspondence de Napoléon*, vol. 15, pp. 433, 448–9, 465–7, 510–11.

77. *Correspondence de Napoléon*, vol. 15, pp. 459–60.
78. Dreyer's two despatches reporting this interview to Christian Bernstorff are printed in full in Holm, *Danmark-Norges* (1875), pp. 387–91.
79. DRA, DUA 2128, desp. 63, Dreyer to C. Bernstorff, 14 August 1807.
80. Eric Lerdrup-Bourgois, *De Tilsit à Fontainebleau: La Correspondence du Ministre Plénipotentiaire de Danemark-Norvège près Napoléon juillet 1807–novembre 1807. Recueil de sources* (Copenhagen, 2003), p. xi.
81. Emmanuel de Waresquiel, *Talleyrand: Le Prince immobile* (Paris, 2003), pp. 373–7; Philip G. Dwyer, *Talleyrand* (London/Harlow, 2002), pp. 108–11.
82. DRA, DUA 2128, desps 59 and 60, Dreyer to C. Bernstorff, 31 July and 3 August 1807.
83. Entry on Dreyer in *DBL*.
84. Holm, *Danmark-Norges* (1875), pp. 387–91.
85. DRA, DUA 2128, desp. 64, Dreyer to C. Bernstorff, 17 August 1807.
86. For the final stage of the Pomeranian campaign, see Björlin, *Sveriges krig*, pp. 202–26.
87. Torvald Höjer, *Carl XIV Johan*, vol. 1, *Den franska tiden* (Stockholm, 1939), p. 368.
88. *Correspondence de Napoléon*, vol. 15, pp. 467–8.
89. For this argument, see, e.g., Holm, *Danmark-Norges* (1875), p. 270; Sørensen (ed.), *Meddelelser*, vol. 3, pp. 14–15; Holm, *Danmark-Norges* (1912), p. 351; and Rodger, *The Command of the Ocean*, p. 549.
90. TNA: PRO, Jackson, 'A Review'.

CHAPTER 9

1. Raeder, *Danmarks Krigs- og Politiske Historie*, vol. 1, p. 113; TNA: PRO, Jackson, 'A Review'.
2. Printed in *Gambier Memorials*, vol. 2, pp. 23–5.
3. Raeder, *Danmarks Krigs- og Politiske Historie*, vol. 1, pp. 108–18.
4. Fortescue, *A History*, p. 67; TNA: PRO, Jackson, 'A Review' (quotation), Raeder, *Danmarks Krigs- og Politiske Historie*, vol. 1, p. 125.
5. TNA: PRO WO 1/188, Cathcart to Castlereagh, 14 October 1807; C.T. Atkinson (ed.), 'Gleanings from the Cathcart MSS, Part VI, The "Conjoint" Expedition to Copenhagen, 1807', *Journal of the Society for Army Historical Research*, vol. 30, no. 122 (1952), pp. 85–6.
6. *A Series of Letters of the First Earl of Malmesbury*, vol. 2, p. 42.
7. TNA: PRO, Jackson, 'A Review'.
8. Saxtorph, 'Det britiske angreb', pp. 7–8.
9. Fortescue, *A History*, p. 68.
10. Raeder, *Danmarks Krigs- og Politiske Historie*, vol. 1, p. 125.
11. H.G. Garde, *Den dansk-norsk Sömagts Historie 1700–1814* (Copenhagen, 1852), pp. 429–31; James, *Naval History*, vol. 4, pp. 203–4.

12. TNA: PRO, Jackson, 'A Review'.
13. Huntington Library MS STG, Garlike to T. Grenville, 18 and 24 August 1807.
14. TNA: PRO, Jackson, 'A Review'; Sørensen, 'Den politiske Krise i 1807', p. 57.
15. TNA: PRO, Jackson, 'A Review'.
16. Entry on Cathcart by M.D. Eddy in ODNB.
17. TNA: PRO, Jackson, 'A Review'.
18. For a defence of Cathcart, see Atkinson (ed.), 'Gleanings from the Cathcart MSS', p. 86.
19. TNA: PRO WO 1/188, Cathcart's Journal for 22 August to 1 September 1807; A Series of Letters of the First Earl of Malmesbury, vol. 2, p. 38.
20. TNA: PRO, Jackson, 'A Review'.
21. Raeder, Danmarks Krigs- og Politiske Historie, vol. 1, pp. 83, 93, 151; Ryan, 'The Navy', p. 205.
22. Entry on Peymann in DBL.
23. Entry on Bille in DBL.
24. Raeder, Danmarks Krigs- og Politiske Historie, vol. 1, pp. 95, 96; Garde, Den dansk-norsk Sömagts Historie, p. 425.
25. Saxtorph, 'Det britiske angreb', p. 8.
26. Raeder, Danmarks Krigs- og Politiske Historie, vol. 1, pp. 96–7.
27. DRA, Søkrigskancelliet – kongens flådetabeller- 1801- arkivnr 509-E-0017 – sk. nr 968.
28. Raeder, Danmarks Krigs- og Politiske Historie, vol. 1, pp. 95–6; Garde, Den dansk-norsk Sömagts Historie, pp. 427–8; Saxtorph, 'Det britiske angreb', pp. 9–10.
29. Garde, Den dansk-norsk Sömagts Historie, p. 447.
30. Ryan, 'The Navy', p. 208.
31. A Series of Letters of the First Earl of Malmesbury, vol. 2, pp. 39, 43.
32. TNA: PRO, Jackson, 'A Review'. See also W.G. Perrin (ed.), 'The Bombardment of Copenhagen, 1807: Journal of Surgeon Charles Chambers of H.M. Fireship Prometheus', The Naval Miscellany, vol. 3, Publications of the Navy Record Society, vol. 63 (1928), p. 387.
33. Perrin (ed.), 'The Bombardment of Copenhagen', p. 387.
34. James, Naval History, vol. 4, p. 206; Saxtorph, 'Det britiske angreb', p. 14.
35. Saxtorph, 'Det britiske angreb', p. 17; James, Naval History, vol. 4, p. 206; Raeder, Danmarks Krigs- og Politiske Historie, vol. 1, p. 215.
36. Gambier Memorials, vol. 2, p. 34.
37. TNA: PRO, Jackson, 'A Review'.
38. Entry on Wellesley (first Duke of Wellington) by Norman Gash in ODNB.
39. Thomas Munch-Petersen, 'Lord Cathcart, Sir Arthur Wellesley and the British Capture of Copenhagen in 1807', in C.M. Woolgar (ed.), Wellington Studies II (Southampton, 1999), pp. 109–10.

40. For the composition of the militia, see Jens Johansen, *Frederik VIs Hær 1784–1814* (Copenhagen, 1948), pp. 52–60, 72–5, and E.O.A. Hedegård, *Krigen på Sjælland 1807* (Copenhagen, 1970), pp. 38–54.

41. Hedegård, *Krigen på Sjælland*, pp. 56–7.

42. Entries on Castenschiold and Oxholm in *DBL*.

43. Raeder, *Danmarks Krigs- og Politiske Historie*, vol. 1, pp. 178–9.

44. *Ibid.*, pp. 178–97; Hedegård, *Krigen på Sjælland*, pp. 55–80; Johansen, *Frederik VIs Hær*, pp. 76–85.

45. *Supplementary Despatches and Memoranda of Field Marshal Arthur Duke of Wellington, KG*, ed. A.R. Wellesley, second Duke of Wellington (15 vols, London, 1858–72), vol. 6, pp. 5–8.

46. *The Dispatches of Field Marshal the Duke of Wellington, KG, during his Various Campaigns . . . from 1799 to 1818*, ed. J. Gurwood (new edn, 13 vols, London, 1837–9), vol. 3, p. 7.

47. *Wellington Supplementary Despatches*, vol. 6, pp. 16–17, 20–1; Raeder, *Danmarks Krigs- og Politiske Historie*, vol. 1, pp. 207, 209.

48. For accounts of the battle of Køge and the events surrounding it, see Fortescue, *A History*, pp. 71–2; *Wellington Dispatches*, vol. 3, pp. 7–8, 10; *Wellington Supplementary Despatches*, vol. 6, pp. 5–8, 10–15, 16–21; Raeder, *Danmarks Krigs- og Politiske Historie*, vol. 1, pp. 194–208; Hedegård, *Krigen på Sjælland*, pp. 79–125.

49. TNA: PRO WO 1/188, Cathcart to Castlereagh, 8 September 1807.

50. Raeder, *Danmarks Krigs- og Politiske Historie*, vol. 1, p. 208; Hedegård, *Krigen på Sjælland*, p. 125.

51. An English translation is printed in *The Annual Register for 1807* (London, 1809), p. 731.

52. Raeder, *Danmarks Krigs- og Politiske Historie*, vol. 1, pp. 372–4.

53. *Ibid.*, pp. 380–4; Sørensen (ed.), *Meddelelser*, vol. 3, pp. 22, 25.

54. Quoted in Holm, *Danmark-Norges* (1875), p. 269, and in Ryan, 'The Navy', p. 206.

55. The declaration is enclosed (in the original French) in DRA, DUA/1920, desp. 46, C. Bernstorff to Dreyer, 23 August 1807, and printed (in a somewhat quaint English translation) in *Annual Register*, pp. 733–5.

56. DRA, DUA/1920, C. Bernstorff to Blome, 10 August 1807.

57. C. Bernstorff to Blome, 31 August 1807, quoted in Holm, *Danmark-Norges* (1875), p. 271.

58. Holm, *Danmark-Norges* (1875), pp. 269–79; Holm, *Danmark-Norges* (1912), pp. 351–61.

59. DRA, GSKA, Frankrig I, C. Bernstorff to Dreyer, desp. 45, 19 August 1807.

60. DRA, DUA/1920, C. Bernstorff to Blome, 31 August 1807.

61. Höjer, *Carl XIV Johan*, pp. 368–9; Sørensen (ed.), *Meddelelser*, vol. 3, pp. 14–15.

62. *Correspondence de Napoléon*, vol. 15, pp. 504–5; Höjer, *Carl XIV Johan*, p. 368.

63. Holm, *Danmark-Norges* (1875), pp. 279–80.
64. *Correspondence George III*, vol. 4, p. 613, n. 2.
65. *Ibid.*, p. 619, n. 2.
66. *Ibid.*, p. 617, n. 2.
67. TNA: PRO WO 6/14, Castlereagh to Cathcart, 3 August 1807.
68. TNA: PRO WO 6/14, Castlereagh to Gambier, 3 August 1807.
69. See pp. 163–4.
70. Martin Robson, 'British Intervention in Portugal, 1806–1808', unpublished Ph.D. dissertation, King's College London, 2003, fo. 185. There is a good succinct account of the Portuguese crisis in Muir, *Britain and the Defeat of Napoleon*, pp. 29–30; and a detailed survey in Fugier, *Napoléon*, pp. 216–64, 346–54.
71. Glete, *Navies and Nations*, p. 400.
72. *Correspondence George III*, vol. 4, p. 621, n. 2 (Canning's emphasis).
73. Robson, 'British Intervention', fo. 187; *Correspondence George III*, vol. 4, pp. 618–19, 620–1, 621, n. 3.
74. Ryan (ed.), *Documents*, pp. 318–20.
75. Canning to Sousa, 7 September 1807, quoted in Robson, 'British Intervention', fo. 191.
76. TNA: PRO PRO 30/29/8/4, Canning to Gower, 5 November 1807.
77. TNA: PRO WO 6/14, desp. 10, Castlereagh to Cathcart, 5 September 1807; *Correspondence of Castlereagh*, vol. 6, p. 182.

CHAPTER 10

1. NLS, Murray Papers, Adv. MS 46.1.12, unsigned and undated report by Paget.
2. *A Series of Letters of the First Earl of Malmesbury*, vol. 2, p. 39.
3. Entry on Murray by S.G.P. Ward in *ODNB*.
4. NLS, Murray Papers, Adv. MS 46.1.12, Plan of attack on Copenhagen submitted by Lieutenant-Colonel Murray to Lord Cathcart, 14 August 1807.
5. *Wellington Supplementary Despatches*, vol. 6, p. 3.
6. NLS, Murray Papers, Adv. MS 46.1.12, Plan of attack on Copenhagen submitted by Lieutenant-Colonel Murray to Lord Cathcart, 14 August 1807.
7. *Wellington Supplementary Despatches*, vol. 6, p. 9.
8. Munch-Petersen, 'Lord Cathcart, Sir Arthur Wellesley', pp. 119–20.
9. TNA: PRO, Jackson, 'A Review'.
10. TNA: PRO WO 1/188, Cathcart to Castlereagh, 22 August 1807.
11. Raeder, *Danmarks Krigs- og Politiske Historie*, vol. 1, pp. 149–50.
12. TNA: PRO WO 1/188, Cathcart to Castlereagh, 22 and 31 August 1807.
13. Ryan (ed.), *Documents*, p. 318.

14. TNA: PRO WO 1/188, Cathcart to Castlereagh, 31 August 1807; see also p. 189.

15. Munch-Petersen, 'Lord Cathcart, Sir Arthur Wellesley', pp. 117–18; *Wellington Supplementary Despatches*, vol. 6, p. 34; Raeder, *Danmarks Krigs- og Politiske Historie*, vol. 1, p. 241.

16. Ryan (ed.), *Documents*, pp. 320–1.

17. *A Series of Letters of the First Earl of Malmesbury*, vol. 2, p. 46.

18. For accounts of the bombardment, see Raeder, *Danmarks Krigs- og Politiske Historie*, vol. 1, pp. 227–42; Marcus Rubin, *1807–14: Studies til Københavns og Danmarks Historie* (Copenhagen, 1892, reprinted 1970), pp. 448–52; S. Cedergren Bech, *Storhandelens by, Københavns historie*, vol. 3, *1728–1830* (Copenhagen, 1981), pp. 294–304. Two eyewitness accounts by British observers of the bombardment are Perrin (ed.), 'The Bombardment of Copenhagen', pp. 405–12, and Roger Norman Buckley (ed.), *The Napoleonic War Journal of Captain Thomas Henry Browne 1807–1816* (Army Records Society) (London, 1987), pp. 56–9.

19. Egon Eriksen and Ole L. Frantzen, *Dansk artilleri i napoleonstiden: Forudsætninger og udvikling 1760–1814* (2nd edn, Copenhagen, 1989), pp. 11–12.

20. Frank H. Winter, *The First Golden Age of Rocketry: Congreve and Hale Rockets of the Nineteenth Century* (Washington and London, 1990), pp. 13–22. For a more detailed account of the use of rockets at Copenhagen, see Frank H. Winter, 'Raketterne ved Københavns belejring – en milepæl i rakettens historie', *Marinehistorisk Tidsskrift*, vol. 12, no. 1 (1979).

21. Perrin (ed.), 'The Bombardment of Copenhagen', pp. 398, 401 (quotation).

22. Eriksen and Frantzen, *Dansk artilleri*, p. 11.

23. Eileen Hathaway (ed.), *A Dorset Rifleman: The Recollections of Benjamin Harris* (Swanage, 1996), p. 28.

24. Raeder, *Danmarks Krigs- og Politiske Historie*, vol. 1, pp. 241–3; *Parl. Deb.*, vol. 10, p. 225.

25. Raeder, *Danmarks Krigs- og Politiske Historie*, vol. 1, pp. 240–1.

26. *Ibid.*, p. 244; *Parl. Deb.*, vol. 10, p. 226.

27. Sørensen (ed.), *Meddelelser*, vol. 3, pp. 124–7; Raeder, *Danmarks Krigs- og Politiske Historie*, vol. 1, pp. 245–6.

28. Raeder, *Danmarks Krigs- og Politiske Historie*, vol. 1, p. 246; *Parl. Deb.*, vol. 10, p. 226 (quotation).

29. TNA: PRO, Jackson, 'A Review'.

30. TNA: PRO WO 1/188, Cathcart to Castlereagh, 8 September 1807.

31. *Wellington Dispatches*, vol. 3, p. 11.

32. Entry on Popham by Hugh Popham in *ODNB*.

33. *Wellington Dispatches*, vol. 3, p. 11.

34. For the negotiations and the terms of capitulations, see *Wellington Dispatches*, vol. 3, pp. 10–11; Sørensen (ed.), *Meddelelser*, vol. 3, pp. 129–32;

Parl. Deb., vol. 10, pp. 227–9; and Raeder, *Danmarks Krigs- og Politiske Historie*, vol. 1, pp. 260–6.

35. Hugh Popham, *A Damned Cunning Fellow: The Eventful Life of Rear-Admiral Sir Home Popham KCB, KCH, KM, FRS 1762–1820* (Tywardreath, 1991), p. 180.
36. Sørensen (ed.), *Meddelelser*, vol. 3, p. 130.
37. Holm, *Danmark-Norges* (1875), p. 269.
38. Sørensen (ed.), *Meddelelser*, vol. 3, p. 50.
39. *Ibid.*, pp. 50 (quotation) and 103.
40. *Ibid.*, p. 27; Raeder, *Danmarks Krigs- og Politiske Historie*, vol. 1, p. 258.
41. TNA: PRO WO 1/188, Cathcart to Castlereagh, 31 August 1807.
42. Henrik Saxtorph, 'Flåden gøres klar til ødelæggelse 1807', *Marinehistorisk Tidsskrift*, vol. 23, no. 4 (1990), pp. 6–8; Sørensen (ed.), *Meddelelser*, vol. 3, p. 132.
43. Sørensen (ed.), *Meddelelser*, vol. 3, pp. 124–8, 132–3; Saxtorph, 'Flåden', pp. 8–17.
44. Raeder, *Danmarks Krigs- og Politiske Historie*, vol. 1, pp. 260–2.
45. *Ibid.*, p. 268.

CHAPTER 11

1. Raeder, *Danmarks Krigs- og Politiske Historie*, vol. 1, pp. 392–5; James, *Naval History*, vol. 4, p. 213; Nicholas Tracy (ed.), *The Naval Chronicle, The Contemporary Record of the Royal Navy at War*, vol. 4, *1807–1810* (London: Chatham Publishing, 1999), pp. 92–4.
2. Sørensen (ed.), *Meddelelser*, vol. 3, pp. 29–32, 65, 67; Raeder, *Danmarks Krigs- og Politiske Historie*, vol. 1, pp. 275–6.
3. Sørensen (ed.), *Meddelelser*, vol. 3, p. 157.
4. See Raeder, *Danmarks Krigs- og Politiske Historie*, vol. 1, pp. 271–354, for a detailed account of the occupation of Copenhagen.
5. Garde, *Den dansk-norsk Sömagts Historie*, p. 468.
6. James, *Naval History*, vol. 4, pp. 208–9; Raeder, *Danmarks Krigs- og Politiske Historie*, vol. 1, pp. 307–10; Garde, *Den dansk-norsk Sömagts Historie*, pp. 464–8; Hans C. Bjerg, 'Flådens ran 1807', *Marinehistorisk Tidsskrift*, vol. 15, no. 2 (1982), pp. 14–31; Tracy (ed.), *Naval Chronicle*, p. 107; *Browne's Journal*, pp. 60–1.
7. LDA, George Canning Papers, HAR/GC/42, Canning to Jackson, 5 September 1807.
8. *Correspondence of Castlereagh*, vol. 6, p. 175.
9. LDA, George Canning Papers, HAR/GC/57, Hammond to Canning, 20 September 1807.
10. LDA, George Canning Papers, HAR/GC/31, Mulgrave to Canning, 20 September 1807.

11. *Correspondence of Castlereagh*, vol. 6, p. 184.

12. *Wellington Supplementary Despatches*, vol. 6, pp. 28–9; LDA, George Canning Papers, HAR/GC/32, Canning to Castlereagh, 1 October 1807; LDA, George Canning Papers, HAR/GC/43, Pierrepont to Canning, 13 October 1807.

13. TNA: PRO WO 1/188, Cathcart to Castlereagh, 18 September 1807.

14. TNA: PRO PRO 30/29/8/4, Canning to Gower, 5 November 1807; printed in Ryan (ed.), *Documents*, p. 325.

15. For British discussions about retaining Zealand, see *Correspondence of Castlereagh*, vol. 6, pp. 175–94; *Wellington Supplementary Despatches*, vol. 6, pp. 24–5, 26–9; TNA: PRO WO 6/14, Castlereagh to Cathcart, 5 September 1807; TNA: PRO WO 1/188, Cathcart to Castlereagh, especially 18 September, 24 September, 14 October and 15 October 1807; *Gambier Memorials*, vol. 2, pp. 61–7.

16. *Correspondence of Castlereagh*, vol. 6, p. 193.

17. TNA: PRO FO 73/41, desp. 43, Pierrepont to Canning, 19 September 1807.

18. LDA, George Canning Papers, HAR/GC/43, Pierrepont to Canning, 21 October 1807.

19. For Swedish policy in September and October 1807, see Carlsson and Höjer, *Den svenska utrikespolitikens historia*, pp. 111–12; Jorgensen, *The Anglo-Swedish Alliance*, pp. 105–10; and Trulsson, *British and Swedish Policies*, pp. 95–123.

20. TNA: PRO WO 1/188, Cathcart to Castlereagh, 21 October 1807.

21. TNA: PRO WO 1/188, Cathcart to Castlereagh, 28 October 1807.

22. Bjerg, 'Flådens ran 1807', pp. 19, 26–8; Garde, *Den dansk-norsk Sömagts Historie*, p. 468; James, *Naval History*, vol. 4, p. 210.

23. James, *Naval History*, vol. 4, p. 210; entry on Cathcart by M.D. Eddy in *ODNB*; *Browne's Journal*, p. 64.

24. Bjerg, 'Flådens ran 1807', p. 28.

25. TNA: PRO WO 6/14, Castlereagh to Cathcart, 5 September 1807.

26. LDA, George Canning Papers, HAR/GC/44, Jackson to Canning, 8 September 1807.

27. TNA: PRO FO 22/54, desp. 10, Jackson to Canning, 14 September 1807 (quotation); TNA: PRO, Jackson, 'A Review'.

28. TNA: PRO WO 6/14, Castlereagh to Cathcart, 19 September 1807.

29. Entry on Anthony Merry by Malcolm Lester in *ODNB*; see also Bindoff *et al.*, *British Diplomatic Representatives*, p. 41; DRA, DUA/1989, desp. 68, Rist to C. Bernstorff, 26 September 1807 (quotation).

30. DRA, DUA/1989, desps 65 and 67, Rist to C. Bernstorff, 18 August and 25 September 1807; Rist to J. Bernstorff, 25 August 1807; Holm, *Danmark-Norges* (1875), p. 340.

31. DRA, DUA/1989, Rist to C. Bernstorff, 28 September 1807.

32. TNA: PRO FO 22/55, desp. 5, Canning to Merry, 2 October 1807.

33. Copies of Rist's and Canning's summaries of the British offer are enclosed in TNA: PRO FO 22/55, desp. 1, Canning to Merry, 27 September 1807 and

DRA, DUA/1989, desp. 68, Rist to C. Bernstorff, 26 September 1807. See also in the same file desp. 69, Rist to C. Bernstorff, 27 September, 28 September and 2 October 1807.

34. *Wellington Supplementary Despatches*, vol. 6, pp. 26–7.
35. *Correspondence George III*, vol. 4, p. 632; *Wellington Supplementary Despatches*, vol. 6, p. 27; DRA, DUA/1989, desp. 68, Rist to C. Bernstorff, 26 September 1807.
36. Holm, *Danmark-Norges* (1912), p. 383 n.
37. Holm, *Danmark-Norges* (1875), pp. 328–34.
38. *Ibid.*, pp. 338–9.
39. DRA, DUA/1920, C. Bernstorff to Rist, 14 October 1807. See also TNA: PRO FO 22/57, Rist to Canning, 30 October 1807.
40. LDA, George Canning Papers, HAR/GC/42, Canning to Rist, 7 and 19 November 1807.
41. Holm, *Danmark-Norges* (1875), pp. 335–9, 349–50; Jespersen and Feldbæk, *Revanche og neutralitet*, pp. 498–9.
42. Granville, *Correspondence*, vol. 2, pp. 277, 279.
43. *Ibid.*, vol. 2, pp. 278–9, 282–3, 292, 295–9, 305–6.
44. For Savary's mission, see Tatistcheff, *Alexandre 1er et Napoléon*, pp. 189–94; Vandal, *Napoléon et Alexandre 1er*, pp. 112–44.
45. LDA, George Canning Papers, HAR/GC/57, Gower to Canning, 17 August 1807.
46. TNA: PRO FO 65/69, desp. 12, Gower to Canning, 2 August 1807; FO 65/70, desp. 16, Gower to Canning, 17 August 1807; LDA, George Canning Papers, HAR/GC/57, Gower to Canning, 1, 17 and 21 August (quotation) and 11 September 1807 (quotation).
47. See p. 135.
48. TNA: PRO FO 65/70, desp. 18, Gower to Canning, 2 September 1807; printed in *Parl. Deb.*, vol. 10, pp. 195–7.
49. TNA: PRO FO 65/70, desp. 19, Gower to Canning, 2 September 1807; partially printed in *Parl. Deb.*, vol. 10, pp. 197–8.
50. LDA, George Canning Papers, HAR/GC/44, Gambier to Canning, 21 August 1807; TNA: PRO FO 65/70, desp. 20, Gower to Canning, 2 September 1807; *Gambier Memorials*, vol. 2, p. 40.
51. Entry on Wilson by R.H. Vetch, rev. Gordon L. Teffeteller, in *ODNB*.
52. *Correspondence George III*, vol. 4, pp. 628–30.
53. LDA, George Canning Papers, HAR/GC/44, Wilson's report to Canning, 20 September 1807; Randolph (ed.), *Wilson*, p. 365.
54. *Correspondence George III*, vol. 4, pp. 629–30; Soviet Foreign Ministry, *Vneshniaia*, vol. 4, pp. 42–4.
55. *Correspondence George III*, vol. 4, p. 624, n. 2 (Canning's emphasis).
56. TNA: PRO FO 65/70, desp. 34, Canning to Gower, 27 September 1807, partially printed in *Parl. Deb.*, vol. 10, pp. 200–6.

57. LDA, George Canning Papers, HAR/GC/59B, d'Antraigues to Canning, 20 August 1807 and Czartoryski to d'Antraigues, 8/20 July 1807.

58. TNA: PRO FO 65/70, unnumbered desp., Canning to Gower, 27 September 1807.

59. TNA: PRO FO 65/70, desps 34, unnumbered, 35 and 37, Canning to Gower, 27, 27, 28 September and 1 October 1807; TNA: PRO PRO 30/29/8/4, Canning to Gower, 29 September, 2 October, 2 October 1807.

60. TNA: PRO FO 65/70, unnumbered desp., Gower to Canning, 9 September 1807.

61. *Sbornik*, vol. 155–6.

62. For Budberg and Rumiantsev, see Patricia Kennedy Grimstead, *The Foreign Ministers of Alexander I: Political Attitudes and the Conduct of Russian Diplomacy, 1801–1825* (Berkeley and Los Angeles, 1969), pp. 151–93.

63. TNA: PRO FO 65/70, desp. 26, Gower to Canning, 1 October 1807 with enclosed exchange of notes between Rumiantsev and Gower.

64. TNA: PRO FO 65/70, desps 26 (quotation) and 28, Gower to Canning, 1 October 1807.

65. TNA: PRO FO 65/70, desp. 31, Gower to Canning, 29 October 1807.

66. TNA: PRO FO 65/70, desps 33 and 34, Gower to Canning, 29 October and 4 November 1807.

67. LDA, George Canning Papers, HAR/GC/57, Gower to Canning, 5 November 1807.

68. Randolph (ed.), *Wilson*, pp. 433–9.

69. TNA: PRO FO 65/70, desp. 36, Gower to Canning, 8 November 1807, enclosing Rumiantsev's note and the Russian proclamation; partially printed in *Parl. Deb.*, vol. 10, pp. 216–21.

70. LDA, George Canning Papers, HAR/GC/57, Gower to Canning, 8 November and 17 November 1807.

71. Crouzet, *L'Économie Britannique*, pp. 252–4.

72. Muir, *Britain and the Defeat of Napoleon*, p. 30; Fugier, *Napoléon*, pp. 216–64, 346–54; Robson, 'British Intervention', fos 195–265.

73. *Correspondence George III*, vol. 4, p. 661 (Canning's emphasis).

74. TNA: PRO PRO 30/29/8/4, Canning to Gower, 2 October 1807.

THE BALANCE SHEET

1. Hinde, *George Canning*, pp. 175–6; Historical Manuscripts Commission, *Report on the Manuscripts of J.B. Fortescue, Esq., Preserved at Dropmore*, vol. 9 (London, 1915), p. 144.

2. *Parl. Deb.*, vol. 10, pp. 122–3.

3. *Ibid.*, p. 63.

4. *Ibid.*, p. 300.

5. *Ibid.*, pp. 46, 55 (quotation), 84, 88–9, 92.

6. *Ibid.*, pp. 94, 453, 658–9, 874, 876, 1190, 1214, 1361.

7. *Ibid.*, pp. 86–7, 94, 304, 357–8, 378–9, 1214.

8. Historical Manuscripts Commission, *Dropmore*, vol. 9, pp. 182–92.

9. *Parl. Deb.*, vol. 10, pp. 252–67.

10. Ryan (ed.), *Documents*, p. 323.

11. *Parl. Deb.*, vol. 10, pp. 267–87.

12. For the debates, there is a brief account in Hinde, *George Canning*, pp. 187–9, and very detailed summaries at various points in *Parl. Deb.*, vol. 10, *passim*.

13. Sørensen (ed.), *Meddelelser*, vol. 3, pp. 38–41; Raeder, *Danmarks Krigs- og Politiske Historie*, vol. 1, pp. 447–86; entry on Peymann in *DBL*.

14. For Corfu and the fate of the Russian Mediterranean fleet, see Piers Mackesy, *The War in the Mediterranean 1803–1810* (Cambridge, Mass., 1957), pp. 216–30; Driault, *Napoléon et l'Europe*, pp. 267–70; Robson, 'British Intervention', fos 251–69.

15. *Parl. Deb.*, vol. 10, pp. 266–7.

16. A.N. Ryan, 'The Defence of British Trade with the Baltic, 1808–1813', *English Historical Review*, vol. 74 (1959), pp. 443–6.

17. Johnson, *Sverige*, pp. 148–55.

18. Päiviö Tommila, *La Finlande dans la politique européenne en 1809–1815* (Helsinki, 1962), pp. 14–20, especially footnote 4 on pp. 18–19; Driault, *Napoléon et l'Europe*, pp. 293–7.

19. There is a huge literature on events in Scandinavia between 1807 and 1814. There is a fairly detailed English-language account in H. Arnold Barton, *Scandinavia in the Revolutionary Era, 1760–1815* (Minneapolis, 1986).

20. Jespersen and Feldbæk, *Revanche og neutralitet*, p. 512.

21. For the later lives of the British figures discussed here, see the *ODNB* references and biographies cited earlier.

22. *Gentleman's Magazine*, January–June 1815, p. 565.

23. Amanda Foreman, *Georgiana, Duchess of Devonshire* (London, 1998), pp. 396–7, 437, n. 21.

24. LDA, George Canning Papers, HAR/GC/32, Canning to Hawkesbury, 6 October 1808.

25. Granville, *Correspondence*, vol. 2, p. 292.

26. TNA: PRO PRO 30/29/8/4, Canning to Gower, 5 August 1807.

27. TNA: PRO PRO 30/29/8/4, Canning to Gower, 9 June 1807.

28. Ryan (ed.), *Documents*, p. 324 (Canning's emphasis).

29. *Correspondence George III*, vol. 4, p. 634.

30. LDA, George Canning Papers, HAR/GC/31, Mulgrave to Canning, 20 September 1807.

SELECT BIBLIOGRAPHY

MANUSCRIPT SOURCES

THE NATIONAL ARCHIVES, PUBLIC RECORD OFFICE, KEW

Foreign Office

Denmark
FO 22/43–57. Correspondence relating to Denmark, 1803–7

France
FO 27/76. Correspondence relating to France, 1807

Hanse Towns
FO 33/31–39. Correspondence relating to Hamburg and the Hanse Towns, 1806–7

'Frontiers of Holland' (Sir Charles Gordon)
FO 38/9 and 10. Reports from Gordon, 1806–7

Prussia
FO 64/74–77. Correspondence relating to Prussia, 1806–7

Russia
FO 65/63–73. Correspondence relating to Russia, 1806–7

Sweden
FO 73/36–44. Correspondence relating to Sweden, 1806–7

Admiralty

ADM 1/5. Baltic 1807
ADM 3/160. Minutes of Board of Admiralty, April–June 1807
ADM 3/161. Minutes of Board of Admiralty, July–September 1807

War Office

WO 1/187. Gambier's reports to Castlereagh, 1807
WO 1/188. Cathcart's reports to Castlereagh, 1807
WO 6/14. Castlereagh's despatches to Cathcart and Gambier, 1807

PRIVATE COLLECTIONS IN THE PRO

Granville Papers

PRO 30/29/8/4. Letters from Canning to Granville Leveson Gower, 1807–9

Francis Jackson's Private Papers

FO 353/29. Jackson's papers relating to Denmark, 1807
FO 353/56. Francis Jackson, 'A Review of the last two months of my Life written at Broadstairs in October 1807'
FO 353/77. Letters from Thornton to Jackson, 1807
FO 353/85. Letters from Wynn to Jackson, 1804–6

Edward Thornton's Private Papers

FO 933/16. Secret intelligence received by Thornton in 1806 from Vienna, The Hague and Munich

PRIVATE COLLECTIONS, UNITED KINGDOM

George Canning Papers, Leeds District Archive

Bundle 22. Canning's correspondence with his wife Joan, 1807
Bundles 31 and 32. Canning's correspondence with other ministers
Bundle 41A. Notes and minutes for the Cabinet, 1807–9
Bundle 42. Correspondence relating to Denmark, Russia and Sweden, 1807–9
Bundle 43. Correspondence relating to Sweden, 1807–9
Bundle 44. Correspondence relating to Denmark, 1807–9
Bundle 50. Correspondence relating to Austria, 1807–9
Bundle 57. Correspondence relating to Russia, 1807–9
Bundles 59, 59A and 59B. Correspondence with d'Antraigues, 1807–9

Second Earl Grey Papers, Durham University Library

B1/5. The admiralty, 1787–1832
B2/4. Grey's correspondence with d'Antraigues, 1806–12
B7/15. Grey's correspondence with Boothby, 1806
B8/14. Grey's correspondence with Butler, 1812
B9A/6. Grey's correspondence with Canning, 1807–12
B15/11. Grey's correspondence with Garlike, 1807–12
B21/2–4. Grey's correspondence with Grenville, 1806–19
B47/2. Grey's correspondence with Pierrepont, 1806–7
B54/12. Grey's correspondence with Thornton, 1806–7
B56/8. Grey's correspondence with Vincent, 1806–7

National Maritime Museum, Greenwich

Duckworth Papers, DUC/13. Duckworth's correspondence for 1807

British Library

Add. MS 58900. Wynn's letters to Grenville, 1799–1813
Add. MS 59035. Grenville's correspondence with d'Antraigues, 1806
Add. MS 59035. Vansittart's correspondence with d'Antraigues, 1806

George Murray Papers, National Library of Scotland, Edinburgh

46.1.12 and 46.1.13. Documents relating to operations in northern Europe, 1807–8

PRIVATE COLLECTION, UNITED STATES

Thomas Grenville Papers, Huntington Library

Huntington Library MS STG. Letters from Garlike to T. Grenville, 1807

DANISH NATIONAL ARCHIVES, COPENHAGEN

Gesandtskabsarkivet (Archives of Danish Missions Abroad)

GskA [372], England I – Instructions from Christian Bernstorff to the Danish envoy in London, 1805–7
GskA [419], Frankrig I – Instructions from Christian Bernstorff to the Danish envoy in Paris, 1807
GskA [398], Rusland I – Instructions from Christian Bernstorff to the Danish envoy in St Petersburg, 1804–7

Departementet for de Udenlandske Anliggender (Archives of the Danish Foreign Ministry)

Reports from the Danish envoy in London to Christian Bernstorff in Kiel
DUA/1988. Despatches, January 1806–April 1807
DUA/1989. Despatches, May–October 1807
DUA/ 1179. Reklamationer, 1802–7 (complaints over the detention of Danish shipping by Britain)
DUA/1919 and 1920. England – Materiale vdr. fredsbruddet med England 1807 (material relating to the outbreak of war with Britain in 1807)
DUA/1945. Sager vdr. Engelske postsager-1807 (material relating to the British postal route through Husum)

Reports from the Danish envoy in Paris to Christian Bernstorff in Kiel
DUA/2127 and 2128. Despatches for 1806 and 1807 respectively

Reports from the Danish envoy in St Petersburg to Christian Bernstorff in Kiel
DUA/2452 and 2453. Despatches for 1807 and 1808

Other Government Departments

Søkrigskancelliet – kongens flådetabeller- 1801- arkivnr 509-E-0017 – sk. nr 968
Søkrigskancelliet – kongens flådetabeller- 1805- arkivnr 509-E-0017 – sk. nr 972
Søkrigskancelliet – kongens flådetabeller- 1806- arkivnr 509-E-0017 – sk. nr 973
Søkrigskancelliet – kongens flådetabeller- 1807- arkivnr 509-E-0017 – sk. nr 974
(Material on the fitting-out, manning and construction of the Danish navy for
     1801, 1805, 1806 and 1807)

Tillæg til søetatens arkiv-skibsjournaler 1675–1900 – år 1807 arkivnr 521-J-01
     protokolnummer 832 (registratur 85 b2)
(Logbooks for the *Princesse Louisa Augusta, Prinds Christian Fredrick* and *Waldemar,*
     1807)

Admiralitetet (søetaten) – generalkopibog m. registre – 1806 – arkivnr 510-C01-
     3 – adm. 309
Admiralitetet (søetaten) – generalkopibog m. registre – 1807 – arkivnr 510-C01-
     03 adm. 310
(Material on the equipment and manning of Trekronor and Prøvesten in 1806
     and 1807 respectively)

Marineministeriet (0008) – 1650–1969 Skibsjournaler – Tre Kroner Batteri 1807
     – nr 850-1–850-5
(Further material on the equipment and manning of Trekroner in 1807)

Generalkommissariatet (søetaten) – 1728–1847 – Kopibøger materialvæsenet
     vedkommende – 1807 – nr 231
(Copy books of the naval commissariat for 1807)

Ingeniørkorpsets danske arkiv – Ind- og udgående kvartalsrapporter ved
     ingeniørkorpset 1804–1807 vedr. rigets fæstninger – ark. nr 240–001 – nr
     290–291
(Quarterly reports of the engineer corps on fortifications)

Søetaten – Orlogsværftets afleveringer 1945 – Udkommando af Flaadens Skibe fra
     Aaret 1677 til 1886 – nr 9 [for 1807]
(List of ships sent to sea, 1677–1866, compiled by Degenkolv in 1892)

Arkivnummer 1474. Kabinetssekretariatet – Kronprins Frederiks Arkiv.
Breve til kronprinsen fra General Walterstorff, 1799–1807 – pakke nr 317
(Letters from General Walterstorff to Prince Fredrick)

PRIVATE COLLECTIONS IN THE DANISH NATIONAL ARCHIVE

Arkivnummer 5128. Privatarkiv for familien Bernstorff Stintenburg. Christian G. Bernstorffs arkiv: Breve fra Joachim Bernstorff, 1789–1835 – Lb. Nr 48
(Bernstorff family archive. Letters from Joachim to Christian Bernstorff, 1789–1835)

Arkivnummer 5890. Admiral Hans Lindholms Arkiv, 1797–1817. Breve fra Kronprins Frederik, 1797–1807
(Admiral Lindholm's archive. Letters from Prince Fredrick, 1797–1807)

PUBLIC AND PRIVATE COLLECTIONS IN EUROPE

Archives du Ministère des Affaires Étrangères (Archives of the French Foreign Ministry), Paris
Fonds Bourbons
vol. 631. Czartoryski's letters to d'Antraigues, 1807–9
vol. 643. Letters of Prince and Princess Troubetzkoi to d'Antraigues, 1805–7

Czartoryski Library, Cracow, Czart. MS
vol. 5481. d'Antraigues's letters to Czartoryski, 1806–7

Swedish National Archives, Stockholm
Anglica/489–490. Reports from Rehausen to Gustavus, 1806–7

National Archives of Finland, Helsinki
Armfelt archive 1:26, microfilm PR 9 and 10. d'Antraigues's letters to Armfelt, 1805–6

PRINTED PRIMARY SOURCES

Jane Austen's Letters, coll. and ed. Deirdre Le Faye (3rd edn, Oxford, 1995)
Mémoires du Général Bennigsen, vol. 2 (Paris, 1906)
The Napoleonic War Journal of Captain Thomas Henry Browne 1807–1816 (Army Records Society) (London, 1987)

Buckingham and Chandos, Duke of, *Memoirs of the Court and Cabinets of George III*, vol. 1 (London, 1855)

Correspondence, Despatches, and Other Papers of Viscount Castlereagh, Second Marquess of Londonderry, ed. C.W. Vane, Marquess of Londonderry (12 vols, London, 1848–53), 2nd series, vol. 6

Atkinson, C.T. (ed.), 'Gleanings from the Cathcart MSS, Part VI, The "Conjoint" Expedition to Copenhagen, 1807', *Journal of the Society for Army Historical Research*, vol. 30, no. 122 (1952)

Perrin, W.G. (ed.), 'The Bombardment of Copenhagen, 1807: Journal of Surgeon Charles Chambers of H.M. Fireship Prometheus', *The Naval Miscellany*, vol. 3, *Publications of the Navy Records Society*, vol. 63 (1928)

Historical Manuscripts Commission, *Report on the Manuscripts of J.B. Fortescue, Esq., preserved at Dropmore*, vols 8 (London, 1912) and 9 (London, 1915)

[Fauche-Borel, Louis], *Mémoires de Fauche-Borel*, vols 3 and 4 (Paris, 1829)

Memorials, Personal and Historical of Admiral Lord Gambier, ed. Georgiana, Lady Chatterton (2nd edn, vol. 2, London, 1861)

Aspinall, A. (ed.), *The Later Correspondence of George III, 1783–1810*, vol. 4 (Cambridge, 1968)

Gower, Lord Ronald (ed.), *Stafford House Letters* (London, 1891)

Granville, Castalia Countess, *Lord Granville Leveson Gower: Private Correspondence*, 2 vols (London, 1916)

Hathaway, Eileen (ed.), *A Dorset Rifleman: The Recollections of Benjamin Harris* (Swanage, 1996)

d'Hauterive, Ernest, *La Police secrète du premier empire: Bulletins quotidiens addressés par Fouché à l'Empereur*, vol. 3, *1806–1807* (Paris, 1922)

The Diaries and Letters of Sir George Jackson, ed. Lady Jackson, 2 vols (London, 1872), vol. 2

Malmesbury, Earl of, *Memoirs of an Ex-Minister* (London, 1884), 2 vols

Diaries and Correspondence of James Harris, First Earl of Malmesbury (London, 1844), vol. 4

A Series of Letters of the First Earl of Malmesbury His Family and Friends from 1745 to 1820 (London, 1870), vol. 2

The Memoirs of Baron de Marbot (London, 1892)

Markham, J. David, *Imperial Glory: The Bulletins of Napoleon's Grande Armée 1805–1814* (London, 2003)

Correspondence de Napoléon 1er, 32 vols (Paris, 1858–70)

The Parliamentary Debates from the Year 1803 to the Present Time, vols 8, 9 and 10 (London, 1812)

Rist, Johan, *Lebenserinnerungen*, 2 vols (2nd edn, Gotha, 1884–6)

Ryan, A.N. (ed.), 'Documents Relating to the Copenhagen Operation, 1807', *The Naval Miscellany*, vol. 5, *Publications of the Navy Records Society*, vol. 125 (1984), pp. 297–329

Sbornik imperatorskogo russkogo istoricheskogo obshchestva (St Petersburg,

1867–1916), vols 82, 83, 88 and 89

Schulz, Hans (ed.), *Briefwechsel des Herzogs Friedrich Christian zu Schleswig-Holstein-Sonderburg-Augustenburg mit König Friedrich VI von Dänemark* (Leipzig, 1908)

Sørensen, C.T. (ed.), *Meddelelser fra Krigarkiverne. Udgivne af Generalstaben*, vol. 2 (Copenhagen, 1885)

—— *Meddelelser fra Krigarkiverne. Udgivne af Generalstaben*, vol. 3 (Copenhagen, 1888)

Soviet Foreign Ministry, *Vneshniaia Politika Rossii XIX i nachala XX veka: dokumenty rossiiskigo ministerstva inostrannykh del*, Series 1, *1801–1815* (Moscow, 1960 and ongoing), vols 3 and 4

Arkhiv knyazya Vorontsova, ed. P. Bartenev, 40 vols (Moscow, 1870–95), vols 15, 18 and 22

The Dispatches of Field Marshal the Duke of Wellington, KG, during his Various Campaigns . . . from 1799 to 1818, ed. J. Gurwood (new edn, 13 vols, London, 1837–9), vol. 3

Supplementary Despatches and Memoranda of Field Marshal Arthur Duke of Wellington, KG, ed. A.R. Wellesley, second Duke of Wellington, 15 vols (London, 1858–72), vol. 6

The Life of General Sir Robert Wilson, ed. Herbert Randolph, vol. 2 (London, 1862)

REFERENCE WORKS

The Annual Register for 1807 (London, 1809)

Bindoff, S.T. *et al.*, *British Diplomatic Representatives, 1789–1852*, Camden Third Series, vol. 50 (London, 1934)

The Gentleman's Magazine, January–June 1815

Robinet, Adolphe, *Dictionnaire historique et biographique de la Révolution et de l'Empire* (Paris, n.d.)

UNPUBLISHED DISSERTATIONS

Ekberger, Maria, 'Københavns sødefension 1777–1807', unpublished dissertation, History Department, Copenhagen University, 1984

Robson, Martin, 'British Intervention in Portugal, 1806–1808', unpublished Ph.D. thesis, King's College London, 2003

Saxtorph, Henrik, 'Københavns søforsvar 1807', unpublished dissertation, History Department, Copenhagen University, 1989

SECONDARY SOURCES

Aspinall, A., 'The Canningite Party', *Transactions of the Royal Historical Society*, Fourth Series, vol. 17 (1934)

Barton, H. Arnold, *Scandinavia in the Revolutionary Era, 1760–1815* (Minneapolis, 1986)

Bistrup, H., 'Premierløjtnant F Grodtschillings Journal under Kjøbenhavns Bombardement 1807', *Tidsskrift for Søvæsen*, vol. 100 (1929)

Bjerg, Hans C., 'Flådens ran 1807', *Marinehistorisk Tidsskrift*, vol. 15, no. 2 (1982), pp. 14–31

Björlin, G., *Sveriges krig i Tyskland åren 1805–1807* (Stockholm, 1882)

Black, Jeremy, *European International Relations 1648–1815* (Basingstoke, 2002)

Bonsdorff, Carl von, *Gustav Mauritz Armfelt: Levnadsskildring*, 4 vols (Helsingfors, 1930–4)

Brooke, John, *King George III* (London, 1972)

Burrows, Simon, 'British Propaganda for Russia in the Napoleonic Wars: The *Courier d'Angleterre*', *New Zealand Slavonic Journal* (1993)

—— 'The Struggle for European Opinion in the Napoleonic Wars: British Francophone Propaganda, 1803–1814', *French History*, vol. 11, no. 1 (1997)

—— *French Exile Journalism and European Politics 1792–1815* (Woodbridge, 2000)

Butterfield, Herbert, *The Peace Tactics of Napoleon 1806–1808* (Cambridge, 1929)

Carlsson, Sten and Höjer, Torvald, *Den svenska utrikespolitikens historia*, vol. 3, nos 1–2 (Stockholm, 1954)

Cedergren Bech, S., *Storhandelens by, Københavns historie*, vol. 3, *1728–1830* (Copenhagen, 1981)

Chandler, David (ed.), *Napoleon's Marshals* (London, 1987)

Crouzet, F., *L'Économie Britannique et le Blocus Continental*, vol. 1 (Paris, 1958)

Desbrière, Édouard, *Projets et tentatives de débarquement aux îles britanniques*, 4 vols (Paris, 1900–2)

Dickinson, H.T. (ed.), *Britain and the French Revolution, 1789–1815* (Basingstoke, 1989)

Dixon, Piers, *Canning: Politician and Statesman* (London, 1976)

Driault, Édouard, *Napoléon et l'Europe: Tilsit. France et Russie sous le premier empire. La Question de Pologne (1806–1809)* (Paris, 1917)

Duckworth, Colin, *The D'Antraigues Phenomenon* (Newcastle, 1986)

Dwyer, Philip G., *Talleyrand* (London/Harlow, 2002)

Elliott, Marianne, *Partners in Revolution: The United Irishmen and France* (New Haven and London, 1982)

Eriksen, Egon and Frantzen, Ole L., *Dansk artilleri i napoleonstiden: Forudsætninger og udvikling 1760–1814* (2nd edn, Copenhagen, 1989)

Fedorak, Charles John, *Henry Addington. Prime Minister, 1801–1804: Peace, War, and Parliamentary Politics* (Akron, Oh., 2002)

Feldbæk, Ole, 'The Anglo-Russian Rapprochement of 1801', *Scandinavian Journal of History*, vol. 3, no. 3 (1978)

—— *Denmark and the Armed Neutrality 1800–1801* (Copenhagen, 1980)

—— 'The Foreign Policy of Tsar Paul I, 1800–1801: An Interpretation', *Jahrbücher für Geschichte Osteuropas*, NS, vol. 30 (1982)

—— [Gyldendals] *Danmarks historie*, vol. 4, *Tiden 1730–1814* (Copenhagen, 1982)

—— 'Eighteenth-Century Danish Neutrality: Its Diplomacy, Economics and Law', *Scandinavian Journal of History*, vol. 8, no. 1 (1983)

—— 'Denmark and the Treaty of Kiel, 1814', *Scandinavian Journal of History*, vol. 15, no. 4 (1990)

—— 'Denmark and the Baltic, 1720–1864', in G. Rystad *et al.* (eds), *In Quest of Trade and Security: The Baltic in Power Politics, 1500–1990*, vol. 1, 1500–1890 (Stockholm, 1994)

—— 'Danmark og Øresund under revolutions- og Napoleonskrigene: Eller hvordan Sjælland blev en ø', in Johan Engström and Ole L. Frantzen (eds), *Øresunds strategiske rolle i et historisk perspektiv* (Lund, 1998)

—— 'Denmark in the Napoleonic Wars: A Foreign Policy Survey', *Scandinavian Journal of History*, vol. 26 (2001)

—— *The Battle of Copenhagen, 1801* (Barnsley, 2002)

Foreman, Amanda, *Georgiana, Duchess of Devonshire* (London, 1998)

Fortescue, J.W., *A History of the British Army*, vol. 6, *1807–1809* (London, 1910)

Frantzen, O.L., *Truslen fra øst: Dansk-norsk flådepolitik 1769–1807* (Copenhagen, 1980)

Fraser, Flora, *The Unruly Queen: The Life of Queen Caroline* (London, 1996)

Fugier, André, *Napoléon et l'Espagne*, vol. 2 (Paris, 1930)

Garde, H.G., *Den dansk-norsk Sömagts Historie 1700–1814* (Copenhagen, 1852)

Gates, David, *The Napoleonic Wars 1803–1815* (reprinted edn, London, 2003)

Geyl, Pieter, *Napoleon: For and Against* (reprinted edn, Harmondsworth, 1965)

Glete, Jan, *Navies and Nations: Warships, Navies and State Building in Europe and America, 1500–1860*, 2 vols (Stockholm, 1993)

Glover, Richard, 'The French Fleet, 1807–1814; Britain's Problem; and Madison's Opportunity', *Journal of Modern History*, vol. 39 (1967)

—— *Britain at Bay: Defence against Bonaparte 1803–14* (London, 1973)

Godechot, Jacques, *Le Comte d'Antraigues: Un espion dans l'Europe des émigrés* (Paris, 1986)

Gomm, Bernhard, *Die Russischen Kriegschiffe 1856–1917*, 2 vols (Wiesbaden, 1991–2)

Grimstead, Patricia Kennedy, *The Foreign Ministers of Alexander 1: Political Attitudes and the Conduct of Russian Diplomacy, 1801–1825* (Berkeley and Los Angeles, 1969)

Hall, Christopher D., *British Strategy in the Napoleonic War 1803–15* (Manchester, 1992)

Hartley, Janet M., *Alexander I* (Harlow, 1994)

Harvey, A.D., 'European Attitudes to Britain during the French Revolutionary and Napoleonic Era', *History*, vol. 63 (1978)

Hedegård, E.O.A., *Krigen på Sjælland 1807* (Copenhagen, 1970)

Hill, Richard, *The Prizes of War: The Naval Prize System in the Napoleonic Wars, 1793–1815* (Stroud, 1998)

Hinde, Wendy, *George Canning* (London, 1973)

Hodge, Jane Aiken, *Passion & Principle: The Loves and Lives of Regency Women* (London, 1996)

Höjer, Torvald, *Carl XIV Johan*, vol. 1, *Den franska tiden* (Stockholm, 1939)

Holland Rose, J., 'Canning and Denmark in 1807', *English Historical Review*, vol. 11 (1896), pp. 82–92

—— 'A British Agent at Tilsit', *English Historical Review*, vol. 16 (1901)

—— 'Canning and the Secret Intelligence from Tilsit', *Transactions of the Royal Historical Society*, NS, vol. 20 (1906)

Holm, E., *Danmark-Norges udenrigske Historie under den franske Revolution og Napoleons Krige fra 1791 til 1807*, vol. 2 (Copenhagen, 1875)

—— *Danmark-Norges udenrigske Historie i Aarene 1800 til 1814*, vol. 7, pt 1, *1800–1807* (Copenhagen, 1912)

Horne, Alistair, *How Far from Austerlitz? Napoleon 1805–1815* (London, 1996)

James, William, *The Naval History of Great Britain, from the Declaration of War by France in 1793 to the Accession of George IV*, vol. 4 (London, 1886)

Jespersen, Knud J.V., *The Besieging of Copenhagen in 1807 and the Map in the Governor's Library in Odense* (Odense, 1974)

—— and Feldbæk, Ole, *Revanche og neutralitet, 1648–1814* (Copenhagen, 2002), vol. 2 of Carsten Due-Nielsen *et al.*, *Dansk udenrigspolitiks historie* (ongoing)

Johansen, Jens, *Frederik VIs Hær 1784–1814* (Copenhagen, 1948)

Johnson, Seved, *Sverige och stormakterna 1800–1804* (Lund, 1957)

Jorgensen, Christer, *The Anglo-Swedish Alliance against Napoleonic France* (Basingstoke, 2004)

Jupp, Peter, *Lord Grenville 1759–1834* (Oxford, 1985)

Lavery, Brian, *Nelson's Navy: The Ships, Men and Organisation 1793–1815* (London, 1989)

Lenotre, G., *L'Affaire Perlet: Drames policiers* (Paris, 1923)

—— *Two Royalist Spies of the French Revolution* (London, 1924)

Lerdrup-Bourgois, Eric, *De Tilsit à Fontainebleau: La Correspondence du Ministre Plénipotentiaire de Danemark-Norvège près Napoléon juillet 1807–novembre 1807. Recueil de sources* (Copenhagen, 2003)

Lindvald, A., 'Bidrag til Oplysning om Danmark-Norges Handel og Skibsfart 1800–1807', (Danish) *Historisk Tidsskrift*, 8th series, vol. 6 (1917)

—— *Kronprins Frederik og hans Regering 1797–1807* (Copenhagen, 1923)

Ludlow Beamish, N., *History of the King's German Legion*, vol. 1 (London, 1832)

Mackesy, Piers, *The War in the Mediterranean 1803–1810* (Cambridge, Mass., 1957)

Macmillan, David S., 'Russo-British Trade Relations under Alexander I', *Canadian–American Slavic Studies*, vol. 9, no. 4 (1975)

Madelin, Louis, *Fouché 1759–1820*, vol. 2, *Ministre de la police* (Paris, 2002)

Madriaga, Isabel de, *Russia in the Age of Catherine the Great* (reissued edn, London, 2002)

Masterson, William H., *Tories and Democrats: British Diplomats in Pre-Jacksonian America* (College Station, Tex., 1985)

Middleton, Charles Ronald, *The Administration of British Foreign Policy 1782–1846* (Durham, NC, 1977)

Møller, E., 'England og Danmark-Norge 1807', (Danish) *Historisk Tidsskrift*, 8th series, vol. 3 (1910–12)

Muir, Rory, *Britain and the Defeat of Napoleon 1807–1815* (London, 1996)

Munch-Petersen, Thomas, 'A Prelude to the British Bombardment of Copenhagen: Viscount Howick and Denmark, 1806–1807', *Scandia*, vol. 65, no. 1 (1999)

—— 'Lord Cathcart, Sir Arthur Wellesley and the British Capture of Copenhagen in 1807', in C.M. Woolgar (ed.), *Wellington Studies II* (Southampton: Hartley Institute, 1999)

—— 'The Secret Intelligence from Tilsit: New Light on the Events Surrounding the British Bombardment of Copenhagen in 1807', (Danish) *Historisk Tidsskrift*, vol. 102, no. 1 (2002)

—— 'Colin Alexander Mackenzie: A British Agent at Tilsit', *Northern Studies*, vol. 37 (2003)

Olrik, H.G., *Fra Rosenborg til Sorø Kirke: Kronjuvelernes Udflugt* (Copenhagen, 1945)

Palmer, Alan, *Alexander I: Tsar of War and Peace* (London, 1974)

Parker, Harold T., *Three Napoleonic Battles* (Durham, NC, 1983)

Petre, F. Loraine, *Napoleon's Campaign in Poland, 1806–1807* (reprinted edn, London, 1989)

Pingaud, Léonce, *Un agent secret sous la Révolution et l'Empire: Le comte d'Antraigues* (2nd edn, Paris, 1894)

Pocock, Tom, *The Terror before Trafalgar: Nelson, Napoleon and the Secret War* (London, 2002)

Popham, Hugh, *A Damned Cunning Fellow: The Eventful Life of Rear-Admiral Sir Home Popham KCB, KCH, KM, FRS 1762–1820* (Tywardreath, 1991)

Raeder, J.v., *Danmarks Krigs- og Politiske Historie fra Krigens Udbrud 1807 til Freden in Jönköping den 10de December 1809*, vol. 1 (Copenhagen, 1845)

Roach, Elmo E., 'Anglo-Russian Relations from Austerlitz to Tilsit', *International History Review*, vol. 5 (1989)

Rodger, N.A.M., *The Command of the Ocean: A Naval History of Britain, 1649–1815* (London, 2004)

Romanov, Nicholas Mikhailovitch, *Portraits Russes*, 5 vols (St Petersburg, 1905–9)

Rubin, Marcus, *1807–14: Studies til Københavns og Danmarks Historie* (Copenhagen, 1892; reprinted 1970)

Ryan, A.N., 'The Causes of the British Attack upon Copenhagen in 1807', *English Historical Review*, vol. 68 (1953)

—— 'The Navy at Copenhagen in 1807', *Mariner's Mirror*, vol. 39 (1953)

—— 'The Defence of British Trade with the Baltic, 1808–1813', *English Historical Review*, vol. 74 (1959)

Saxtorph, Henrik, 'Det britiske angreb of Københavns søforsvar 1807', *Marinehistorisk Tidsskrift*, vol. 23, no. 3 (1990)

—— 'Flåden gøres klar til ødelæggelse 1807', *Marinehistorisk Tidsskrift*, vol. 23, no. 4 (1990)

Schroeder, Paul W., 'Napoleon's Foreign Policy: A Criminal Enterprise', *Journal of Military History*, vol. 54, no. 2 (1990)

—— *The Transformation of European Politics 1763–1848* (Oxford, 1994)

Sheehan, James J., *German History 1770–1866* (Oxford, 1989)

Smith, E.A., *Lord Grey 1764–1845* (Stroud, 1996)

Søby Andersen, H., *En lus mellem to negle: Dansk-norsk neutralitetspolitik 1801–1807* (Odense, 1991)

Sørensen, C.T., 'Den politiske Krise i 1807', (Danish) *Historisk Tidsskrift*, 6th series, vol. 1 (1887–8)

Sparrow, Elizabeth, *Secret Service: British Agents in France 1792–1815* (Woodbridge, 1999)

Tatistcheff, Serge, *Alexandre 1er et Napoléon d'après leur correspondance inédite* (Paris, 1894)

Tommila, Päiviö, *La Finlande dans la politique européenne en 1809–1815* (Helsinki, 1962)

Tracy, Nicholas (ed.), *The Naval Chronicle: The Contemporary Record of the Royal Navy at War*, vol. 4, *1807–1810* (London: Chatham Publishing, 1999)

Trulsson, S.G., *British and Swedish Policies and Strategies in the Baltic after the Peace of Tilsit in 1807* (Lund, 1976)

Vandal, Albert, *Napoléon et Alexandre 1er: L'Alliance russe sous le premier empire*, vol. 1, *De Tilsit à Erfurt* (Paris, 1911)

Waresquiel, Emmanuel de, *Talleyrand: Le Prince immobile* (Paris, 2003)

Whitcomb, Edward A., *Napoleon's Diplomatic Service* (Durham, NC, 1979)

Wilkinson, David, *The Duke of Portland: Politics and Party in the Age of George III* (Basingstoke, 2003)

Wilson, Frances, *The Courtesan's Revenge: Harriette Wilson, the Woman who Blackmailed the King* (London, 2003)

Winter, Frank H., 'Raketterne ved Københavns belejring – en milepæl i rakettens istorie', *Marinehistorisk Tidsskrift*, vol. 12, no. 1 (1979)

—— *The First Golden Age of Rocketry: Congreve and Hale Rockets of the Nineteenth Century* (Washington and London, 1990)

Zawadzki, W.H., *A Man of Honour: Adam Czartoryski as a Statesman of Russia and Poland 1795–1831* (Oxford, 1993)

INDEX

instructions 140, 191, 192, 193, 197–8
  Zealand 189–90, 212, 213, 216
casualties 185, 200
Cathcart, Lord William Schaw
  career 172–3, 216, 240
  Copenhagen, siege of 193, 194, 197,
    199
  Copenhagen, surrender 202, 203, 204,
    205, 213
  headquarters 170
  instructions 108, 140, 196, 198
  and Jackson 169
  Køge, battle of 182
  Pomerania 145, 146
  Swan Mill 177
  troops 171
  and Wellesley 180
  Zealand 161, 212, 215
Catherine the Great 25, 27
ceasefire, Copenhagen 212
Chambers, Charles 201
Champagny, Jean-Baptiste Nompère, Count
    de 165, 222
Charles XIII: 239
Charles of Kirkaldy 178
Charlottenlund, Zealand 171
Christian VII: 39, 159, 221, 236
Cockburn, Alexander 86, 87, 98
'Congreve rockets' 201–2
Congreve, William 201
Constantine, Grand Duke 26–7
continental system 26, 130, 163, 237,
    238, 239
Copenhagen 174
  battle of (1801) 42, 50, 99
  bombardment 195, 196, 199–202
  British debates about 233, 234
  casualties 200
  ceasefire 212
  council of war 203, 207, 208
  fighting around 174–9
  fires 199, 200
  floating batteries 78–9
  naval stores 212
  navy 52–3, 76–7, 79, 144, 175
  sea forts 79, 98–9

siege of 170–1, 193–202
  surrender 202–9, 213
  Thornton's suggestion 88
council of war, Copenhagen 203, 207, 208
Czartoryski, Adam, Prince
  and Alexander I: 123
  d'Antraigues 118, 120, 122, 227
  and Gower 124, 125, 224
  Zealand 226

Danican, Louis-Michel-Auguste 91–4
d'Antraigues, Count see Antraigues,
    Count d'
decision-making, for attack on Denmark
    98–9, 106–12
Denmark
  army 43, 48, 99, 156, 174
  Britain 42, 45–6, 56, 151–2, 218–22
  declaration of war 185
  France 164, 187–8, 220, 221, 222
  international support sought 186–7
  militia 174–5, 181, 182, 200, 202
  monarchy 39–40
  Napoleonic Wars 238
  navy see navy (Danish)
  neutrality 31, 39, 45, 72, 74, 219, 228,
    243
  old kingdom 40, 239
  Prussia 43
  Russia 41, 43, 186
  Sweden 41, 51
  see also Copenhagen; Fredrick, Crown
    Prince; Holstein; Jutlandic peninsula;
    Schleswig; Zealand
detained Danish ships 65–7
Douglas, Admiral 141
Dreyer, Christopher Vilhelm 164, 165, 222
Duckworth, Sir John 53, 58
Dunbar, James 52, 80
Duroc, General 19, 20–1

Elbe blockade 46, 58, 62, 63–4
Eldon, Lord 103
escalated British objectives 106–12
Essington, Rear-Admiral 141, 145
Eylau, battle of 2